**Structural Equation Models
in the Social Sciences**

QUANTITATIVE STUDIES IN SOCIAL RELATIONS

Consulting Editor: Peter H. Rossi

THE JOHNS HOPKINS UNIVERSITY
BALTIMORE, MARYLAND

Structural Equation Models in the Social Sciences

Edited by

ARTHUR S. GOLDBERGER

Department of Economics
University of Wisconsin
Madison, Wisconsin

OTIS DUDLEY DUNCAN

Department of Sociology and Population Studies Center
University of Michigan
Ann Arbor, Michigan

SEMINAR PRESS New York and London   1973

A Subsidiary of Harcourt Brace Jovanovich, Publishers

SEMINAR PRESS, INC.
111 Fifth Avenue, New York, New York 10003

United Kingdom Edition published by
SEMINAR PRESS LIMITED
24/28 Oval Road, London NW1

Library of Congress Cataloging in Publication Data

Conference on Structural Equation Models, Madison,
    Wis., 1970.
    Structural equation models in the social sciences.

    (Quantitative studies in social relations)
    "Revisions of papers presented at a conference co-
sponsored by the Social Science Research Council and
the Social Systems Research Institute of the University
of Wisconsin."
    Bibliography: p.
    1.   Social sciences–Mathematical models–Congresses.
2.   Social sciences–Methodology–Congresses.
I.   Goldberger, Arthur Stanley, DATE   ed.
II.   Duncan, Otis Dudley, ed.   III.   Social Science
Research Council. IV. Wisconsin. University. Social
Systems Research Institute.   V.   Title.
H61.C585   1970   300´.1´5118   72–7701
ISBN 0–12–839950–3

Contents

1. Structural Equation Models: An Overview
Arthur S. Goldberger

2. Identification, Parameter Estimation, and Hypothesis Testing in Recursive Sociological Models
Kenneth C. Land

7. Efficient Estimation in Overidentified Models: An Interpretive Analysis

Arthur S. Goldberger

8. Cross-Lagged and Synchronous Common Factors in Panel Data

David A. Kenny

9. Diagnosing Indicator Ills in Multiple Indicator Models

Herbert L. Costner and Ronald Schoenberg

10. Ratio Variables and Path Models

Karl Schuessler

11. Psychological and Cultural Factors in the Process of Occupational Achievement

Otis Dudley Duncan and David L. Featherman

12. Disaggregating a Social-Psychological Model of Educational Attainment

Robert M. Hauser

13. Education, Income, and Ability

Zvi Griliches and William M. Mason

List of Contributors

Numbers in parentheses indicate the pages on which the authors' contributions begin.

HERBERT L. COSTNER (167), Department of Sociology, University of Washington, Seattle, Washington

OTIS DUDLEY DUNCAN (229), Population Studies Center, University of Michigan, Ann Arbor, Michigan

DAVID L. FEATHERMAN (229), Department of Rural Sociology, University of Wisconsin, Madison, Wisconsin

ARTHUR S. GOLDBERGER (1, 131), Department of Economics, University of Wisconsin, Madison, Wisconsin

ZVI GRILICHES (285), Department of Economics, Harvard University, Cambridge, Massachusetts

ROBERT M. HAUSER (255), Department of Sociology, University of Wisconsin, Madison, Wisconsin

NEIL W. HENRY (51), Department of Sociology, Cornell University, Ithaca, New York

JOHN E. JACKSON (329), Department of Government, Harvard University, Cambridge, Massachusetts

KARL G. JÖRESKOG* (85), Educational Testing Service, Princeton, New Jersey

* Present address: Department of Statistics, Uppsala University, Uppsala, Sweden.

DAVID A. KENNY* (153), Department of Psychology, Northwestern University, Evanston, Illinois

KENNETH C. LAND (19), Russell Sage Foundation, New York, New York

WILLIAM M. MASON (285), Department of Sociology, Duke University, Durham, North Carolina

MARC NERLOVE (317), Department of Economics, University of Chicago, Chicago, Illinois

RONALD SCHOENBERG (168), Department of Sociology, University of Washington, Seattle, Washington

KARL SCHUESSLER (201), Department of Sociology, Indiana University, Bloomington, Indiana

T. PAUL SCHULTZ† (317), Population Program, The RAND Corporation, Santa Monica, California

HENRI THEIL (113), Center for Mathematical Studies in Business and Economics, University of Chicago, Chicago, Illinois

DAVID E. WILEY (69), Department of Education, University of Chicago, Chicago, Illinois

* Present address: Department of Psychology and Social Relations, Harvard University, Cambridge, Massachusetts.
† Present address: Department of Economics, University of Minnesota, Minneapolis, Minnesota.

Foreword

The articles contained in this book are revisions of papers presented at a conference cosponsored by the Social Science Research Council and the Social Systems Research Institute of the University of Wisconsin, November 12–16, 1970. The conference was organized and chaired by Professor Arthur S. Goldberger, coeditor of this volume, and was held at Madison. The Russell Sage Foundation generously provided funds for the expenses of the conference and preparation of the papers for publication.

The Conference on Structural Equation Models is a milestone in the history of social science methodology, for it brought together the widest variety of social scientists whose research interests lay in the development and use of quantitative methods for analyzing causation in non-experimental data. The conferees came from economics, education, political science, psychology, and sociology. Their topical interests ranged across occupational mobility, educational achievement, Congressional voting, conflict resolution, and macroeconomic policy. They spent five days together, having read each other's prepared papers beforehand, in intensive and obviously fruitful discovery of communalities of method and technique amidst the great diversity of topical and disciplinary areas. One participant, not noted for his effusiveness, later described the conference as "the most exciting intellectual experience of my life."

The conference had its origin in an interdisciplinary, though highly informal, discussion during the 1968 Annual Meeting of the Directors of the Social Science Research Council, when James Coleman, Lee Cronbach, Frederick Mosteller, and Herbert Simon foregathered with the writer (who was at that time Vice President of the Council) to talk about possible SSRC activities in the realm of methodology. They quickly agreed on the urgent need to encourage developments in methods for analyzing causative influences in complex social phenomena. This conclusion emerged in a context of concern for improving both the design and the evaluation of social interventions—that is, programs designed to produce changes in social conditions, social processes, or individual behavior in areas such as education, welfare, housing, and health; but the fundamental scientific nature of the problem was recognized and it was urged that a beginning be made on a methodological level.

The first result of this discussion was the decision to explore recent developments in causal analysis, for it seemed that a number of technical developments had been taking place simultaneously and almost independently in several disciplines and were being tried out on a variety of social scientific problems. A preliminary conference of about a dozen specialists was convened at the Social Science Research Council in New York in January 1970 for a two-day discussion. The participants quickly discovered a number of parallel lines of inquiry in their different fields, which had problems in common. They also identified other related work and active scholars who were not represented at the conference but whose research was relevant. The conferees recommended that a longer, intensive working conference be held to allow exploration of these problems in depth.

Fortunately, Arthur Goldberger was an energetic and stimulating participant in the January meeting, and agreed to organize the longer meeting, and suggested the Social Systems Research Institute join as cosponsor. Orville Brim immediately recognized the importance of the proposal and gave enthusiastic support to a request to the Russell Sage Foundation, which provided the necessary funds.

The Conference on Structural Equation Models was attended by all those whose revised papers appear herein and, in addition, by Hayward Alker and George Bohrnstedt, whose participation in the discussion was of great value. After the meeting, Otis Dudley Duncan joined Arthur Goldberger in editing the revised papers for publication.

The impact of the conference on the participants is already clear, but they can, I believe, confidently expect their work to influence a much wider audience through this volume. It represents a true pooling of talent and interest to consolidate advances in social science research methods. Besides being a significant contribution in its own right, it exemplifies the highest, and perhaps the most significant type of interdisciplinary collaboration—the meaningful conjunction of previously separate streams of investigation which, in coming together, move our whole enterprise forward more swiftly.

HENRY W. RIECKEN
*Center for Advanced Study
in the Behavioral Sciences*

1

Structural Equation Models: An Overview

ARTHUR S. GOLDBERGER

1. Introduction

The invitation to prospective participants in our conference ran, in part:

> Over the past ten years there has been an upsurge of interest in structural equation models within the social sciences. In subject matter terms, the interest has been generated in studies of macroeconomic policy formation, intergenerational occupational mobility, racial discrimination in employment and earnings, scholastic achievement, congressional constituency representation, and evaluation of social action programs, among others. In methodological terms, the models have been referred to as simultaneous equation systems, linear causal schemes, path analysis, structural equation models, dependence analysis, test score theory, multitrait–multimethod matrices, and the cross-lagged panel correlation technique.
>
> Behind all this diversity of subject matter and terminology, several common features can be identified. One relates to the analysis of *nonexperimental data*: the absence of laboratory conditions demands that statistical procedures substitute for conventional experimental controls. A second one concerns *hypothetical constructs*: many of the models contain latent variables which, while not directly observed, have operational implications for relationships among observable variables. A third common element relates to *systems*: the models are typically built up of several or many equations which interact together.
>
> These features call for statistical tools which are based upon, but which go well beyond, conventional regression and analysis of variance. Within the several disciplines, as you know, a substantial amount of effort has been and is

being devoted to the development of the statistical tools. The time seems ripe for a consolidation of the progress which has been made and for a clarification of the remaining issues.

  With this in mind, we are planning a working conference of a small group who are actively engaged in this broad area. . . . The plan is that each participant prepare a paper which will form the basis for a two-hour session at which it will be presented and discussed. There may be several papers of the survey type, but I expect that most participants will want to report on their own current research on structural equation models, be it substantive or methodological. I believe that each of those invited has some acquaintance with the relevant literature in one or more disciplines besides his own. Thus there should be enough overlap of language as well as community of interest. A major objective of the conference, obviously, is to bridge the gaps between the several disciplines, and I believe that this will be accomplished by the discussion as well as by the papers themselves.

The participants did find—or rather, make—the conference productive; readers of this volume may judge for themselves. Ultimately, the success of the conference will be measured by the extent to which the ideas, approaches, and results reported here prove useful in further social science research with structural equation models. To assist in this process, we sketch out some of the main issues alluded to in the invitation and developed in the chapters which follow.

2. Regression and Structure: The Issue of Invariance

In a structural equation model each equation represents a causal link rather than a mere empirical association. In a regression model, on the other hand, each equation represents the conditional mean of a dependent variable as a function of explanatory variables. It is this distinction that makes conventional regression analysis an inadequate tool for estimating structural equation models. If, in a sample of observations, we fit the regression of y on x, we will be estimating the conditional expectation of y as a function of x. This is all very well if we are content to trace out the course of the mean value of y as x varies. But as a rule, it will not serve us well if we wish to characterize the mechanism that generated the observations in terms of more fundamental parameters.

Three cases stand out as ones in which least-squares regression of y on x is an inappropriate estimation procedure. Economists are inclined to describe these situations by saying that the least-squares estimates are "biased." But it is more instructive to concede that least-squares estimation will provide "unbiased" estimates of the conditional expectation function $E(y \mid x)$. The objection to least-squares regression will then rest on the assertion that the parameters of $E(y \mid x)$ do not correspond to the fundamental parameters of the mechanism that generated the data.

The three cases referred to involve (i) unobservable variables (= errors of measurement), (ii) simultaneity (= reciprocal causation), (iii) omitted variables (= inadequate control). We consider these briefly in turn.

Case (i) Unobservable variables

Consider the structural model

$$x = x^* + u, \qquad y = \beta x^* + v, \tag{1}$$

where x^*, u, and v are independently distributed with zero expectations. (The zero-expectation assumption, introduced as a matter of convenience, will be retained without further notice throughout this chapter.) The model purports to describe the mechanism that generates values of the observable random variables x and y—they have a common unobservable cause x^* as well as unique unobservable causes u and v. We might think of x as a measurement of the construct x^* and of y as an effect of x^*, but in a sense, both x and y are erroneous measurements of x^*. The model produces a joint distribution of x and y, with zero expectations, and variances and covariance:

$$\sigma_{xx} = \sigma_{**} + \sigma_{uu}, \qquad \sigma_{xy} = \beta\sigma_{**},$$

$$\sigma_{yy} = \beta^2\sigma_{**} + \sigma_{vv}.$$

The conditional expectation of y given x (or population linear regression of y on x) is therefore

$$E(y \mid x) = (\sigma_{xy}/\sigma_{xx})x = (\beta\kappa)x, \tag{2}$$

where $\kappa = \sigma_{**}/(\sigma_{**} + \sigma_{uu})$ is a variance ratio that lies between zero and one. (We have implicitly assumed that the conditional expectation of y varies linearly with x. For convenience, we retain this assumption throughout the chapter. The linear regression defined by (2) may always be interpreted as the best linear approximation to a conditional expectation function when the latter is nonlinear.) The parameter $\beta\kappa$ which characterizes the population linear regression clearly differs from the structural parameter β. Thus, had we used x as a "proxy" for x^*, our sample least-squares regression of y on x would have estimated $\beta\kappa$, and *precisely for that reason*, failed to estimate β. If our interest is in β, the basic objection to least squares is not that it is biased, but rather that it is unbiased for the wrong parameter.

Case (ii) *Simultaneity*

Consider the structural model

$$y = \beta x + v, \qquad x = \alpha y + u, \tag{3}$$

where u and v are independent unobservable disturbances. The model purports to describe the mechanism that generates values of the observable random variables x and y—they cause each other. It produces a joint distribution of x and y with

$$\sigma_{xx} = (\sigma_{uu} + \alpha^2 \sigma_{vv})/(1 - \alpha\beta)^2, \qquad \sigma_{xy} = (\beta\sigma_{uu} + \alpha\sigma_{vv})/(1 - \alpha\beta)^2,$$
$$\sigma_{yy} = (\beta^2\sigma_{uu} + \sigma_{vv})/(1 - \alpha\beta)^2. \tag{4}$$

(To compute these moments, we first solved (3) for y and x in terms of u and v, obtaining $y = (\beta u + v)/(1 - \alpha\beta)$ and $x = (u + \alpha v)/(1 - \alpha\beta)$.) The population linear regression of y on x is therefore

$$E(y \mid x) = (\sigma_{xy}/\sigma_{xx})x = (\beta\kappa + (1/\alpha)(1 - \kappa))x,$$

where $\kappa = \sigma_{uu}/(\sigma_{uu} + \alpha^2\sigma_{vv})$ is a variance ratio that lies between zero and one. The parameter $\beta\kappa + (1/\alpha)(1 - \kappa)$ which characterizes the population linear regression differs from the structural parameter β. A sample least-squares regression of y on x will estimate $\beta\kappa + (1/\alpha)(1 - \kappa)$, and precisely for that reason, fail to estimate β.

Case (iii) *Omitted variables*

Consider the structural model

$$y = \beta_1 x_1 + \beta_2 x_2 + v,$$

where v is an unobserved disturbance distributed independently of the observed random variables x_1 and x_2, which have variances σ_{11}, σ_{22}, and covariance σ_{12}. This model describes a mechanism in which x_1 and x_2 combine to determine y. It generates a joint distribution of x_1 and y with

$$\sigma_{1y} = \beta_1\sigma_{11} + \beta_2\sigma_{12}, \qquad \sigma_{yy} = \beta_1^2\sigma_{11} + \beta_2^2\sigma_{22} + 2\beta_1\beta_2\sigma_{12} + \sigma_{vv}.$$

The population linear regression of y on x_1 is

$$E(y \mid x_1) = (\sigma_{1y}/\sigma_{11}) x_1 = (\beta_1 + \kappa\beta_2) x_1$$

where $\kappa = \sigma_{12}/\sigma_{11}$ is the slope in the population linear regression of x_2 on x_1. The parameter $\beta_1 + \kappa\beta_2$ which characterizes $E(y \mid x_1)$ differs from the structural parameter β_1. Sample least-squares regression of y on x_1 will estimate the former, not the latter.

Having distinguished the three cases, we should recognize that the distinctions are not very sharp. For example, we can convert the unobservable-variable case into an omitted-variable case by writing

$$y = \beta x^* + v = \beta(x - u) + v = \beta x - \beta u + v,$$

and viewing u as the omitted variable. More fundamentally, the common element in the three cases is the following. The structural model is specified in terms of a set of parameters. The model generates for the observable variables a joint distribution which, among other things, traces out the conditional expectation function of one of the observables given the others, i.e., specifies how the mean value of one varies with the others. The parameters of this population linear regression are mixtures of the structural parameters. Least-squares regression estimates these mixtures rather than the individual structural parameters.

Now, a mixture of parameters is also a parameter. For example, in case (i), $\beta\kappa$, is, like its components β, σ_{**}, and σ_{uu}, a characteristic of the mechanism that generated the observable variables. To sustain the objection to least-squares regression as a tool for estimating a structural model, we must make the case that the structural parameters are somehow more fundamental than the regression parameters. The key to this case is the notion that the regression parameters are *mixtures* of the structural parameters; if one structural parameter changes, *all* regression coefficients may change.

Suppose the population that produced our data is the only relevant population; i.e., the mechanism that generated our sample will continue to generate all samples in the future. If so, over the relevant universe, all structural parameters will remain the same *and* all regression parameters will also remain the same. The latter are just as fundamental as the former. But suppose the population that generated our data will not continue to generate all data in the future. Specifically, suppose that for the next population, one and only one of the structural parameters changes its value. Then that next population may well have all its regression parameters different.

For example, in case (i) suppose that β, σ_{uu}, and σ_{vv} remain unchanged while σ_{**} is increased to $\bar{\sigma}_{**}$. Then κ will increase to $\bar{\kappa} = \bar{\sigma}_{**}/(\bar{\sigma}_{**}+\sigma_{uu})$, and the slope of the regression of y on x will increase to $\beta\bar{\kappa}$. The slope of the regression of x on y will also change, from

$$\sigma_{xy}/\sigma_{yy} = \beta\sigma_{**}/(\beta^2\sigma_{**} + \sigma_{vv}) = (1/\beta)\lambda,$$

where $\lambda = \beta^2 \sigma_{**}/(\beta^2 \sigma_{**} + \sigma_{vv})$, to $(1/\beta)\bar{\lambda}$, where $\bar{\lambda} = \beta^2 \bar{\sigma}_{**}/(\beta^2 \bar{\sigma}_{**} + \sigma_{vv})$. Similarly, in case (iii) suppose that β_1, β_2, σ_{11}, σ_{22}, and σ_{vv} remain unchanged, while σ_{12} changes. Then the regression slope of y on x_1 and the regression slope of y on x_2 will both change.

This line of argument leads to the conclusion that the search for structural parameters is a search for invariant features of the mechanisms that generate observable variables. Invariant features are those which remain stable—or vary individually—over the set of populations in which we are interested. When regression parameters have this invariance, they are proper objects of research, and regression is an appropriate tool. But when, as appears to be the case in many social science areas, regression parameters lack this invariance, the proper objects of research are more fundamental parameters; and statistical tools which go beyond conventional regression are required.

Surprisingly enough, discussions of this issue are rather scarce in the literature. We can point to Marschak (1953), Simon (1953), and to Malinvaud (1970, pp. 60–63), which ends as follows:

> It often happens that the model chosen as the basis for econometric investigation relative to one group or during one period of time may not be suitable, just as it is, for another group or another period of time. Certain of the model's laws will still apply but others will have to be modified. Only an exact knowledge of the structures can provide the basis for the necessary revision. . . . In short, if it is not enough to know the distribution of the observed variables, if we wish to determine all the parameters occurring in the original formulation of the model, then we are really considering these parameters, taken individually, to be more stable, less often subject to revision, more "autonomous" than the directly observable distributions.

In the papers which follow, readers may not find any detailed discussion of this issue. But it looms in the background throughout, justifying, if only implicitly, the participants' concern with sophisticated estimation procedures.

3. Unobservables and Observables: The Issue of Identification

Population regressions among observable variables have a great virtue: their parameters can be directly deduced from the population moments of the observable variables. Since these moments can be estimated by sample moments, there is no essential problem in estimating regression parameters. But once our interest is thrown back onto structural parameters, the issue of identification arises: Is it possible to deduce uniquely the values of the structural parameters from the population moments of the observable variables ("observable moments")?

This question was explored in a variety of contexts and ways at our conference. To provide a unifying thread, we start with case (i) of the previous section, reparameterizing and relabeling it as follows:

$$y_1 = \beta_1 x^* + u, \qquad y_2 = \beta_2 x^* + v. \tag{5}$$

Here x^*, u, and v are independent unobservables, and we take $\sigma_{**} = 1$ as a normalization instead of taking the first slope equal to 1 as we did in (1). The model implies three equations connecting observable moments to structural parameters, namely

$$\sigma_{11} = \beta_1^2 + \sigma_{uu}, \qquad \sigma_{12} = \beta_1 \beta_2,$$
$$\sigma_{22} = \beta_2^2 + \sigma_{vv}. \tag{6}$$

Clearly, these three equations will not suffice to determine uniquely the four structural parameters β_1, β_2, σ_{uu}, σ_{vv}. The structural parameters are not identified.

If, however, we observed three, rather than two indicators (= erroneous measurements) of the unobservable x^*, the situation improves. Consider the model

$$y_1 = \beta_1 x^* + u, \qquad y_2 = \beta_2 x^* + v, \qquad y_3 = \beta_3 x^* + w, \tag{7}$$

where x^*, u, v, w are independent unobservables with $\sigma_{**} = 1$. The model implies six equations connecting observable moments to structural parameters, namely

$$\sigma_{11} = \beta_1^2 + \sigma_{uu}, \qquad \sigma_{12} = \beta_1 \beta_2, \qquad \sigma_{13} = \beta_1 \beta_3,$$
$$\sigma_{22} = \beta_2^2 + \sigma_{vv}, \qquad \sigma_{23} = \beta_2 \beta_3,$$
$$\sigma_{33} = \beta_3^2 + \sigma_{ww}. \tag{8}$$

These six equations will just suffice to determine uniquely the six structural parameters, β_1, β_2, β_3, σ_{uu}, σ_{vv}, σ_{ww}. Explicitly, the solutions are

$$\beta_1 = (\sigma_{12}\sigma_{13}/\sigma_{23})^{1/2}, \qquad \beta_2 = (\sigma_{12}\sigma_{23}/\sigma_{13})^{1/2}, \qquad \beta_3 = (\sigma_{13}\sigma_{23}/\sigma_{12})^{1/2},$$
$$\sigma_{uu} = \sigma_{11} - \sigma_{12}\sigma_{13}/\sigma_{23}, \quad \sigma_{vv} = \sigma_{22} - \sigma_{12}\sigma_{23}/\sigma_{13}, \quad \sigma_{ww} = \sigma_{33} - \sigma_{13}\sigma_{23}/\sigma_{12}.$$

The structural parameters are identified.

If we observe still more indicators of x^*, the observable moments provide more than enough information to identify the structural parameters. Consider the model

$$y_m = \beta_m x^* + u_m, \qquad m = 1,...,M, \tag{9}$$

where $x^*, u_1, ..., u_M$ are independent unobservables with $\sigma_{**} = 1$. In matrix form, we write this as

$$y = \beta x^* + u, \tag{10}$$

where $y = (y_1, ..., y_M)'$, $\beta = (\beta_1, ..., \beta_M)'$, $u = (u_1, ..., u_M)'$, and express the normalization and independence by

$$\sigma_{**} = E(x^* x^*) = 1, \qquad E(x^* u') = 0, \qquad E(uu') = \Theta \quad \text{diagonal}, \tag{11}$$

where the diagonal elements of Θ are the variances of the elements of u. Let Σ denote the covariance matrix of the observables, so that σ_{mn} $(m, n = 1, ..., M)$ denotes $C(y_m, y_n)$, the covariance of y_m and y_n [for $m = n$, $\sigma_{mm} = C(y_m, y_m) = V(y_m)$, the variance of y_m]. This multiple-indicator model implies

$$\Sigma = E(yy') = E((\beta x^* + u)(x^* \beta' + u')) = \beta\beta' + \Theta. \tag{12}$$

This represents a system of q equations in p unknowns, where $q = M(M + 1)/2$ is the number of distinct elements in the symmetric matrix Σ, and $p = 2M$ is the number of elements in β plus the number of nonzero elements in Θ. Since $q - p = (M - 3)M/2$ is positive for $M > 3$, we see that when there are more than three indicators of the common unobservable x^*, the structural parameters are not only identified but actually overidentified: the same values of the structural parameters can be deduced uniquely from the observable moments in several distinct ways. This overidentification creates possibilities for improved inference from a sample; these will be touched on in the next section. For present purposes, the point is that the structural parameters are uniquely determined in terms of the observable moments.

What we have called the multiple-indicator model is merely a special case of the classical factor analysis model, special in that it has a single common factor. The general factor analysis model specifies that a set of M observable variables $y_1, ..., y_M$ (indicators) are determined linearly by a set of K unobservable variables $x_1^*, ..., x_K^*$ (common factors) and a set of M unobservable disturbances $u_1, ..., u_M$ (unique factors). In matrix form this structural model is

$$y = Bx^* + u$$

$$E(x^* x^{*\prime}) = \Phi, \qquad E(x^* u') = 0, \qquad E(uu') = \Theta \quad \text{diagonal}. \tag{13}$$

It implies that

$$\Sigma = E(yy') = B\Phi B' + \Theta. \tag{14}$$

To avoid a trivial indeterminancy, we temporarily adopt the normalization rules

$$\Phi = I, \qquad B'\Theta^{-1}B = \Delta \quad \text{diagonal.}$$

Then (14) represents a system of q equations in p unknowns, where $q = M(M + 1)/2$ is the number of distinct elements in Σ, and $p = M(K + 1) - K(K - 1)/2$ is the number of unknown structural parameters. [The value of p is computed as follows: MK (elements in B) plus M (nonzero elements in Θ) plus K (nonzero elements in Δ) minus $K(K + 1)/2$ (distinct constraints in $B'\Theta^{-1}B = \Delta$).] If

$$q - p = ((M - K)^2 - (M + K))/2 \geqslant 0,$$

these equations should suffice to determine the unknown structural parameters. However, the normalization rules are essentially arbitrary, and it is possible to undo them by transformations designed to reveal a simpler parametric structure. Transformed factors $z = Ax^*$ are sought such that $\bar{B} = BA^{-1}$ and $\bar{\Phi} = E(zz') = AA'$ have neat patterns. These transformations, or rotations, are widely used in conventional *exploratory* factor analysis.

Exploratory factor analysis, as sketched here, may have limited appeal as a basis for structural modeling. It treats all observables symmetrically, as indicators of the unobservable common factors, and it permits ex post redefinition of variables and parameters. These characteristics, no doubt, have inhibited its use in those social science areas where fairly clear chains of causation and fairly well-defined variables are available. In those areas, it is natural to incorporate more structural assumptions in advance. For example, it may be appropriate to specify that certain observables depend on certain common factors, or that certain common factors are correlated in a particular manner. Thus values of some elements in B and Φ are fixed in advance. When enough such assumptions are made, rotation is ruled out. In this manner one arrives at models of *confirmatory* factor analysis, discussed in Lawley & Maxwell (1963, Chapter 6) and Jöreskog (1969). Proceeding in the same spirit, it may be natural to formulate a structural model for the factors themselves, in which event the elements of Φ are derivable from more fundamental parameters. In this manner one is led to second-order factor analysis and then to Jöreskog's (1970a) general covariance structure model. Participants in our conference drew on these modern versions of factor analysis rather than on the more traditional exploratory factor analysis.

We have now seen how identification is attained when multiple indicators (= effects) are observable. Some structural models rely instead on observable determinants (= causes) of the unobservables. Consider the structural model

$$y_1 = \beta_1 x^* + u, \qquad y_2 = \beta_2 x^* + v, \qquad x^* = \alpha x + w, \qquad (15)$$

where the disturbances u, v, w are mutually independent, and independent of the observable x, which is a cause of x^*. In conjunction with the normalization rule $\sigma_{**} = 1$, the model implies

$$\sigma_{11} = \beta_1{}^2 + \sigma_{uu}, \qquad \sigma_{12} = \beta_1 \beta_2, \qquad \sigma_{1x} = \beta_1 \alpha$$

$$\sigma_{22} = \beta_2{}^2 + \sigma_{vv}, \qquad \sigma_{2x} = \beta_2 \alpha.$$

These five equations together with $\alpha^2 \sigma_{xx} + \sigma_{ww} = \sigma_{**} = 1$ suffice to identify the six structural parameters β_1, β_2, α, σ_{uu}, σ_{vv}, σ_{ww}.

Additional causes, like additional indicators, may occur. Adopting a matrix formulation, we consider the following multiple-indicator–multiple-cause structural model

$$y = \beta x^* + u, \qquad x^* = \alpha' x, \qquad E(xu') = 0, \qquad (16)$$

where y is the $M \times 1$ vector of observable indicators, x the $K \times 1$ vector of causes, u the $M \times 1$ disturbance vector, and β and α are respectively $M \times 1$ and $K \times 1$ parameter vectors. The model, in conjunction with $\alpha' E(xx') \alpha = \sigma_{**} = 1$, implies the following relationships between observable moments and structural parameters:

$$E(yy') = \beta\beta' + \Theta, \qquad E(xy') = E(xx')\alpha\beta', \qquad (17)$$

where $\Theta = E(uu')$. (We are not assuming Θ diagonal, but are ruling out the disturbance in the equation determining x^*.) The right-hand equations, in conjunction with the normalization $\alpha' E(xx')\alpha = 1$, express $q = KM$ observable moments in terms of $p = M + K - 1$ structural parameters. Provided that $q - p \geqslant 0$, this will identify β and α; then the left-hand equations identify Θ.

An alternative analysis, more natural to economists, may be instructive. Solving (16) for the observable indicators in terms of the observable causes, we obtain the "reduced form"

$$y' = x'\alpha\beta' + u' = x'\Pi + u' \qquad (18)$$

say. Since $E(xu') = 0$, the mth column of Π gives the coefficients in the population linear regression of y_m on the x's. Regression equations in observable variables are always identified in terms of moments; so β and α will be identified if they can be determined from the reduced-form coefficient matrix Π. They can, using the normalization rule, if $q - p \geqslant 0$. When $q - p > 0$ the model is in fact overidentified. This reduced-form analysis is equivalent to the previous population-moment analysis, since $\Pi = [E(xx')]^{-1}E(xy')$ is just a nonsingular transformation of the right-hand equations in (17).

This multiple-indicator–multiple-cause model, discussed by Zellner (1970), Hauser & Goldberger (1971), and Goldberger (1972), appears in various guises in the papers which follow. Some of the empirical studies use recursive models in which unobservable variables appear both as causes and as effects of observables.

Having come this far with case (i), let us turn to case (ii), the simultaneous-equation scheme

$$y = \beta x + v, \qquad x = \alpha y + u,$$

where u and v are independent disturbances. Clearly the three equations relating the observable moments $\sigma_{xx}, \sigma_{yy}, \sigma_{xy}$ to the four structural parameters β, α, σ_{uu}, σ_{vv} will not suffice to determine the latter. The structural parameters are not identified. Suppose, however, we had the following, richer, simultaneous equation model:

$$y_1 = \alpha_1 y_2 + \alpha_2 x_1 + u_1, \qquad y_1 = \beta_1 y_2 + \beta_2 x_2 + \beta_3 x_3 + u_2, \qquad (19)$$

where the disturbances u_1 and u_2 (not necessarily mutually independent) are independent of the observable exogenous variables x_1, x_2, and x_3.

To analyze the situation, it is convenient to solve the structural equations for the reduced form which gives y_1 and y_2 in terms of x_1, x_2, x_3:

$$y_1 = (-\alpha_2 \beta_1/\Delta) x_1 + (\alpha_1 \beta_2/\Delta) x_2 + (\alpha_1 \beta_3/\Delta) x_3 + v_1 \qquad (20a)$$

$$y_2 = (-\alpha_2/\Delta) \quad x_1 + \quad (\beta_2/\Delta) x_2 + \quad (\beta_3/\Delta) x_3 + v_2, \qquad (20b)$$

where the symbols $\Delta = \alpha_1 - \beta_1$, $v_1 = (\alpha_1 u_1 - \beta_1 u_2)/\Delta$, and $v_2 = (u_2 - u_1)/\Delta$ have been introduced to simplify the formulas. Noting that v_1 and v_2, being functions of u_1 and u_2, share the latter's independence from x_1, x_2, x_3, we first deduce equations relating the observable moments to the structural coefficients $\alpha_1, \alpha_2, \beta_1, \beta_2, \beta_3$. These equations are obtained as follows: Multiply (20a) through by x_1 and take expected values; multiply (20a) through by x_2 and take expected values; multiply (20a) through by x_3 and take expected values. Repeat these steps for (20b). The six equations thus produced (more than) suffice to determine the five structural coefficients. Then we deduce equations relating the observable moments to the structural disturbance parameters

$V(u_1)$, $V(u_2)$, $C(u_1, u_2)$. This second set of equations is obtained as follows: Multiply (20a) by itself and take expected values; multiply (20b) by itself and take expected values; multiply (20a) by (20b) and take expected values. The three equations thus produced suffice, in conjunction with the previous results, to determine the three structural disturbance parameters. Thus all structural parameters are identified.

An alternative analysis is more customary in econometrics. Each of the reduced-form equations in (20) represents a population regression function of a y given the x's. Regression functions are, as usual, identified, so the structural coefficients will be identified if they can be determined from the reduced-form regression coefficients. There being five of the former and six of the latter, identifiability of the former is indicated. Identification of the disturbance parameters follows as before.

Generalizing this example leads us to the standard simultaneous-equation model of econometrics. The structural model is

$$y'\Gamma = x'B + u', \qquad E(xu') = 0, \tag{21}$$

where y is the $M \times 1$ vector of endogenous variables, x the $K \times 1$ vector of exogenous variables, u the $M \times 1$ vector of disturbances, and Γ and B are $M \times M$ and $K \times M$ structural coefficient matrices. The matrix Γ is nonsingular, and the covariance matrix of the structural disturbances, $E(uu') = \Theta$, is positive definite. To avoid a trivial indeterminancy, one element in each column of Γ is normalized at unity. Certain other elements of Γ and B are specified to be zero to capture the behavioral assumptions of the model; let s denote the number of such prior restrictions. The reduced form of the model, obtained by solving for y in terms of x, is

$$y' = x'B\Gamma^{-1} + u'\Gamma^{-1} = x'\Pi + v', \tag{22}$$

where $\Pi = B\Gamma^{-1}$ and $v' = u'\Gamma^{-1}$. The columns of Π, being coefficients of population linear regressions, are automatically identified in terms of the moments of the observable variables x and y. Identifiability of the structural coefficients B and Γ thus rests on the possibility of solving the $q = KM$ equations $\Pi = B\Gamma^{-1}$ for the $p = M(K + M) - s$ free parameters in B and Γ. Roughly speaking, identifiability of all the structural coefficients is possible if $q - p \geqslant 0$, i.e., if $s \geqslant M^2$. Once the structural coefficients are identified, the remaining structural parameters can be obtained from $\Theta = \Gamma'E(vv')\Gamma$. This conventional econometric analysis can be rephrased in terms of moments. Since x is independent of v, (22) implies

$$E(yy') = \Gamma^{-1'}B'E(xx')B\Gamma^{-1} + \Gamma^{-1'}\Theta\Gamma^{-1}, \qquad E(xy')\Gamma = E(xx')B. \tag{23}$$

Identifiability of B and Γ is determined by the right-hand equations; then identifiability of Θ follows from the left-hand equations.

For simultaneous-equation models, detailed rules for determining identifiability have been developed in the econometric literature; for factor analysis models, detailed rules for determining identifiability have been developed in the psychometric literature. (The counting rules we have been using here are suggestive, rather than decisive.) Years ago, Koopmans & Reiersøl (1950) discussed identification in fairly general terms, referring to psychometrics as well as to econometrics. Still, fresh issues of identification arise in the papers which follow. The explanation is that many of these studies are concerned with models that incorporate both simultaneity *and* measurement error. The conjunction of reciprocal causation and unobservables was a leitmotiv of the conference. It evoked a loss of inhibition—economists recognizing that identifiability is attainable in the presence of measurement error, psychologists recognizing that identifiability is attainable in the presence of simultaneity. In this process, sociologists played a vital role; their path analysis approach was receptive to both themes.

4. Efficiency and Testing: The Issue of Overidentification

When the moments of observable variables (or equivalently the parameters of regressions among observable variables) provide more than enough information to determine the structural parameters, the model is overidentified. In that event, we have restrictions, or constraints, on the observable moments. These restrictions may be used in at least two distinct ways when we have a sample in hand. First, if the model is taken to be valid, the restrictions may be exploited to obtain "more efficient" estimates (i.e. estimates with smaller sampling variability) of the unknown structural parameters. Second, if the validity of the model is in doubt, the restrictions may be utilized to "test" the model.

If the model is valid, then all the equations relating moments to parameters, no matter how numerous they may be, will hold in the population. However, since sample moments inevitably deviate from their population counterparts, in overidentified models the sample analogues of the moment-parameter equations will conflict with one another, and cannot be solved directly for estimates of the parameters. In the psychometric literature, as in the econometric literature, a large variety of procedures have been developed for efficient estimation of overidentified models. In some instances, these procedures are, in effect, devices for reconciling the conflicting sample equations by minimizing some measure of the difference between the sample moment matrix and its parametric structure; cf. Goldberger (1971). Thus, factor analysis estimation procedures choose values of B, Φ, and Θ to minimize some scalar measure of $S_{yy} - (B\Phi B' + \Theta)$; econometric estimation procedures choose values of B and Γ to minimize some scalar measure of $(S_{xy}\Gamma - S_{xx}B)'(S_{xy}\Gamma - S_{xx}B)$. Here S_{yy}, S_{xx}, and S_{xy} are sample moment matrices. When models falling outside the conventional boundaries of simultaneous equations and factor analysis arise, as happens in several of the papers which follow, variations on the standard estimation procedures are called for.

If the model is invalid, certain of the restrictions will be violated in the population. Hence, if population moments were known, the validity of the model (or rather of its restrictions) could be determined unequivocally. However, since sample moments deviate from population moments, the failure of the former to satisfy restrictions on the latter might be attributable to sampling variability. From this point of view, the restrictions are seen as null hypotheses, which are to be probed by significance tests. It should be emphasized that it is the restrictions—the null hypotheses—which are tested, rather than the model per se—the maintained hypotheses. A just-identified model is after all not really testable. Readers will find testing procedures developed and employed in several of the papers. On most occasions, they are employed in a constructive, rather than mechanical, manner. That is, rejection of a null hypothesis is taken as a clue to the part of the model that needs revision, rather than as an incentive to discard the entire model out of hand.

5. Identification and Inference in Linear Models

We now introduce in turn the papers in the first part of the volume, in which the emphasis is on theory and methods.

Kenneth Land considers a fully recursive model. With disturbances independent and measurement errors absent, the system of structural equations decomposes into a sequence of regression equations. Since each structural equation gives the conditional expectation of one variable given causally prior variables, equation-by-equation least-squares regressions do provide desirable structural estimates. Still, Land shows that even this least-troublesome structural model demands modification of the classical regression model to capture the stochastic nature of the explanatory variables and to cover cross-equation constraints.

Neil Henry also works with a recursive model with independent disturbances. But here an unobservable dichotomy is the underlying variable. Casting his measurement model in linear terms, Henry develops the relationships identifying structural parameters in terms of the population moments of the observable measurements, also dichotomous. The analysis exploits the special properties of dichotomous variables, but also develops analogies with continuous-variable models.

David Wiley explores the problems of identification and estimation which arise when hypothetical, or erroneously measured, variables occur in multi-equation models. Working through a series of illustrative recursive models, he calls attention to the possibility of attaining identification by obtaining multiple measurements of the variables. Wiley carries this idea over to a simultaneous-equation model, and offers some guidelines for determining identifiability.

Karl Jöreskog tackles a general linear model which incorporates simultaneity and errors of measurement. The model subsumes as special cases the conventional simultaneous-equation model of econometrics (in which measurement error is absent) and the factor analysis model of psychometrics (in which behavioral disturbances are absent). The relationships between population moments and structural parameters are obtained, but not analyzed for identifiability. On the condition that the model is identified, Jöreskog draws on the maximum-likelihood principle to develop the algorithm for obtaining efficient estimates of the structural parameters and testing overidentifying restrictions. Econometric model-builders will find that his paper opens up new possibilities for handling those empirical situations in which accurate measurements are not available.

For estimating a conventional overidentified simultaneous equation model (no measurement error), economists most frequently use the two-stage least-squares (2SLS) procedure, originated by Henri Theil. The first stage of 2SLS calls for estimation of the unrestricted reduced-form parameters. But in economic contexts, where models are large and samples small, this may be impossible, the number of predetermined variables exceeding the number of observations. Theil here adapts 2SLS to handle such undersized samples in a straightforward manner.

In a variety of overidentified situations, efficient estimation procedures can be viewed as devices for reconciling the conflicting moment equations. Arthur Goldberger translates this into the idea that the efficient estimation procedures produce weighted averages of basic estimates. Illustrations are drawn from multiple-regression, unobservable-variable, and simultaneous-equation models.

David Kenny recasts the "cross-lagged panel correlation" approach in a structural equation framework. The time path of a set of measured variables is traced back to the time path of common unobservable factors. Kenny's concern is to distinguish a structural model in which common-factor effects are instantaneous from one in which they are also delayed. Here the overidentifying restrictions play their second role—that of testable hypotheses.

This role is further developed by Herbert Costner and Ronald Schoenberg who work with a simple confirmatory factor analysis model. Violations of overidentifying restrictions are viewed as clues to the location of misspecifications in a tentative structural model. Using real-world as well as artificial data, Costner and Schoenberg attempt to build, on the basis of significance test statistics, a systematic procedure for diagnosing and correcting a structural model.

The variables that enter structural equation models are often trans-formations of raw data. Karl Schuessler updates the well-seasoned literature on ratio variables by tying it into the recent work on structural equation models. Ratio variables were featured in the earliest discussions of "spurious correlation," and a concern with spurious correlation was one of the forces which stimulated the development of structural models. Schuessler's paper reminds us that questions of spuriousness can only be resolved within the framework of a structural model.

6. Empirical Analysis of Social, Economic, and Political Processes

In the second part of the volume, the emphasis is on empirical analysis. These chapters, which stand on their own as substantive contributions to sociology, economics, and political science, also serve to flesh out the issues of specification, identification, and estimation which are treated in theoretical terms in the first part.

Dudley Duncan and David Featherman construct a model of occupa-tional achievement which proceeds from family background through motivations and aspirations to occupation and education. In their block-recursive model one finds latent variables used as causes, and also finds feedback between observables and unobservables. To test theories that emphasize motivational variables, Duncan and Featherman adopt the strategy of giving those variables as much rope as possible in the course of model specification.

Robert Hauser is also concerned with recursively modeling educational achievement on the basis of background and ability. Substantively, the model features youngsters' perceptions of the expectations which others hold for their educational achievement. Hauser's discussion clarifies the distinction between treating measured variables as causes and as effects of unobservables. In the course of his analysis he develops the algorithm for efficient estimation of a multiple-indicator–multiple-cause model with extra exogenous variables.

Next, Zvi Griliches and William Mason take up the background–ability–education–income nexus. Their motivation is to sharpen economists' estimates of the rate of return to education, by examining the bias which arises when ability is omitted. Griliches and Mason treat ability as a latent variable, erroneously measured by test scores which may be contaminated by education itself. Their estimation procedure is an adaptation of 2SLS. Readers may want to trace out the similarities and differences in the approaches to similar empirical problems taken by sociologists in the two previous papers and by an economist–sociologist team in this one.

Marc Nerlove and Paul Schultz summarize their detailed model of Puerto Rican demography, which covers births, female labor force participation, marriage, income, and migration. Their summary illuminates the intimate relationship among simultaneity, measurement error, and omitted variables. Nerlove and Schultz sketch out a variance-component scheme which, in effect, specifies a factor-analysis model for regression disturbances.

John Jackson's empirical analysis of senate voting concludes the volume. To validate regression results on the effects of constituencies and colleagues on senators' votes, Jackson uses a model designed to do justice to the nonmetric character of the data. Unobservable variables appear as hypothetical metric constructs underlying the observations.

7. Conclusion

As this overview indicates, the scope of the topics covered in this volume is, in a sense, severely limited. Certainly, no all-purpose strategy for empirical research emerges. Rather, our attention is confined to situations in which fairly well-developed causal theories are already available, and in which the objective of the empirical research is to confront the theories with data. Even over this domain, the stochastic models considered here may not be applicable. Quite possibly, they fail to do justice to the nonlinearities, learning mechanisms, and goal-determined responses of some social processes. At the conference, this argument, and the case for the more flexible simulation approach, was made, forcefully, by Hayward Alker.

What the experience of our multidisciplinary group does indicate is that the structural equation approach is usable in all of the social sciences. It is striking how similar the analytical problems which arise in sociology, economics, political science, and psychology actually are. To be sure, they come in different settings and are couched in different languages. But, as we found, the effort needed to overcome such natural barriers is not enormous, and is, in any event, well repaid.

2

Identification, Parameter Estimation, and Hypothesis Testing in Recursive Sociological Models

KENNETH C. LAND

1. Introduction

The use of simultaneous-equation systems to analyze sociological data has had a gradual acceptance over the past decade. Initially, the simultaneous-equation approach was greatly stimulated by the explorations of Hubert M. Blalock, Jr., into the problems of causal inferences in nonexperimental research (see, e.g., Blalock, 1964). A second source of considerable influence has been Otis Dudley Duncan's extensive use of simultaneous-equation path-analytic models to unravel the factors involved in the process of social stratification (see, e.g., Blau & Duncan, 1967; Duncan, Featherman, & Duncan, 1968). There have been numerous other applications of simultaneous-equation models in the recent sociological literature.

Certain general features characterize the typical applications of simultaneous-equation models in sociology. First, the models typically consist of a set of equations each of which possesses a random disturbance or error term that summarizes the influence of unmeasured or unknown variables on the mechanism of interest. In short, the models are typically *stochastic* rather than exact or deterministic. Second, the variables of sociological models typically are not functions of time and hence are not dated. This is primarily a consequence of the fact that most of the applications to date have been concerned with variables measured in cross-sectional surveys. Thus, the equations defining sociological models are typically *static* rather than dynamic. Third, most of the models that have been constructed to date rule out two-way causation among the variables of the system. Thus, the models are *recursive*. Fourth, most simultaneous-equation sociological models are *linear* in the variables and the disturbances. Fifth, most sociological models have imposed the assumption that the disturbance terms are contemporaneously *independent*. Finally, although there have been several recent attempts to introduce measurement errors or "errors-in-variables" into the models, it has generally been assumed that the variables of the system are *measured without error*.

As the use of simultaneous-equation models has diffused through the profession, sociological statisticians have addressed the problems of the proper estimation procedures for such systems and of the relation of causal inferences to hypothesis testing (see, e.g., Blalock, 1964; Duncan, 1966; Boudon, 1968; Heise, 1969b; Land, 1969). However, certain troublesome issues have not yet been systematically treated in the social statistical literature. For example, the literature on simultaneous-equation path-analytic models offers no systematic guidance on the estimation of overidentified models. (Indeed, this problem is sufficiently complex that I found it necessary to restrict my earlier exposition of path models (Land, 1969) to just-identified recursive models with uncorrelated normally distributed disturbances.) Furthermore, given systematic parameter estimation procedures, the relation of over-identification to hypothesis testing or model evaluation has not yet been completely resolved.

The purpose of this paper is (1) to bring the general statistical literature to bear on these problems as well as (2) to attempt to give a systematic reconciliation of the various parameter estimation and hypothesis testing methods which have been proposed in the sociological literature. We confine our attention to recursive models with independent disturbances. First, we derive necessary and sufficient conditions for the identifiability of the class of models under consideration. Second, we show that the ordinary least-squares method of estimation applied to each equation of the model provides optimal estimators. Third, we point out how tests of hypotheses concerning structural parameters of the model can be based on the sampling distribution of the estimators. In this discussion, we also exhibit overidentification test statistics for evaluating the empirical adequacy of a recursive model.

2. Sociological Examples

To begin, it is useful to cite a few examples from the sociological literature that illustrate the substantive applications of the models. The first example is familiar to most sociologists—Duncan's basic model of the process of social stratification (Blau & Duncan, 1967). This model is noteworthy in several respects. First, the data from which the parameters of the model were estimated constitute a highly representative and reliable set of observations on the American population. The variables were measured on a sample of approximately 20,000 American men aged 20–64 in 1962; and, as Siegel & Hodge (1968) have shown, the measurements of the variables are highly reliable for this data set. Second, Duncan has carefully elaborated his basic model to include other variables and models of related social processes; see Duncan, Featherman, & Duncan (1968).

Duncan's basic model of the process of social stratification can be written as the following set of structural equations (Blau & Duncan, 1967, p. 170) where the format of the equations follows that defined in the next section:

$$y_1 \qquad\qquad -.310z_1 - .279z_2 = .859u_1$$

$$-.440y_1 + \quad y_2 \qquad\qquad -.224z_2 = .818u_2 \qquad\qquad (1)$$

$$-.281y_1 - .394y_2 + y_3 \qquad -.115z_2 = .753u_3 \,,$$

where z_1 is father's education, z_2 is father's occupation, y_1 is son's education, y_2 son's first full-time occupation, y_3 son's occupation in 1962, and u_1, u_2, u_3 are mutually independent stochastic disturbance terms. In the terminology that will be developed in this paper, Blau and Duncan assumed that father's educational attainment and father's occupation are exogenous variables, while the son's education, first full-time occupation, and occupation in 1962 were taken as endogenous variables in a recursive model of the process of social stratification. The recursivity of the model derives from the nature of the causal processes that are assumed to govern the process of status attainment. That is, first z_1 and z_2 determine y_1, then z_2 and y_1 determine y_2, and, finally, z_2, y_1, and y_2 determine y_3. All variables, including the stochastic disturbance terms, are measured with zero means in standard deviation units. The numerical coefficients shown in Eqs. (1) were estimated by techniques that will be derived in subsequent sections of the paper.

The second example is one of Duncan's modifications of his basic model (Duncan, 1968). It can be written as the following set of equations:

$$y_1 \qquad\qquad - .16z_1 - .20z_2 + .15z_3 - .40z_4 = .76u_1$$

$$-.52y_1 + \quad y_2 \quad - .04z_1 - .12z_2 + .04z_3 - .08z_4 = .75u_2 \qquad (2)$$

$$-.11y_1 - .26y_2 + y_3 - .03z_1 \qquad\qquad - .10z_4 = .91u_3 \, ,$$

where z_1 is the father's education, z_2 is father's occupation, z_3 is number of siblings, z_4 is intelligence (circa age 12), and y_1 is son's education, y_2 is son's 1964 occupation, y_3 is son's 1964 earnings, and u_1, u_2, u_3 are mutually independent stochastic disturbance terms. The parameters in this set of equations were estimated for the cohort of white men in the United States aged 25 to 34 in 1964. Again, the variables were standardized, and the parameters were estimated as above.

As a final example, we cite a study by Sewell & Shah (1968) of the relation of family social class and parental encouragement to educational aspirations of high school seniors. Sewell and Shah's model can be written as:

$$y_1 \qquad - .32z_1 - .25z_2 = .89u_1$$

$$-.34y_1 + y_2 - .22z_1 - .24z_2 = .79u_2 \, , \qquad (3)$$

where z_1 is the family socioeconomic status, z_2 is student's intelligence, y_1 student's parental encouragement, y_2 student's college plans, and u_1, u_2 are mutually independent stochastic disturbance terms. The parameters in (3) were estimated on the basis of measurements on approximately 5000 male seniors who constituted about a one-third random sample of all 1957 male seniors in Wisconsin.

On the basis of the examples of recursive sociological models reviewed here, several questions could be generated. Are the equations of the models identified? Are the statistical techniques that have been used to estimate the parameters optimal in some well-defined sense? Can the hypotheses embodied in the models be subjected to statistical tests of significance? Before addressing these or other questions, we pause to define the general characteristics of this class of models.

3. The General Model

We consider a *model* which consists of G linear equations in H observable variables and G unobservable disturbances. We thus write

$$Ax_n = u_n \, , \qquad (4)$$

where n ($n = 1,..., N$) denotes the different observations, A is a $G \times H$ matrix of parameters to be estimated, x_n is an H-component column vector whose typical element x_{hn} is the value of the hth variable for the nth observation, and u_n is a G-component column vector whose typical element u_{gn} is the value of the gth random disturbance for the nth observation. When a specific matrix is subsituted for A and a specific probability distribution is assumed for the elements of u_n, the resulting subcase of the model is called a *structure*.

We must now distinguish between two kinds of variables: (1) those which the model determines, called *endogenous*, and (2) those which are independently determined outside of the model, called *exogenous*. Corresponding to this distinction, we partition x_n, reordering the variables if necessary, so that the first G components of x_n are the values of the endogenous variables for the nth observation. We denote the G-component column vector of those values by y_n, and the $(H - G)$-component column vector of the values of the exogenous variables for the nth observation by z_n. We set $K = H - G$. Correspondingly, we partition A as $A = (B, \Gamma)$ where B is the $G \times G$ matrix of coefficients of the endogenous variables and Γ is the $G \times K$ matrix of coefficients of the exogenous variables. We now rewrite (4) as

$$By_n + \Gamma z_n = u_n, \tag{5}$$

where y_n, z_n, u_n are column vectors of G, K, and G elements respectively.

Equation (5) is a set of linear relations which are assumed to hold for each individual n ($n = 1,..., N$) in a (random or stratified-random) sample of sociological units (persons or organizations). The model is regarded as a theory explaining the determination of the endogenous variables y_{gn} ($g = 1,..., G$) in terms of the exogenous variables z_{kn} ($k = 1,..., K$) and the stochastic disturbances u_{gn} ($g = 1,..., G$), for $n = 1,..., N$. It is the function of sociological theory to specify that some of the coefficients of the B and Γ matrices in (5) are zero. If it did not, then statistical estimation would of course be impossible since all relations in the model would look alike statistically, so that one could not distinguish between them. The form of the variables will be specified in the context below. That is, we shall state explicitly whether we are dealing with the actual variables, deviations of the variables from arithmetic means, or ratios of the deviations from the means to the standard deviations of the variables. If we are dealing with the actual variables, then a constant term in each relation may be allowed for by setting one of the z variables at unity. We also adopt the normalization

convention that the diagonal elements of B are equal to unity: $\beta_{gg} = 1$
$(g = 1,..., G)$.

We continue to establish notation and terminology. First, if the model is to explain the determination of the endogenous variables in terms of the exogenous variables and disturbances, then we must assume that the rank of B in Eq. (5) is G. Therefore, B^{-1} exists and the system of equations can be solved uniquely for y_n in terms of z_n and u_n. Thus

$$y_n = -B^{-1}\Gamma z_n + B^{-1}u_n = \Pi z_n + v_n . \tag{6}$$

The system of equations (6) is called the *reduced form* of the model (5). Here, $\Pi = -B^{-1}\Gamma$ is a $G \times K$ matrix of reduced-form coefficients and $v_n = B^{-1}u_n$ $(n = 1,..., N)$ is a column vector of G reduced-form disturbances.

With respect to the structural disturbances, we specify that they are random variables drawn from a multivariate probability distribution with

$$E(u_n) = 0 \qquad (n = 1,..., N) , \tag{7}$$

where E denotes the expectation operator. In words, each disturbance vector (the set of G disturbances for each observation) has a zero expectation, so $E(u_{gn}) = 0$ for all g and n. Furthermore, the population variance–covariance matrix of the disturbances at each observation is

$$\Sigma = E(u_n u_n') = \begin{bmatrix} \sigma_{11} & \cdots & \sigma_{1G} \\ \vdots & & \vdots \\ \sigma_{G1} & \cdots & \sigma_{GG} \end{bmatrix} \tag{8}$$

where the prime denotes transposition. In words, the covariance matrix of the disturbances in the different equations is the same for all observations. The expectation of the reduced-form disturbance vector is thus $E(v_n) = B^{-1}E(u_n) = 0$, and its variance–covariance matrix at each observation is

$$\Omega = E(v_n v_n') = \begin{bmatrix} \omega_{11} & \cdots & \omega_{1G} \\ \vdots & & \vdots \\ \omega_{G1} & \cdots & \omega_{GG} \end{bmatrix}$$

$$= E(B^{-1}u_n u_n' B^{-1'}) = B^{-1}E(u_n u_n') B^{-1'} = B^{-1}\Sigma B^{-1'}. \tag{9}$$

The third equality here results from substituting $B^{-1}u_n$ for v_n, the fourth from the constancy of B, the fifth from applying the definition of Σ. We shall assume that Σ is positive definite, a necessary condition for which is that all identities have been removed from the model. Therefore, Σ will be nonsingular and since B^{-1} is also nonsingular, it follows that Ω is nonsingular, and indeed positive definite.

We shall sometimes use the following notation. Let N be the total number of observations in the sample. Denote by Y, Z, U, and V, respectively, the $N \times G$, $N \times K$, $N \times G$, and $N \times G$ *observation matrices* whose nth rows are y_n', z_n', u_n', and v_n', where the prime, as before, denotes transposition. Then we may rewrite Eq. (5) as

$$YB' + Z\Gamma' = U. \tag{10}$$

The use of transposes here will allow us to maintain the usual notation for least-squares theory while keeping the model in a form that seems most natural for discussion of identifiability. A form equivalent to that of Eq. (10) is

$$BY' + \Gamma Z' = U', \tag{11}$$

so that the reduced form can now be written as

$$Y' = -B^{-1}\Gamma Z' + B^{-1}U' = \Pi Z' + V'. \tag{12}$$

We note that the general forms of the B and Γ matrices are

$$B = \begin{bmatrix} \beta_{11} & \beta_{12} & \cdots & \beta_{1G} \\ \beta_{21} & \beta_{22} & \cdots & \beta_{2G} \\ \vdots & \vdots & & \vdots \\ \beta_{G1} & \beta_{G2} & \cdots & \beta_{GG} \end{bmatrix} \tag{13}$$

and

$$\Gamma = \begin{bmatrix} \gamma_{11} & \gamma_{12} & \cdots & \gamma_{1K} \\ \gamma_{21} & \gamma_{22} & \cdots & \gamma_{2K} \\ \vdots & \vdots & & \vdots \\ \gamma_{G1} & \gamma_{G2} & \cdots & \gamma_{GK} \end{bmatrix}. \tag{14}$$

For recursive systems, the matrix B takes a special form, so that the equation system (5) can be written as follows:

$$
\begin{aligned}
y_{1n} && + \sum_{k=1}^{K} \gamma_{1k} z_{kn} &= u_{1n} \\
\beta_{21} y_{1n} + \quad y_{2n} && + \sum_{k=1}^{K} \gamma_{2k} z_{kn} &= u_{2n} \\
\beta_{31} y_{1n} + \beta_{32} y_{2n} + y_{3n} && + \sum_{k=1}^{K} \gamma_{3k} z_{kn} &= u_{3n} \\
\vdots \qquad\qquad & & \vdots \qquad\qquad \vdots & \\
\beta_{G1} y_{1n} + \beta_{G2} y_{2n} + \beta_{G3} y_{3n} + \cdots + y_{Gn} && + \sum_{k=1}^{K} \gamma_{Gk} z_{kn} &= u_{Gn}.
\end{aligned} \tag{15}
$$

Specifically, the B matrix is *triangular* in a recursive system. This amounts to placing zero restrictions on B. In addition to the zeros above the diagonal in B, other elements of B and Γ may be set equal to zero a priori which means, in terms of sociological theory, that certain causally prior variables are assumed a priori to have no "direct effect" on certain endogenous variables. For models with independent disturbances, the Σ matrix is *diagonal*.

We shall have to take such a priori restrictions on the model into account in our discussions of identification, parameter estimation, and hypothesis testing. In order to analyze these issues, we shall have to make additional stochastic specifications about how the observations have been generated. We summarize these together with the specifications made above in the following two sets of assumptions.

ASSUMPTION 3.1. First, we summarize those assumptions which are commonly used to specify the general *simultaneous-equation model*:

 a. $E(u_n) = 0$ $(n = 1,..., N)$;
 b. the u_n are independently distributed $(n = 1,..., N)$;
 c. $E(u_n u_n') = \Sigma$, where Σ is positive definite $(n = 1,..., N)$;
 d. $Z = (z_1 ,..., z_K)$ is a set of N observations on the K exogenous variables; exogenous means here that the variables are stochastically independent of all random disturbances, i.e., the disturbances are distributed independently of the exogenous variables;
 e. Z has rank K;
 f. all observables are measured without error;
 g. the matrix B has rank G.

All of the above assumptions are assumed to apply throughout this paper. In addition, we shall often also specify that:

 h. the u_n $(n = 1,..., N)$ have a multivariate normal distribution. Then assumptions a and c can be compactly written as $u_n \sim N(0, \Sigma)$.

ASSUMPTION 3.2. In addition to Assumption 3.1, two specifications suffice to define the class of *recursive models with independent disturbances*:

 a. the matrix B is triangular;
 b. the matrix Σ is diagonal.

With respect to each of the G equations in the model (5), Assumption 3.1.a states that the u_{gn} are random variables with zero expectation. Assumptions 3.1.b and 3.1.c imply that the disturbances are homoscedastic (that is, that the u_{gn} have constant variance σ_{gg}) and that the u_{gn} $(n = 1,..., N)$ values are stochastically independent, which implies that $E(u_{gn}u_{gm}) = 0$ for $n \neq m$. This is the consequence of specifying random or stratified random sampling. Assumption 3.1.e is that no exact linear relations exist between any of the z variables. Assumption 3.1.f implies that the measurements of all of the variables are perfectly reliable.

With respect to the set of equations in the model, Assumption 3.1.g states that the model can be solved for y_n in terms of z_n and u_n, and Assumption 3.1.c says that the covariance matrix of the disturbances in the different equations is the same for all n. Assumption 3.2.a specifies that we are here dealing with a recursive model. Assumption 3.2.b states that the disturbances of the set of G structural relations are mutually independent, that is, the us in different equations for the same individual are independent. As noted above, this assumption has been an essential characteristic of most applications of recursive models in sociology. Finally, Assumption 3.1.h is that the disturbances at each observation have a G-variate normal distribution, which implies that each u_{gn} has a univariate normal distribution. This assumption is needed for some of the results given below (those which refer to the form of the sampling distributions of estimators), but not to others (those which refer to unbiasedness and consistency). If one prefers to make no explicit assumption about the form of the distribution, then one may appeal to the central limit theorem to justify the distributional results.

4. Identification

The first issue that we must dispose of with regard to the general model described above is the identification of the equations of the model. Specifically, we wish to show that the equations of a recursive model with independent disturbances are identifiable. The approach to the identification problem taken here follows closely that given in Fisher's (1966) treatise on the subject. In particular, we shall summarize here several general definitions and theorems that provide a natural context in which to analyze the identifiability of the present class of models.

Informally, the identification problem refers to the limits of observational information in distinguishing true structural equations from other plausible candidates. That is, we want to be assured that we can distinguish (identify) the equations of the matrix A in Eq. (4) in such a way that we can obtain unique estimates of the coefficients. The problem arises because observational (a posteriori) information can only distinguish the true equations from certain kinds of equations as specified in Theorem 4.1.

For the sake of definiteness (and without loss of generality), we shall here be concerned with the estimation of the coefficients of the first equation of (4)—the estimation of the first row of A. We denote that row by A_1 and similarly denote the first rows of B and Γ by B_1 and Γ_1, respectively. We start with:

THEOREM 4.1. An H-component row vector α can be distinguished from the true A_1 on the basis of observational information if and only if α is not a linear combination of the rows of A.

Proof: See Fisher (1966, pp. 20–21).

Briefly, this theorem assures us that observational information can only distinguish the true first equation from candidates which *are not* linear combinations of the equations of the model. Therefore, the identification issue revolves around whether or not the a priori information, that is, the theoretical specification of the coefficient matrix A, is sufficient to distinguish each equation of the model from any other possible linear combination of the equations of the model.

Equivalently, so far as observational information is concerned, the true set of structural equations cannot be distinguished from a false set in which each structural equation is replaced by a linear combination of the equations. Let F be any $G \times G$ matrix and premultiply Eq. (4) by F to obtain

$$A^*x_n = u_n{}^* \tag{16}$$

where

$$A^* = FA \qquad \text{and} \qquad u_n{}^* = Fu_n . \tag{17}$$

Observational information cannot distinguish (16) from the true model (4) if A^* has rank G as A does. Therefore, we will add the restriction that F be nonsingular. This specification gives us our definition of observationally admissible transformations:

DEFINITION 4.2. A linear transformation denoted by a $G \times G$ matrix F is called *observationally admissible* if and only if:

a. F is nonsingular,
b. $A^* = FA$ satisfies all a priori restrictions on A, and
c. $\Sigma^* = F\Sigma F'$ satisfies all a priori restrictions on Σ, where Σ is the variance–covariance matrix of the disturbances of (4) and Σ^* is the variance–covariance matrix of the transformed disturbances.

We are now ready to give a precise definition of identification. We shall do this in terms of an arbitrary equation of the model (4). We shall also assume that everything we know about an equation is true for all different normalization rules (the "homogeneous" case). Let i_g be an H-component row vector whose gth element is unity and whose remaining elements are zero.

DEFINITION 4.3.   The gth equation of the model is *identifiable* under the a priori restrictions if and only if the gth row of the matrix of every observationally admissible linear transformation is some scalar multiple of i_g.

We shall sometimes omit the words "under the a priori restrictions" and we shall sometimes use "identified" in place of "identifiable."

THEOREM 4.4.   For the general model—Eq. (4) or (5)—where Σ is not necessarily triangular, if it is possible to find a *nondiagonal* matrix F which is observationally admissible, then the G equations of A are not all identifiable.

Proof: Follows directly from Definitions 4.2 and 4.3. Boudon (1968, p. 203) gives a similar statement as a *definition* of identifiability.

DEFINITION 4.5.   An equation of the model that is not identifiable is *underidentified*.

DEFINITION 4.6.   A set of independent prior restrictions *just-identify* an equation of the model if and only if that equation is identified under all restrictions in the set but is not identified under any proper subset of the restrictions. If all the available a priori restrictions taken together just-identify a particular equation, that equation is *just-identified*.

DEFINITION 4.7.   An equation of the model is *overidentified* if and only if there exist two different (not necessarily disjoint) sets of a priori restrictions each of which just-identify the equation and the union of the two sets is an independent set of restrictions.

In order to represent the prior information (J independent restrictions) on each equation of the model, we construct $H \times J$ matrices ϕ_g, $g = 1,..., G$, such that all prior information on the gth equation of the model takes the form

$$A_g \phi_g = 0. \tag{18}$$

The columns of ϕ_g are formed from the coefficients of particular linear restrictions. For example, an exclusion restriction which sets the hth element of A_g equal to zero is expressed by a column of ϕ_g whose hth element is unity and whose remaining elements are zero. Then we have the following theorem and its corollary.

THEOREM 4.8 (Rank Condition). A necessary and sufficient condition for the identifiability of the gth equation of the model under restrictions (18) is

$$\text{rank}(A\phi_g) = G - 1. \tag{19}$$

Proof: See Fisher (1966, pp. 36–37).

COROLLARY 4.9 (Order Condition). A necessary (but not sufficient) condition for the identifiability of the gth equation of the model is that

$$\text{rank}(\phi_g) \geqslant G - 1. \tag{20}$$

In other words, there must be at least $G - 1$ independent restrictions expressed by Eq. (18).

Proof: See Fisher (1966, p. 39).

Consider now the case where all a priori restrictions are exclusion restrictions. That is, suppose that all restrictions correspond to setting some element of the gth row of A in (4) equal to zero, which means that no "direct effect" is postulated for the corresponding variable in the gth equation. Then the rank and order conditions have somewhat simpler forms. In this case, every column of ϕ_g has one and only one nonzero element which is equal to unity. Since the position of a unit element corresponds to a restriction that the corresponding element of A_g be zero, the order condition can be restated as follows.

COROLLARY 4.10 (Order Condition). A necessary (but not sufficient) condition for the identifiability of the gth equation under exclusion restrictions is that there be at least $G - 1$ variables excluded a priori from that equation.

Moreover, since the matrix $A\phi_g$ in this case will consist of the columns of A corresponding to the excluded variables, the rank condition becomes:

COROLLARY 4.11 (Rank Condition). A necessary and sufficient condition for the identifiability of the gth equation under exclusion restrictions is that it be possible to form at least one nonvanishing determinant of order $G - 1$ from the columns of A corresponding to the variables excluded a priori from that equation.

This completes our review of the general results in the theory of identification in linear models. This theory can be found in several econometrics textbooks. It has been given here both because it gives a logical completeness to this presentation of the identification problem and because it is a natural prelude to proving the identifiability of linear recursive systems with independent disturbances. First, we need the following definition.

DEFINITION 4.12. A variable is *exogenous with respect to a particular equation* if and only if it is stochastically independent of the disturbance of that equation.

Note, first, that exogenous variables are exogenous with respect to every equation of the system. In general, however, endogenous variables are not exogenous with respect to any equation in the system, for

$$Y' = \Pi Z' + V' \tag{21}$$

implies

$$E(Y'U) = \Pi E(Z'U) + E(V'U) = 0 + E(B^{-1}U'U) = NB^{-1}\Sigma, \tag{22}$$

and in general linear systems there are no restrictions on $B^{-1}\Sigma$. But in recursive models with independent disturbances, the triangularity of B and the diagonality of Σ together imply that $B^{-1}\Sigma$ is triangular, so that u_h is uncorrelated with y_g ($g = 1,..., h - 1$). Furthermore, in recursive systems, since the endogenous variable y_g is not an explicit function of the endogenous variables $y_{g+1},..., y_G$, we know that the only possible source of stochastic dependence between y_g and $u_{g+1},..., u_G$ is a dependence between u_g and $u_{g+1},..., u_G$. For the present class of models, however, the disturbances are independent. Therefore, y_g is independent of $u_{g+1},..., u_G$. Consequently, for purposes of identifying the hth equation, the gth ($g < h$) endogenous variable in such a system may be added to the list of K exogenous variables. This is equivalent to raising K by 1 *and* dropping G by 1, thus reducing for the hth equation the crucial number ($G - 1$) of pieces of additional a priori information necessary for its identification.

By the immediately preceding argument, we deduce from the fact that the gth ($g = 1,..., h - 1$) and the hth ($h = 1,..., G$) disturbances are independent, the result that the endogenous variables $y_1,..., y_{h-1}$ may be thought of as exogenous with respect to the hth equation. Therefore, $G - 1$ in Corollary 4.10 becomes $G - 1 - (h - 1) = G - h$.

Moreover, since B is triangular, it follows that the $G - h$ endogenous variables $y_{h+1},..., y_G$ do not appear in the hth equation. Furthermore, since the diagonal elements of the equations for the $G - h$ variables $y_{h+1},..., y_G$ are all equal to unity, it is possible to form at least one non-vanishing determinant of order $G - h$ from the columns of A corresponding to the variables excluded from the hth equation. By the preceding argument, it follows that $G - 1$ in Corollary 4.11 is reduced to $G - 1 - (h - 1) = G - h$. Thus:

THEOREM 4.13 (Identifiability of Recursive Models with Independent Disturbances). In the general model—(4) or (5)—as specified by Assumptions 3.1 and 3.2, every equation is identifiable.

Proof: By the preceding discusson, for the hth equation, the $G - h$ restrictions that endogenous variables $h + 1,..., G$ do not appear in the hth equation suffice to identify it.   Q.E.D.

In summary, following Fisher (1966), we have shown that the equations of the class of recursive models with independent disturbances are identifiable with no additional a priori exclusion restrictions.

5. Parameter Estimation

Now that we have shown that the class of models specified by Assumptions 3.1 and 3.2 is identifiable we can proceed to the derivation of estimators of the parameters of the models, estimators which possess certain desirable statistical properties. That is, for our general recursive model with independent disturbances, we should like to possess techniques for estimating the values of the elements of the B, Γ, and Σ matrices from given sets of observations on the variables. By way of background, we review standard concepts of estimation theory in general terms. We give definitions in terms of random vectors; the reader can specialize the definitions to the case of random vectors of one dimension, i.e., random variables.

Suppose that the vector of parameters to be estimated is denoted by

$$\theta = \begin{bmatrix} \theta_1 \\ \vdots \\ \theta_P \end{bmatrix}.$$

Then, if the set of observations is denoted by X, the function d, where $\hat{\theta} = d(X)$, is called an *estimator* of θ. The value taken by an estimator when a specific set of sample observations are inserted in the function is called an *estimate*.

Let us briefly examine some statistical properties that we would like our estimators to possess. First, it is desirable that an estimator be unbiased in the sense that its expected value is equal to the true population value. Second, of the set of unbiased estimators, we might like to choose that estimator which is best in the sense of possessing a sampling distribution with smallest variance. Finally, since linear functions are the simplest to work with, we might prefer to choose our minimum variance unbiased estimators out of the class of linear estimators. We summarize these properties in the following definition.

DEFINITION 5.1. Suppose that θ is a vector of parameters to be estimated. Then

a. $\hat{\theta}$ is an *unbiased estimator* of θ if and only if $E(\hat{\theta}) = \theta$.

b. $\hat{\theta}$ is a *minimum variance unbiased estimator* (MVUE) of θ if and only if $\hat{\theta}$ is unbiased and $E[(\tilde{\theta} - \theta)(\tilde{\theta} - \theta)'] - E[(\hat{\theta} - \theta)(\hat{\theta} - \theta)']$ is nonnegative definite where $\tilde{\theta}$ is any other unbiased estimator of θ.

c. $\hat{\theta}$ is a *minimum variance linear unbiased estimator* (MVLUE) of θ if and only if $\hat{\theta}$ is a linear estimator, unbiased, and is the minimum variance estimator within the class of linear unbiased estimators.

The properties above refer to the distribution of $\hat{\theta}$ for every sample size. Generally, the expectation and variance of $\hat{\theta}$ will depend on sample size. Therefore, it is useful to consider properties that refer to the analogous asymptotic (i.e., large-sample) distribution, which are summarized in the following definition.

DEFINITION 5.2. Suppose that θ is a vector of parameters to be estimated. Let $\hat{\theta}_N$ denote an estimator of θ for sample size N. Let $E(\hat{\theta}_N)$ denote the expectation of $\hat{\theta}$ for sample size N. Then

a. $\hat{\theta}$ is an *asymptotically unbiased estimator* of θ if and only if $\lim_{N \to \infty} E(\hat{\theta}_N) = \theta$.

b. $\hat{\theta}$ is a *consistent estimator* of θ if and only if for every $\epsilon > 0$,

$$\lim_{N \to \infty} \text{prob}\{| \hat{\theta}_N - \theta | > \epsilon\} = 0.$$

c. $\hat{\theta}$ is an *asymptotically efficient estimator* of θ if and only if $\hat{\theta}$ is consistent and

$$(1/N) \lim_{N \to \infty}\{NE[(\tilde{\theta}_N - \theta)(\tilde{\theta}_N - \theta)']\} - (1/N) \lim_{N \to \infty}\{NE[(\hat{\theta}_N - \theta)(\hat{\theta}_N - \theta)']\}$$

is nonnegative definite where $\tilde{\theta}$ is any other consistent estimator of θ.

d. $\hat{\theta}$ is an *asymptotically normal estimator* of θ if and only if $N^{1/2}(\hat{\theta}_N - \theta)$ approaches the multivariate normal distribution with mean 0 and variance–covariance matrix $\Sigma_{\theta\theta}$ as $N \to \infty$.

e. $\hat{\theta}$ is the *best asymptotically normal estimator* (BAN) of θ if and only if it is consistent, asymptotically normal, and asymptotically efficient.

With these properties of estimators defined, we move now to the derivation of estimators for the model specified above. First, we define a convenient notation for the estimation process. Consider the estimation of the hth equation of the model (5). By the results of our discussion on identification, all of the endogenous variables y_g ($g = 1,..., h - 1$) determined in the preceding $h - 1$ equations in the model can be considered as exogenous with respect to the hth equation. For this equation, there is no longer a need to distinguish between the zs and the $y_1,..., y_{h-1}$. Considering all of these together, suppose that P_h ($\leqslant K + h - 1$) appear with nonzero coefficients in the equation. We relabel these $x_1,..., x_{P_h}$. Denote the $N \times P_h$ matrix of observations on the exogenous variables for the hth equation by $X_h = (x_1,..., x_{P_h})$ where x_1 is a vector of unit elements since we are here dealing with the *observed values of the variables*. Likewise, denote the N-component column vector of observations on the endogenous variable by y_h. Then the matrix equation composing our model for the estimation of the hth equation of (5) can be written as

$$y_h = X_h \beta_h{}^* + u_h, \tag{23}$$

where X_h is assumed to have full column rank, and y_h, $\beta_h{}^*$, and u_h are column vectors of N, P_h, and N components, respectively. Note that each of the $\beta_h{}^*$ parameters in Eq. (23) is equal to minus one times the corresponding parameter of the hth equation of the general model (5).

The $\beta_h{}^*$ vector and the common variance of the elements of u_h in (23) are unknown, and our problem is to obtain estimators of these unknowns. In order to do this, we shall first adopt all of the specifications of Assumptions 3.1 and 3.2 except the assumption of multivariate normality of the disturbances. Specifically, those assumptions will allow us to use the notation of Eq. (23) to develop estimators for each of the G equations of the model considered separately. Essentially, we will do this by restating standard single-equation linear regression theory. Therefore, we will drop the subscript h for the present discussion, rewriting (23) as $y = X\beta^* + u$ with rank $X = P$, and reintroduce it only when we again consider several structural equations.

Let b denote a column vector of estimates of β^*. Then we may write

$$y = Xb + e \tag{24}$$

where $e = y - Xb$ denotes the column vector of N observed residuals. Then the *ordinary least-squares estimator* (OLS) of β^* is the value of b that minimizes the sum of squares of the residuals e, that is, $\sum_{n=1}^{N} e_n{}^2$. The sum of squared residuals is

$$\sum_{n=1}^{N} e_n{}^2 = e'e = (y - Xb)'(y - Xb) = y'y - 2b'X'y + b'X'Xb, \tag{25}$$

using the fact that $b'X'y$ is a scalar and thus equal to its transpose. To find the value of b that minimizes the sum of squared residuals we differentiate (25):

$$\partial(e'e)/\partial b = -2X'y + 2X'Xb. \tag{26}$$

Equating (26) to zero gives

$$X'Xb = X'y, \tag{27}$$

and from the assumption that X has rank P,

$$b = (X'X)^{-1} X'y. \tag{28}$$

This is the ordinary least-squares estimator in matrix form. It gives b as a function of y. That (28) locates a minimum is verified by the fact that $\partial^2(e'e)/\partial b^2 = 2X'X$ is positive definite.

To find the expectation of b, we substitute the model $y = X\beta^* + u$ into (28), which gives

$$b = (X'X)^{-1} X'(X\beta^* + u) = \beta^* + (X'X)^{-1} X'u. \tag{29}$$

Equation (29) expresses b as a linear function of the true but unknown β^* and the disturbance values u. In repeated samples, the values of X and u will differ (even if the fully exogenous variables—the zs—are fixed in repeated samples, the ys which enter this equation will not be) so that the vector b will vary from sample to sample. Taking expected values of both sides of (29) gives

$$E(b) = E(\beta^*) + E[(X'X)^{-1} X'u] = \beta^* + E[(X'X)^{-1} X'] E(u) = \beta^*, \tag{30}$$

where the second equality follows since the exogenous variables X are stochastically independent of the disturbances u, and the third equality follows from Assumption 3.1.a. Thus, b is *unbiased*.

Next, we derive an estimate of the variance of the disturbance of Eq. (23). Since we have dropped the subscript h in the present discussion, we will denote the population variance of u by σ^2. Consider the residual vector

$$e = y - Xb = X\beta^* + u - X[(X'X)^{-1} X'(X\beta^* + u)]$$
$$= u - X(X'X)^{-1} X'u = [I_N - X(X'X)^{-1} X']u = Mu, \tag{31}$$

where

$$M = I_N - X(X'X)^{-1} X'. \tag{32}$$

The following results show that M is a symmetric idempotent matrix:

$$M' = I_N - X(X'X)^{-1} X' = M, \tag{33}$$

and

$$
\begin{aligned}
M^2 &= [I_N - X(X'X)^{-1} X'][I_N - X(X'X)^{-1} X'] \\
&= I_N - 2X(X'X)^{-1} X' + X(X'X)^{-1} X'X(X'X)^{-1} X' \\
&= I_N - X(X'X)^{-1} X' \\
&= M.
\end{aligned}
\tag{34}
$$

Hence, the sum of squared residuals is

$$e'e = u'M'Mu = u'Mu = u'[I_N - X(X'X)^{-1} X']u. \tag{35}$$

Taking expectations, we have

$$
\begin{aligned}
E(e'e) &= \sigma^2 \operatorname{tr} E[I_N - X(X'X)^{-1} X'] \\
&= \sigma^2 \{\operatorname{tr} I_N - \operatorname{tr} E[X(X'X)^{-1} X']\} \\
&= \sigma^2 \{N - \operatorname{tr} E[(X'X)^{-1} (X'X)]\} \\
&= (N - P)\sigma^2,
\end{aligned}
\tag{36}
$$

where the first equality follows from our specifications 3.1.b of the u variables, the second equality follows since the trace operation is distributive, the third equality follows from the result that $\operatorname{tr}(ABC) = \operatorname{tr}(BCA) = \operatorname{tr}(CAB)$, and the fourth equality follows since $X'X$ is of order P so that $(X'X)^{-1}(X'X) = I_P$. Thus

$$s^2 = (e'e)/(N - P) \tag{37}$$

is *an unbiased estimator of* σ^2.

Now consider the variances and covariances of the elements of the $P \times 1$ vector b. Subtracting β^* from both sides of (29), we have

$$b - \beta^* = (X'X)^{-1} X'u \tag{38}$$

so that

$$
\begin{aligned}
\operatorname{var}(b) &= E[(b - \beta)(b - \beta)'] \\
&= E[(X'X)^{-1} X'uu'X(X'X)^{-1}] \\
&= E\{E[X'X)^{-1} X'uu'X(X'X)^{-1} \mid X]\} \\
&= E\{(X'X)^{-1} X'E(uu' \mid X) X(X'X)^{-1}\} \\
&= E\{(X'X)^{-1} X'\sigma^2 I_N X(X'X)^{-1}\} \\
&= \sigma^2 E\{X'X)^{-1} X'X(X'X)^{-1}\} \\
&= \sigma^2 E(X'X)^{-1},
\end{aligned}
\tag{39}
$$

where the second equality follows on substitution from Eq. (38), the third equality follows from the fact that any expectation can be computed as the expectation of conditional expectations, the fourth follows since, conditional on X, X is constant and thus can be factored out of the expectation, the fifth equality follows because the stochastic independence of u and X implies that $E(uu' \mid X) = E(uu') = \sigma^2 I_N$, and the sixth equality follows from the fact that σ^2 is a scalar. Thus, Eq. (39) expresses the variance–covariance matrix of the sampling distribution of the least-squares estimators of β^*.

We can proceed to inquire as to whether or not b posseses any optimal minimum-variance properties. We note that in classical linear regression, where the X variables are fixed in repeated samples, the famous "Gauss–Markov theorem on least-squares" states that b is the MVLUE of β^*. In the nonexperimental sciences, the assumption of "fixed regressors" typically must be replaced by the assumption of "stochastic regressors" (i.e., random exogenous z variables) as in Assumption 3.1 of the present paper. Conditional on X, the Gauss–Markov theorem still applies, cf. Christ (1966, pp. 370–372). However, in the present case, equation (23) represents the hth equation of a recursive model with independent disturbances. For h greater than one, X presumably contains not only "fully exogenous" z variables but also endogenous y_g variables with $g < h$, which thus are only "exogenous with respect to the hth equation" of the model. Conditioning on X would require that these latter are fixed, which in turn requires that the $u_g(g < h)$ are constant in repeated samples of size N. Thus, in order to prove a conditional Gauss–Markov theorem for recursive models with independent disturbances, one must condition on all variables that have been determined in equations prior to the one under consideration, as in the derivation of Eq. (39). One may well question the merits of such restrictive conditioning. It is nevertheless possible to establish a weaker version of the Gauss–Markov theorem.

THEOREM 5.3 (Gauss–Markov Theorem for Stochastic Regressors). Let $y = X\beta^* + u$, where $E(u \mid X) = 0$ and $E(uu' \mid X) = \sigma^2 I$ for all X, and the stochastic matrix X has full column rank. Then, within the class of estimators *which, conditional on every X, are linear and unbiased*, the least-squares estimator $b = (X'X)^{-1}X'y$ has the minimum variance.

Proof: The class of estimators under consideration is defined by

$$\beta^* = C'y, \qquad E(\beta^* \mid X) = \beta^* \qquad \text{for all } X, \qquad (40)$$

where C' is constant conditional on X. Substituting (23) into (40), we find

$$\beta^* = C'(X\beta^* + u) = C'X\beta^* + C'u,$$

the conditional expectation of which is

$$E(\hat{\beta}^* \mid X) = C'X\beta^* + E(C'u \mid X) = C'X\beta^* + C'E(u \mid X) = C'X\beta^*. \quad (41)$$

For $E(\hat{\beta}^* \mid X) = \beta^*$ to hold, therefore, it must be true that

$$C'X = I. \quad (42)$$

In that event we have

$$\hat{\beta}^* - E(\hat{\beta}^* \mid X) = C'u, \quad (43)$$

which says that conditional on X, the sampling error of the estimator is linear in the disturbance vector. Proceeding, the conditional variance–covariance matrix of $\hat{\beta}^*$ is

$$\mathrm{var}(\hat{\beta}^* \mid X) = E\{[\hat{\beta}^* - E(\hat{\beta}^* \mid X)][\hat{\beta}^* - E(\hat{\beta}^* \mid X)]' \mid X\} \quad (44)$$

$$= E(C'uu'C \mid X) = C'E(uu' \mid X)C = \sigma^2 C'C. \quad (45)$$

The least-squares estimator is a member of this class, namely $b = \hat{C}'y$, where $\hat{C}' = (X'X)^{-1}X'$; its conditional variance–covariance matrix is $\mathrm{var}(b \mid X) = \sigma^2\hat{C}'\hat{C} = \sigma^2(X'X)^{-1}$. Without loss of generality we may write any C' as

$$C' = (X'X)^{-1}X' + D' = \hat{C}' + D', \quad (46)$$

by choosing an appropriate D', which like C' and $\hat{C}'$, is constant conditional on X. The unbiasedness condition (42) translates into $D'X = 0$, whence

$$D'\hat{C} = 0. \quad (47)$$

Thus the conditional covariance matrix above can be written as

$$\mathrm{var}(\hat{\beta}^* \mid X) = \sigma^2 C'C = \sigma^2(\hat{C}' + D')(\hat{C} + D) = \sigma^2(\hat{C}'\hat{C} + D'D)$$
$$= \sigma^2\hat{C}'\hat{C} + \sigma^2 D'D = \mathrm{var}(b \mid X) + \sigma^2 D'D.$$

Since for any D, the matrix $D'D$ is nonnegative definite, we conclude that

$$\mathrm{var}(\hat{\beta}^* \mid X) - \mathrm{var}(b \mid X) = \sigma^2 D'D \quad (48)$$

is nonnegative definite. This establishes that, *conditional on X*, b has the minimum variance in the class of estimators under consideration, which is merely a restatement of the standard Gauss–Markov theorem.

The present theorem, however, refers to *unconditional* properties. The unconditional variance is obtained by taking expectations over X of the conditional variances (since the conditional expectations are constant over X). This shows that

$$\text{var}(\beta^*) - \text{var}(b) = E[\text{var}(\beta^* \mid X)] - E[\text{var}(b \mid X)] = \sigma^2 E(D'D) \quad (49)$$

is nonnegative definite, which establishes Theorem 5.3.

Note that our theorem restricts attention to estimators which are unbiased *conditional on every* X. This leaves open the possibility that there is an unbiased linear estimator with smaller variance–covariance matrix than b. Such an estimator would be biased conditional on X, but unbiased unconditionally. Being biased conditionally, its conditional variance–covariance matrices could be smaller than those of b, and could be sufficiently small that the unconditional variance–covariance matrix would be smaller than that of b. This possibility can, in fact, be ruled out; see Hurwicz (1950).

For each equation in our recursive model with independent errors, the assumptions of Theorem 5.3 hold, so that least squares is an optimal estimation procedure.

Thus far we have used no explicit assumption about the form of the distribution of the u_n ($n = 1,..., N$). Several additional properties of the least-squares estimator for single equations of the model may be proven if we assume that the u_n are jointly normally distributed. If we prefer to make no explicit assumption about the form of the distribution, then we may appeal to the central limit theorem to justify the statement that the results below are approximately correct as was noted above. First, we need the following two definitions.

DEFINITION 5.4.   The *likelihood function* of N random variables $x_1 ,..., x_N$ is the joint density of the N random variables $g(x_1 ,..., x_N; \theta)$ considered to be a function of the vector of parameters θ. In particular, if $(x_1 ,..., x_N)$ is a random sample from the density $f(x; \theta)$, then the likelihood function is

$$g(x_1 ,..., x_N) = f(x_1 ; \theta) f(x_2 ; \theta) \cdots f(x_N ; \theta).$$

DEFINITION 5.5.   Let $L(\theta) = g(x_1 ,..., x_N; \theta)$ be the likelihood function for the random variables $x_1 ,..., x_N$. If the vector $\hat{\theta} = d(x_1 ,..., x_N)$ is the value of θ which maximizes $L(\theta)$, then $\hat{\theta}$ is the *maximum-likelihood estimator* (MLE) of θ.

We shall proceed to apply the maximum-likelihood method of estimation to Eq. (23). That is, we shall find the maximum-likelihood estimators of β^* and σ^2 for any single equation of our recursive model with independent disturbances. The virtue of these estimators lies in the fact that under very general conditions on the regularity of the likelihood function (see, e.g., Wilks, 1962, pp. 358–365, 379–381), they possess desirable asymptotic properties. In particular, the normal distribution satisfies these regularity conditions. Moreover, for the estimation problem considered here, the following theorem establishes a most useful identity of the single-equation maximum-likelihood estimators with the OLS estimators for single equations.

THEOREM 5.6. Conditional on the observed X, and under the assumption that the disturbances are normally distributed, the single-equation maximum-likelihood estimators of (23) possess the following properties:

a. the ML estimator $\hat{\beta}^*$ of β^* is identical with the OLS estimator b;
b. the ML estimator $\hat{\sigma}^2$ of σ^2 is $e'e/N$ where e is the $N \times 1$ vector of least-squares residuals;
c. the asymptotic variance–covariance matrix of $\hat{\beta}^*$ is $\mathrm{var}(\hat{\beta}^*) = \sigma^2(X'X)^{-1}$;
d. $\hat{\beta}^*$ and $\hat{\sigma}^2$ are consistent, asymptotically normal, asymptotically efficient, and hence BAN estimators of β^* and σ^2.

Proof: First, we note that (d) is a general characteristic of maximum-likelihood estimators; see, e.g., Wilks (1962, Chapter 12). Hence, we shall be content here to give the standard proofs of properties (a) and (b), from which (c) also follows as a general property of maximum-likelihood estimators. The likelihood of the sample u in this model is, in accordance with Definition 5.4 and the definition of the normal density function, given by

$$L = (2\pi\sigma^2)^{-N/2} \exp\{-u'u/(2\sigma^2)\}, \tag{50}$$

whence the logarithmic likelihood is

$$L^* = -\tfrac{1}{2}N \log(2\pi\sigma^2) - \tfrac{1}{2}(\sigma^2)^{-1} u'u. \tag{51}$$

Replacing u by $y - X\beta^*$ we obtain the logarithmic likelihood expressed in terms of the observations y and X and the parameters β^* and σ^2:

$$L^* = -\tfrac{1}{2}N \log(2\pi\sigma^2) - (2\sigma^2)^{-1} (y - X\beta^*)' (y - X\beta^*). \tag{52}$$

Differentiating:

$$\partial L^*/\partial\beta^* = (2\sigma^2)^{-1} 2X'(y - X\beta^*), \tag{53}$$

$$\partial L^*/\partial\sigma^2 = -\tfrac{1}{2}N(\sigma^2)^{-1} + \tfrac{1}{2}(\sigma^2)^{-1} (y - X\beta^*)' (y - X\beta^*). \tag{54}$$

Setting the derivatives equal to zero and solving gives the equations determining the maximum-likelihood estimators $\hat{\beta}*$ and $\hat{\sigma}^2$:

$$\hat{\beta}* = (X'X)^{-1} X'y = b, \tag{55}$$

$$\hat{\sigma}^2 = N^{-1}(y - X\hat{\beta}*)' (y - X\hat{\beta}*) = e'e/N, \tag{56}$$

which proves assertions (a) and (b). That these estimators indeed determine a maximum is confirmed by the fact that $\partial^2 L*/\partial\beta*^2 = -(\sigma^2)^{-1}X'X$ is negative definite. Finally, by a general result for the method of maximum-likelihood estimation (see, e.g., Wilks, 1962, p. 380), the asymptotic variance–covariance matrix of $\hat{\beta}*$ is given by $\text{var}(\hat{\beta}*) = (-\partial^2 L*/\partial\beta*^2)^{-1} = \sigma^2(X'X)^{-1}$, which shows property (c).

Two comments are in order concerning Theorem 5.6. First, we note that the proof of this theorem conditions on the observed values of all variables that are exogenous with respect to Eq. (23). Removal of this constraint creates no essential difficulties; cf. Koopmans and Hood (1953, pp. 147–151), Christ (1966, pp. 372–374). We shall shortly indicate how the key conclusions carry over when we condition only on the values of the z variables that are exogenous with respect to the model as a whole.

A second observation which is pertinent at this point is that all of the results derived above in Theorems 5.3 and 5.6 have been properties of single-equation estimators. That is, the estimators derived heretofore have utilized as a priori information only the constraints or restrictions on the coefficients of one equation together with the results on identification from Section 4. In particular, we have not yet taken into account the fact that each equation is embedded in a set of equations which constitutes our recursive model with independent disturbances. Thus, we need an optimal estimation method which is adressed to the joint estimation of the parameters of the system of equations that make up the model. As several authors (e.g., Johnston, 1972, pp. 377–380; Goldberger, 1964, pp. 352–356) have noted, such an ideal method is the classical *full-information maximum-likelihood* (FIML) method (see Koopmans, Rubin, & Leipnik, 1950). Essentially, this method is simply an application of the maximum-likelihood principle simultaneously to the set of the G equations of the model. Its outstanding attribute is that it draws on *all* of the a priori restrictions which are incorporated into the equations of the model in the derivation of estimators. For the general case of simultaneous-equation models, the method produces extremely cumbersome nonlinear estimation equations. But, for recursive models with independent disturbances, these complications do not arise, and, subject to one qualification, FIML reduces to equation-by-equation least-squares regression.

The qualification is that there be no a priori *cross-equation constraints* on the coefficients of the model. Examples of cross-equation constraints are: (1) a (nonzero) coefficient in one equation is known to be equal to a coefficient in another equation; and (2) the sum of two (nonzero) coefficients in two different equations is known to be equal to some particular number. Although such constraints have not occurred in past sociological applications of recursive models with independent disturbances, it is worthwhile to recognize that FIML can handle them if they do occur. Moreover, cross-equation constraints pin down the distinction between equation-by-equation and model-as-a-whole maximum-likelihood estimation for this class of models. The basic result is:

THEOREM 5.7. For a recursive model with independent disturbances, full-information maximum-likelihood estimation reduces to equation-by-equation least squares, provided that there are no cross-equation constraints on the coefficients.

Proof. Consider again Eqs. (5) as specified by Assumptions 3.1 and 3.2:

$$By_n + \Gamma z_n = u_n \qquad (n = 1,..., N). \tag{57}$$

Assumption 3.1.h specifies that the column vector u_n is multivariate normal $N(0, \Sigma)$. Furthermore, the conditional probability of y_n for given z_n (note that we condition only on those variables which are exogenous with respect to the model as a whole) is

$$p(y_n \mid z_n) = p(u_n \mid z_n) \mid \partial u_n/\partial y_n \mid = p(u_n) \mid \partial u_n/\partial y_n \mid, \tag{58}$$

since u_n is independent of all exogenous variables by Assumption 3.1.d. Here, $\mid \partial u_n/\partial y_n \mid$ indicates the absolute value of the determinant formed from the $G \times G$ matrix of the partial derivatives of the u_{gn} with respect to the y_{gn} (i.e., the Jacobian of the transformation). Since the structural equations in (57) are linear, this matrix of partial derivatives is merely the the coefficient matrix B. Hence, (58) may be written

$$p(y_n \mid z_n) = \mid \det B \mid p(u_n). \tag{59}$$

Thus, the likelihood of the values of a random sample of size N, conditional upon the values of z_n, is given by

$$L = p(y_1 ,..., y_N \mid z_1 ,..., z_N) = \mid \det B \mid^N p(u_1) \cdots p(u_N). \tag{60}$$

Since the u_n ($n = 1,..., N$) are multivariate normal, it follows that (60) can be written as

$$L = \frac{|\det B|^N}{(\det \Sigma)^{N/2} (2\pi)^{NG/2}} \exp\left\{-\frac{1}{2} \sum_{n=1}^{N} u_n' \Sigma^{-1} u_n\right\}. \tag{61}$$

Then the log of the likelihood function is

$$L^* = N \log |\det B| - \tfrac{1}{2}NG \log(2\pi) - \tfrac{1}{2}N \log \det \Sigma - \tfrac{1}{2} \sum_{n=1}^{N} u_n' \Sigma^{-1} u_n. \tag{62}$$

Because of Assumption 3.2.a and our normalization rule which sets the diagonal elements of B equal to unity, $\det B = 1$, so that (62) reduces to

$$L^* = -\tfrac{1}{2}NG \log(2\pi) - \tfrac{1}{2}N \log \det \Sigma - \tfrac{1}{2} \sum_{n=1}^{N} u_n' \Sigma^{-1} u_n. \tag{63}$$

But Σ is diagonal so

$$\det \Sigma = \sigma_{11} \cdots \sigma_{GG} \tag{64}$$

and

$$\Sigma^{-1} = \begin{bmatrix} 1/\sigma_{11} & 0 & \cdots & 0 \\ 0 & 1/\sigma_{22} & \cdots & 0 \\ \vdots & \vdots & & \vdots \\ 0 & 0 & \cdots & 1/\sigma_{GG} \end{bmatrix}. \tag{65}$$

Thus

$$L^* = -\tfrac{1}{2}NG \log(2\pi) - \tfrac{1}{2}N \sum_{g=1}^{G} \log \sigma_{gg} - \tfrac{1}{2} \sum_{g=1}^{G} u_g' u_g / \sigma_{gg}$$

$$= \sum_{g=1}^{G} L_g^*, \tag{66}$$

where

$$L_g^* = -\tfrac{1}{2}N \log(2\pi) - \tfrac{1}{2}N \log \sigma_{gg} - \tfrac{1}{2}(y_g - X_g \beta_g^*)' (y_g - X_g \beta_g^*)/\sigma_{gg}$$

$$(g = 1,..., G). \tag{67}$$

We see that the log-likelihood for the model as a whole turns out to be the sum of the log-likelihoods for the individual equations. In the absence of cross-equation constraints, therefore, the log-likelihood for the model as a whole is maximized with respect to all its arguments when each L_g^* is maximized with respect to its own arguments. As we have seen in Theorem 5.6, the latter is accomplished by choosing the least-squares values $\hat{\beta}_g^* = b_g$ and $\hat{\sigma}_{gg} = e_g'e_g/N$. If cross-equation constraints were present, these would have to be imposed in the maximization of L^*, in which case FIML would not reduce to equation-by-equation least squares.

For future reference, we note that the maximized value of L_g^* is

$$
\begin{aligned}
\hat{L}_g^* &= -\tfrac{1}{2}N \log(2\pi) - \tfrac{1}{2}N \log \hat{\sigma}_{gg} - \tfrac{1}{2}e_g'e_g/\hat{\sigma}_{gg} \\
&= -\tfrac{1}{2}N \log(2\pi) - \tfrac{1}{2}N \log \hat{\sigma}_{gg} - \tfrac{1}{2}N\hat{\sigma}_{gg}/\hat{\sigma}_{gg} \\
&= -\tfrac{1}{2}N(\log 2\pi + 1) - \tfrac{1}{2}N \log \hat{\sigma}_{gg}
\end{aligned}
\tag{68}
$$

and so the maximized value of L is

$$
\hat{L}^* = -\tfrac{1}{2}GN(\log 2\pi + 1) - \tfrac{1}{2}N \sum_{g=1}^{G} \log \hat{\sigma}_{gg} .
\tag{69}
$$

In brief, Theorems 5.6 and 5.7 verify that the method of least squares applied equation by equation is equivalent to the maximum-likelihood method applied to the model as a whole for recursive models with independent disturbances in the case of no cross-equation constraints on the parameters. This condition has been met in all applications of such models in sociology to date. Thus, the optimality of the least-squares estimation procedures is confirmed.

Before proceeding to a discussion of hypothesis testing, we pause to note that the results derived above also hold when the observations are expressed in *standard-score form*. This has been a particularly important form of variables in sociological models and it occurs in the theory of path analysis as several authors have noted (see, e.g., Duncan, 1966; Heise, 1969b; Land, 1969).

To conclude this discussion of parameter estimation, we can summarize by saying that we have found that the ordinary single-equation least-squares estimators of the parameters of recursive models with independent disturbances possess highly desirable small- and large-sample distribution properties. Specifically, Theorems 5.3, 5.6, and 5.7 show, in essence, that one cannot improve on these estimators. Furthermore, these results follow regardless of the degree of over-identification of the model. Thus, there is no need to define new estimators when some additional structural coefficients are known to be zero as Boudon (1968, pp. 213–215) has proposed. Such an effort will only produce an estimator with a larger sampling variance, as Goldberger (1970a) has shown with a specific example.

6. Hypothesis Testing

Now that we have derived statistical estimators of the parameters of recursive models with independent disturbances, we can enter into a discussion of the process of model appraisal. Essentially, we would like to evaluate both the a priori specification of the model and the particular values of the parameters that are computed for, and conditional upon, a given set of observations. First, concerning inferences about the estimated coefficients, we note that, if one conditions on the observed values of all variables which are exogenous with respect to a particular equation as in Theorems 5.3 and 5.6, then the standard t- and F-tests of parametric statistical inference—see, e.g., Mood & Graybill (1963, pp. 350–353)—can be applied directly to the estimated structural coefficients of that equation. If the disturbance is normally distributed, then the theorems apply exactly. If not, then the results are, of course, only approximate.

Second, we should emphasize a conclusion which was alluded to above, by noting that one can systematically handle questions of overidentification for the present class of models by standard statistical procedures. In recursive models with independent disturbances, overidentification is produced by an a priori specification that more than $G - h$ variables are excluded from the hth equation of the model. As an example, consider Duncan's basic model of the process of stratification given above as Eqs. (1) where z_1 is excluded from the second structural equation. The model is identified without that exclusion, so that the exclusion over-identifies the model. Such overidentifying restrictions are themselves subject to formal statistical testing.

Thus, at this point, we need standard procedures for evaluating the a priori specification of a recursive model with independent disturbances. When the overidentifying restrictions pertain only to a single equation of the model, we can apply standard t- and F-tests to assess their validity; cf. Malinvaud (1970, pp. 679–681). These t- and F-tests are the likelihood ratio tests under our specifications, so that they possess certain optimal statistical properties; cf. Wilks, (1962, pp. 405–408).

The sociological practice has been to "test" the overidentifying restrictions by seeing whether the correlations among the variables implied by the estimated model ("reproduced correlations") are close to the actual observed correlations. (In the absence of overidentifying restrictions, the estimated model would reproduce the observed correlations exactly.) While this informal device has intuitive appeal, it is clear that a formal procedure is required, particularly when more than a single equation in the model is overidentified.

The standard likelihood-ratio procedure meets this need. Let L^{*0} denote the maximized value of the log-likelihood function when no overidentifying restrictions are present, and L^{*1} denote the maximized value of the log-likelihood when all the overidentifying restrictions are imposed. Then, on the null hypothesis that the overidentifying restrictions are correct, the statistic $-2(L^{*1} - L^{*0})$ is asymptotically distributed as χ^2 with degrees of freedom equal to the number of overidentifying restrictions; cf. Wilks (1962, pp. 408–411).

For our recursive model with independent errors (and no cross-equation constraints), we see from (69) that the test statistic is simply

$$N \sum_{g=1}^{G} \log(\hat{\sigma}_{gg}^1/\hat{\sigma}_{gg}^0) \qquad (70)$$

where $\hat{\sigma}_{gg}^0$ is the estimate of the gth disturbance variance (i.e., the mean squared residual) obtained when y_g is regressed on all antecedent variables (i.e., on $y_{g-1}, ..., y_1, z_1, ..., z_K$), and $\hat{\sigma}_{gg}^1$ is the estimate of the gth disturbance variance obtained when y_g is regressed on all antecedent variables except those which are excluded a priori from the gth equation. Clearly $\hat{\sigma}_{gg}^1/\hat{\sigma}_{gg}^0 \geqslant 1$, and the magnitude of this ratio measures the extent to which imposition of the constraints worsens the fit to the sample data. A significantly large value of the statistic indicates that the worsening of the fit is too large to be attributable to chance, and thus is evidence against the set of overidentifying restrictions. (When there are cross-equation constraints, the likelihood-ratio test statistic still has the form of (70) but the $\hat{\sigma}_{gg}^1$ are no longer obtained from equation-by-equation least squares.)

Thus, to conclude this discussion, we can say that the classical theory of hypothesis testing can be applied to test the validity of particular a priori restrictions. Viewed in this manner, the classical t- and F-tests provide us with "overidentification test statistics" for recursive models with independent disturbances. In the presence of more than one overidentified equation, one may use Eq. (70) as an overidentification test statistic. It may be possible, however, for the individual coefficient test statistics to be nonsignificant while the model test statistic of Eq. (70) is significant. Therefore, in practice, a good strategy for models with multiple constraints may be to use both the model chi-square test statistic and the individual coefficient t-tests to evaluate the fit of a model to a given set of data.

7. Concluding Comments

In this chapter, we have specialized the standard theories of identification, parameter estimation, and hypothesis testing to the class of recursive models with independent disturbances, which recently has been so widely applied in sociology. This has included the statement of theorems on the identifiability of recursive models with independent disturbances, on the optimal statistical estimators for such models, and, finally, on hypothesis testing procedures for the evaluation of overidentifying a priori restrictions. For additional discussions of recursive models, the reader should consult the econometric literature; see, in particular Goldberger (1964, pp. 354–356), Christ (1966, pp. 454–455), Wonnacott & Wonnacott (1970, pp. 193–194), Malinvaud (1970, pp. 611–617, 641–644, 678–681), Theil (1971, pp. 460–463), and Johnston (1972, pp. 377–380).

In concluding this paper, consider briefly what happens to a recursive model when Σ is not diagonal, i.e., when the disturbances are correlated between equations. Then the proof of Theorem 4.13 no longer holds. Thus, one must fall back to the rank and order conditions of Corollaries 4.10 and 4.11 to establish the identifiability of a particular model by exclusion restrictions. As the reader will recall, these corollaries involve the exclusion of at least $G - 1$ variables (endogenous or exogenous) as a condition for the identifiability of a particular structural equation. Thus, the triangularity of the B matrix alone in recursive models with correlated disturbances is not sufficient to identify all of the equations of the models. In fact, the triangularity of the B matrix is a sufficient condition to identify only the first equation of the model since it implies that the remaining $G - 1$ endogenous variables are excluded from that equation. In order to identify the other equations of the model, one is forced to utilize additional a priori information such as the exclusion of additional variables from that equation. As an example, consider the following simple model, where z is exogenous, y_1 and y_2 are endogenous, the disturbances u_1 and u_2 have nonzero covariance σ_{12}, and (for convenience) all variables have zero expectations:

$$y_1 \quad + \gamma z = u_1 \tag{71a}$$

$$\beta y_1 + y_2 \quad = u_2. \tag{71b}$$

The least-squares estimator of $\beta^* = -\beta$ is

$$b = \sum y_1 y_2 \Big/ \sum y_1{}^2 \tag{72}$$

where the summation runs over the sample observations. Multiplying (71b) by y_1 and summing, we find

$$\sum y_1 y_2 = \beta^* \sum y_1{}^2 + \sum y_1 u_2 . \tag{73}$$

Upon division by $\sum y_1{}^2$ we have, recalling (72),

$$b = \beta^* + \sum y_1 u_2 \Big/ \sum y_1{}^2 = \beta^* + \left(\sum y_1 u_2 / N\right) \Big/ \left(\sum y_1{}^2 / N\right),$$

so that the asymptotic expectation of b is not β^*, but rather

$$\lim_{N \to \infty} E(b) = \beta^* + \sigma_{12}/\sigma_{y_1}^2 . \tag{74}$$

Thus, as this example suggests, if the disturbances are contemporaneously correlated between equations, the least-squares estimators are biased and inconsistent. We note that a similar, although slightly more complicated, proof can be given to show that least-squares estimators are biased and inconsistent for nonrecursive models (see, e.g., Johnston, 1972, pp. 341–344; Goldberger, 1964, pp. 289–292; Christ, 1966, pp. 459–463).

That this condition of correlated disturbances can easily arise in sociological practice is illustrated by the fact that Duncan (1968) has shown that number of siblings and intelligence (c. age 12) have nonzero effects on son's educational and occupational attainment. Yet these variables were not included in Duncan's original specification of the basic model of stratification—Eqs. (1). Therefore, the disturbances in the basic model are correlated and the least-squares estimates are biased. Apart from the admonition that all exogenous variables that possess nonzero coefficients should be included in the model—an admonition that is generally impossible to adhere to in sociological research—we offer the suggestion that one should consider statistical estimators which do not assume that disturbances are uncorrelated and which have desirable statistical properties, provided that the requisite instrumental variables are available.

Such estimators have been developed in econometrics primarily for the class of completely nonrecursive simultaneous-equation models, i.e., for models with nondiagonal Σ and nontriangular B. However, the estimators can also be applied to recursive models with correlated disturbances, and the reader is referred to the standard texts cited above for details. As an example of the application of one of these methods to the estimation of a recursive model with correlated disturbances, consider again the simple model of (71). Note, in particular, that both equations are just-identified. Furthermore, since u_1 is correlated with u_2, and since u_1 contributes to y_1, y_1 itself will be correlated with u_2. The two-stage least-squares (2SLS) estimator for the second equation is

$$\hat{\beta} = -\hat{\pi}_2/\hat{\pi}_1 \tag{75}$$

where $\hat{\pi}_1 = \sum zy_1/\sum z^2$ and $\hat{\pi}_2 = \sum zy_2/\sum z^2$ are the ordinary least-squares estimators of the reduced-form coefficients $\pi_1 = -\gamma$ and $\pi_2 = \beta\gamma$, respectively.

The meaning of Eq. (75) becomes clearer when it is compared with the estimation procedure for the model (71) which one derives from a path analysis framework. *We now assume that the variables were standardized.* Applying the principles of path analysis (Duncan, 1966; Land, 1969), one would write the following estimation equations:

$$\hat{\gamma} = -r_{y_1z} \tag{76}$$

and

$$\hat{\beta}(-r_{y_1z}) = r_{y_2z} \tag{77}$$

or

$$\hat{\beta} = -r_{y_2z}/r_{y_1z} \tag{78}$$

where the rs denote sample correlation coefficients. Since the variables are measured in standard deviation units (in which case bivariate regression coefficients are identical to correlation coefficients), it is readily seen that estimators (78) and (75) are identical. Thus, properly applied, path analysis yields 2SLS estimators for just-identified recursive models with correlated disturbances. For just-identified models that are more complicated than (71), it becomes computationally advantageous to use the standard two-stage least-squares computational algorithms. When the model is overidentified, two-stage least-squares provides a straightforward procedure for handling the excess equations.

3

Measurement Models for Continuous and Discrete Variables

NEIL W. HENRY

1. Introduction

Several recent papers have used the path analysis framework to present a formal description of measurement problems. In some of these the emphasis is on the imperfect measurement of a single variable at several different points in time (Heise, 1969a; Wiley & Wiley, 1970; Jöreskog, 1970b; Werts, Jöreskog, & Linn, 1971), while in others a more general multivariate system is discussed (Costner, 1969; Blalock, 1969a). In all cases, however, the variables discussed are real valued (continuous), so that regression models are appropriate to the analysis. In this paper we shall present a simple probabilistic model for errors of measurement when all variables are dichotomies. Our aim is to show how the assumptions of models of the path-analytic type closely parallel those for dichotomies. While the style is meant to be expository, a few new results extending the work of Coleman (1964) and Lazarsfeld & Henry (1968) will be developed.

Before discussing models for dichotomies, however, we shall review the basic characteristics of the simplest continuous-variable models.

2. Repeated Measurement of One Continuous Variable

2.1 The General Model

Suppose that F is a real-valued variable, and that X is an imperfect observation of the value F. The linear additive model in its most general form is

$$X = c + aF + e, \tag{1}$$

where e is a random variable independent of F, with mean zero and variance σ^2. In factor analysis one assumes that there are several different measurements X available for a given factor with (possibly) different parameters c and a for each (Harman, 1967). Since in that context there is no information about the zero point or the scale of F, it is conventionally assumed to have mean 0 and variance 1. This permits c to be identified as the mean of X. The parameters a can be identified if there are as few as three different measures X.

In contrast we shall suppose that only one measure is available at any point in time, and furthermore, that F changes with time according to a linear additive *chain* model,

$$F_{t+1} = d_t + b_t F_t + U_{t+1} \qquad (t = 1, 2,..., T - 1). \tag{2}$$

Here U_{t+1} has mean zero, variance τ_{t+1}^2, and is uncorrelated with F_t and the other Us. While these "random shocks" (Coleman, 1964) have zero means, it is no longer reasonable to assume that the mean or the variance of F_t is constant. For, the sequence of means depends on the parameters of the system:

$$E(F_2) = d_1 + b_1 E(F_1) \tag{3}$$

$$E(F_3) = d_2 + b_2 E(F_2) = d_2 + b_2 d_1 + b_2 b_1 E(F_1), \qquad \text{etc.}, \tag{4}$$

as do the variances:

$$V(F_2) = b_1^2 V(F_1) + \tau_2^2 \tag{5}$$

$$V(F_3) = b_2^2 V(F_2) + \tau_3^2 = b_2^2 b_1^2 V(F_1) + b_2^2 \tau_2^2 + \tau_3^2, \quad \text{etc.} \tag{6}$$

In this model, with the latent variables connected by a causal chain, we might set the zero point and scale by assuming arbitrarily that $E(F_1) = 0$ and $V(F_1) = 1$; but standardizing *all* the factors constrains the model unnecessarily. Wiley & Wiley (1970), for instance, made the point that it is unrealistic to expect the variances of the F_t to remain constant under the influence of the shocks U_t.

When the repeated measurements X_t are considered, the general model is

$$X_t = c_t + a_t F_t + e_t ,\qquad (7)$$

with the added assumptions that the e_t are independent of each other. In an operational sense the parameters a_t and c_t, together with the variance σ_t^2 of e_t, are characteristics of the measurement procedure. In this general model we allow them to vary in time, not requiring identical procedures at each point.

From (7), recalling that e is supposed to have mean zero and be independent of F, we find that

$$E(X_t) = c_t + a_t E(F_t)\qquad (8)$$

and

$$V(X_t) = a_t^2 V(F_t) + \sigma_t^2.\qquad (9)$$

Next, using Eqs. (3)–(6) and assuming that F_1 is standardized, we derive the following relations:

$$
\begin{aligned}
E(X_1) &= c_1 , \\
E(X_2) &= c_2 + a_2 d_1 , \\
E(X_3) &= c_3 + a_3 d_2 + a_3 b_2 d_1 , \quad \text{etc.;}
\end{aligned}
\qquad (10)
$$

$$
\begin{aligned}
V(X_1) &= a_1^2 + \sigma_1^2, \\
V(X_2) &= a_2^2(b_1^2 + \tau_2^2) + \sigma_2^2, \\
V(X_3) &= a_3^2 b_2^2(b_1^2 + \tau_2^2) + a_3^2 \tau_3^2 + \sigma_3^2, \quad \text{etc.}
\end{aligned}
\qquad (11)
$$

If the as and ds were known, the cs could be estimated from the observed means (10); if, in addition, bs and τs were known, the error variances σ_t^2 could be estimated from the observed variances (11). From this perspective we see that there is little hope of identifying all the parameters in the general model, since there are more parameters a_t, b_t, d_t, and τ_t, than there are covariances.

To illustrate, we calculate covariances of the observed variables X_t. From (7), when $s > 0$,

$$C(X_t , X_{t+s}) = a_t a_{t+s} C(F_t , F_{t+s}).\qquad (12)$$

From (2), on the other hand,

$$C(F_t , F_{t+s}) = b_{t+s-1} C(F_t , F_{t+s-1}),$$

whence by induction,

$$C(F_t, F_{t+s}) = V(F_t) \prod_{i=1}^{s} b_{t+i-1}, \qquad s > 0. \tag{13}$$

Consequently, we have

$$C(X_1, X_2) = a_1 a_2 b_1, \quad C(X_1, X_3) = a_1 a_3 b_1 b_2, \quad C(X_1, X_4) = a_1 a_4 b_1 b_2 b_3$$

$$C(X_2, X_3) = a_2 a_3 b_2 V(F_2), \qquad C(X_2, X_4) = a_2 a_4 b_2 b_3 V(F_2),$$

$$C(X_3, X_4) = a_3 a_4 b_3 V(F_3), \quad \text{etc.} \tag{14}$$

While these equations generate *predictions* about the observed variables, e.g.,

$$C(X_2, X_4) \, C(X_1, X_3) = C(X_1, X_4) \, C(X_2, X_3),$$

and thus permit weak tests of the model, the individual parameter values cannot be identified without additional assumptions.

While higher-order moments could be examined in an attempt to achieve identifiability, there are two reasons for not continuing along that path here: first, these moments are traditionally ignored in psychometrics and econometrics, and second, if the various random variables have joint-normal distributions (as is often assumed for purposes of testing statistical hypotheses) the higher-order moments add no information whatsoever to that contained in the means and covariance matrix. We turn, therefore, to more restricted models.

2.2 Identification of a Restricted Model

The first restriction that seems to be made by most authors is to require that all variables have zero means. There are two aspects to this assumption: first, that the measurement X does not have a systematic bias; second, that the mean value of F does not change in time. We shall only consider here the restriction on Eq. (7) made by Wiley & Wiley (1970). They set $c_t = 0$ and $a_t = 1$:

$$X_t = F_t + e_t \qquad \text{for all} \quad t. \tag{15}$$

Thus X has the same mean as F, $E(X_t) = E(F_t)$, and also $E(X_t \mid F_t) = F_t$. The fact that the coefficient of F is one means that the *scale* of F is the same as that of the observed variable X. These two assumptions, while arbitrary, seem to be a reasonable solution to the problem of deciding on a scale and zero point for F.

With these two parameters eliminated from consideration for each t, Eqs. (10), (11), (14), relating the observable moments of the X_t to the unknown parameters, simplify as shown in Table 1. Because of the scale-defining assumptions made in (15), we do *not* assume that $V(F_1) = 1$ in this section. To simplify notation somewhat, we shall define $h_t = V(F_t)$.

TABLE 1

ACCOUNTING EQUATIONS FOR THE MODIFIED WILEY AND WILEY MODEL

$E(X_2) = d_1$	$C(X_1, X_2) = b_1 h_1$
$E(X_3) = d_2 + b_2 b_1$	$C(X_1, X_3) = b_1 b_2 h_1$
$E(X_4) = d_3 + b_3(d_2 + b_2 d_1)$, etc	$C(X_1, X_4) = b_1 b_2 b_3 h_1$
	$C(X_2, X_3) = b_2 h_2 = b_2(b_1{}^2 h_1 + \tau_2{}^2)$
$V(F_t) = h_t = b_{t-1}^2 h_{t-1} + \tau_t{}^2$	$C(X_2, X_4) = b_2 b_3 h_2 = b_2 b_3(b_1{}^2 h_1 + \tau_2{}^2)$
	$C(X_3, X_4) = b_3 h_3 = b_2{}^2 h_2 + \tau_3{}^2$, etc.
$V(X_1) = h_1 + \sigma_1{}^2$	
$V(X_2) = b_1{}^2 h_1 + \tau_2{}^2 + \sigma_2{}^2$	
$V(X_3) = b_2{}^2(b_1{}^2 h_1 + \tau_2{}^2) + \tau_3{}^2 + \sigma_3{}^2$, etc.	

Examination of the equations in Table 1 shows that many of the parameters can be identified. If $X_1, X_2, ..., X_T$ are available, then $b_2, b_3, ..., b_{T-1}$ are calculable as simple ratios of covariances, e.g.,

$$b_2 = C(X_1, X_3)/C(X_1, X_2).$$

All the ds, which indicate how the means of the F_t are changing, can then be calculated, e.g.,

$$d_2 = E(X_3) - b_2 E(X_1).$$

The variances of $F_2, ..., F_{T-1}$ are also identified, e.g.,

$$h_2 = C(X_2, X_3)/b_2, \quad h_3 = C(X_3, X_4)/b_3,$$

and in turn this permits the random shock variances $\tau_3{}^2, ..., \tau_{T}{}^2_{-1}$ to be calculated, e.g.,

$$\tau_3{}^2 = h_3 - b_2{}^2 h_2.$$

Finally, the measurement error variances $\sigma_2{}^2, ..., \sigma_{T-1}$ can be identified, e.g.,

$$\sigma_2{}^2 = V(X_2) - h_2.$$

We are left, however, with several parameters that cannot be identified. These include b_1, h_1, τ_2^2, σ_1^2, from the beginning of the sequence, and τ_T^2 and σ_T^2 from the end of the sequence. Certain combinations of these are known however:

$$b_1 h_1 = C(X_1, X_2), \qquad h_1 + \sigma_1^2 = V(X_1), \qquad b_1^2 h_1 + \tau_2^2 = h_2,$$

and

$$\sigma_T^2 + \tau_T^2 = V(X_T) - b_{T-1}^2 h_{T-1}.$$

Therefore, b_1, σ_1^2, and τ_1^2 can be evaluated relative to h_1, the variance of F_1.

The identifiability of the parameters connected with the variables *internal* to the sequence $X_1, ..., X_T$ has been noted by Werts, Jöreskog, & Linn (1971). The introduction of nonzero d_t in this paper provides a relatively trivial extension of their results.

3. A Measurement Model for Dichotomous Attributes

3.1 THE GENERAL MODEL

There are two ways of developing measurement models for dichotomous attributes. One way is to treat the variables as number-valued (binary or "dummy"), associating the value 1 with one of the two responses and 0 with the other. The linear additive model is then applied and the statistical analysis is carried out in a framework very much like that for continuous variables. The other approach is simply to define conditional probabilities of response uncertainty and change under various conditions, leading to a style of analysis that is comparable to Markov chain analysis (Coleman, 1964; Lazarsfeld & Henry, 1968, Chapter 9). The advantage of this is that extensions to discrete (nominal or ordinal) variates with more than two categories can be made easily, using matrix notation. We shall follow the latter approach here, occasionally drawing attention to parallel development in Section 2.

We assume that an observed dichotomous attribute (X) is an imperfect representation of an underlying dichotomy (F). The actual response of an individual depends probabilistically on his true state through a matrix $Q = (q_{ij})$ of conditional response probabilities, as shown in Table 2. Here q_{ij} is the probability of giving response j when the latent state is i; q_{12}, for instance, is the probability of giving the "wrong" response $(-)$ when the true state is $+$, q_{21} being the other uncertainty parameter. In the

3. MEASUREMENT MODELS FOR CONTINUOUS AND DISCRETE VARIABLES 57

present context we would expect these two parameters to be substantially less than 0.5, but there is no necessity to assume that is actually the case.[†]
If the latent distribution is $(v, 1 - v)$, i.e., a proportion v are $+$, the expected proportion responding positively will be

$$p = vq_{11} + (1 - v) q_{21}. \tag{16}$$

A matrix representation can be made as follows:

$$(p, 1 - p) = (v, 1 - v) \begin{pmatrix} q_{11} & q_{12} \\ q_{21} & q_{22} \end{pmatrix}, \tag{17}$$

or

$$\mathbf{p}' = \mathbf{v}'Q. \tag{18}$$

where $\mathbf{p}' = (p, 1 - p)$ and $\mathbf{v}' = (v, 1 - v)$.

TABLE 2

CONDITIONAL PROBABILITIES OF RESPONSE GIVEN A LATENT ("TRUE") STATE

| | | Manifest response | |
		+	−
Latent attribute	+	$q_{11} = 1 - q_{12}$	q_{12}
	−	q_{21}	$q_{22} = 1 - q_{21}$

If the latent attribute remained fixed, and several different indicators X were available, we would have the simple model of two latent classes discussed by Lazarsfeld & Henry (1968, Chapter 2). In the analogous situation in Section 2, we saw that the development for continuous variables led to the classic factor analysis model. If observations are repeated in time, however, one usually expects that some real changes will occur. The natural parallel to the simple causal chain defined for the F variables in the previous section is the Markov chain for discrete states.

[†] We occasionally use the terms "error," "right," "wrong," etc., in keeping with common conventions. It should be understood that in most social applications there is no right or wrong response: we should not describe someone as being "in error" simply because he makes a response that has a low probability.

Consider then, the following model: individuals change their latent state according to a Markov chain. Let $M_t = (m_{ijt})$ be the matrix of transition probabilities from time t to time $t + 1$. That is, m_{ijt} is the probability of being in state j at time $t + 1$, conditional on having been in state i at time t. These probabilities are permitted to vary with time. The Markov assumption states that the conditional probability m_{ijt} is not affected by the development of the process *before* time t. If $M(t, t + s)$ is defined to be the matrix of transition probabilities from t to $t + s$, the Markov assumption implies that

$$M(t, t + s) = M_t M_{t+1} \cdots M_{t+s-1} . \tag{19}$$

Next we let v_t be the probability of being positive on the latent attribute at time t $(=1, 2,..., T)$; let $\mathbf{v}_t{}' = (v_t, 1 - v_t)$ be the corresponding row vector. The definitions imply that

$$\mathbf{v}'_{t+1} = \mathbf{v}_t{}' M_t , \tag{20}$$

whence by a recursive argument and (19), we have

$$\mathbf{v}'_{t+1} = \mathbf{v}_1{}' M_1 M_2 \cdots M_t = \mathbf{v}_1{}' M(1, t + 1). \tag{21}$$

Equation (18) shows how the latent state is transformed into the manifest response. We shall consider the general model, in which the response probability matrix Q may vary with time:

$$\mathbf{p}_t{}' = \mathbf{v}_t{}' Q_t . \tag{22}$$

If the uncertainty parameters q_{12} and q_{21} are interpreted as measurement error probabilities, variation in Q_t over time may indicate changes in the measuring procedures.

The derived equation

$$\mathbf{p}_t{}' = \mathbf{v}_1{}' M(1, t) Q_t \tag{23}$$

shows how this general model is defined by the response probability matrices $Q_1, Q_2,..., Q_t$; the latent transition probability matrices $M_1, M_2,..., M_{T-1}$; and the initial latent distribution $\mathbf{v}_1$.

3.2 IDENTIFICATION OF THE MODEL

In order to compute the expected proportions of combinations of responses at different times we have to make explicit the assumption of local independence: when the latent states are known, manifest responses occur independently of one another. This is analogous to assuming in the continuous-variable model that the measurement error variables e_t are independent of one another. To compute the probability of giving positive responses at times t *and* $t + s$, for instance, we need to take into account the four possible combinations of latent states and their respective probabilities:

$$v_{++}(t, t + s) = v_t m_{11}(t, t + s) \tag{24}$$

$$v_{+-}(t, t + s) = v_t m_{12}(t, t + s) \tag{25}$$

$$v_{-+}(t, t + s) = (1 - v_t)\, m_{21}(t, t + s) \tag{26}$$

$$v_{--}(t, t + s) = (1 - v_t)\, m_{22}(t, t + s), \tag{27}$$

where the $m_{ij}(t, t + s)$ are the elements of $M(t, t + s)$. The manifest probability of two positive responses is obtained by multiplying (24) by $q_{11t}q_{11,t+s}$ (the probability of making no error); (25) by $q_{11t}q_{21,t+s}$; (26) by $q_{21t}q_{11,t+s}$; (27) by $q_{21t}q_{21,t+s}$ (the probability of making the positive response both times when the negative is called for); and adding these four terms together. A convenient matrix formula is available as soon as we define the diagonal matrix

$$V_t = \begin{pmatrix} v_t & 0 \\ 0 & 1 - v_t \end{pmatrix}$$

and the 2×2 matrix of joint response probabilities $P(t, t + s)$:

$$\begin{array}{c} \text{Response at } t + s \\ \begin{array}{cc} + & \quad - \end{array} \end{array}$$

$$\text{Response at } t \quad \begin{array}{c} + \\ - \end{array} \begin{pmatrix} p_{11}(t, t + s) & p_{12}(t, t + s) \\ p_{21}(t, t + s) & p_{22}(t, t + s) \end{pmatrix}.$$

Note that $p_{11}(t, t + s) + p_{12}(t, t + s) + p_{21}(t, t + s) + p_{22}(t, t + s) = 1$. The general form of the matrix equation is

$$P(t, t + s) = Q_t' V_t M(t, t + s) Q_{t+s}, \qquad s > 0. \tag{28}$$

To see how this matrix equation arises, we develop the product on the right of (28) for $t = 1$ and $s = 1$:

$$\begin{pmatrix} q_{111} & q_{211} \\ q_{121} & q_{221} \end{pmatrix} \begin{pmatrix} v_1 & 0 \\ 0 & 1 - v_1 \end{pmatrix} \begin{pmatrix} m_{11}(1, 2) & m_{12}(1, 2) \\ m_{21}(1, 2) & m_{22}(1, 2) \end{pmatrix} \begin{pmatrix} q_{112} & q_{122} \\ q_{212} & q_{222} \end{pmatrix}.$$

The (1,1) entry works out to be

$$\begin{aligned} p_{11}(1, 2) = \; & v_1 q_{111}[m_{11}(1, 2)\, q_{112} + m_{12}(1, 2)\, q_{212}] \\ & + (1 - v_1)\, q_{211}[m_{21}(1, 2)\, q_{112} + m_{22}(1, 2)\, q_{212}], \end{aligned}$$

which illustrates the sequence of steps involved in giving two consecutive positive responses: at $t = 1$ one may be $+$ on the latent attribute with probability v_1, and then give the positive response with probability q_{111}; over the interval $(1, 2)$ a move may be made to the second latent state with probability $m_{12}(1, 2)$, followed by the positive response that then has probability q_{212}, or no change in latent state followed by the positive response, $m_{11}(1, 2)q_{112}$. Alternatively, the initial latent state might be $-$ with probability $1 - v_1$, response positive with probability q_{211}, followed by change or no change of the latent state which determines the probability of positive response at $t = 2$.

Using the observable data in the form of (28) we can identify many of the parameters of the process. From (28) and (19),

$$P(1, 2) = Q_1'V_1M_1Q_2, \tag{29}$$

$$P(1, 3) = Q_1'V_1M_1M_2Q_3, \tag{30}$$

$$P(2, 3) = Q_2'V_2M_2Q_3. \tag{31}$$

A little algebra will show that

$$P(2, 3)\,P(1, 3)^{-1}\,P(1, 2) = Q_2'V_2Q_2. \tag{32}$$

The matrix $Q_2'V_2Q_2$, by the way, has an interesting interpretation. It is a theoretical cross-classification of two responses, both subject to measurement error, at time $t = 2$. Coleman (1964), operating in continuous rather than discrete time, could define it as the limit of $P(t, t + s)$ as s approaches zero; he calls the off-diagonal entries "unreliabilities."

In this general model, which is almost exactly analogous to the general model for continuous variables discussed in Section 2.1, no further identification of parameters is possible if we restrict observation to the joint probabilities of response at *pairs* of time points. In Section 3.3 we consider two interesting special cases, but now we will show how higher-order probabilities, involving more than two time points, can be used to obtain a general solution. The style of the solution is not new (Lazarsfeld and Henry, 1968, p. 256), but its application to the general model developed here is.

Consider the probability of giving the positive response at time 1, again at time 2, and again at time 3. We need to consider that the latent state may change, and that all eight latent patterns have a certain probability of occurring. The manifest probability requires a sum of products over the eight possible latent types; each product involves the latent probability and three different response probabilities, e.g.,

$$v_{+++}q_{111}q_{112}q_{113} \quad \text{or} \quad v_{+-+}q_{111}q_{212}q_{113}.$$

We construct a "stratified" manifest matrix $P_+(1, 3; 2)$ by considering only those individuals who give the positive response at time 2. The i, j entry of this matrix, denoted by $p_{ij;1}(1, 3; 2)$, is the probability of giving response i at time 1, response j at time 3, *and* response $+$ at time 2. We can write

$$p_{ij;1}(1, 3; 2) = \sum_{\beta, \gamma} [v_1 m_{1\beta}(1, 2)\, m_{\beta\gamma}(2, 3)\, q_{1i1} q_{\beta12} q_{\gamma j3}$$

$$+ (1 - v_1)\, m_{2\beta}(1, 2)\, m_{\beta\gamma}(2, 3)\, q_{2i1} q_{\beta12} q_{\gamma j3}].$$

By defining a diagonal matrix

$$D_+(2) = \begin{pmatrix} q_{112} & 0 \\ 0 & q_{212} \end{pmatrix},$$

which contains the probabilities of responding positively at time 2 within each of the two latent classes, the stratified matrix $P_+(1, 3; 2)$ can be shown to be

$$P_+(1, 3; 2) = Q_1' V_1 M_1 D_+(2)\, M_2 Q_3 , \tag{33}$$

a simple expression which is quite similar to Eq. (30). The similarity suggests the following manipulation:

$$P_+(1, 3; 2)\, P(1, 3)^{-1} = Q_1' V_1 M_1 D_+(2)\, M_2 Q_3 Q_3^{-1} M_2^{-1} M_1^{-1} V_1^{-1} Q_1'^{-1}$$

$$= A_1 D_+(2)\, A_1^{-1}, \tag{34}$$

where

$$A_1 = Q_1' V_1 M_1 . \tag{35}$$

Equation (34), however, implies that the two diagonal entries of $D_+(2)$ are the characteristic roots of the matrix $P_+(1, 3; 2)\, P(1, 3)^{-1}$, which can be calculated by well-known procedures. This calculation means that Q_2 is now known, since the other two entries of Q_2 are simply $q_{122} = 1 - q_{112}$ and $q_{222} = 1 - q_{212}$. As long as the trivial special case $q_{112} = q_{212}$ does not occur, Q_2 will be nonsingular and V_2 can be identified using (20):

$$\mathbf{v_2}' = \mathbf{p_2}' Q_2^{-1}. \tag{36}$$

If $T > 3$, the above procedure can be used to identify each V_t and each Q_t except for the first and last in the sequence. To see this, simply replace 3 by T and 2 by t in Eqs. (33)–(36). Thus the latent distribution and the response probabilities at each intermediate time point can be identified as long as the indicated matrix inversions are permitted. Any transition matrix *between* intermediate points, i.e., M_2, M_3,..., M_{T-2}, can also be identified. Consider, for instance, $P(2, 3) = Q_2'V_2M_2Q_3$. Then

$$M_2 = V_2^{-1}Q_2'^{-1}P(2, 3)Q_3^{-1}, \tag{37}$$

where V_2, Q_2, and Q_3 have already been shown to be computable when $T > 3$. In this model Q_1, Q_T, M_1, M_{T-1}, and V_1 remain unidentified, although certain combinations of these matrices can be calculated, i.e., $M_{T-1}Q_T$ and $Q_1'V_1M_1$.

Our general result is very similar to that developed for continuous variables in Section 2. The response probabilities Q_t play the role of error variances σ_t^2; the transition matrices M_t and the latent distributions V_t are analogous to the parameters of the latent process d_t, b_t, and τ_t^2. In both cases, these parameters are identified for intermediate t. The major difference in the exposition was due to the fact that we needed to look at third-order probabilities (i.e., third-order moments) in order to identify the general dichotomous model.

3.3   RESTRICTED MODELS

We shall now consider two ways of restricting the general model for dichotomous variables: (i) assuming that Q_t is constant over time, and (ii) assuming that Q_t varies with time, but is symmetric.

i. *Constant Error Probabilities*

Suppose that $Q_t = Q$ for all t. That is, as time goes on, the "measuring instrument" retains exactly the same characteristics. The two probabilities that determine the relation between latent state and manifest response remain constant. This assumption is analogous to that made by Wiley and Wiley (1970) in their analysis of the continuous variable model: they supposed that the error variances σ_t^2 were constant.

From the general analysis with three time points we know how to compute $Q'V_2Q$; and indeed, for any *intermediate* point t, $Q'V_tQ$ is computable $(1 < t < T)$. Suppose that $T > 3$. With $Q'V_2Q$ and $Q'V_3Q$ known we can calculate

$$(Q'V_2Q)^{-1}Q'V_3Q = Q^{-1}V_2^{-1}V_3Q \tag{38}$$

as long as Q and V_2 are nonsingular. Since $V_2^{-1}V_3$ is a diagonal matrix, its two diagonal entries $(v_3/v_2$ and $(1 - v_3)/(1 - v_2))$ are the characteristic roots of the given matrix, while the rows of Q are the associated characteristic vectors, well defined as long as the two roots are distinct. In other words, when $T > 3$, this model implies that

$$P(1, 2)^{-1} P(1, 3) P(2, 3)^{-1} P(3, 4) P(2, 4)^{-1} P(2, 3) = Q^{-1}V_2^{-1}V_3Q, \quad (39)$$

and therefore v_2, v_3, and Q can be identified from the characteristic roots and vectors of the matrix on the left of (24) as long as $v_2 \neq v_3$.

Next we see that M_2 (and, in general M_t for $1 < t < T$) can be identified since $P(2, 3) = Q'V_2M_2Q$ implies that

$$M_2 = V_2^{-1}Q'^{-1}P(2, 3)Q^{-1}. \quad (40)$$

Once again we are able to determine parameters at intermediate time points, but V_1 and M_1 remain indeterminate in this model. (The product V_1M_1 *is* identifiable.)

The response probabilities of order greater than two add no further information. The parameters are thus overidentified, and the third-order probabilities are available as a test of the model, for instance, by comparing $P_+(1, 3; 2)$ with the product $P(1, 2)Q^{-1}D_+M_2Q$, after Q and M_2 have been estimated by the methods described above.

ii. *The Homoscedastic Model*

Suppose that the matrices Q_t are symmetric:

$$Q_t = \begin{pmatrix} 1 - q_t & q_t \\ q_t & 1 - q_t \end{pmatrix} \quad (41)$$

This is interpreted most easily by thinking of q_t as the probability of an error *of either type*. We call this "homoscedastic" because the conditional variance of response does not depend on the latent state when Q_t is symmetric.

The term homoscedastic is usually used in the analysis of linear models for continuous variables. In the situation where X_t is the dependent variable and F_t the independent, it is assumed that the conditional variance of X_t, given F_t, is constant and equal to the overall error variance σ_t^2. Typically, when distributional assumptions are made it is assumed that the conditional distribution of the measurement error e_t given F_t is normal with mean 0 and variance σ_t^2. Assuming homoscedasticity for the dichotomous model makes it more comparable to the continuous variable model where only one variance parameter, σ_t^2, is specified.

Consider the conditional variances in our general dichotomous model: when the latent state is positive the probability of a positive response is

q_{11t}, and so the variance of response is $q_{11t}(1 - q_{11t})$. When the latent state is negative, the probability of a positive response is q_{21t}, and the variance is $q_{21t}(1 - q_{21t})$. These two conditional variances are equal only if $q_{11t} = q_{21t}$, the trivial case that gives us a singular Q_t; or when $q_{11t} = 1 - q_{21t}$, the more interesting symmetric case that we shall examine here.

Once again we recall that $Q_t'V_tQ_t$ can be computed from manifest probabilities for $1 < t < T$. In this special case, however,

$$Q_t'V_tQ_t = \begin{pmatrix} 1 - q_t & q_t \\ q_t & 1 - q_t \end{pmatrix}\begin{pmatrix} v_t & 0 \\ 0 & 1 - v_t \end{pmatrix}\begin{pmatrix} 1 - q_t & q_t \\ q_t & 1 - q_t \end{pmatrix}$$

$$= \begin{pmatrix} q_t^2 + (1 - 2q_t)\,v_t & (1 - q_t)\,q_t \\ (1 - q_t)\,q_t & (1 - q_t)^2 - (1 - 2q_t)\,v_t \end{pmatrix}.$$

The value of q_t can be found from the off-diagonal element of this matrix and then v_t from either of the diagonal elements.

With Q_t and V_t identified, M_t can be computed in the usual way for $1 < t < T - 1$:

$$M_t = V_t^{-1}Q_t'^{-1}P(t, t + 1)Q_{t+1}^{-1}, \tag{42}$$

while Q_1, V_1, M_1, M_{T-1}, and Q_T cannot be identified.

4. Conclusion

In this section we explore the possibility of dealing with dichotomous items within the framework of Section 2 by defining binary ("dummy") variables, then conclude by indicating how the model discussed in Section 3 can be generalized to handle items with more than two categories.

4.1 COMPARISON WITH BINARY VARIABLE ANALYSIS

In the initial model of Section 2.1 we now suppose that the variables X_t and F_t take on only two values 1 and 0 according as the response is positive or negative. The equation

$$F_{t+1} = d_t + b_tF_t + U_{t+1}, \tag{43}$$

along with the assumption that $E(U_{t+1}) = 0$, implies that

$$E(F_{t+1}) = d_t + b_tE(F_t). \tag{44}$$

In the notation of Section 3, $E(F_t) = v_t$, the probability of being in the positive latent state at time t. Hence

$$v_{t+1} = d_t + b_t v_t = d_t(1 - v_t) + (d_t + b_t) v_t,\tag{45}$$

so that

$$(v_{t+1}, 1 - v_{t+1}) = (v_t, 1 - v_t)\begin{pmatrix}d_t + b_t & 1 - d_t - b_t\\ d_t & 1 - d_t\end{pmatrix}.\tag{46}$$

Note how this equation resembles Eq. (20) of Section 3, $\mathbf{v}'_{t+1} = \mathbf{v}'_t M_t$, indicating that d_t and $d_t + b_t$ are interpretable as transition probabilities of the latent Markov chain.

Similarly, since

$$X_t = c_t + a_t F_t + e_t\tag{47}$$

and $E(e_t) = 0$, we have

$$E(X_t) = c_t + a_t E(F_t).\tag{48}$$

In the notation of Section 3, therefore,

$$p_t = c_t + a_t v_t = c_t(1 - v_t) + (c_t + a_t) v_t.\tag{49}$$

In matrix form

$$(p_t, 1 - p_t) = (v_t, 1 - v_t)\begin{pmatrix}c_t + a_t & 1 - c_t - a_t\\ c_t & 1 - c_t\end{pmatrix},$$

which resembles Eq. (22) of Section 3, $\mathbf{p}_t' = \mathbf{v}_t' Q_t$. The parameters c_t and $c_t + a_t$ are thus interpreted as the response probabilities q_{21t} and q_{11t}, respectively, in the matrix Q_t.

A major difference in the analysis of the regression equations for the binary variables is that the *variances* of the X_t add no new information to that contained in their means, since $V(F_t) = E(F_t)(1 - E(F_t)) = v_t(1 - v_t)$ and $V(X_t) = E(X_t)(1 - E(X_t)) = p_t(1 - p_t)$. Using the usual assumption of uncorrelatedness of F_t and e_t, we derive from (47)

$$V(X_t) = a_t^2 V(F_t) + \sigma_t^2\tag{50}$$

or

$$p_t(1 - p_t) = a_t^2 v_t(1 - v_t) + \sigma_t^2.\tag{51}$$

In the continuous-variable model, σ_t^2, the error variances, are independent parameters, free to vary. When dichotomous variables are analyzed, however, the σ_t^2 are restricted functions of the other parameters. Substituting (49) into (51), we find that

$$\sigma_t^2 = c_t(1 - c_t) + a_t v_t(1 - a_t - 2c_t).\tag{52}$$

In like fashion we see that the $\tau_t{}^2$ (the variance of U_t) are not free parameters either. Rewrite

$$V(F_{t+1}) = b_t{}^2 V(F_t) + \tau_t{}^2 \tag{53}$$

as $v_{t+1}(1 - v_{t+1}) = b_t{}^2 v_t (1 - v_t) + \tau_t{}^2$; then substitute (45), to get

$$\tau_t{}^2 = d_t(1 - d_t) + b_t v_t(1 - b_t - 2d_t). \tag{54}$$

Now suppose we used the Wiley and Wiley specification Eq. (15) to determine location and scale of the F_t. We would find that $p_t = v_t$ and the covariance of X_t and F_t is equal to 1. The first condition, that the manifest probability of a positive response is equal to the corresponding latent probability, would certainly be an artificial constraint on the model discussed here. The second cannot be satisfied at all: the covariance of two binary variables can never exceed .25 in absolute value. The reason for the apparent contradiction is that there are no location or scale problems in the usual sense when a variable can take on only two values. The nature of the variables imposes its own restrictions [namely (52) and (54)] on the number of free parameters in the model. This fact, coupled with the information available from third-order moments in the binary variable model, explains why the "general" model of Section 3 could be identified, while the "general" model of Section 2.1 had to be restricted in 2.2 before identification of intermediate parameters was possible. The models are in fact quite analogous, but parameter specifications that seem natural for continuous variables may be unnecessary or contradictory when analyzing dichotomous variables.

4.2 POLYTOMOUS QUALITATIVE VARIABLES

Suppose that we were dealing with qualitative variables X with more than two categories. It is not hard to see that the matrix equations set down in Section 3 would still hold, as long as we made the appropriate assumptions about the latent variables F. In particular, if we assume that F has the same number of categories as X, then all the matrices remain square and the proofs that parameters are identifiable are unchanged. Of course, the various results hold only if all indicated matrix inversions can be carried out, and these conditions can be violated in nontrivial ways when there are a large number of categories (Madansky, 1960).

One might not want to define a latent state to correspond to each manifest state, however; F may have more or fewer categories than X. In the latter case the latent structure is "simpler" than the manifest structure. Suppose, for instance, that there were only two types of individuals, "Anomic" and "Eunomic," but for various reasons a five-point response scale had been constructed (Miller and Butler, 1966). Then the matrices Q_t would have two rows and five columns and could not be inverted. By restricting attention to only two of the five scale categories, however, square matrices could be constructed and the columns of Q_t would be identified two at a time, using the methods of Section 3. The former case, where the response structure is simpler than the latent structure, cannot be analyzed by these procedures. Despite the fact that this case is theoretically more interesting, we know of no *general* results on identifiability of parameters when X has fewer categories than F.

In the regression analysis literature a k-category qualitative variable is analyzed by defining $k - 1$ binary variables. This scheme is useful when the variable in question is an independent variable, but less so when, like X, it is a dependent variable. The causal scheme then would have to become multivariate, dealing with $k - 1$ variables at each time t, complicating the analysis greatly. The direct qualitative analysis of Section 3 seems a more straightforward way of dealing with such data.

In this paper we have dealt with only two of the four possible models relating latent and manifest variables: X and F continuous, and X and F discrete. The other two, X continuous and F discrete, X discrete and F continuous, deserve some attention also, for some interesting special cases will undoubtedly arise when repeated observations are made.

4

The Identification Problem for Structural Equation Models with Unmeasured Variables

DAVID E. WILEY

1. Introduction

This paper has four goals. The first is to present a general framework for the consideration of models with error in the measured variables and/or constructs which were not measured directly. The second goal is to present some of the difficulties inherent in the use of standard analytic procedures when the appropriate model has these properties. The third objective is to propose a strategy for the design of measurement operations together with a general class of models which incorporate those operations as well as structural parameters. The strategy, together with the model, point to some solutions to the difficulties encountered with standard analyses. The last goal is to present some initial ideas concerning the identifiability of particular models in the general class.

A primary specification that should be made in building a causal model is the designation of each term in the model as either a random variable or a fixed constant. When n variables are considered exogenous to m other variables, a linear model might be specified as

$$\underset{(m \times N)}{Y} = \underset{(m \times n)}{B} \underset{(n \times N)}{X} + \underset{(m \times N)}{\mathcal{E}}. \tag{1}$$

If the N units, which are each characterized by $m + n$ measurements, include the population of X vectors about which inferences are to be made, and if the Y vectors corresponding to each X vector are a random sample from the population of such Y vectors, the random vectors in $\mathcal{E}$ will be uncorrelated with the vectors in X, and the model specified by Eq. (1) may be fitted by least squares.

If, on the other hand, the N units are sampled from a larger population of units to which inferences are to be generalized, then the matrix X is a matrix of random variables. In such a case, the model might be better phrased as follows:

$$\underset{(m \times 1)}{y} = \underset{(m \times 1)}{\mu_y} + \underset{(m \times n)}{B} \underset{(n \times 1)}{(x - \mu_x)} + \underset{(m \times 1)}{\epsilon} , \tag{2}$$

where

$$\mu_x = E(x) \quad \text{and} \quad E((x - \mu_x) \epsilon') = \underset{(n \times m)}{0} .$$

If we assume that x and ϵ, and therefore y, have a multivariate normal distribution, then the parameters to be estimated are $\mu_y = E(y)$, μ_x, B, $\Sigma_{xx} = E((x - \mu_x)(x - \mu_x)')$, and $\Sigma_{\epsilon\epsilon} = E(\epsilon\epsilon')$. The mean vector and covariance matrix of the observable random vector $z = \binom{y}{x}$ are

$$E(z) = \binom{\mu_y}{\mu_x} \quad \text{and} \quad \Sigma = \begin{pmatrix} B\Sigma_{xx}B' + \Sigma_{\epsilon\epsilon} & B\Sigma_{xx} \\ \Sigma_{xx}B' & \Sigma_{xx} \end{pmatrix}.$$

The sufficient statistics for these parameters are the sample mean vector

$$\bar{z} = \binom{\bar{x}}{\bar{y}}$$

and the sample covariance matrix

$$S = \begin{pmatrix} S_{yy} & S_{yx} \\ S_{xy} & S_{xx} \end{pmatrix}.$$

Since the model is just-identified (if Σ_{xx} is of full rank), the maximum-likelihood estimates of the covariance structure parameters are

$$\hat{\Sigma}_{xx} = S_{xx} , \tag{3}$$

$$\hat{B} = S_{yx}S_{xx}^{-1} , \tag{4}$$

and

$$\hat{\Sigma}_{\epsilon\epsilon} = S_{yy} - \hat{B}\hat{\Sigma}_{xx}\hat{B}' = S_{yy} - S_{yx}S_{xx}^{-1}S_{xy} . \tag{5}$$

The maximum-likelihood estimate $\hat{B}$ in model (2) is numerically equal to the least-squares estimate of B in model (1). However, the probability distributions of these estimates are quite different owing to the differing assumptions in the models. For example, it is clear that in the univariate case, a sample regression coefficient $b = s_{xy}/s_{xx}$ has a nonnormal distribution when s_{xx} is a random variable rather than a fixed constant.

If we accept the second model as a more realistic one for sociology and psychology, we should recognize the implications for standardization. The usual practice in implementing a structural model is to standardize the scores of random variables so that they have a mean of zero and unit variance in the sample. This results in data analyses based on the sample correlation matrix R rather than the sample covariance matrix S which was used above. However, there are definite reasons for presenting a parameterization in terms of Σ (the population covariance matrix) rather than P (the population correlation matrix). Under a broad class of biased selections from a population, e.g., selections of subpopulations that result in changes in range (changes in values of Σ_{xx} or $\Sigma_{\epsilon\epsilon}$), the regression coefficients B will remain invariant. This will not be true, however, of the standardized regression coefficients (based on P). Thus, more comparability across discrepant studies should result if one uses the original covariance matrix; see Tukey (1954) and Blalock (1967).

2. Measurement Error in Nonsimultaneous Models

At this point we shall add a specification of measurement error to the models given above and explore the consequences. In this section the major concern is with model specification and parameter identification and not with estimation. Consequently, the discussion will be phrased in terms of population parameters and not in terms of sample statistics or estimates based on them.

Suppose we take a simple model with one independent and one dependent variable:

$$x \sim N(0, \sigma_x{}^2), \quad \epsilon \sim N(0, \sigma_\epsilon{}^2), \quad y = \alpha x + \epsilon, \quad C(x, \epsilon) = 0.$$

Then the covariance matrix of the observable vector $\binom{x}{y}$ is

$$\Sigma = \begin{pmatrix} \sigma_x{}^2 & \alpha\sigma_x{}^2 \\ \alpha\sigma_x{}^2 & \alpha^2\sigma_x{}^2 + \sigma_\epsilon{}^2 \end{pmatrix}.$$

We may note that there are three parameters and three estimable variances and covariances. The parameters are identifiable and consistent estimates are available.

If we modify the model and assume that the variables are measured with errors independent of the true values, we would have the following (with a change in notation):

$$\eta = \alpha\xi + \theta, \qquad y_1 = \xi + \epsilon_1, \qquad y_2 = \eta + \epsilon_2 = \alpha\xi + \theta + \epsilon_2,$$

$$\xi \sim N(0, \sigma_\xi^2), \qquad \theta \sim N(0, \sigma_\theta^2), \qquad C(\xi, \theta) = 0,$$

$$\epsilon_i \sim N(0, \sigma_i^2), \qquad C(\epsilon_i, \xi) = C(\epsilon_i, \theta) = 0, \qquad (i = 1, 2).$$

Thus the covariance matrix of the observable vector $\binom{y_1}{y_2}$ is

$$\Sigma = \begin{pmatrix} \sigma_\xi^2 + \sigma_1^2 & \alpha\sigma_\xi^2 \\ \alpha\sigma_\xi^2 & \alpha^2\sigma_\xi^2 + \sigma_\theta^2 + \sigma_2^2 \end{pmatrix}.$$

We now have five parameters and only three variances and covariances. Therefore the parameters are not identified without two independent restrictions. One possible set of restrictions is (i) $\sigma_\theta^2 = 0$, (ii) $\sigma_1^2 = \sigma_2^2 = \sigma^2$, which is equivalent to assuming that (i) each of the variables y_1 and y_2 is a measure of a common trait (which is y_1 in the absence of measurement error) and (ii) the measurement errors have equal variance. Another possible restriction is $\sigma_1^2 = 0$, which implies that the first variable is measured without error. If we also absorb the measurement error in the second variable into the disturbance, the remaining parameters are identifiable.

Now suppose we have two measures, rather than one measure, of each of ξ and η. Suppose further that the measures have the following characteristics:

$$y_1 = \xi + \epsilon_1 \qquad\qquad\qquad y_2 = \gamma_1\xi + \epsilon_2$$

$$y_3 = \eta + \epsilon_3 = \alpha\xi + \theta + \epsilon_3 \qquad y_4 = \gamma_2\eta + \epsilon_4 = \gamma_2(\alpha\xi + \theta) + \epsilon_4.$$

Then the covariance matrix of the observables is

$$\Sigma = \begin{bmatrix} \sigma_\xi^2 + \sigma_1^2 & & & \\ \gamma_1\sigma_\xi^2 & \gamma_1^2\sigma_\xi^2 + \sigma_2^2 & & \\ \alpha\sigma_\xi^2 & \gamma_1\alpha\sigma_\xi^2 & (\alpha^2\sigma_\xi^2 + \sigma_\theta^2) + \sigma_3^2 & \\ \gamma_2\alpha\sigma_\xi^2 & \gamma_1\gamma_2\alpha\sigma_\xi^2 & \gamma_2(\alpha^2\sigma_\xi^2 + \sigma_\theta^2) & \gamma_2^2(\alpha^2\sigma_\xi^2 + \sigma_\theta^2) + \sigma_4^2 \end{bmatrix}.$$

Denoting the elements in this matrix by $\sigma_{ij} = C(y_i, y_j)$, we find that the parameters in this model are all identifiable in terms of the σ_{ij}.

Explicitly,

$$\sigma_\xi^2 = \sigma_{12}\sigma_{13}/\sigma_{23} \qquad\qquad \sigma_\theta^2 = \alpha_{34}/\gamma_2 - \alpha^2\sigma_\xi^2$$

$$\sigma_1^2 = \sigma_{11} - \sigma_\xi^2 \qquad\qquad \sigma_2^2 = \sigma_{22} - \gamma_1^2\sigma_\xi^2$$

$$\gamma_1 = \sigma_{12}/\sigma_\xi^2 \quad (=\sigma_{23}/\sigma_{13} = \sigma_{24}/\sigma_{14}) \qquad \sigma_3^2 = \sigma_{33} - (\alpha^2\sigma_\xi^2 + \sigma_\theta^2)$$

$$\alpha = \sigma_{13}/\sigma_\xi^2 \quad (=\sigma_{23}/\sigma_{12}) \qquad\qquad \sigma_4^2 = \sigma_{44} - \gamma_2^2(\alpha^2\sigma_\xi^2 + \sigma_\theta^2)$$

$$\gamma_2 = \sigma_{14}/\alpha\sigma_\xi^2 \quad (=\sigma_{14}/\sigma_{13} = \sigma_{24}/\sigma_{23}).$$

Indeed, the parameters are overidentified, since the ten elements of Σ are expressed in terms of only nine parameters. The single overidentifying constraint is

$$\sigma_{14}\sigma_{23} = \sigma_{13}\sigma_{24}. \qquad (6)$$

If this constraint is not met in the population, the model is incorrect. The fault may lie with the replicate measurements, i.e., they may not be truly measuring the same constructs. That misspecification is only detectable when it results in unexpected covariance across the variables, i.e., violates (6).

The structural characteristics of this example suggest for the design of studies a general strategy that assures the identification of relevant structural parameters. The strategy consists of generating two nominally parallel measurements for each latent exogenous variable in the model. Nominally parallel measurements have two properties: (i) their latent variables are linearly dependent, and (ii) their measurement errors are independent.

If we specify a vector of true exogenous variables ξ and two vectors of observable variables

$$x_1 = \xi + \epsilon_1, \qquad x_2 = \Gamma\xi + \epsilon_2,$$

where Γ is a diagonal matrix and the errors are all mutually independent, then the covariance matrix of the xs is

$$\Sigma = \begin{bmatrix} \Sigma_{\xi\xi} + \Psi_1 & \Sigma_{\xi\xi}\Gamma' \\ {\scriptstyle(n\times n)} & {\scriptstyle(n\times n)} \\ \Gamma\Sigma_{\xi\xi} & \Gamma\Sigma_{\xi\xi} + \Psi_2 \\ {\scriptstyle(n\times n)} & {\scriptstyle(n\times n)} \end{bmatrix}, \qquad (7)$$

where $\Psi_i = E(\epsilon_i\epsilon_i')$, $(i = 1, 2)$, and $\Sigma_{\xi\xi} = E(\xi\xi')$, are the relevant covariance matrices. Under these circumstances, the matrix $\Sigma_{\xi\xi}$ is identifiable under fairly general conditions provided that the number of elements in ξ is greater than or equal to two. Given that $\Sigma_{\xi\xi}$ is identified and nonsingular, the matrix of coefficients relating ξ and the other variables is identified since $\Gamma = (\Gamma\Sigma_{\xi\xi})(\Sigma_{\xi\xi})^{-1}$.

3. Recursive Models and the Effect of Measurement Error

In this section we present an example of a recursive model and explore the effects of various assumptions on identification and estimation, with and without the presence of measurement error.

The structural model is

$$\eta_1 = \alpha_{12}\eta_2 + \beta_{11}\xi_1 + \theta_1 \tag{8}$$

$$\eta_2 = \beta_{21}\xi_1 + \beta_{22}\xi_2 + \theta_2 , \tag{9}$$

where the ξs are exogenous, the ηs are endogenous, and the θs are disturbance terms (which are independent of the ξs). The reduced form of this model is

$$\eta_1 = \gamma_{11}\xi_1 + \gamma_{12}\xi_2 + \phi_1 \tag{10}$$

$$\eta_2 = \beta_{21}\xi_1 + \beta_{22}\xi_2 + \theta_2 , \tag{11}$$

where $\gamma_{11} = \alpha_{12}\beta_{21} + \beta_{11}$, $\gamma_{12} = \alpha_{12}\beta_{22}$, and $\phi_1 = \alpha_{12}\theta_2 + \theta_1$.

3.1. ESTIMATION

Case I: If we assume that $C(\theta_1 , \theta_2) = 0$, the model is overidentified—nine parameters, ten variances and covariances. Least-squares fitting of (8) and (9) gives estimates $\hat{\alpha}_{12}$, $\hat{\beta}_{12}$, $\hat{\beta}_{21}$, $\hat{\beta}_{22}$, which, under normality, are full-information maximum-likelihood (FIML) estimates of the structural parameters.

Case II: If we assume that $C(\theta_1 , \theta_2) \neq 0$, then the system is just-identified—ten parameters, ten variances and covariances. Least-squares fitting of (10) and (11) gives estimates $\hat{\gamma}_{11}$, $\hat{\gamma}_{12}$, $\hat{\beta}_{21}$, $\hat{\beta}_{22}$, $\hat{\sigma}^2_{\phi_1}$, $\hat{\sigma}^2_{\theta_2}$, $\hat{\sigma}_{\theta_2\phi_1}$ which can be translated into FIML estimates of the structural parameters. The translation is as follows, tildes denoting FIML estimates:

$$\tilde{\beta}_{21} = \hat{\beta}_{21} \tag{12}$$

$$\tilde{\beta}_{22} = \hat{\beta}_{22} \tag{13}$$

$$\tilde{\sigma}^2_{\theta_2} = \hat{\sigma}^2_{\theta_2} \tag{14}$$

$$\tilde{\alpha}_{12} = \hat{\gamma}_{12}/\hat{\beta}_{22} \tag{15}$$

$$\tilde{\beta}_{11} = \hat{\gamma}_{11} - \hat{\beta}_{21}\tilde{\alpha}_{12} \tag{16}$$

$$\tilde{\sigma}_{\theta_1\theta_2} = \hat{\sigma}_{\theta_2\phi_1} - \tilde{\alpha}_{12}\tilde{\sigma}^2_{\theta_2} \tag{17}$$

$$\tilde{\sigma}^2_{\theta_1} = \hat{\sigma}^2_{\phi_1} - \tilde{\alpha}^2_{12}\tilde{\sigma}^2_{\theta_2} - 2\tilde{\alpha}_{12}\tilde{\sigma}_{\theta_1\theta_2} . \tag{18}$$

Clearly in both models the structural parameters are identified. But the direct least-squares estimates appropriate for Case I are not consistent for Case II. (The "indirect least-squares" estimates appropriate for Case II are consistent, but not efficient, for Case I.)

Now suppose there are errors in the endogenous variables. That is, instead of observing η_1 and η_2, we observe y_1 and y_2 where

$$y_1 = \eta_1 + \epsilon_1 \quad \text{and} \quad y_2 = \eta_2 + \epsilon_2,$$

the ϵs being independent of the θs and the ξs (and therefore the ηs). The reduced-form equations are now:

$$y_1 = \gamma_{11}\xi_1 + \gamma_{12}\xi_2 + \phi_1 + \epsilon_1 \tag{19}$$

$$y_2 = \beta_{21}\xi_1 + \beta_{22}\xi_2 + \theta_2 + \epsilon_2. \tag{20}$$

Coefficient estimates obtained by least-squares regression on (8) with y_2 in place of η_2 are not consistent. For, the estimate of α_{12} is attenuated by the error of measurement in y_2 and that of β_{11} is biased (upward or downward depending on whether the product of α_{12} and the covariance of η_2 and ξ_1 is positive or negative). An alternative way of viewing this phenomenon is that y_2 is correlated with the disturbance in Eq. (8).

3.2 AN EMPIRICAL EXAMPLE OF THE EFFECTS OF MEASUREMENT ERROR

Sewell, Haller, & Ohlendorf (1970) report a structural analysis of the status attainment process for a large sample of individuals who were high school seniors in Wisconsin in 1957. From their model it is possible to separate out the following three-equation submodel:

$$\eta_1 = \beta_{11}\xi_1 + \theta_1 \tag{21}$$

$$\eta_2 = \alpha_{21}\eta_1 + \beta_{21}\xi_1 + \beta_{22}\xi_2 + \theta_2 \tag{22}$$

$$\eta_3 = \alpha_{31}\eta_1 + \alpha_{32}\eta_2 + \theta_3. \tag{23}$$

To this model we have added

$$y_2 = \eta_2 + \epsilon. \tag{24}$$

The variables are ξ_1 = mental ability, ξ_2 = socioeconomic status, η_1 = academic performance, η_2 = true significant others' influence, η_3 = educational aspiration, and y_2 = observed significant others' influence.

A path diagram for the model is given in Fig. 1. Summary data are found in Table 1.

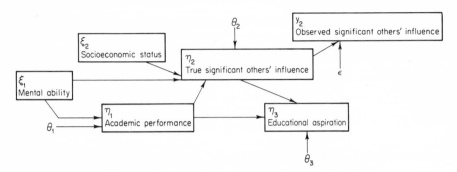

Figure 1.   Path diagram for a submodel of Sewell *et al.* (1970).

TABLE 1

CORRELATIONS AND STANDARD DEVIATIONS FROM SEWELL *et al.* (1970).

	MA	SES	AP	SO	EA
Mental ability	1.000				
Socioeconomic status	.288	1.000			
Academic performance	.589	.194	1.000		
Significant others' influence	.438	.359	.473	1.000	
Educational aspiration	.418	.380	.459	.611	1.000
Standard deviations	29.165	11.088	27.050	1.710	.942

One of the variables in the submodel (the one termed significant others' influence) is a composite of questionnaire items reflecting encouragement of college attendance by parents and teachers, together with one reflecting friends' college plans. It would seem likely that this variable is subject to large measurement errors. This is the reasoning behind the inclusion of Eq. (24). As in the original, we have assumed that all the disturbances are uncorrelated with each other and the other variables which they do not help define.

The first three equations represent the structural model for the true scores and the last equation represents the errorful nature of y_2. We are assuming no measurement error for ξ_1, ξ_2, η_1, and η_3, but measurement error in η_3 could be absorbed into θ_3.

The reduced form is

$$\eta_1 = \beta_{11}\xi_1 + \theta_1 \tag{25}$$

$$y_2 = (\alpha_{21}\beta_{11} + \beta_{21})\,\xi_1 + \beta_{22}\xi_2 + (\theta_2 + \alpha_{21}\theta_1 + \epsilon) \tag{26}$$

$$\eta_3 = [\alpha_{32}(\alpha_{21}\beta_{11} + \beta_{21}) + \alpha_{31}\beta_{11}]\,\xi_1 + \alpha_{32}\beta_{22}\xi_2$$
$$+ [\alpha_{32}(\theta_2 + \alpha_{21}\theta_1) + \alpha_{31}\theta_1 + \theta_3]. \tag{27}$$

Given the absence of measurement error in ξ_1, ξ_2, η_1, and η_3, Eqs. (25), (26), and (27) may be estimated by least squares. These estimates are sufficient to produce unique estimates for all the structural coefficients. The following estimates are obtained (the original estimates are listed for comparative purposes):

	Estimates from Sewell *et al.* (1970)	New estimates
β_{11}	0.60	0.60
β_{21}	0.18	0.18
β_{22}	0.25	0.25
α_{21}	0.32	0.35
α_{31}	0.22	0.13
α_{32}	0.51	1.11

As the reanalysis indicates, measurement error may have a dramatic effect.

3.3 ERRORS IN THE EXOGENOUS VARIABLES

If we assume errors of measurement in both exogenous variables in (8) and (9), none of the structural parameters of the model are identified without additional information. If, however, we follow the strategy of design presented above, and obtain two alternative measures of each exogenous variable, the reduced-form coefficients will generally be identified. Since the original model, free of measurement error, is identified, all of the structural coefficients are identified. The logical structure of these deductions will be discussed more completely in Sections 5 and 6, where a general model is presented.

4. Recursive Models with Unmeasured Variables

In this section we will present a simple example of a recursive model with an unmeasured variable and explore the effects of various assumptions on identification. "Unmeasured" is used here to indicate that there is no operational variable which was intended to directly measure a construct which is symbolized in the model. The model presented is a version of that discussed by Hauser & Goldberger (1971).

The structural model is

$$\eta_1 = \beta_{11}\xi_1 + \beta_{12}\xi_2 + \theta_1 \tag{28}$$

$$\eta_2 = \alpha_{21}\eta_1 + \theta_2 \tag{29}$$

$$\eta_3 = \alpha_{31}\eta_1 + \theta_3 \,, \tag{30}$$

where the θs are independent of the ξs, and η_1 is an unmeasured variable. The reduced form in terms of the measured variables is

$$\eta_2 = \alpha_{21}\beta_{11}\xi_1 + \alpha_{21}\beta_{12}\xi_2 + (\alpha_{21}\theta_1 + \theta_2) \tag{31}$$

$$\eta_3 = \alpha_{31}\beta_{11}\xi_1 + \alpha_{31}\beta_{12}\xi_2 + (\alpha_{31}\theta_1 + \theta_3). \tag{32}$$

We must introduce restrictions in order to identify any structural parameters. At this point there are 13 parameters: three elements of the covariance matrix of ξ_1 and ξ_2, four structural coefficients, and six elements of the covariance matrix of θ_1, θ_2, and θ_3. The ten observable variances and covariances provide only nine pieces of information because they are subject to one (nonlinear) restriction. Therefore, there must be four independent restrictions on the model parameters to achieve full identifiability. Many choices of restrictions are available. A common and fairly natural set of choices are the following:

i. $C(\theta_1, \theta_2) = C(\theta_1, \theta_3) = C(\theta_2, \theta_3) = 0$,
ii. $\text{var}(\eta_1) = 1$.

These restrictions impart sufficient information about the structural parameters through the covariances of the reduced-form disturbances to allow identification of the structural coefficients.

The second assumption above—or some substitute (e.g., $\alpha_{21} = 1$)— seems to be necessary. If the variable η_1 is completely unspecified with respect to metric, it is necessary to induce a normalization to ensure identifiability.

5. Specification of a General Model

This section will introduce a general model for a simultaneous equation system in the presence of measurement error and unmeasured variables and will then discuss the implication of various constraints on the parameter matrices for identifiability.

An important distinction, long made in psychometrics, is between latent and manifest variables. Latent variables are variables which are of direct interest in a theoretical specification of the model, but which are rarely equivalent to the manifest variables that are actually measured in an experiment. Our strategy is to treat the specifications of the total model in three parts: (1) a simultaneous equation model relating latent exogenous and latent endogenous variables; (2) a measurement model for the exogenous variables relating manifest exogenous variables to latent exogenous variables; (3) a measurement model relating manifest endogenous to latent endogenous variables. These parts will then be assembled into the complete model.

5.1 PART 1

We let the random vector ξ represent the n latent exogenous variables, the random vector η represent the m latent endogenous variables, and the random vector θ represent the m structural disturbances. The model is specified as

$$\eta = A\eta + B\xi + \theta. \tag{33}$$

We assume that the disturbances are independent of the exogenous variables, but we impose no restrictions on their covariances. The reduced form of the model is

$$\eta = (I - A)^{-1} B\xi + (I - A)^{-1} \theta. \tag{34}$$

It should be noted that the standard normalization rules (see for example, Malinvaud, 1970, Chapter 18) form a specification that all diagonal entries in A are identically equal to zero. Given this model the structural characteristics of Σ^*, the covariance matrix of the latent variables, are

$$\Sigma^* = \begin{pmatrix} \underset{(n \times n)}{\Sigma_{\xi\xi}} & \underset{(n \times m)}{\Sigma_{\xi\xi}B'(I - A')^{-1}} \\ \underset{(m \times n)}{(I - A)^{-1} B\Sigma_{\xi\xi}} & \underset{(m \times m)}{(I - A)^{-1} B\Sigma_{\xi\xi}B'(I - A')^{-1} + (I - A)^{-1} \Sigma_{\theta\theta}(I - A')^{-1}} \end{pmatrix}. \tag{35}$$

Here $\Sigma_{\xi\xi}$ and $\Sigma_{\theta\theta}$ are the covariance matrices of ξ and θ respectively. If $\Sigma_{\xi\xi}$ is identifiable, the identification conditions for A, B, and $\Sigma_{\theta\theta}$ can be expressed as follows:

  i. $\Sigma_{\xi\xi}$ is nonsingular.
 ii. The equation $\Pi^* = (I - A)^{-1}B$ has a unique solution for A and B.

It is clear then that general requirements for identification in simultaneous equation models—lack of collinearity in the exogenous variables

and the rank and order conditions (see Malinvaud 1970, Chapter 18)—
hold when the exogenous variables are considered random rather than
fixed. The nonsingularity conditions for $\Sigma_{\xi\xi}$ play a role identical to those
on the cross-product matrix in a fixed model.

5.2   PART 2

We let the random vector x represent the k manifest exogenous
variables. We specify the model as

$$x = D\xi + \epsilon \tag{36}$$

where D is $k \times n$ and the errors ϵ are independent of the true variables ξ.
Consequently,

$$\underset{(k\times k)}{\Sigma_{xx}} = \underset{(k\times n)}{D} \ \underset{(n\times n)}{\Sigma_{\xi\xi}} \ \underset{(n\times k)}{D'} + \underset{(k\times k)}{\Psi_1} \tag{37}$$

where $\Sigma_{\xi\xi}$ and Ψ_1 are the covariance matrices of ξ and ϵ, respectively.
This model has the form of the Lawley version of the factor-analysis
model (see, for example, Jöreskog, 1967a).

5.3   PART 3

We let the random vector y represent the l manifest endogenous
variables and specify the model as

$$y = C\eta + \delta \tag{38}$$

where C is $l \times m$ and δ is independent of η. Consequently,

$$\underset{(l\times l)}{\Sigma_{yy}} = \underset{(l\times m)}{C} \ \underset{(m\times m)}{\Sigma_{\eta\eta}} \ \underset{(m\times l)}{C'} + \underset{(l\times l)}{\Psi_2}. \tag{39}$$

5.4   THE COMPLETE MODEL

Assuming that θ, δ, and ϵ are mutually independent, the three submodels yield the following covariance structure for the observable
variables:

$$\Sigma = \begin{pmatrix} \underset{(k\times k)}{D\Sigma_{\xi\xi}D' + \Psi_1} & \underset{(k\times l)}{D\Sigma_{\xi\xi}B'(I - A')^{-1}C'} \\ \underset{(l\times k)}{C(I - A)^{-1}B\Sigma_{\xi\xi}D'} & \underset{(l\times l)}{\begin{array}{c} C(I - A)^{-1}B\Sigma_{\xi\xi}B'(I - A')^{-1}C' \\ + C(I - A)^{-1}\Sigma_{\theta\theta}(I - A')^{-1}C' + \Psi_2 \end{array}} \end{pmatrix}.$$

In particular applications, the matrices D and C may take on specific forms. For example, if we have two nominally parallel measures of each exogenous variable, then

$$D = \begin{pmatrix} I \\ \Gamma \end{pmatrix}$$

is a $2n \times n$ matrix, Γ being an $n \times n$ diagonal matrix. In the case of unmeasured endogenous variables the matrix C may take on the relatively simple form of a row-censored identity matrix. In the example of (28)–(30),

$$C = \begin{pmatrix} 0 & 1 & 0 \\ 0 & 0 & 1 \end{pmatrix}.$$

A fuller discussion of this general model is given in Keesling (1972).

6. Identification of the Parameters of the General Model

The identification problem for our general model is a very difficult one to solve, but a sequential set of sufficient conditions for identifiability can be stated. This procedure was the one used at the end of Section 2 in the case of double measurement of the exogenous variables. In the more general case, this procedure consists of:

(i) demonstrating the identifiability of $\Sigma_{\xi\xi}$ and D in terms of Σ,

(ii) demonstrating the identifiability of A, B, and C in terms of $\Pi = C(I - A)^{-1}B$.

These two demonstrations are all that are required for total identifiability since (i) together with the nonsingularity of $\Sigma_{\xi\xi}$ implies that Π is identifiable; see Section 5.1. It should be noted that if sufficient conditions were separately established for (i) and (ii), the union of them might not be necessary since A, B, and C might be sufficiently restricted to yield information about D and $\Sigma_{\xi\xi}$.

A theorem by Wald (1950) on the identification problem appears to have important application here. In language relevant to the above model Wald's theorem is this: Consider two sets of parameters, one set which is identifiable and which is also a function of the second set. If M, the matrix of partial derivatives of the first set with respect to the second set, has rank equal to the number of parameters in the second set, then the second set of parameters is locally identifiable.

Of course, the first-derivative matrix itself involves parameters, so that its rank will depend on unknown parameter values. Still, if we can find a parameter vector for which the matrix has the appropriate rank, then the model is locally identifiable in a region containing that vector. This suggests the following procedure for tentatively determining the identifiability of the complete model:

(i)   calculate the derivative matrix algebraically,
(ii) substitute some reasonable numerical values for the parameters,
(iii) evaluate the rank of the resulting matrix.

This process is probably not very burdensome (except for accuracy determinations) when programmed for a computer. It might be made a a part of the estimation program.†

Alternatively, we may rely on the information matrix; cf. Rao (1965, p. 349). The information matrix of the parameters of interest is equal to $M' \mathscr{J} M$ where M is the matrix of partial derivatives of the elements of the covariance matrix of the observed variables with respect to the structural parameters and $\mathscr{J}$ is the information matrix for the covariance matrix of the observable variables. Since $\mathscr{J}$ is nonsingular (the covariance matrix is, after all, identified), the rank of $M' \mathscr{J} M$ is equal to the rank of M. If an estimation program already computes a numerical estimate of the information matrix for the parameters—as in Jöreskog (this volume)—an evaluation of its rank for reasonable parameter values will

---

† A useful case where these partial derivatives are simple to write symbolically is that of identifying A, B, and C when $\Pi = C(I - A)^{-1}B$ is identifiable. We define a string operator S for matrices such that $S(X)$ is a vector array of the elements of the $m \times n$ matrix X, $S(X) = (x_{11}, x_{12}, ..., x_{1n}, ..., x_{mn})$. We can define, if X is a function of the elements of a matrix Y, the matrix of partial derivatives $\partial S(X)/\partial S(Y)$; the column order of this matrix is equal to the product of the dimensions of X and the row order is the same for Y. In the above case we want the partial derivatives of $S(\Pi)$ with respect to $S(A)$, $S(B)$, and $S(C)$. These are given below where the symbol $\otimes$ represents the Kronecker product:

$$\partial S(\Pi)/\partial S(C) = I_l \otimes (I - A)^{-1}B \tag{40}$$

$$\partial S(\Pi)/\partial S(A) = [(I - A')^{-1} \otimes (I - A)^{-1}](I_m \otimes B)(C' \otimes I_n) \tag{41}$$

$$\partial S(\Pi)/\partial S(B) = [(I - A')^{-1}C'] \otimes I_n \tag{42}$$

where the subscript on the identity indicates its order. Then the matrix of these derivatives with respect to all elements of A, B, and C would be

$$F = \begin{bmatrix} \partial S(\Pi)/\partial S(C) \\ \partial S(\Pi)/\partial S(A) \\ \partial S(\Pi)/\partial S(B) \end{bmatrix}, \tag{43}$$

with rows corresponding to zero restrictions and normalization rules omitted. Substitution of reasonable values for the parameters and the determination of the latent roots or the determinant of FF' should provide evidence of identifiability.

give good assurance as to the identifiability of the parameters. It is useful to note that this approach provides an analogue to the collinearity problem in ordinary linear models. As M becomes ill conditioned, so does $M'\mathscr{J}M$, and the standard errors of the parameter estimates (the square roots of the diagonal elements of $(M'\mathscr{J}M)^{-1}$) become large.

Acknowledgments

The author would like to thank Richard G. Wolfe for many useful comments and suggestions. This paper was begun while the author was a Resident Advisor to the Venezuelan Ministry of Education, Directorate of Planning, under the auspices of the University of Wisconsin and the Ford Foundation; and was completed while the author was a Fellow at the Center for Advanced Study in the Behavioral Sciences.

5

A General Method for Estimating a Linear Structural Equation System

KARL G. JÖRESKOG

1. Introduction

We shall describe a general method for estimating the unknown coefficients in a set of linear structural equations. In its most general form the method will allow for both errors in equations (residuals, disturbances) and errors in variables (errors of measurement, observational errors) and will yield estimates of the disturbance variance–covariance matrix and the measurement-error variances as well as estimates of the unknown coefficients in the structural equations, provided that all these parameters are identified. Models of this kind have been studied under the name of path analysis by biometricians (e.g., Wright, 1934, 1954; Turner & Stevens, 1959), sociologists (e.g., Duncan, 1966; Land, 1969; Heise, 1969b; Blalock, 1969a, 1971a; Costner, 1969; Hauser & Goldberger, 1971), and psychologists (e.g., Werts & Linn, 1970). After giving the results for the general case, two special cases will be considered. The first is the case when there are errors in equations but no errors in variables. This case has been studied extensively by econometricians (e.g., Klein, 1953; Wold & Jureen, 1953; Goldberger, 1964; Fisher, 1966; Malinvaud, 1970; Johnston, 1972). The second case is when there are errors in variables but no errors in equations. Models of this kind are related to factor analysis and covariance structure models studied by Jöreskog (1970a).

In the first special case referred to above, where there are no errors of measurement in the observed variables, the general method to be presented is equivalent to the *full-information maximum-likelihood* (FIML) method of Koopmans, Rubin, & Leipnik (1950), provided that no constraints are imposed on the disturbance variance–covariance matrix and the variance–covariance matrix of the independent variables. However, with the general method described here, it is possible to assign fixed values to some elements of these matrices and also to have equality constraints among the remaining elements.

2. The General Model

Consider random vectors $\eta' = (\eta_1, \eta_2, ..., \eta_m)$ and $\xi' = (\xi_1, \xi_2, ..., \xi_n)$ of true dependent and independent variables, respectively, and the following system of linear structural relations

$$\mathbf{B}\eta = \Gamma\xi + \zeta, \tag{1}$$

where $\mathbf{B}(m \times m)$ and $\Gamma(m \times n)$ are coefficient matrices and $\zeta' = (\zeta_1, \zeta_2, ..., \zeta_m)$ is a random vector of disturbances (errors in equations). Without loss of generality it may be assumed that $E(\eta) = E(\zeta) = \mathbf{0}$ and $E(\xi) = \mathbf{0}$. It is furthermore assumed that ζ is uncorrelated with ξ and that $\mathbf{B}$ is nonsingular.

The vectors η and ξ are not observed, but instead vectors $\mathbf{y}' = (y_1, y_2, ..., y_m)$ and $\mathbf{x}' = (x_1, x_2, ..., x_n)$ are observed, such that

$$\mathbf{y} = \mu + \eta + \epsilon \tag{2}$$

$$\mathbf{x} = \nu + \xi + \delta, \tag{3}$$

where $\mu = E(\mathbf{y})$, $\nu = E(\mathbf{x})$, and ϵ and δ are vectors of errors of measurement in $\mathbf{y}$ and $\mathbf{x}$, respectively. It is convenient to refer to $\mathbf{y}$ and $\mathbf{x}$ as the observed variables and η and ξ as the true variables. The errors of measurement are assumed to be uncorrelated with the true variates and among themselves. It should be emphasized that there is only one observed variable for each true variable.

Let $\Phi(n \times n)$ and $\Psi(m \times m)$ be the variance–covariance matrices of ξ and ζ, respectively, $\Theta_\epsilon^2(m \times m)$ and $\Theta_\delta^2(n \times n)$ the diagonal matrices of error variances for $\mathbf{y}$ and $\mathbf{x}$, respectively. Then it follows, from the above assumptions, that the variance–covariance matrix $\boldsymbol{\Sigma}[(m + n) \times (m + n)]$ of $\mathbf{z} = (\mathbf{y}', \mathbf{x}')'$ is

$$\boldsymbol{\Sigma} = \begin{pmatrix} \mathbf{B}^{-1}\boldsymbol{\Gamma}\boldsymbol{\Phi}\boldsymbol{\Gamma}'\mathbf{B}'^{-1} + \mathbf{B}^{-1}\boldsymbol{\Psi}\mathbf{B}'^{-1} + \boldsymbol{\Theta}_\epsilon^2 & \mathbf{B}^{-1}\boldsymbol{\Gamma}\boldsymbol{\Phi} \\ \boldsymbol{\Phi}\boldsymbol{\Gamma}'\mathbf{B}'^{-1} & \boldsymbol{\Phi} + \boldsymbol{\Theta}_\delta^2 \end{pmatrix}. \qquad (4)$$

The elements of $\boldsymbol{\Sigma}$ are functions of the elements of $\mathbf{B}$, $\boldsymbol{\Gamma}$, $\boldsymbol{\Phi}$, $\boldsymbol{\Psi}$, $\boldsymbol{\Theta}_\delta$, and $\boldsymbol{\Theta}_\epsilon$. In applications some of these elements are fixed and equal to assigned values. In particular this is so for elements in $\mathbf{B}$ and $\boldsymbol{\Gamma}$, but we shall allow for fixed values even in the other matrices. For the remaining nonfixed elements of the six parameter matrices, one or more subsets may have identical but unknown values. Thus parameters in $\mathbf{B}$, $\boldsymbol{\Gamma}$, $\boldsymbol{\Phi}$, $\boldsymbol{\Psi}$, $\boldsymbol{\Theta}_\delta$, and $\boldsymbol{\Theta}_\epsilon$ are of three kinds: (i) *fixed parameters* that have been assigned given values, (ii) *constrained parameters* that are unknown but equal to one of more other parameters, and (iii) *free parameters* that are unknown and not constrained to be equal to any other parameter.

Before an attempt is made to estimate a model of this kind, the identification problem must be examined. Identifiability depends on the specification of fixed, constrained, and free parameters. Under a given specification, a given structure $\mathbf{B}$, $\boldsymbol{\Gamma}$, $\boldsymbol{\Phi}$, $\boldsymbol{\Psi}$, $\boldsymbol{\Theta}_\delta$, $\boldsymbol{\Theta}_\epsilon$ generates one and only one $\boldsymbol{\Sigma}$, but there may be several structures generating the same $\boldsymbol{\Sigma}$. If two or more structures generate the same $\boldsymbol{\Sigma}$, the structures are said to be equivalent. If a parameter has the same value in all equivalent structures, the parameter is said to be identified. If all parameters of the model are identified, the whole model is said to be identified. When a model is identified one can usually find consistent estimates of all its parameters. Identification problems under various special cases of the general model are discussed by Koopmans & Reiersøl (1950), Fisher (1966), Geraci & Goldberger (1971), and Wiley (this volume).

The model is scale-free in the following sense. Suppose the model is normalized by fixed unities in the diagonal of $\mathbf{B}$, that all other fixed elements in $\mathbf{B}$, $\boldsymbol{\Gamma}$, $\boldsymbol{\Phi}$, $\boldsymbol{\Psi}$, $\boldsymbol{\Theta}_\delta$, $\boldsymbol{\Theta}_\epsilon$ are zeros, and that no parameters are constrained. Furthermore, suppose the units of measurement in each of the observed variables are changed so that $\mathbf{y}$ is replaced by $\mathbf{y}^* = \mathbf{D}_y\mathbf{y}$ and $\mathbf{x}$ is replaced by $\mathbf{x}^* = \mathbf{D}_x\mathbf{x}$, where $\mathbf{D}_y$ and $\mathbf{D}_x$ are diagonal matrices of scale factors. This will change the parameter matrices $\mathbf{B}$, $\boldsymbol{\Gamma}$, $\boldsymbol{\Phi}$, $\boldsymbol{\Psi}$, $\boldsymbol{\Theta}_\delta$, $\boldsymbol{\Theta}_\epsilon$ to $\mathbf{B}^* = \mathbf{D}_y\mathbf{B}\mathbf{D}_y^{-1}$, $\boldsymbol{\Gamma}^* = \mathbf{D}_y\boldsymbol{\Gamma}\mathbf{D}_x^{-1}$, $\boldsymbol{\Phi}^* = \mathbf{D}_x\boldsymbol{\Phi}\mathbf{D}_x$, $\boldsymbol{\Psi}^* = \mathbf{D}_y\boldsymbol{\Psi}\mathbf{D}_y$, $\boldsymbol{\Theta}_\delta^* = \mathbf{D}_x\boldsymbol{\Theta}_\delta$, $\boldsymbol{\Theta}_\epsilon^* = \mathbf{D}_y\boldsymbol{\Theta}_\epsilon$, respectively. Thus it is possible to obtain the parameters corresponding to one set of units from those corresponding to another, knowing only the scale factors. If the units of measurement in the observed variables are arbitrary, as in many studies in the behavioral sciences, one may analyze the correlation matrix $\mathbf{R}$ instead of the variance–covariance matrix $\mathbf{S}$.

3. Estimation of the General Model

Let z_1, z_2 ,.... z_N be N independent observations on $z = (y', x')'$ from a multinormal distribution with mean vector $(\mu', \nu')'$ and variance–covariance matrix Σ. The assumption of independent observations rules out dynamic models which include lagged endogenous variables observed with measurement errors. In that case, the method to be described is consistent, but not maximum likelihood. When measurement errors are absent as in Section 5, no difficulty arises.

Since no constraints are imposed on the mean vector, the maximum-likelihood estimate of this is the usual sample mean vector $\bar{z} = (\bar{y}', \bar{x}')'$. Let

$$S = [1/(N-1)] \sum_{t=1}^{N} (z_t - \bar{z})(z_t - \bar{z})' \tag{5}$$

be the usual sample variance–covariance matrix, partitioned as

$$S[(m+n) \times (m+n)] = \begin{bmatrix} S_{yy}(m \times m) & S_{yx}(m \times n) \\ S_{xy}(n \times m) & S_{xx}(n \times n) \end{bmatrix}. \tag{6}$$

The logarithm of the likelihood function, omitting a function of the observations, is given by (see e.g., Anderson, 1958, p. 159)

$$\log L = -[(N-1)/2][\log |\Sigma| + \mathrm{tr}(S\Sigma^{-1})]. \tag{7}$$

This is regarded as a function of the independent parameters in $\mathbf{B}$, $\mathbf{\Gamma}$, $\mathbf{\Phi}$, $\mathbf{\Psi}$, $\mathbf{\Theta}_\delta$, and $\mathbf{\Theta}_\epsilon$, and is to be maximized with respect to these, taking into account that some elements may be fixed and some may be constrained to be equal to some others. Maximizing $\log L$ is equivalent to minimizing

$$F = \tfrac{1}{2}[\log |\Sigma| + \mathrm{tr}(S\Sigma^{-1})]. \tag{8}$$

Such a minimization problem may be formalized as follows.

Let $\lambda' = (\lambda_1, \lambda_2, ..., \lambda_p)$ be a vector of *all* the elements of $\mathbf{B}$, $\mathbf{\Gamma}$, $\mathbf{\Phi}$, $\mathbf{\Psi}$, $\mathbf{\Theta}_\delta$, and $\mathbf{\Theta}_\epsilon$ arranged in a prescribed order. Then F may be regarded as a function $F(\lambda)$ of λ_1, λ_2 ,..., λ_p, which is continuous and has continuous derivatives $\partial F/\partial \lambda_s$ and $\partial^2 F/\partial \lambda_s \partial \lambda_t$ of first and second order, except where Σ is singular. The totality of these derivatives is represented by a gradient vector $\partial F/\partial \lambda$ and a symmetric matrix $\partial^2 F/\partial \lambda \partial \lambda'$. Now let some $p - q$ of the λs be fixed and denote the remaining λs by π_1, π_2 ,..., π_q, $q \leqslant p$. The function F is now considered as a function $G(\pi)$ of $\pi' = (\pi_1, \pi_2, ..., \pi_q)$. Derivatives $\partial G/\partial \pi$ and $\partial^2 G/\partial \pi \partial \pi'$ are obtained from $\partial F/\partial \lambda$ and $\partial^2 F/\partial \lambda \partial \lambda'$ by omitting rows and columns corresponding to the fixed λs. Among $\pi_1, \pi_2, ..., \pi_q$, let there be just r distinct parameters denoted $\kappa_1, \kappa_2, ..., \kappa_r$, $r \leqslant q$, so that each π_i is equal to one and only one κ_j, but possibly several πs equal the same κ. Let $\mathbf{K} = (k_{ij})$ be a matrix of order $q \times r$ with elements $k_{ij} = 1$ if $\pi_i = \kappa_j$ and $k_{ij} = 0$ otherwise. The function G is now a function $H(\mathbf{\kappa})$ of $\mathbf{\kappa}' = (\kappa_1, \kappa_2, ..., \kappa_r)$ and we have

$$\partial H/\partial \mathbf{\kappa} = \mathbf{K}'(\partial G/\partial \pi) \tag{9}$$

$$\partial^2 H/\partial \mathbf{\kappa}\, \partial \mathbf{\kappa}' = \mathbf{K}'(\partial^2 G/\partial \pi\, \partial \pi')\mathbf{K}. \tag{10}$$

Thus, the derivatives of H are simple sums of the derivatives of G.

The minimization of $H(\mathbf{\kappa})$ is a straightforward application of the Davidon–Fletcher–Powell method (Fletcher & Powell, 1963) using a computer program by Gruvaeus and Jöreskog (1970). This method makes use of a matrix $\mathbf{E}$, which is evaluated in each iteration. Initially $\mathbf{E}$ is any positive definite matrix approximating the inverse of $\partial^2 H/\partial \mathbf{\kappa}\, \partial \mathbf{\kappa}'$. In subsequent iterations $\mathbf{E}$ is improved using the information built up about the function, so that ultimately $\mathbf{E}$ converges to an approximation of the inverse of $\partial^2 H/\partial \mathbf{\kappa}\, \partial \mathbf{\kappa}'$ at the minimum. If there are many parameters, the number of iterations may be excessive, but can be considerably decreased by the provision of a good initial estimate of $\mathbf{E}$. Such an estimate may be obtained by inverting

$$E(\partial^2 H/\partial \mathbf{\kappa}\, \partial \mathbf{\kappa}') = \mathbf{K}'E(\partial^2 G/\partial \pi\, \partial \pi')\mathbf{K}, \tag{11}$$

where $E(\partial^2 G/\partial \pi\, \partial \pi')$ is obtained from

$$E(\partial^2 F/\partial \lambda\, \partial \lambda') = (N - 1)\, E[(\partial F/\partial \lambda)(\partial F/\partial \lambda)'] \tag{12}$$

by omitting rows and columns corresponding to the fixed λs. When the minimum of H has been found, the inverse of the information matrix may be computed again to obtain standard errors of all the parameters in $\mathbf{\kappa}$. A general method for obtaining the elements of $E[(\partial F/\partial \lambda)(\partial F/\partial \lambda)']$ is given in Appendix A2.

The application of the Fletcher–Powell method requires formulas for the derivatives of F with respect to the elements of $\mathbf{B}, \mathbf{\Gamma}, \mathbf{\Phi}, \mathbf{\Psi}, \mathbf{\Theta}_\delta$, and $\mathbf{\Theta}_\epsilon$. These may be obtained by matrix differentiation as shown in Appendix A1. Writing $\mathbf{A} = \mathbf{B}^{-1}$, $\mathbf{D} = \mathbf{B}^{-1}\mathbf{\Gamma}$, and

$$\mathbf{\Omega} = \begin{pmatrix} \mathbf{\Omega}_{yy} & \mathbf{\Omega}_{yx} \\ \mathbf{\Omega}_{xy} & \mathbf{\Omega}_{xx} \end{pmatrix} = \mathbf{\Sigma}^{-1}(\mathbf{\Sigma} - \mathbf{S})\, \mathbf{\Sigma}^{-1}, \tag{13}$$

the derivatives are

$$\partial F/\partial \mathbf{B} = -(\mathbf{A}'\Omega_{yy}\mathbf{D}\Phi\mathbf{D}' + \mathbf{A}'\Omega_{yy}\mathbf{A}\Psi\mathbf{A}' + \mathbf{A}'\Omega_{yx}\Phi\mathbf{D}') \qquad (14)$$

$$\partial F/\partial \Gamma = (\mathbf{A}'\Omega_{yy}\mathbf{D}\Phi + \mathbf{A}'\Omega_{yx}\Phi) \qquad (15)$$

$$\partial F/\partial \Phi = \tfrac{1}{2}(\mathbf{D}'\Omega_{yy}\mathbf{D} + \mathbf{D}'\Omega_{yx} + \Omega_{xy}\mathbf{D} + \Omega_{xx}) \qquad (16)$$

$$\partial F/\partial \Psi = \tfrac{1}{2}\mathbf{A}'\Omega_{yy}\mathbf{A} \qquad (17)$$

$$\partial F/\partial \Theta_\delta = \Omega_{xx}\Theta_\delta \qquad (18)$$

$$\partial F/\partial \Theta_\epsilon = \Omega_{yy}\Theta_\epsilon . \qquad (19)$$

In obtaining these expressions we have used the symmetry of $\mathbf{S}$, Σ, Ω, Φ, and Ψ, but in the differentiation *all* the elements of $\mathbf{B}$, Γ, Φ, Ψ, Θ_δ, and Θ_ϵ have been treated as free parameters. In the minimization the off-diagonal zero elements of Θ_δ and Θ_ϵ are treated as fixed parameters and the symmetric off-diagonal elements of Φ and Ψ are treated as constrained parameters.

When the maximum-likelihood estimates of the parameters have been obtained, the goodness of fit of the model may be tested, in large samples, by the likelihood-ratio technique. Let H_0 be the null hypothesis of the model under the given specifications of fixed, constrained, and free parameters. The maintained hypothesis H_1 is that Σ may be any positive definite matrix. Under H_1, the maximum of $\log L$ is (see, e.g., Anderson, 1958, Chapter 3),

$$\log L_1 = -[(N-1)/2](\log |\mathbf{S}| + m + n).$$

Under H_0, the maximum of $\log L$ is equal to minus $(N-1)$ times the minimum value F_0 of F. Thus -2 times the logarithm of the likelihood ratio becomes

$$(N-1)[2F_0 - \log |\mathbf{S}| - (m+n)]. \qquad (20)$$

If the model holds, this is distributed, in large samples, as χ^2 with

$$d = \tfrac{1}{2}(m+n)(m+n+1) - r \qquad (21)$$

degrees of freedom, where, as before, r is the total number of independent parameters estimated under H_0.

4. Analysis of Artificial Data

To illustrate the ideas and methods of the previous section we shall use a hypothetical model. An analysis based on real data is presented in Section 8.

The equations of the hypothetical model are

$$\eta_1 = -\beta_{12}\eta_2 - \beta_{13}\eta_3 + \zeta_1 \tag{22}$$

$$\eta_2 = -\beta_{24}\eta_4 + \gamma_{23}\xi_3 + \zeta_2 \tag{23}$$

$$\eta_3 = \eta_4 - \eta_2 - \xi_1 \tag{24}$$

$$\eta_4 = \eta_1 + \xi_2, \tag{25}$$

or in matrix form

$$\begin{pmatrix} 1 & \beta_{12} & \beta_{13} & 0 \\ 0 & 1 & 0 & \beta_{24} \\ 0 & 1 & 1 & -1 \\ -1 & 0 & 0 & 1 \end{pmatrix} \begin{pmatrix} \eta_1 \\ \eta_2 \\ \eta_3 \\ \eta_4 \end{pmatrix} = \begin{pmatrix} 0 & 0 & 0 \\ 0 & 0 & \gamma_{23} \\ -1 & 0 & 0 \\ 0 & 1 & 0 \end{pmatrix} \begin{pmatrix} \xi_1 \\ \xi_2 \\ \xi_3 \end{pmatrix} + \begin{pmatrix} \zeta_1 \\ \zeta_2 \\ 0 \\ 0 \end{pmatrix}. \tag{26}$$

The variables η_1, η_2, η_3, η_4, ξ_1, ξ_2, and ξ_3 involved in this model are assumed to be true variables that cannot be measured without errors of measurement. Each of the corresponding observed variables y_1, y_2, y_3, y_4, x_1, x_2, and x_3 is the sum of a true variable and an error of measurement as in (2) and (3). Equations (22) and (23) contain random disturbance terms ζ_1 and ζ_2. Equations (24) and (25) are identities assumed to hold for the true variables. These do not hold exactly for the observed variables, however, due to the errors of measurement. To illustrate the idea of a constrained parameter, we shall assume that the error variance in y_4 is the same as the error variance in x_3.

There are 19 independent parameters in this model, namely four in $\mathbf{B}$ and $\mathbf{\Gamma}$, six in

$$\mathbf{\Phi} = \begin{pmatrix} \sigma_{\xi_1}^2 & & \\ \sigma_{\xi_1\xi_2} & \sigma_{\xi_2}^2 & \\ \sigma_{\xi_1\xi_3} & \sigma_{\xi_2\xi_3} & \sigma_{\xi_3}^2 \end{pmatrix},$$

three in

$$\mathbf{\Psi} = \begin{pmatrix} \sigma_{\zeta_1}^2 & & & \\ \sigma_{\zeta_1\zeta_2} & \sigma_{\zeta_2}^2 & & \\ 0 & 0 & 0 & \\ 0 & 0 & 0 & 0 \end{pmatrix}, \tag{27}$$

and six in $\mathbf{\Theta}_\delta = \mathrm{diag}(\sigma_{\delta_1}, \sigma_{\delta_2}, \sigma_{\delta_3})$ and $\mathbf{\Theta}_\epsilon = \mathrm{diag}(\sigma_{\epsilon_1}, \sigma_{\epsilon_2}, \sigma_{\epsilon_3}, \sigma_{\epsilon_4})$. Note that since (24) and (25) are error-free equations, $\mathbf{\Psi}$ has the form (27) with zero variances and covariances for ζ_3 and ζ_4. Also, since $\sigma_{\epsilon_4} = \sigma_{\delta_3}$, there are only six independent elements in $\mathbf{\Theta}_\delta$ and $\mathbf{\Theta}_\epsilon$.

Population moments were generated from this model by assigning the following values to each of the 19 parameters:

$$\beta_{12} = -0.8 \qquad \beta_{13} = -0.4 \qquad \beta_{24} = -0.3 \qquad \gamma_{23} = 0.2$$

$$\sigma^2_{\xi_1} = 1.0 \qquad \sigma^2_{\xi_2} = 2.0 \qquad \sigma^2_{\xi_3} = 3.0$$

$$\sigma_{\xi_1\xi_2} = 0.1 \qquad \sigma_{\xi_1\xi_3} = 0.2 \qquad \sigma_{\xi_2\xi_3} = 0.1$$

$$\sigma^2_{\zeta_1} = 0.2 \qquad \sigma^2_{\zeta_2} = 0.3 \qquad \sigma_{\zeta_1\zeta_2} = 0.1$$

$$\sigma_{\delta_1} = 0.4 \qquad \sigma_{\delta_2} = 0.6 \qquad \sigma_{\delta_3} = 0.5$$

$$\sigma_{\epsilon_1} = 0.5 \qquad \sigma_{\epsilon_2} = 0.6 \qquad \sigma_{\epsilon_3} = 0.9 \qquad \sigma_{\epsilon_4} = 0.5.$$

The resulting Σ, obtained from (4) and rounded to three decimals, is

	y_1	y_2	y_3	y_4	x_1	x_2	x_3
y_1	4.599						
y_2	2.481	2.069					
y_3	4.659	2.159	7.514				
y_4	6.449	3.731	7.409	10.799			
x_1	−0.692	−0.138	−1.454	−0.592	1.160		
x_2	2.100	1.250	2.750	4.100	0.100	2.360	
x_3	0.442	0.763	−0.421	0.542	0.200	0.100	3.250.

$$(28)$$

For the purpose of illustrating the estimation method of Section 3, the above matrix is regarded as a sample dispersion matrix S to be analyzed. The order of the vector λ is 78, since there are all together 78 elements in B, Γ, Φ, Ψ, Θ_δ, and Θ_ϵ. Of these, 54 are fixed and 24 are nonfixed, so that π is of order 24. Because of the symmetry of Φ and Ψ and the imposed equality of σ_{ϵ_4} and σ_{δ_3}, there are 19 independent parameters, so that the order of $\varkappa$ is 19.

The minimization of $H(\varkappa)$ started at the point

$$\beta_{12} = -0.6 \qquad \beta_{13} = -0.3 \qquad \beta_{24} = -0.4 \qquad \gamma_{23} = 0.1$$

$$\sigma^2_{\xi_1} = 2.0 \qquad \sigma^2_{\xi_2} = 2.0 \qquad \sigma^2_{\xi_3} = 2.0$$

$$\sigma_{\xi_1\xi_2} = \sigma_{\xi_1\xi_3} = \sigma_{\xi_2\xi_3} = 0.0$$

$$\sigma^2_{\zeta_1} = 0.3 \qquad \sigma^2_{\zeta_2} = 0.3 \qquad \sigma_{\zeta_1\zeta_2} = 0.0$$

$$\sigma_{\delta_1} = 0.4 \qquad \sigma_{\delta_2} = 0.6 \qquad \sigma_{\delta_3} = 0.5$$

$$\sigma_{\epsilon_1} = 0.5 \qquad \sigma_{\epsilon_2} = 0.6 \qquad \sigma_{\epsilon_3} = 0.9 \qquad \sigma_{\epsilon_4} = 0.5.$$

From this point seven steepest-descent iterations were performed. Thereafter Davidon–Fletcher–Powell iterations starting with $\mathbf{E} = \mathbf{I}$ were used and it took 23 such iterations to reach a point where all derivatives were less than 0.00005 in absolute value. At this point, the solution was correct to four decimals and the $\boldsymbol{\Sigma}$ in (28) was reproduced exactly. The 23 Davidon–Fletcher–Powell iterations required for convergence were not considered excessive since no information about second-order derivatives was used.

5. The Special Case of No Errors of Measurement

If there are no errors of measurement in $\mathbf{y}$ and $\mathbf{x}$, the model (1) may be written

$$\mathbf{By} = \boldsymbol{\Gamma}\mathbf{x} + \mathbf{u} \tag{29}$$

where we have written $\mathbf{u}$ instead of $\boldsymbol{\zeta}$. In (29) we have altered the model slightly, compared to (1), (2), and (3), in that the mean vectors have been eliminated. This is no limitation, however, since constant terms in the equations can be handled by using an x variable that has the value 1 for every observation. The likelihood function is now given by (7) with N instead of $N - 1$ and with $\mathbf{S}$ being the raw moment matrix instead of the dispersion matrix.

This type of model has been studied for many years by econometricians under the names *simultaneous equation* and *recursive* systems (e.g., Hood & Koopmans, 1953 and Wold & Jureen, 1953). In the econometric terminology, the variables are classified as *exogenous* and *endogenous* variables, the idea being that the exogenous variables are given from the outside and the endogenous variables are accounted for by the model. From a statistical point of view the distinction is actually between the independent or *predetermined* variables $\mathbf{x}$ and the dependent or current endogenous variables $\mathbf{y}$. The disturbance $\mathbf{u}$ represents a random term assumed to be independent of the predetermined variables. Observations $\mathbf{y}_t$ and $\mathbf{x}_t$ on $\mathbf{y}$ and $\mathbf{x}$ are usually in the form of a time series.

Equation (29) is referred to as the *structural form* of the model. When (29) is premultiplied by $\mathbf{B}^{-1}$ one obtains the *reduced form*

$$\mathbf{y} = \boldsymbol{\Pi}\mathbf{x} + \mathbf{u}^*, \tag{30}$$

where $\boldsymbol{\Pi} = \mathbf{B}^{-1}\boldsymbol{\Gamma}$ is the reduced-form coefficient matrix, and $\mathbf{u}^* = \mathbf{B}^{-1}\mathbf{u}$ is the reduced-form disturbance vector.

In this case, $\mathbf{\Theta}_\delta$ and $\mathbf{\Theta}_\epsilon$ in (4) are zero and therefore $|\mathbf{\Sigma}|$ and $\mathbf{\Sigma}^{-1}$ in (7) can be written explicitly. It is readily verified that

$$|\mathbf{\Sigma}| = |\mathbf{B}|^{-2}|\mathbf{\Phi}||\mathbf{\Psi}|$$

and

$$\mathbf{\Sigma}^{-1} = \begin{pmatrix} \mathbf{B}'\mathbf{\Psi}^{-1}\mathbf{B} & -\mathbf{B}'\mathbf{\Psi}^{-1}\mathbf{\Gamma} \\ -\mathbf{\Gamma}'\mathbf{\Psi}^{-1}\mathbf{B} & \mathbf{\Gamma}'\mathbf{\Psi}^{-1}\mathbf{\Gamma} + \mathbf{\Phi}^{-1} \end{pmatrix}.$$

Using the above results, $\log L$ becomes

$$\log L = -\tfrac{1}{2}N[\log|\mathbf{\Phi}| + \operatorname{tr}(\mathbf{S}_{xx}\mathbf{\Phi}^{-1})] - \tfrac{1}{2}N\{\log|\mathbf{\Psi}| - \log|\mathbf{B}|^2$$
$$+ \operatorname{tr}[(\mathbf{B}\mathbf{S}_{yy}\mathbf{B}' - \mathbf{B}\mathbf{S}_{yx}\mathbf{\Gamma}' - \mathbf{\Gamma}\mathbf{S}_{xy}\mathbf{B}' + \mathbf{\Gamma}\mathbf{S}_{xx}\mathbf{\Gamma}')\,\mathbf{\Psi}^{-1}]\}.$$

If $\mathbf{\Phi}$ is unconstrained, maximizing $\log L$ with respect to $\mathbf{\Phi}$ gives $\hat{\mathbf{\Phi}} = \mathbf{S}_{xx}$, which is to be expected, since $\mathbf{\Phi}$ in this case is the variance–covariance matrix of $\mathbf{x}$. After the likelihood has been maximized with respect to $\mathbf{\Phi}$, the concentrated likelihood is equal to a constant plus

$$\log L^* = -\tfrac{1}{2}N\{\log|\mathbf{\Psi}| - \log|\mathbf{B}|^2$$
$$+ \operatorname{tr}[(\mathbf{B}\mathbf{S}_{yy}\mathbf{B}' - \mathbf{B}\mathbf{S}_{yx}\mathbf{\Gamma}' - \mathbf{\Gamma}\mathbf{S}_{xy}\mathbf{B}' + \mathbf{\Gamma}\mathbf{S}_{xx}\mathbf{\Gamma}')\,\mathbf{\Psi}^{-1}]\}. \qquad (31)$$

If also $\mathbf{\Psi}$ is unconstrained, further simplification can be obtained, for then (31) is maximized with respect to $\mathbf{\Psi}$ when $\mathbf{\Psi}$ is equal to

$$\mathbf{\Psi} = \mathbf{B}\mathbf{S}_{yy}\mathbf{B}' - \mathbf{B}\mathbf{S}_{yx}\mathbf{\Gamma}' - \mathbf{\Gamma}\mathbf{S}_{xy}\mathbf{B}' + \mathbf{\Gamma}\mathbf{S}_{xx}\mathbf{\Gamma}'. \qquad (32)$$

Consequently, the function to be maximized with respect to $\mathbf{B}$ and $\mathbf{\Gamma}$ is a constant plus

$$\log L^{**} = -\tfrac{1}{2}N[\log|\mathbf{\Psi}| - \log|\mathbf{B}|^2] = -\tfrac{1}{2}N\log(|\mathbf{\Psi}|/|\mathbf{B}|^2)$$
$$= -\tfrac{1}{2}N\log|\mathbf{B}^{-1}\mathbf{\Psi}\mathbf{B}'^{-1}| = -\tfrac{1}{2}N\log|\mathbf{\Psi}^*|, \qquad (33)$$

where

$$\mathbf{\Psi}^* = \mathbf{S}_{yy} - \mathbf{S}_{yx}\mathbf{\Pi}' - \mathbf{\Pi}\mathbf{S}_{xy} + \mathbf{\Pi}\mathbf{S}_{xx}\mathbf{\Pi}'. \qquad (34)$$

In deriving (33), we started from the likelihood function (7) based on the assumption of multinormality of $\mathbf{y}$ and $\mathbf{x}$. Such an assumption may be very unrealistic in most economic applications. Koopmans, Rubin, & Leipnik (1950) derived (31) and (33) from the assumption of multi-normal disturbances $\mathbf{u}$, without a distributional assumption on $\mathbf{x}$. Clearly, with $\mathbf{\Phi}$ unconstrained, the criterion (33) has intuitive appeal regardless of distributional assumptions and connections with the maximum–likelihood method. The matrix $\mathbf{\Psi}$ in (32) is the residual variance–covariance matrix in the structural form (29), and the matrix $\mathbf{\Psi}^*$ in (34) is the residual variance–covariance matrix in the reduced form (30). Maximizing (33) is equivalent to minimizing $|\mathbf{\Psi}^*|$, as noted by Goldberger (1964, pp. 352–356). Several other estimation criteria based on $\mathbf{\Psi}^*$ have been proposed. Brown (1960) suggested the minimization of $\mathrm{tr}(\mathbf{\Psi}^*)$. Malinvaud (1970, Chapter 19) considered the family of estimation criteria $\mathrm{tr}(\mathbf{A}\mathbf{\Psi}^*)$ with arbitrary positive definite weighting matrices $\mathbf{A}$. One possible choice of $\mathbf{A}$, which is suggested by the argument in Zellner (1962), is $(\mathbf{S}_{yy} - \mathbf{S}_{yx}\mathbf{S}_{xx}^{-1}\mathbf{S}_{xy})^{-1}$.

Since the original article by Koopmans, Rubin, & Leipnik (1950), several authors have contributed to the development of their FIML method (Chernoff & Divinsky, 1953; Klein, 1953, 1969; Brown, 1959; Eisenpress, 1962; Eisenpress & Greenstadt, 1966; Rothenberg & Leenders, 1964; Rothenberg, 1966; Chow, 1968; Wegge, 1969). This paper will add another computational algorithm to those already existing.

Minimizing $|\mathbf{\Psi}^*|$ is equivalent to minimizing

$$F = \tfrac{1}{2}[\log|\mathbf{\Psi}| - \log|\mathbf{B}|^2]. \tag{35}$$

Matrix derivatives of F with respect to $\mathbf{B}$ and $\mathbf{\Gamma}$ may be obtained by matrix differentiation as shown in Appendix A3. The results are

$$\partial F/\partial\mathbf{B} = \mathbf{\Psi}^{-1}(\mathbf{B}\mathbf{S}_{yy} - \mathbf{\Gamma}\mathbf{S}_{xy}) - \mathbf{B}'^{-1} \tag{36}$$

$$\partial F/\partial\mathbf{\Gamma} = \mathbf{\Psi}^{-1}(\mathbf{\Gamma}\mathbf{S}_{xx} - \mathbf{B}\mathbf{S}_{yx}). \tag{37}$$

The function F is to be minimized with respect to the elements of $\mathbf{B}$ and $\mathbf{\Gamma}$, taking into account that some elements are fixed and others are constrained. As will be demonstrated in Section 6, allowing for equalities among the elements of $\mathbf{B}$ and $\mathbf{\Gamma}$ is not sufficient to handle some economic applications. Instead, more general constraints may be involved. Usually these constraints are linear, but even models with nonlinear constraints have been studied, e.g., Cobb–Douglas functions, by Nerlove (1965). Such constraints can be handled as follows.

Let $\mathbf{\lambda}' = (\lambda_1, \lambda_2, ..., \lambda_p)$ be the vector of all elements in $\mathbf{B}$ and $\mathbf{\Gamma}$. Some of these elements are fixed a priori. Let $\mathbf{\pi}' = (\pi_1, \pi_2, ..., \pi_q)$ be the vector of all nonfixed elements. Each of these elements may be a known linear or nonlinear function of $\mathbf{\varkappa}' = (\kappa_1, \kappa_2, ..., \kappa_r)$, the parameters to be estimated, i.e.,

$$\pi_i = f_i(\mathbf{\varkappa}) \qquad (i = 1, 2, ..., q).$$

Then F is regarded as a function $H(\mathbf{\varkappa})$ of $\kappa_1, \kappa_2, ..., \kappa_r$. The first derivatives of H are again given by (9), but now $\mathbf{K}$ is the matrix of order

$q \times r$ whose ijth element is $\partial f_i/\partial \kappa_j$. The second derivatives of H are obtained from

$$\partial^2 H/\partial \varkappa \, \partial \varkappa' = \mathbf{K}'(\partial^2 G/\partial \pi \, \partial \pi')\mathbf{K} + \sum_{i=1}^{q} \partial G/\partial \pi_i(\partial^2 f_i/\partial \varkappa \, \partial \varkappa').$$

Both the exact values and the probability limits of the elements of the second-order derivative matrix $\partial^2 F/\partial \lambda \, \partial \lambda'$ are given in Appendix A4. In this case, when exact second-order derivatives are available, probably the best way of minimizing H is to use the Newton–Raphson procedure. Let $\mathbf{g}^{(s)}$ and $\mathbf{G}^{(s)}$ denote the column vector $\partial H/\partial \varkappa$ and the matrix of second-order derivatives $\partial^2 H/\partial \varkappa \, \partial \varkappa'$ in the sth iteration, respectively. The iteration procedure may then be written

$$\mathbf{G}^{(s)}\boldsymbol{\delta}^{(s)} = \mathbf{g}^{(s)} \tag{38}$$

$$\varkappa^{(s+1)} = \varkappa^{(s)} - \boldsymbol{\delta}^{(s)}, \tag{39}$$

where $\boldsymbol{\delta}^{(s)}$ is a vector of corrections determined by (38). The exact matrix of second-order derivatives obtained from (10) and (A33), (A34), (A35) may not be positive definite in the beginning. Therefore the approximation given by (A38), (A39), and (A40), which is always positive definite, is used in the beginning and until one has reached a quadratic region where the exact second-order derivative matrix is positive definite. This procedure is relatively easy to apply even in the nonlinear case and the iterations converge from an arbitrary starting point to a minimum of the function, although there is no guarantee that this is the absolute minimum if several local minima exist. Convergence is quadratic in a neighborhood of the minimum.

When the minimum of H has been found, the approximate second-order derivative matrix may be computed at the minimum to give the information matrix $\mathbf{G}^*$. Then $N^{-1/2}$ times the square root of the diagonal elements of $\mathbf{G}^{*-1}$ gives the standard errors of the estimated parameters.

6. An Economic Application

In this section we apply the method of Section 5 to a small economic model taken from the literature. The model is Klein's (1950) model of United States economy as presented in Goldberger (1964, pp. 303–325):

Consumption:	$C = a_0 + a_1 P + a_2 P_{-1} + a_3 W + u_1$	(40a)
Investment:	$I = b_0 + b_1 P + b_2 P_{-1} + b_3 K_{-1} + u_2$	(40b)
Private wages:	$W^* = c_0 + c_1 E + c_2 E_{-1} + c_3 A + u_3$	(40c)
Product:	$Y + T = C + I + G$	(40d)
Income:	$Y = P + W$	(40e)
Capital:	$K = K_{-1} + I$	(40f)
Wages:	$W = W^* + W^{**}$	(40g)
Private product:	$E = Y + T - W^{**}.$	(40h)

The endogenous variables are

C	consumption	Y	national income
I	investment	K	end-of-year capital stock
W^*	private wage bill	W	total wage bill
P	profits	E	private product

and the predetermined variables are the lagged endogenous variables P_{-1}, K_{-1}, and E_{-1} and the exogenous variables

1	unity	G	government expenditures
W^{**}	government wage bill	A	time in years from 1931
T	indirect taxes		

All variables except 1 and A are in billions of 1934 dollars.

This model contains eight dependent variables and eight predetermined variables. There are three equations involving disturbance terms. The other five equations are identities. Using the five identities (40d)–(40h), P, Y, K, W, and E may be solved for and substituted into (40a)–(40c). This gives a model with the structural form

$$\begin{pmatrix} 1 - a_1 & -a_1 & a_1 - a_3 \\ -b_1 & 1 - b_1 & b_1 \\ -c_1 & -c_1 & 1 \end{pmatrix} \begin{pmatrix} C \\ I \\ W^* \end{pmatrix}$$

$$= \begin{pmatrix} a_0 & a_3 - a_1 & -a_1 & a_1 & 0 & a_2 & 0 & 0 \\ b_0 & -b_1 & -b_1 & b_1 & 0 & b_2 & b_3 & 0 \\ c_0 & -c_1 & 0 & c_1 & c_3 & 0 & 0 & c_2 \end{pmatrix} \begin{pmatrix} 1 \\ W^{**} \\ T \\ G \\ A \\ P_{-1} \\ K_{-1} \\ E_{-1} \end{pmatrix}. \quad (41)$$

There are 24 nonfixed elements in $\mathbf{B}$ and $\mathbf{\Gamma}$. These are all linear functions of the 12 unknown coefficients in (40a)–(40c) as shown in (42).

$$
\begin{bmatrix}
\beta_{11} \\ \beta_{12} \\ \beta_{13} \\ \beta_{21} \\ \beta_{22} \\ \beta_{23} \\ \beta_{31} \\ \beta_{32} \\ \gamma_{11} \\ \gamma_{12} \\ \gamma_{13} \\ \gamma_{14} \\ \gamma_{16} \\ \gamma_{21} \\ \gamma_{22} \\ \gamma_{23} \\ \gamma_{24} \\ \gamma_{26} \\ \gamma_{27} \\ \gamma_{31} \\ \gamma_{32} \\ \gamma_{34} \\ \gamma_{35} \\ \gamma_{38}
\end{bmatrix}
=
\begin{bmatrix}
0 & -1 & 0 & 0 & 0 & 0 & 0 & 0 & 0 & 0 & 0 & 0 \\
0 & -1 & 0 & 0 & 0 & 0 & 0 & 0 & 0 & 0 & 0 & 0 \\
0 & 1 & 0 & -1 & 0 & 0 & 0 & 0 & 0 & 0 & 0 & 0 \\
0 & 0 & 0 & 0 & 0 & -1 & 0 & 0 & 0 & 0 & 0 & 0 \\
0 & 0 & 0 & 0 & 0 & -1 & 0 & 0 & 0 & 0 & 0 & 0 \\
0 & 0 & 0 & 0 & 0 & 1 & 0 & 0 & 0 & 0 & 0 & 0 \\
0 & 0 & 0 & 0 & 0 & 0 & 0 & 0 & 0 & -1 & 0 & 0 \\
0 & 0 & 0 & 0 & 0 & 0 & 0 & 0 & 0 & -1 & 0 & 0 \\
1 & 0 & 0 & 0 & 0 & 0 & 0 & 0 & 0 & 0 & 0 & 0 \\
0 & -1 & 0 & 1 & 0 & 0 & 0 & 0 & 0 & 0 & 0 & 0 \\
0 & -1 & 0 & 0 & 0 & 0 & 0 & 0 & 0 & 0 & 0 & 0 \\
0 & 1 & 0 & 0 & 0 & 0 & 0 & 0 & 0 & 0 & 0 & 0 \\
0 & 0 & 1 & 0 & 0 & 0 & 0 & 0 & 0 & 0 & 0 & 0 \\
0 & 0 & 0 & 0 & 1 & 0 & 0 & 0 & 0 & 0 & 0 & 0 \\
0 & 0 & 0 & 0 & 0 & -1 & 0 & 0 & 0 & 0 & 0 & 0 \\
0 & 0 & 0 & 0 & 0 & -1 & 0 & 0 & 0 & 0 & 0 & 0 \\
0 & 0 & 0 & 0 & 0 & 1 & 0 & 0 & 0 & 0 & 0 & 0 \\
0 & 0 & 0 & 0 & 0 & 0 & 1 & 0 & 0 & 0 & 0 & 0 \\
0 & 0 & 0 & 0 & 0 & 0 & 0 & 1 & 0 & 0 & 0 & 0 \\
0 & 0 & 0 & 0 & 0 & 0 & 0 & 0 & 1 & 0 & 0 & 0 \\
0 & 0 & 0 & 0 & 0 & 0 & 0 & 0 & 0 & -1 & 0 & 0 \\
0 & 0 & 0 & 0 & 0 & 0 & 0 & 0 & 0 & 1 & 0 & 0 \\
0 & 0 & 0 & 0 & 0 & 0 & 0 & 0 & 0 & 0 & 0 & 1 \\
0 & 0 & 0 & 0 & 0 & 0 & 0 & 0 & 0 & 0 & 1 & 0
\end{bmatrix}
\begin{bmatrix}
a_0 \\ a_1 \\ a_2 \\ a_3 \\ b_0 \\ b_1 \\ b_2 \\ b_3 \\ c_0 \\ c_1 \\ c_2 \\ c_3
\end{bmatrix}
+
\begin{bmatrix}
1 \\ 0 \\ 0 \\ 0 \\ 1 \\ 0 \\ 0 \\ 0 \\ 0 \\ 0 \\ 0 \\ 0 \\ 0 \\ 0 \\ 0 \\ 0 \\ 0 \\ 0 \\ 0 \\ 0 \\ 0 \\ 0 \\ 0 \\ 0
\end{bmatrix}
$$

$$(42)$$

From annual observations, United States, 1921–1941, the following raw moment matrices are obtained:

$$
\mathbf{S}_{yy} = \begin{array}{c} C \\ I \\ W^* \end{array}
\begin{pmatrix}
62166.63 & & \\
1679.01 & 286.02 & \\
42076.78 & 1217.92 & 28560.86
\end{pmatrix},
\quad
\begin{array}{ccc} C & I & W^* \end{array}
$$

	C	I	W^*
1	1133.90	26.60	763.60
W^{**}	5977.33	103.80	4044.07
T	7858.86	160.40	5315.62
G	11633.68	243.19	7922.46
A	577.70	−105.60	460.90
P_{-1}	18929.37	655.33	12871.73
K_{-1}	227767.38	5073.25	153470.56
E_{-1}	66815.25	1831.13	45288.51

$$\mathbf{S}_{xy} = \quad ,$$

$$
\mathbf{S}_{xx} = \begin{array}{c}
 \\
1 \\
W^{**} \\
T \\
G \\
A \\
P_{-1} \\
K_{-1} \\
E_{-1}
\end{array}
\begin{array}{ccc}
1 & W^{**} & T \\
21.00 & & \\
107.50 & 626.87 & \\
142.90 & 789.27 & 1054.95 \\
208.20 & 1200.19 & 1546.11 \\
0.00 & 238.00 & 176.00 \\
343.90 & 1746.22 & 2348.48 \\
4210.40 & 21683.18 & 28766.23 \\
1217.70 & 6364.43 & 8436.53
\end{array}
$$

$$
\begin{array}{ccccc}
G & A & P_{-1} & K_{-1} & E_{-1} \\
2369.94 & & & & \\
421.70 & 770.00 & & & \\
3451.86 & -11.90 & 5956.29 & & \\
42026.14 & 590.60 & 69073.54 & 846132.70 & \\
12473.50 & 495.60 & 20542.22 & 244984.77 & 72200.03
\end{array}
$$

The following estimated model was obtained

$$
\begin{aligned}
C &= 18.318 - 0.229P + 0.384P_{-1} + 0.802W + u_1 \\
I &= 27.278 - 0.797P + 1.051P_{-1} - 0.148K_{-1} + u_2 \\
W^* &= 5.766 + 0.235E + 0.284E_{-1} + 0.234A + u_3 \, ,
\end{aligned}
\tag{43}
$$

with

$$
\hat{\Psi} = \begin{pmatrix}
43.775 & & \\
80.456 & 265.856 & \\
9.834 & 80.247 & 37.540
\end{pmatrix}.
\tag{44}
$$

These estimates agree with those reported by Chernoff & Divinsky (1953) and Chow (1968). The relationships between the coefficients of Chow's equations and those of ours are

$$
\begin{array}{lll}
\beta_{12} = -(1 - a_3)/(1 - a_1) & \beta_{13} = 1/(1 - a_1) & \gamma_{12} = a_2/(1 - a_1) \\
\beta_{21} = c_1/(1 - c_1) & \gamma_{24} = c_3/(1 - c_1) & \gamma_{27} = c_2/(1 - c_1) \\
\beta_{31} = b_1 & \gamma_{32} = b_2 & \gamma_{33} = 1 + b_3 \, .
\end{array}
$$

Chow gives β_{31} with the wrong sign.

7. The Special Case of No Disturbances

When there are no disturbances in (1), the relations between η and ξ are exact. The joint distribution of η and ξ is singular and of rank n. In Eq. (4) for Σ, the second term in Σ_{yy} vanishes. In general, when there are fixed and constrained elements in $\mathbf{B}$ and $\boldsymbol{\Gamma}$ or in $\boldsymbol{\Phi}$, $\boldsymbol{\Theta}_\delta$, and $\boldsymbol{\Theta}_\epsilon$, this model may be estimated by the method of Section 3. This may be done by setting $\boldsymbol{\Psi} = \mathbf{0}$ and specifying the fixed elements and the constraints as described in that section.

The matrix $\boldsymbol{\Sigma}$ can also be written

$$\boldsymbol{\Sigma} = \boldsymbol{\Lambda}\boldsymbol{\Phi}\boldsymbol{\Lambda}' + \boldsymbol{\Theta}^2, \tag{45}$$

where

$$\boldsymbol{\Lambda} = \begin{pmatrix} \mathbf{B}^{-1}\boldsymbol{\Gamma} \\ \mathbf{I} \end{pmatrix} \quad \text{and} \quad \boldsymbol{\Theta} = \begin{pmatrix} \boldsymbol{\Theta}_\epsilon & \mathbf{0} \\ \mathbf{0} & \boldsymbol{\Theta}_\delta \end{pmatrix}, \tag{46}$$

from which it is seen that the model is identical to a certain restricted factor-analysis model. Several special cases will now be considered.

If $\mathbf{B} = \mathbf{I}$ and $\boldsymbol{\Gamma}$ is unconstrained, i.e., all elements of $\boldsymbol{\Gamma}$ are regarded as free parameters, model (45) is formally equivalent to an unrestricted factor model (Jöreskog, 1969). The matrix $\boldsymbol{\Lambda}$ in (46) may be obtained from *any* $\boldsymbol{\Lambda}^*$ of order $(m + n) \times n$ satisfying

$$\boldsymbol{\Sigma} = \boldsymbol{\Lambda}^*\boldsymbol{\Lambda}^{*\prime} + \boldsymbol{\Theta}^2 \tag{47}$$

by a transformation of $\boldsymbol{\Lambda}^*$ to a reference variables solution (Jöreskog, 1969) where the xs are used as reference variables. Maximum-likelihood estimates of $\boldsymbol{\Lambda}^*$ and $\boldsymbol{\Theta}$ may be obtained by the method of Jöreskog (1967a,b) which also yields a large-sample χ^2 test of goodness of fit. Let the estimate of $\boldsymbol{\Lambda}^*$ be partitioned as

$$\hat{\boldsymbol{\Lambda}}^* = \begin{bmatrix} \hat{\boldsymbol{\Lambda}}_1^* \\ \hat{\boldsymbol{\Lambda}}_2^* \end{bmatrix}, \tag{48}$$

where $\hat{\boldsymbol{\Lambda}}_1^*$ is of order $m \times n$ and $\hat{\boldsymbol{\Lambda}}_2^*$ of order $n \times n$. Then the maximum-likelihood estimates of $\boldsymbol{\Gamma}$ and $\boldsymbol{\Phi}$ are

$$\hat{\boldsymbol{\Gamma}} = \hat{\boldsymbol{\Lambda}}_1^* \hat{\boldsymbol{\Lambda}}_2^{*-1}, \tag{49}$$

$$\hat{\boldsymbol{\Phi}} = \hat{\boldsymbol{\Lambda}}_2^* \hat{\boldsymbol{\Lambda}}_2^{*\prime}. \tag{50}$$

If $\mathbf{B} = \mathbf{I}$ and $\boldsymbol{\Gamma}$ is constrained to have some fixed elements while the remaining elements in $\boldsymbol{\Gamma}$ are free parameters, model (45) is formally equivalent to a restricted factor model in the sense of Jöreskog (1969). This model may be estimated by the procedure described in the same paper and, in large samples, standard errors of the estimates and a goodness of fit test can also be obtained. A computer program ACOVS for this procedure is available (Jöreskog, Gruvaeus, & van Thillo, 1970). A more general case is when **B** is lower triangular. The structural equation system for the true variates is then recursive. In general such a recursive system may be estimated by the method described in Section 3 of this chapter, though there may be simpler methods. One example occurs when the system is normalized by fixing one element in each row of **Γ** to unity and **B** has the form

$$\mathbf{B} = \begin{bmatrix} \beta_{11} & 0 & \cdots & 0 \\ \beta_{21} & \beta_{22} & \cdots & 0 \\ \vdots & \vdots & & \vdots \\ \beta_{m1} & \beta_{m2} & \cdots & \beta_{mm} \end{bmatrix}$$

where all the βs are free parameters. Then there is a one-to-one transformation between the free parameters of **B** and the free elements of $\mathbf{A} = \mathbf{B}^{-1}$. One may therefore estimate **A** instead of **B**. In this case, the variance–covariance matrix **Σ** is of the form

$$\Sigma = \mathbf{B}^{*}\Lambda\Phi\Lambda'\mathbf{B}^{*'} + \Theta^{2} \tag{51}$$

where

$$\mathbf{B}^{*} = \begin{pmatrix} \mathbf{A} & 0 \\ 0 & \mathbf{I} \end{pmatrix}, \quad \Lambda = \begin{pmatrix} \Gamma \\ \mathbf{I} \end{pmatrix}, \quad \Theta = \begin{pmatrix} \Theta_{\epsilon} & 0 \\ 0 & \Theta_{\delta} \end{pmatrix}. \tag{52}$$

Model (51) is a special case of a general model for covariance structures developed by Jöreskog (1970a) and may also be estimated using the computer program ACOVS (Jöreskog *et al.*, 1970). In this model **Γ**, **Φ**, Θ_{δ}, and Θ_{ϵ} may contain fixed parameters and even parameters constrained to be equal in groups. The computer program gives maximum-likelihood estimates of the free parameters in **A**, **Γ**, **Φ**, Θ_{δ}, and Θ_{ϵ} and, in large samples, standard errors of these estimates and a test of overall goodness of fit of the model can also be obtained.

More generally, the above mentioned method may be used whenever **Σ** can be written in the form (51) such that there is a one-to-one correspondence between the free parameters in **B** and **Γ** and the distinct free elements in **B*** and **Λ**. For a less trivial example, see Jöreskog (1970a, Section 2.6).

8. A Psychological Application

In this section we consider a simplified model for the prediction of achievements in mathematics (M) and science (S) at different grade levels. This model illustrates the combination of errors in equations and errors in variables. To estimate the model we make use of longitudinal data from a growth study conducted at Educational Testing Service (Anderson & Maier, 1963; Hilton, 1969). In this study a nationwide sample of fifth graders was tested in 1961 and then again in 1963, 1965, and 1967 as seventh, ninth, and eleventh graders, respectively. The test scores are the verbal (V) and quantitative (Q) parts of SCAT (Scholastic Aptitude Test) obtained in 1961 and the achievement tests in mathematics (M_5, M_7, M_9, M_{11}) and science (S_5, S_7, S_9, S_{11}) obtained in 1961, 1963, 1965, and 1967, respectively.

The model is depicted in the path diagram in Fig. 1, where V, Q, M_5, M_7, M_9, M_{11}, S_5, S_7, S_9, and S_{11} denote the true scores of the

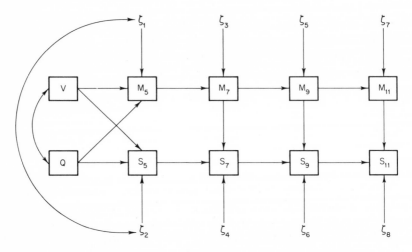

Figure 1.   Model for achievements in mathematics and science.

tests and ζ_1, ζ_2,..., ζ_8 the corresponding disturbances. The model for the true scores is

$$
\begin{aligned}
M_5 &= a_1 V + a_2 Q + \zeta_1 & S_5 &= b_1 V + b_2 Q + \zeta_2 \\
M_7 &= c_1 M_5 + \zeta_3 & S_7 &= d_1 S_5 + d_2 M_7 + \zeta_4 \\
M_9 &= e_1 M_7 + \zeta_5 & S_9 &= f_1 S_7 + f_2 M_9 + \zeta_6 \\
M_{11} &= g_1 M_9 + \zeta_7 & S_{11} &= h_1 S_9 + h_2 M_{11} + \zeta_8 .
\end{aligned}
\tag{53}
$$

This model postulates the major influences on a student's achievement in mathematics and science at various grade levels. At grade 5 the main determinants of student's achievements are his verbal and quantitative abilities at that stage. At higher grade levels, however, the achievements are mainly determined by his achievements in the earlier grades. Thus, achievement in mathematics in grade i is determined mainly by the achievement in mathematics in grade $i - 2$, whereas achievement in science in grade i is determined mainly by the achievement in science in grade $i - 2$ and in mathematics in grade i; $i = 7, 9, 11$.

The structural form of this model is

$$
\begin{bmatrix}
1 & 0 & 0 & 0 & 0 & 0 & 0 & 0 \\
0 & 1 & 0 & 0 & 0 & 0 & 0 & 0 \\
-c_1 & 0 & 1 & 0 & 0 & 0 & 0 & 0 \\
0 & -d_1 & -d_2 & 1 & 0 & 0 & 0 & 0 \\
0 & 0 & -e_1 & 0 & 1 & 0 & 0 & 0 \\
0 & 0 & 0 & -f_1 & -f_2 & 1 & 0 & 0 \\
0 & 0 & 0 & 0 & -g_1 & 0 & 1 & 0 \\
0 & 0 & 0 & 0 & 0 & -h_1 & -h_2 & 1
\end{bmatrix}
\begin{bmatrix}
M_5 \\ S_5 \\ M_7 \\ S_7 \\ M_9 \\ S_9 \\ M_{11} \\ S_{11}
\end{bmatrix}
=
\begin{bmatrix}
a_1 & a_2 \\
b_1 & b_2 \\
0 & 0 \\
0 & 0 \\
0 & 0 \\
0 & 0 \\
0 & 0 \\
0 & 0
\end{bmatrix}
\begin{pmatrix} V \\ Q \end{pmatrix}
+
\begin{bmatrix}
\zeta_1 \\ \zeta_2 \\ \zeta_3 \\ \zeta_4 \\ \zeta_5 \\ \zeta_6 \\ \zeta_7 \\ \zeta_8
\end{bmatrix}.
$$

$$(54)$$

We assume that each of the observables is related to the corresponding true variable according to (2) and (3).

The model is a causal chain and can be estimated by the method described in Section 3, provided some assumption is made about the correlations of $\zeta_1, \zeta_2, ..., \zeta_8$. Without such an assumption the model is not identified. We have chosen to make the assumption that all disturbances are uncorrelated except ζ_1 and ζ_2. This assumption does not seem to be too unrealistic.

The data that we use consist of a random sample of 730 boys taken from all the boys that took all tests at all occasions. The correlation matrices of the observable variables are

	M_5	S_5	M_7	S_7	M_9	S_9	M_{11}	S_{11}
M_5	1.000							
S_5	.755	1.000						
M_7	.730	.664	1.000					
S_7	.651	.700	.710	1.000				
M_9	.712	.636	.763	.673	1.000			
S_9	.619	.683	.671	.740	.736	1.000		
M_{11}	.644	.581	.663	.566	.735	.621	1.000	
S_{11}	.576	.632	.611	.648	.659	.721	.638	1.000

$\mathbf{S}_{yy} = $ (above),

	M_5	S_5	M_7	S_7	M_9	S_9	M_{11}	S_{11}
V	.726	.781	.654	.672	.630	.621	.561	.583
Q	.764	.684	.703	.600	.693	.547	.614	.519

$\mathbf{S}_{xy} = $ (above),

$$\mathbf{S}_{xx} = \begin{array}{c} V \\ Q \end{array} \begin{pmatrix} \overset{V \quad\quad Q}{1.000} & \\ .696 & 1.000 \end{pmatrix}.$$

The estimated model is

$$M_5 = 0.612V + 0.367Q + \zeta_1 \qquad S_5 = 1.092V - 0.086Q + \zeta_2$$
$$M_7 = 0.901M_5 + \zeta_3 \qquad\quad S_7 = 0.360S_5 + 0.560M_7 + \zeta_4$$
$$M_9 = 0.972M_7 + \zeta_5 \qquad\quad S_9 = 0.584S_7 + 0.379M_9 + \zeta_6 \qquad (55)$$
$$M_{11} = 0.858M_9 + \zeta_7 \qquad\quad S_{11} = 0.730S_9 + 0.186M_{11} + \zeta_8 .$$

The estimated variance–covariance matrix of the true scores V and Q is

$$\hat{\mathbf{\Phi}} = \begin{array}{c} V \\ Q \end{array} \begin{pmatrix} \overset{V \quad\quad Q}{.771} & \\ .696 & .930 \end{pmatrix}.$$

Estimated disturbance variances and error variances for each measure are given in Table 1. The estimated correlation between ζ_1 and ζ_2 is 0.17.

TABLE 1

Measure	Disturbance Variance	Error Variance
V	—	0.228
Q	—	0.070
M_5	0.079	0.194
S_5	0.137	0.067
M_7	0.138	0.208
S_7	0.194	0.166
M_9	0.118	0.133
S_9	0.125	0.171
M_{11}	0.362	0.000
S_{11}	0.105	0.250

The estimated reduced form for the true scores is

$$M_5 = 0.612V + 0.367Q + \zeta_1{}^* \qquad S_5 = 1.092V - 0.086Q + \zeta_2{}^*$$
$$M_7 = 0.551V + 0.331Q + \zeta_3{}^* \qquad S_7 = 0.702V + 0.154Q + \zeta_4{}^*$$
$$M_9 = 0.536V + 0.321Q + \zeta_5{}^* \qquad S_9 = 0.613V + 0.212Q + \zeta_6{}^* \qquad (56)$$
$$M_{11} = 0.460V + 0.276Q + \zeta_7{}^* \qquad S_{11} = 0.533V + 0.206Q + \zeta_8{}^*.$$

The relative contributions of V and Q, the disturbance ζ^*, and the error, to each test's total variance are shown in Table 2.

TABLE 2

Measure	V and Q	Disturbance	Error
M_5	0.73	0.08	0.19
S_5	0.80	0.13	0.07
M_7	0.59	0.20	0.21
S_7	0.55	0.28	0.17
M_9	0.56	0.31	0.13
S_9	0.51	0.32	0.17
M_{11}	0.41	0.59	0.00
S_{11}	0.41	0.34	0.25

It is not easy to give a clear-cut interpretation of these results. Inspecting first the equations for M_7, M_9, and M_{11} in (55), it is seen that the effect of M_{i-2} on M_i first increases and then decreases. This is perhaps because mathematics becomes more differentiated at the higher grade levels. The large disturbance variance ζ_7 indicates that M_9 alone is not sufficient to account for M_{11}. This is perhaps due to the fact that mathematics courses at the higher grades change character from being mainly "arithmetic computation" to involving more "algebraic reasoning."

Inspecting next the equations for S_7, S_9, and S_{11} in (55) describing science achievements, it is seen that the influence of mathematics on science tends to decrease at the higher grades. This is natural since science courses in the lower grades are based mainly on "logical reasoning" whereas in the higher grades they are based on "memorization of facts." The effect of science achievements on science two years later increases steadily.

9. Summary and Conclusion

We have described a general model involving linear structural equations among a set of true variables that can only be observed with errors of measurement. By allowing parameters of the model to be fixed, free, or constrained, great flexibility is obtained in that the general model contains a wide range of specific models. When a model is specified in such a way that each parameter is identified, i.e., just-identified or over-identified, the model may be estimated by the maximum-likelihood method based on the assumption that the observed variables have a multinormal distribution. The likelihood function is maximized numerically using the Davidon–Fletcher–Powell method and the information matrix. When the estimates have been obtained, this matrix may be used to compute standard errors of the estimated parameters.

A special case of the general model is when there are no errors of measurement in the observed variables. This case is considered separately. In this case, the assumption that the observed variables are multinormal may not always be appropriate. Instead, one may only want to assume, as is usually done in econometrics, that the conditional distribution of the dependent variables, given the independent variables, is multinormal. This leads to such simplification that the likelihood function may be written as a function of the coefficients of the structural equations only and second derivatives of the likelihood function may be readily computed. For this reason the likelihood function is best minimized by the Newton–Raphson procedure.

It should be pointed out that in the general model there is one observed variable for each true variable. However, in several models recently studied by sociologists (see e.g., Blalock, 1969a), there are multiple indicators of the same underlying true variable. Such models could be handled by replacing (2) and (3) by

$$\mathbf{y} = \boldsymbol{\mu} + \boldsymbol{\Lambda}_y \boldsymbol{\eta} + \boldsymbol{\epsilon} \qquad (57)$$

$$\mathbf{x} = \boldsymbol{\nu} + \boldsymbol{\Lambda}_x \boldsymbol{\xi} + \boldsymbol{\delta}, \qquad (58)$$

where $\boldsymbol{\Lambda}_y(p \times m)$ and $\boldsymbol{\Lambda}_x(q \times n)$ are matrices of the form, say

$$
\begin{bmatrix}
* & 0 & 0 \\
* & 0 & 0 \\
* & 0 & 0 \\
0 & * & 0 \\
0 & * & 0 \\
0 & * & 0 \\
0 & 0 & * \\
0 & 0 & * \\
0 & 0 & *
\end{bmatrix},
$$

with three indicators of each of three unobserved variables. The author is presently working on such an extension of the model.

Separate computer programs have been written in Fortran IV for the general model (LISREL) and for the case of no errors of measurement (FIELES). These programs have been successfully used for the illustrations of this paper. Both programs are currently being revised and experimented with. For practical applications, there are at least two questions that need further study. One is the choice of initial values and its effect on convergence and on rate of convergence. The other is the feasibility of the programs for models involving a large number of equations and parameters.

Appendix: Mathematical Derivations

A1. Matrix Derivatives of Function F in Section 3

The function defined by

$$2F = \log | \, \Sigma \, | + \text{tr}(S\Sigma^{-1}) \tag{A1}$$

is regarded as a function of $\mathbf{B}, \, \boldsymbol{\Gamma}, \, \boldsymbol{\Phi}, \, \boldsymbol{\Psi}, \, \boldsymbol{\Theta}_\delta, \, \boldsymbol{\Theta}_\epsilon$ via (4). To derive the matrix derivatives, we shall make use of matrix differentials. In general, $d\mathbf{X} = (dx_{ij})$ will denote a matrix of differentials, and if F is a function of $\mathbf{X}$ and $dF = \text{tr}(\mathbf{C} \, d\mathbf{X}')$ then $\partial F / \partial \mathbf{X} = \mathbf{C}$.

Writing $\mathbf{A} = \mathbf{B}^{-1}$ and $\mathbf{D} = \mathbf{B}^{-1}\boldsymbol{\Gamma} = \mathbf{A}\boldsymbol{\Gamma}$ we have

$$d\mathbf{A} = -\mathbf{B}^{-1} \, d\mathbf{B} \, \mathbf{B}^{-1} = -\mathbf{A} \, d\mathbf{B} \, \mathbf{A} \tag{A2}$$

$$d\mathbf{D} = \mathbf{B}^{-1} \, d\boldsymbol{\Gamma} + d\mathbf{A} \, \boldsymbol{\Gamma} = \mathbf{A} \, d\boldsymbol{\Gamma} - \mathbf{A} \, d\mathbf{B} \, \mathbf{A}\boldsymbol{\Gamma} = \mathbf{A} \, d\boldsymbol{\Gamma} - \mathbf{A} \, d\mathbf{B} \, \mathbf{D}. \tag{A3}$$

Furthermore, we have

$$d \log | \, \Sigma \, | = \text{tr}(\Sigma^{-1} \, d\Sigma) \tag{A4}$$

and

$$d \, \text{tr}(S\Sigma^{-1}) = \text{tr}(S \, d\Sigma^{-1}) = -\text{tr}(S\Sigma^{-1} \, d\Sigma \, \Sigma^{-1}) = -\text{tr}(\Sigma^{-1}S\Sigma^{-1} \, d\Sigma). \tag{A5}$$

Hence, from (A1) we obtain

$$
\begin{aligned}
2 \, dF &= d \log | \, \Sigma \, | + d \, \text{tr}(S\Sigma^{-1}) = \text{tr}(\Sigma^{-1} \, d\Sigma) - \text{tr}(\Sigma^{-1}S\Sigma^{-1} \, d\Sigma) \\
&= \text{tr}[(\Sigma^{-1} - \Sigma^{-1}S\Sigma^{-1}) \, d\Sigma] = \text{tr}(\Omega \, d\Sigma) \\
&= \text{tr}(\Omega_{yy} \, d\Sigma_{yy} + \Omega_{yx} \, d\Sigma_{xy} + \Omega_{xy} \, d\Sigma_{yx} + \Omega_{xx} \, d\Sigma_{xx}),
\end{aligned} \tag{A6}
$$

where $\Omega = \Sigma^{-1}(\Sigma - S)\Sigma^{-1}$ as in (13) and $d\Sigma$ is partitioned as Ω was in (13).

From (4) and the definitions of $\mathbf{A}$ and $\mathbf{D}$ we have

$$\begin{pmatrix} \Sigma_{yy} & \Sigma_{yx} \\ \Sigma_{xy} & \Sigma_{xx} \end{pmatrix} = \begin{pmatrix} \mathbf{D}\boldsymbol{\Phi}\mathbf{D}' + \mathbf{A}\boldsymbol{\Psi}\mathbf{A}' + \boldsymbol{\Theta}_\epsilon{}^2 & \mathbf{D}\boldsymbol{\Phi} \\ \boldsymbol{\Phi}\mathbf{D}' & \boldsymbol{\Phi} + \boldsymbol{\Theta}_\delta{}^2 \end{pmatrix}, \tag{A7}$$

from which we obtain

$$d\Sigma_{yy} = \mathbf{D\Phi}\,d\mathbf{D}' + \mathbf{D}\,d\mathbf{\Phi}\,\mathbf{D}' + d\mathbf{D}\,\mathbf{\Phi}\mathbf{D}' + \mathbf{A\Psi}\,d\mathbf{A}' + \mathbf{A}\,d\mathbf{\Psi}\,\mathbf{A}'$$
$$+ d\mathbf{A}\,\mathbf{\Psi}\mathbf{A}' + 2\mathbf{\Theta}_\epsilon\,d\mathbf{\Theta}_\epsilon \tag{A8}$$

$$d\Sigma_{xy} = \mathbf{\Phi}\,d\mathbf{D}' + d\mathbf{\Phi}\,\mathbf{D}' \tag{A9}$$

$$d\Sigma_{xx} = d\mathbf{\Phi} + 2\mathbf{\Theta}_\delta\,d\mathbf{\Theta}_\delta. \tag{A10}$$

Substitution of $d\mathbf{A}$ and $d\mathbf{D}$ from (A2) and (A3) into (A8) and (A9) gives

$$d\Sigma_{yy} = \mathbf{D\Phi}\,d\mathbf{\Gamma}'\,\mathbf{A}' - \mathbf{D\Phi}\mathbf{D}'\,d\mathbf{B}'\,\mathbf{A}' + \mathbf{A}\,d\mathbf{\Gamma}\,\mathbf{\Phi}\mathbf{D}' - \mathbf{A}\,d\mathbf{B}\,\mathbf{D\Phi}\mathbf{D}'$$
$$- \mathbf{A\Psi}\mathbf{A}'\,d\mathbf{B}'\,\mathbf{A}' - \mathbf{A}\,d\mathbf{B}\,\mathbf{A\Psi}\mathbf{A}' + \mathbf{D}\,d\mathbf{\Phi}\,\mathbf{D}' + \mathbf{A}\,d\mathbf{\Psi}\,\mathbf{A}' + 2\mathbf{\Theta}_\epsilon\,d\mathbf{\Theta}_\epsilon \tag{A11}$$

$$d\Sigma_{xy} = \mathbf{\Phi}\,d\mathbf{\Gamma}'\,\mathbf{A}' - \mathbf{\Phi}\mathbf{D}'\,d\mathbf{B}'\,\mathbf{A}' + d\mathbf{\Phi}\,\mathbf{D}'. \tag{A12}$$

Substitution of (A11), (A12), and (A10) into (A6), noting that $\mathrm{tr}(\mathbf{C}'\,d\mathbf{X}) = \mathrm{tr}(d\mathbf{X}'\,\mathbf{C}) = \mathrm{tr}(\mathbf{C}\,d\mathbf{X}')$, and collecting terms, shows that the matrices multiplying $d\mathbf{B}'$, $d\mathbf{\Gamma}'$, $d\mathbf{\Phi}$, $d\mathbf{\Psi}$, $d\mathbf{\Theta}_\delta$ and $d\mathbf{\Theta}_\epsilon$ are the matrices on the right sides of Eqs. (14), (15), (16), (17), (18), and (19) respectively. These are therefore the corresponding matrix derivatives.

A2. Information Matrix for the General Model of Section 3

In this section we shall prove a general theorem concerning the expected second-order derivatives of any function of the type (8) and show how this theorem can be applied to compute all the elements of the matrix in (12). This matrix times $N - 1$ is the information matrix. The inverse of the information matrix provides the asymptotic variance-covariance matrix of the maximum likelihood estimates.

We first prove the following:

Lemma. Let

$$\mathbf{S} = [1/(N-1)]\sum_{t=1}^{N}(\mathbf{z}_t - \bar{\mathbf{z}})(\mathbf{z}_t - \bar{\mathbf{z}})',$$

where $\mathbf{z}_1$, $\mathbf{z}_2$,..., $\mathbf{z}_N$ are independently distributed according to $N(\mu, \Sigma)$. Then the asymptotic distribution of the elements of $\mathbf{\Omega} = \mathbf{\Sigma}^{-1}(\mathbf{\Sigma} - \mathbf{S})\mathbf{\Sigma}^{-1}$ is multivariate normal with means zero and variances and covariances given by

$$(N-1)\,E(\omega_{\alpha\beta}\omega_{\mu\nu}) = \sigma^{\alpha\mu}\sigma^{\beta\nu} + \sigma^{\alpha\nu}\sigma^{\beta\mu}. \tag{A13}$$

Proof. The proof follows immediately by multiplying $\omega_{\alpha\beta} = \sum_g \sum_h \sigma^{\alpha g}(\sigma_{gh} - s_{gh})\sigma^{h\beta}$ and $\omega_{\mu\nu} = \sum_i \sum_j \sigma^{\mu i}(\sigma_{ij} - s_{ij})\sigma^{j\nu}$, and using the fact that the asymptotic variances and covariances of **S** are given by

$$(N - 1) E[(\sigma_{gh} - s_{gh})(\sigma_{ij} - s_{ij})] = \sigma_{gi}\sigma_{hj} + \sigma_{gj}\sigma_{hi} ,$$

see Anderson (1958, Theorem 4.2.4).

We can now prove the following general theorem.

THEOREM. Under the conditions of the lemma let the elements of $\boldsymbol{\Sigma}$ be functions of two parameter matrices $\mathbf{M} = (\mu_{gh})$ and $\mathbf{N} = (\nu_{ij})$ and let $F(\mathbf{M}, \mathbf{N}) = \frac{1}{2}[\log| \boldsymbol{\Sigma} | + \mathrm{tr}(\mathbf{S}\boldsymbol{\Sigma}^{-1})]$ with $\partial F/\partial\mathbf{M} = \mathbf{A}\boldsymbol{\Omega}\mathbf{B}$ and $\partial F/\partial\mathbf{N} = \mathbf{C}\boldsymbol{\Omega}\mathbf{D}$, where $\mathbf{A}, \mathbf{B}, \mathbf{C}, \mathbf{D}$ are independent of **S**. Then we have asymptotically

$$E(\partial^2 F/\partial\mu_{gh}\,\partial\nu_{ij}) = (\mathbf{A}\boldsymbol{\Sigma}^{-1}\mathbf{C}')_{gi}\,(\mathbf{B}'\boldsymbol{\Sigma}^{-1}\mathbf{D})_{hj} + (\mathbf{A}\boldsymbol{\Sigma}^{-1}\mathbf{D})_{gj}\,(\mathbf{B}'\boldsymbol{\Sigma}^{-1}\mathbf{C}')_{hi}\,. \quad \text{(A14)}$$

Proof. Writing $\partial F/\partial\mu_{gh} = a_{g\alpha}\omega_{\alpha\beta}b_{\beta h}$ and $\partial F/\partial\nu_{ij} = c_{i\mu}\omega_{\mu\nu}d_{\nu j}$, where it is assumed that every repeated subscript is to be summed over, we have (cf. Kendall & Stuart, 1961, Eq. 18.57)

$$E(\partial^2 F/\partial\mu_{gh}\,\partial\nu_{ij}) = (N - 1)\,E(\partial F/\partial\mu_{gh}\,\partial F/\partial\nu_{ij}) = (N - 1)\,E(a_{g\alpha}\omega_{\alpha\beta}b_{\beta h}c_{i\mu}\omega_{\mu\nu}d_{\nu j})$$
$$= (N - 1)\,a_{g\alpha}b_{\beta h}c_{i\mu}d_{\nu j}E(\omega_{\alpha\beta}\omega_{\mu\nu}) = a_{g\alpha}b_{\beta h}c_{i\mu}d_{\nu j}(\sigma^{\alpha\mu}\sigma^{\beta\nu} + \sigma^{\alpha\nu}\sigma^{\beta\mu})$$
$$= (a_{g\alpha}\sigma^{\alpha\mu}c_{i\mu})(b_{\beta h}\sigma^{\beta\nu}d_{\nu j}) + (a_{g\alpha}\sigma^{\alpha\nu}d_{\nu j})(b_{\beta h}\sigma^{\beta\mu}c_{i\mu})$$
$$= (\mathbf{A}\boldsymbol{\Sigma}^{-1}\mathbf{C}')_{gi}\,(\mathbf{B}'\boldsymbol{\Sigma}^{-1}\mathbf{D})_{hj} + (\mathbf{A}\boldsymbol{\Sigma}^{-1}\mathbf{D})_{gj}\,(\mathbf{B}'\boldsymbol{\Sigma}^{-1}\mathbf{C}')_{hi}\,.$$

It should be noted that the theorem is quite general in that both **M** and **N** may be row or column vectors or scalars and **M** and **N** may be identical in which case, of course, $\mathbf{A} \equiv \mathbf{C}$ and $\mathbf{B} \equiv \mathbf{D}$.

We now show how the above theorem can be applied repeatedly to compute all the elements of the information matrix (12). To do so we write the derivatives (14)–(19) in the form required by the theorem.

Let $\mathbf{A} = \mathbf{B}^{-1}$ and $\mathbf{D} = \mathbf{B}^{-1}\boldsymbol{\Gamma}$, as before, and

$$\mathbf{T}[m \times (m + n)] = [\mathbf{A}' \quad \mathbf{0}] \qquad \text{(A15)}$$

$$\mathbf{P}[(m + n) \times m] = \begin{bmatrix} \mathbf{D}\boldsymbol{\Phi}\mathbf{D}' + \mathbf{A}\boldsymbol{\Psi}\mathbf{A}' \\ \boldsymbol{\Phi}\mathbf{D}' \end{bmatrix} \qquad \text{(A16)}$$

$$\mathbf{Q}[(m + n) \times n] = \begin{pmatrix} \mathbf{D}\boldsymbol{\Phi} \\ \boldsymbol{\Phi} \end{pmatrix} \qquad \text{(A17)}$$

$$\mathbf{R}[(m + n) \times n] = \begin{pmatrix} \mathbf{D} \\ \mathbf{I} \end{pmatrix}. \qquad \text{(A18)}$$

Then it is readily verified that

$$\partial F/\partial \mathbf{B} = -\mathbf{T}\Omega\mathbf{P} \tag{A19}$$

$$\partial F/\partial \mathbf{\Gamma} = \mathbf{T}\Omega\mathbf{Q} \tag{A20}$$

$$\partial F/\partial \mathbf{\Phi} = \tfrac{1}{2}\mathbf{R}'\Omega\mathbf{R} \tag{A21}$$

$$\partial F/\partial \mathbf{\Psi} = \tfrac{1}{2}\mathbf{T}\Omega\mathbf{T}' \tag{A22}$$

$$\partial F/\partial \mathbf{\Theta} = \Omega\mathbf{\Theta}. \tag{A23}$$

In the last equation we have combined (18) and (19) using

$$\mathbf{\Theta} = \begin{pmatrix} \mathbf{\Theta}_\delta & \mathbf{O} \\ \mathbf{O} & \mathbf{\Theta}_\epsilon \end{pmatrix}.$$

A3.   MATRIX DERIVATIVES OF FUNCTION F IN SECTION 5

The function is defined by

$$2F = \log |\,\mathbf{\Psi}\,| - \log |\,\mathbf{B}\,|^2, \tag{A24}$$

where

$$\mathbf{\Psi} = \mathbf{B}\mathbf{S}_{yy}\mathbf{B}' - \mathbf{B}\mathbf{S}_{yx}\mathbf{\Gamma}' - \mathbf{\Gamma}\mathbf{S}_{xy}\mathbf{B}' + \mathbf{\Gamma}\mathbf{S}_{xx}\mathbf{\Gamma}'. \tag{A25}$$

It is convenient to express the results in terms of the matrices

$$\mathbf{U} = \mathbf{B}\mathbf{S}_{yy} - \mathbf{\Gamma}\mathbf{S}_{xy}, \tag{A26}$$

$$\mathbf{V} = \mathbf{\Gamma}\mathbf{S}_{xx} - \mathbf{B}\mathbf{S}_{yx}. \tag{A27}$$

One then finds immediately that

$$\begin{aligned} d\mathbf{\Psi} &= d\mathbf{B}\,\mathbf{S}_{yy}\mathbf{B}' + \mathbf{B}\mathbf{S}_{yy}\,d\mathbf{B}' - d\mathbf{B}\,\mathbf{S}_{yx}\mathbf{\Gamma}' - \mathbf{B}\mathbf{S}_{yx}\,d\mathbf{\Gamma}' \\ &\quad - d\mathbf{\Gamma}\,\mathbf{S}_{xy}\mathbf{B}' - \mathbf{\Gamma}\mathbf{S}_{xy}\,d\mathbf{B}' + d\mathbf{\Gamma}\,\mathbf{S}_{xx}\mathbf{\Gamma}' + \mathbf{\Gamma}\mathbf{S}_{xx}\,d\mathbf{\Gamma}' \\ &= d\mathbf{B}\,\mathbf{U}' + \mathbf{U}\,d\mathbf{B}' + d\mathbf{\Gamma}\,\mathbf{V}' + \mathbf{V}\,d\mathbf{\Gamma}'. \end{aligned} \tag{A28}$$

Hence

$$\begin{aligned} 2dF &= \mathrm{tr}(\mathbf{\Psi}^{-1}\,d\mathbf{\Psi}) - 2\,\mathrm{tr}(\mathbf{B}'^{-1}\,d\mathbf{B}') \\ &= \mathrm{tr}(\mathbf{\Psi}^{-1}\,d\mathbf{B}\,\mathbf{U}' + \mathbf{\Psi}^{-1}\mathbf{U}\,d\mathbf{B}' + \mathbf{\Psi}^{-1}\,d\mathbf{\Gamma}\,\mathbf{V}' + \mathbf{\Psi}^{-1}\mathbf{V}\,d\mathbf{\Gamma}' - 2\mathbf{B}'^{-1}\,d\mathbf{B}') \\ &= 2\,\mathrm{tr}[(\mathbf{\Psi}^{-1}\mathbf{U} - \mathbf{B}'^{-1})\,d\mathbf{B}'] + 2\,\mathrm{tr}(\mathbf{\Psi}^{-1}\mathbf{V}\,d\mathbf{\Gamma}'). \end{aligned}$$

The derivatives of F are therefore given by

$$\partial F/\partial \mathbf{B} = \mathbf{\Psi}^{-1}\mathbf{U} - \mathbf{B}'^{-1} \tag{A29}$$

$$\partial F/\partial \mathbf{\Gamma} = \mathbf{\Psi}^{-1}\mathbf{V} \tag{A30}$$

which are the same as in (36) and (37).

A4. SECOND-ORDER DERIVATIVES AND INFORMATION MATRIX FOR THE MODEL OF SECTION 5

Denoting the matrix derivatives in (A29) and (A30) by $\mathbf{X}$ and $\mathbf{Y}$ respectively, the second-order derivatives are obtained by differentiating $\mathbf{X}$ and $\mathbf{Y}$. We have first

$$d\mathbf{U} = d\mathbf{B}\,\mathbf{S}_{yy} - d\mathbf{\Gamma}\,\mathbf{S}_{xy} \tag{A31}$$

$$d\mathbf{V} = d\mathbf{\Gamma}\,\mathbf{S}_{xx} - d\mathbf{B}\,\mathbf{S}_{yx} \; ; \tag{A32}$$

and secondly from (A28), (A31), and (A32)

$$
\begin{aligned}
d\mathbf{X} &= \mathbf{\Psi}^{-1}\,d\mathbf{U} + d\mathbf{\Psi}^{-1}\,\mathbf{U} - d\mathbf{B}'^{-1} \\
&= \mathbf{\Psi}^{-1}\,d\mathbf{B}\,\mathbf{S}_{yy} - \mathbf{\Psi}^{-1}\mathbf{U}\,d\mathbf{B}'\,\mathbf{\Psi}^{-1}\mathbf{U} - \mathbf{\Psi}^{-1}\,d\mathbf{B}\,\mathbf{U}'\mathbf{\Psi}^{-1}\mathbf{U} \\
&\quad + \mathbf{B}'^{-1}\,d\mathbf{B}'\,\mathbf{B}'^{-1} - \mathbf{\Psi}^{-1}\,d\mathbf{\Gamma}\,\mathbf{S}_{xy} - \mathbf{\Psi}^{-1}\mathbf{V}\,d\mathbf{\Gamma}\,\mathbf{\Psi}^{-1}\mathbf{U} - \mathbf{\Psi}^{-1}\,d\mathbf{\Gamma}\,\mathbf{V}'\mathbf{\Psi}^{-1}\mathbf{U} \\
d\mathbf{Y} &= \mathbf{\Psi}^{-1}\,d\mathbf{V} + d\mathbf{\Psi}^{-1}\,\mathbf{V} = \mathbf{\Psi}^{-1}\,d\mathbf{\Gamma}\,\mathbf{S}_{xx} - \mathbf{\Psi}^{-1}\mathbf{V}\,d\mathbf{\Gamma}'\,\mathbf{\Psi}^{-1}\mathbf{V} - \mathbf{\Psi}^{-1}\,d\mathbf{\Gamma}\,\mathbf{V}'\mathbf{\Psi}^{-1}\mathbf{V} \\
&\quad - \mathbf{\Psi}^{-1}\,d\mathbf{B}\,\mathbf{S}_{yx} - \mathbf{\Psi}^{-1}\mathbf{U}\,d\mathbf{B}'\,\mathbf{\Psi}^{-1}\mathbf{V} - \mathbf{\Psi}^{-1}\,d\mathbf{B}\,\mathbf{U}'\mathbf{\Psi}^{-1}\mathbf{V}.
\end{aligned}
$$

From these results the second-order derivatives are obtained as

$$\partial^2 F/\partial\beta_{gh}\partial\beta_{ij} = \psi^{gi}s_{jh}^{yy} - (\mathbf{\Psi}^{-1}\mathbf{U})_{gj}\,(\mathbf{\Psi}^{-1}\mathbf{U})_{ih} - \psi^{gi}(\mathbf{U}'\mathbf{\Psi}^{-1}\mathbf{U})_{jh} + \beta^{jg}\beta^{hi} \tag{A33}$$

$$\partial^2 F/\partial\beta_{gh}\partial\gamma_{mn} = -\psi^{gm}s_{nh}^{xy} - (\mathbf{\Psi}^{-1}\mathbf{V})_{gn}\,(\mathbf{\Psi}^{-1}\mathbf{U})_{mh} - \psi^{gm}(\mathbf{V}'\mathbf{\Psi}^{-1}\mathbf{U})_{nh} \tag{A34}$$

$$\partial^2 F/\partial\gamma_{kl}\partial\gamma_{mn} = \psi^{km}s_{nl}^{xx} - (\mathbf{\Psi}^{-1}\mathbf{V})_{kn}\,(\mathbf{\Psi}^{-1}\mathbf{V})_{ml} - \psi^{km}(\mathbf{V}'\mathbf{\Psi}^{-1}\mathbf{V})_{nl}\,. \tag{A35}$$

The information matrix may be obtained by taking the probability limits of these second-order derivatives. In doing so we shall make use of the following well-known result (see e.g., Wilks, 1962, p. 103): If $\mathbf{C} = (c_{ij})$ is a matrix whose elements are continuous functions of random variables $x_1, x_2, ..., x_m$ and if $\mathrm{plim}\,x_k = \xi_k$ exists and is finite for all k, then $\mathrm{plim}\,\mathbf{C}(\mathbf{x}) = \mathbf{C}(\xi)$. Moreover, $\mathrm{plim}(\mathbf{AB}) = (\mathrm{plim}\,\mathbf{A})(\mathrm{plim}\,\mathbf{B})$ if $\mathbf{A}$ and $\mathbf{B}$ are matrices with finite probability limits. In what follows, $\mathbf{B}$, $\mathbf{\Gamma}$, and $\mathbf{\Psi}$ denote the true population values as distinguished from the mathematical variables used previously. From (30) it follows that

$$E(\mathbf{yx}' \mid \mathbf{x}) = \mathbf{\Pi}\mathbf{xx}', \qquad E(\mathbf{yy}' \mid \mathbf{x}) = \mathbf{\Pi}\mathbf{xx}'\mathbf{\Pi}' + E(\mathbf{u}^*\mathbf{u}^{*\prime} \mid \mathbf{x}),$$

so that

$$E(\mathbf{S}_{yx} \mid \mathbf{S}_{xx}) = \mathbf{\Pi}\mathbf{S}_{xx}\,, \qquad E(\mathbf{S}_{yy} \mid \mathbf{S}_{xx}) = \mathbf{\Pi}\mathbf{S}_{xx}\mathbf{\Pi}' + \mathbf{\Psi}^*,$$

where $\mathbf{\Pi} = \mathbf{B}^{-1}\mathbf{\Gamma}$ and $\mathbf{\Psi}^* = \mathbf{B}^{-1}\mathbf{\Psi}\mathbf{B}'^{-1}$, as before. Let plim $\mathbf{S}_{xx} = \mathbf{\Phi}$. Then we have

$$\text{plim } \mathbf{S}_{yx} = \mathbf{\Pi}\mathbf{\Phi}, \tag{A36}$$

$$\text{plim } \mathbf{S}_{yy} = \mathbf{\Pi}\mathbf{\Phi}\mathbf{\Pi}' + \mathbf{\Psi}^*. \tag{A37}$$

Furthermore, from (A26) and (A27) we have

$$\text{plim } \mathbf{U} = \mathbf{\Psi}\mathbf{B}'^{-1}, \qquad \text{plim } \mathbf{V} = 0,$$

so that $\text{plim}(\mathbf{\Psi}^{-1}\mathbf{U}) = \mathbf{B}'^{-1}$, $\text{plim}(\mathbf{U}'\mathbf{\Psi}^{-1}\mathbf{U}) = \mathbf{\Psi}^*$, $\text{plim}(\mathbf{\Psi}^{-1}\mathbf{V}) = 0$, $\text{plim}(\mathbf{V}'\mathbf{\Psi}^{-1}\mathbf{V}) = 0$, and $\text{plim}(\mathbf{U}'\mathbf{\Psi}^{-1}\mathbf{V}) = 0$. From these results we find the probability limits of the second-order derivatives to be

$$\text{plim } \partial^2 F/\partial\beta_{gh} \, \partial\beta_{ij} = \psi^{gi}(\mathbf{\Pi}\mathbf{\Phi}\mathbf{\Pi}')_{jh}, \tag{A38}$$

$$\text{plim } \partial^2 F/\partial\beta_{gh} \, \partial\gamma_{mn} = -\psi^{gm}(\mathbf{\Pi}\mathbf{\Phi})_{hn}, \tag{A39}$$

$$\text{plim } \partial^2 F/\partial\gamma_{kl} \, \partial\gamma_{mn} = \psi^{km}\phi_{nl}. \tag{A40}$$

These results may be written in compact form as (cf. Rothenberg & Leenders, 1964, Eq. 4.26):

$$\text{plim } \partial^2 F/\partial\lambda \, \partial\lambda' = \mathbf{\Psi}^{-1} \otimes \begin{pmatrix} \mathbf{\Pi} \\ \mathbf{I} \end{pmatrix} \mathbf{\Phi}(\mathbf{\Pi}', \mathbf{I}) \tag{A41}$$

where $\otimes$ denotes the Kronecker product.

Acknowledgments

This research has been supported in part by grant NSF-GB-12959 from the National Science Foundation. The author wishes to thank Dr. Michael Browne for his comments on an earlier draft of the paper, and Marielle van Thillo, who wrote the computer programs, checked the mathematical derivations, and gave other valuable assistance throughout the work.

6

A Simple Modification of the Two-Stage Least-Squares Procedure for Undersized Samples

HENRI THEIL

1. The Problem

Consider a complete linear system of L simultaneous structural equations and write n for the number of observations on each of the $K + L$ variables, where K is the number of predetermined variables and L that of the jointly dependent variables. The jth equation is written as

$$y_j = Y_j \gamma_j + X_j \beta_j + \epsilon_j \,, \tag{1}$$

where y_j is the n-element column vector of values taken by the dependent variable whose behavior is described by the equation; Y_j is the $n \times L_j$ matrix of values taken by the L_j variables that are jointly dependent in the system but explanatory variables in the jth equation; X_j is the $n \times K_j$ matrix of values taken by the K_j predetermined variables occurring in this equation; γ_j and β_j are unknown parameter vectors consisting of L_j and K_j elements, respectively; ϵ_j is a random disturbance vector which is postulated to have zero mean and a scalar covariance matrix:

$$E(\epsilon_j) = 0 \quad \text{and} \quad E(\epsilon_j \epsilon_j') = \sigma_{jj} I \quad (0 < \sigma_{jj} < \infty). \tag{2}$$

113

Here σ_{jj} is the variance of the disturbances of the jth equation and I the $n \times n$ identity matrix.

A useful alternative notation is

$$y_j = Z_j \delta_j + \epsilon_j , \tag{3}$$

where

$$Z_j = [Y_j \ X_j], \qquad \delta_j = \begin{bmatrix} \gamma_j \\ \beta_j \end{bmatrix}, \qquad N_j = K_j + L_j , \tag{4}$$

N_j being the number of columns of Z_j and the number of rows of δ_j .

Write X for the $n \times K$ matrix of values taken by all K predetermined variables of the system and premultiply (3) by the transpose of X:

$$X'y_j = X'Z_j \delta_j + X'\epsilon_j . \tag{5}$$

Assume that all predetermined variables are purely exogenous. This is a restrictive assumption which is relaxed in the Appendix; it is made here because it enables us to treat the elements of X as fixed numbers. The vector $X'\epsilon_j$ has then zero mean and covariance matrix $\sigma_{jj}X'X$. The two-stage least-squares (2SLS) estimator of δ_j , written d_j , is obtained from (5) by applying Aitken's theorem on the basis of this covariance matrix:

$$Z_j'X(X'X)^{-1} X'y_j = Z_j'X(X'X)^{-1} X'Z_j d_j . \tag{6}$$

The estimator d_j does not exist when $K < N_j$, because (5) then consists of fewer equations than there are elements of δ_j to be estimated. The jth structural equation is then underidentified. The estimator does exist when $X'Z_j$ has rank N_j , which requires $K \geqslant N_j$, provided that X has full column rank (i.e., rank K). But if the rank of X is less than K, the matrix $X'X$ is singular, so that it is impossible to obtain d_j from (6).

The rank of X is *always* less than K when there are fewer observations than predetermined variables in the system ($n < K$), in which case the sample is said to be *undersized*. Thus the 2SLS estimator does not exist when $K < N_j$, because the equation is then underidentified, or when the sample is undersized ($K > n$). The latter possibility is much more serious in practice because it occurs so much more frequently. In econometrics, almost all large models and many medium-sized models (including, for example, the Klein–Goldberger model) have the number of predetermined variables exceeding the number of observations. The problem is not confined to 2SLS estimation. Limited-information maximum-likelihood also uses the inverse of $X'X$; full-information methods such as three-stage least-squares and linearized maximum-likelihood use 2SLS estimates as basic ingredients and are hence inapplicable when 2SLS is not applicable.

The next section contains a brief description of previous attempts to solve the problem. The motivation for this chapter is not only a certain degree of dissatisfaction regarding the results of these attempts, but also the uneasy feeling that it just does not seem reasonable that the use of (5) for the estimation of δ_j should cause difficulties when it consists of too many equations ($K > n$). A priori one would expect troubles when there are too few instead of too many. The procedure proposed is described in intuitive terms in Sections 3–5 and applied numerically in Section 6; the Appendix contains derivations.

2. Previous Attempts to Solve the Problem

The earlier work in this area can be arranged conveniently under four headings.

1. Perhaps the most natural procedure is to apply to (5) a generalization of Aitken's theorem based on a singular covariance matrix $\sigma_{jj}X'X$. This approach was pursued by Swamy & Holmes (1971), but it turns out that this is simply equivalent to a least-squares regression of y_j on Z_j. It is perhaps tempting to consider this result as a justification of the simple least-squares method in the case of undersized samples, but this is not entirely satisfactory. The reason is that Aitken's theorem and its generalization are not fully applicable to (5) because $X'Z_j$ contains $X'Y_j$ as a submatrix, which is correlated with the disturbance vector $X'\epsilon_j$. This correlation is of no concern for large n, but it should cause concern when the sample is undersized.

2. The first attempt to solve the problem, by Kloek & Mennes (1960), replaces certain columns of X by principal components of predetermined variables. A major disadvantage of this procedure is its several sources of arbitrariness. One is the number of components to be used; another is the choice of the normalization rule on the variables that is required for the computation of the principal components; a third is the question of whether these components should refer to all predetermined variables of the system or only to those which are excluded from the equation estimated.

3. Another procedure, proposed by Fisher (1965), is based on causal orderings within the equation system. A disadvantage of this method is that it is difficult to apply without a rather extensive prior knowledge of the system.

4. Finally, there are iterative methods (or truncated iterative methods) which go back and forth between the structural equations and the reduced form of the equation system. The relevant references include Klein (1970) and Mosbaek & Wold (1970).

It is important to note that the procedures 3 and 4 are not really "limited-information" methods in the sense that the only specifications required are that of the equation estimated plus the list of all predetermined variables in the system as a whole. Both 3 and 4 require knowledge of which variables occur in each equation, for any equation to be estimated. In comparison, the 2SLS method—and also the first two procedures listed above—have not only the virtue of conceptual and computational simplicity, but also the merit of being invariant under specification errors in equations other than the one that is estimated. The objective of this chapter is to describe an estimator for undersized samples which is (i) simple and straightforward in application, (ii) not subject to the arbitrariness which characterizes the principal component procedure, and (iii) of the limited-information type as described above.

3. A Class of Estimators for Undersized Samples

Additional insight into the 2SLS procedure is obtained by writing the N_j estimation equations (6) in the notation of (1):

$$\begin{bmatrix} Y_j'X(X'X)^{-1}X'y_j \\ X_j'y_j \end{bmatrix} = \begin{bmatrix} Y_j'X(X'X)^{-1}X'Y_j & Y_j'X_j \\ X_j'Y_j & X_j'X_j \end{bmatrix} \begin{bmatrix} c_j \\ b_j \end{bmatrix}, \qquad (7)$$

where

$$\begin{bmatrix} c_j \\ b_j \end{bmatrix} = d_j \quad \text{is the 2SLS estimator of} \quad \begin{bmatrix} \gamma_j \\ \beta_j \end{bmatrix} = \delta_j .$$

The N_j estimation equations are thus partitioned into two subsets, the first containing L_j and the second K_j equations. It is important for what follows to consider these two subsets separately.

The second subset takes the form

$$X_j'y_j = X_j'[Y_j \quad X_j]\begin{bmatrix} c_j \\ b_j \end{bmatrix} = X_j'Z_jd_j , \qquad (8)$$

which clearly shows that this subset does not involve the (singular or nonsingular) matrix $X'X$ at all. As a matter of fact, (8) is a set of estimation equations which is common to all limited-information estimators of the k-class type, including limited-information maximum-likelihood and least-squares regression of y_j on Z_j. Also, (8) guarantees that if the jth equation is "in reduced form" $(L_j = 0)$, the estimator is simply that of least squares, as one would expect it to be: $X_j'y_j = X_j'X_jb_j$. These are cogent reasons for retaining (8). We shall therefore impose

$$X_j'y_j = X_j'Z_jd_j^*, \tag{9}$$

where d_j^* is the estimator of δ_j that will be proposed. In other words, we shall use (8) to estimate β_j from

$$b_j = (X_j'X_j)^{-1}(X_j'y_j - X_j'Y_jc_j).$$

This estimation is possible once the γ_j estimator has been defined, provided that X_j has full column rank. This proviso requires

$$n \geqslant K_j. \tag{10}$$

The first subset of (7) consisting of L_j equations involves $(X'X)^{-1}$ and is therefore the "controversial subset" of the 2SLS estimation equations. Note that $(X'X)^{-1}X'$, which occurs on both sides of the equation, is the matrix that generates the least-squares coefficients of the reduced-form equations. Given that the number of degrees of freedom available for the estimation of the reduced form is negative when the sample is undersized, it seems preferable to bypass the reduced form for the estimation of a structural equation. To make further progress, we partition X as

$$X = [X_j \quad \bar{X}_j] \tag{11}$$

so that $\bar{X}_j$ is the $n \times (K - K_j)$ matrix of values taken by the $K - K_j$ predetermined variables that are excluded from the jth structural equation. Equation (5) may then be considered as consisting of two components:

$$X_j'y_j = X_j'Z_j\delta_j + X_j'\epsilon_j, \tag{12}$$

which is the population counterpart of (9), and

$$\bar{X}_j'y_j = \bar{X}_j'Z_j\delta_j + \bar{X}_j'\epsilon_j. \tag{13}$$

The disturbance vector $\bar{X}_j'\epsilon_j$ of (13) consists of $K - K_j$ elements and it has zero mean and covariance matrix $\sigma_{jj}\bar{X}_j'\bar{X}_j$ when the predetermined variables are exogenous. This covariance matrix is singular when

$$n < K - K_j, \tag{14}$$

so that we still face the same problem.

To solve this dilemma it is appropriate to realize that the standard properties of the 2SLS estimator are asymptotic. Therefore, what really counts for these properties as far as the second moments of the predetermined variables are concerned is the behavior of $n^{-1}X'X$ for large n. It is typically assumed that this matrix converges to a positive definite matrix as $n \to \infty$, so that the same is true for $n^{-1}\bar{X}_j'\bar{X}_j$ and the singularity problem described below (13) ceases to exist for large n. But if (14) is true, the matrix $n^{-1}\bar{X}_j'\bar{X}_j$ is a poor approximation of its own limit for $n \to \infty$; the singularity is just one aspect of the low quality of this approximation. This suggests that it is better not to rely on Aitken's theorem on the basis of the covariance matrix $\sigma_{jj}\bar{X}_j'\bar{X}_j$, which is impossible anyhow under (14), but to replace this matrix by $\sigma_{jj}D_j$, where D_j is some positive definite matrix consisting of $K - K_j$ rows and columns. At this stage we provide no further specifications on D_j, so that a class of estimators (which may be called the D_j-class) will be derived. Thus, for any given D_j, the estimator d_j* is obtained by minimizing, subject to (9), the quadratic form

$$Q(d_j*) = (\bar{X}_j'y_j - \bar{X}_j'Z_jd_j*)' \, D_j^{-1}(\bar{X}_j'y_j - \bar{X}_j'Z_jd_j*)$$
$$= (y_j - Z_jd_j*)' \, C_j(y_j - Z_jd_j*), \tag{15}$$

where

$$C_j = \bar{X}_jD_j^{-1}\bar{X}_j'. \tag{16}$$

To find d_j* we form the Lagrangian function,

$$F(d_j*, \lambda_j) = \tfrac{1}{2}Q(d_j*) - \lambda_j'(X_j'y_j - X_j'Z_jd_j*)$$
$$= -y_j'C_jZ_jd_j* + \tfrac{1}{2}d_j*'Z_j'C_jZ_jd_j* - \lambda_j'(X_j'y_j - X_j'Z_jd_j*) + \text{const.,} \tag{17}$$

where λ_j is a column consisting of K_j Lagrangian multipliers. Differentiating $F(\cdot)$ with respect to d_j* and equating the result to zero gives

$$-Z_j'C_jy_j + Z_j'C_jZ_jd_j* + Z_j'X_j\lambda_j = 0.$$

We combine this equation with (9) to obtain

$$\begin{bmatrix} Z_j'C_jZ_j & Z_j'X_j \\ X_j'Z_j & 0 \end{bmatrix}\begin{bmatrix} d_j* \\ \lambda_j \end{bmatrix} = \begin{bmatrix} Z_j'C_jy_j \\ X_j'y_j \end{bmatrix}, \tag{18}$$

from which d_j* can be solved if the square matrix on the left is non-singular.

Note that $d_j{}^*$ does not require X to have full column rank; the inverse of $X'X$ plays no role at all. The existence of $d_j{}^*$ requires only that the left-hand square matrix in (18), which has $N_j + K_j = 2K_j + L_j$ rows and columns, be nonsingular. It is shown in the next paragraph that this is the case when $X'Z_j$ has full column rank (i.e., rank N_j). This is a weak condition, asymptotically equivalent to the rank condition of identification, which is also required for the solution of the 2SLS estimator d_j from (6).

The left-hand matrix in (18) is singular if and only if

$$\begin{bmatrix} Z_j'C_jZ_j & Z_j'X_j \\ X_j'Z_j & 0 \end{bmatrix}\begin{bmatrix} a_j \\ b_j \end{bmatrix} = 0,$$

or, equivalently, if and only if

$$Z_j'C_jZ_ja_j + Z_j'X_jb_j = 0 \qquad (19)$$

and

$$X_j'Z_ja_j = 0 \qquad (20)$$

hold for two vectors a_j and b_j consisting of N_j and K_j elements, respectively, which are not both zero vectors. Premultiplication of (19) by a_j' gives

$$a_j'Z_j'C_jZ_ja_j + a_j'Z_j'X_jb_j = 0,$$

which implies $a_j'Z_j'C_jZ_ja_j = 0$ because of (20). Application of (16) shows that this is equivalent to

$$(\bar{X}_j'Z_ja_j)' \, D_j^{-1}(\bar{X}_j'Z_ja_j) = 0,$$

implying $\bar{X}_j'Z_ja_j = 0$ because D_j and hence also D_j^{-1} are positive definite. We combine this result with (20) to conclude that $X'Z_ja_j = 0$, and hence $a_j = 0$ because $X'Z_j$ has full column rank by assumption. Thus, singularity of the left-hand matrix in (18) requires, in view of (19), $Z_j'X_jb_j = 0$ for some $b_j \neq 0$. This amounts to

$$\begin{bmatrix} Y_j' \\ X_j' \end{bmatrix} X_jb_j = \begin{bmatrix} Y_j'X_jb_j \\ X_j'X_jb_j \end{bmatrix} = \begin{bmatrix} 0 \\ 0 \end{bmatrix} \qquad \text{for some} \quad b_j \neq 0,$$

which implies singularity of $X_j'X_j$, and hence that the columns of X_j are linearly dependent. (Note that there cannot be such a linear dependence if X_j has full column rank [see the discussion above (10)].) But if the columns of X_j are linearly dependent, so are those of $Z_j = [Y_j \ X_j]$, which contradicts the assumption that $X'Z_j$ has full column rank. Therefore, this assumption does guarantee that $d_j{}^*$ can be solved from (18).

4. A Particularly Simple Estimator

Any special estimator of the D_j-class is obtained by choosing a particular matrix D_j. The two main considerations for this choice problem are simplicity and statistical efficiency. This is fully comparable with the classical theory of simultaneous equation estimation in which all k-class estimators with $n^{1/2}(k - 1)$ converging to zero have the same asymptotic distribution, the case $k = 1$ (2SLS) dominating all others as far as simplicity is concerned.

We know that $D_j = \bar{X}_j'\bar{X}_j$ is not a feasible specification when (14) holds, and we also know that $n^{-1}\bar{X}_j'\bar{X}_j$ is an unsatisfactory approximation of its own probability limit when n is not large. Nevertheless, given that the covariance matrix of $\bar{X}_j'\epsilon_j$ of (13) is $\sigma_{jj}\bar{X}_j'\bar{X}_j$ when the predetermined variables are exogenous, it is clearly desirable to specify D_j so that it has certain features in common with $\bar{X}_j'\bar{X}_j$, but obviously subject to the constraint that D_j be nonsingular. The most straightforward approach is to choose for D_j the $(K - K_j) \times (K - K_j)$ diagonal matrix whose diagonal coincides with that of $\bar{X}_j'\bar{X}_j$. The criterion function (15) then agrees with Aitken's theorem as far as the variances of the disturbance vector $\bar{X}_j'\epsilon_j$ of (13) are concerned. There is no agreement for the covariances, but these are precisely the source of the singularity complication. If we write x_h for the hth column of X, this choice of D_j implies the following specification of C_j in (15)–(18):

$$C_j = \sum_h (1/x_h'x_h)\, x_h x_h' \tag{21}$$

where the summation is over the subscripts of all predetermined variables that are excluded from the jth equation.

A method proposed by Boudon (1968) has some similarity to the proposal made here but is much cruder. Basically, Boudon suggests writing the K equations (5) in correlation form (by standardizing all variables) and then applying least squares to the resulting K "observations" in order to estimate δ_j. In the special case considered by him this leads to an estimator which is inferior to the least-squares estimator; see Goldberger (1970a).

In summary, both the 2SLS estimator d_j and the special estimator $d_j{}^*$ proposed above are based on the K equations that constitute the vector equation (5). This vector equation is partitioned into two parts, (12) and (13), and both d_j and $d_j{}^*$ use (12) in identically the same way (by requiring that the residual vector be orthogonal to each column of X_j). The difference between d_j and $d_j{}^*$ is confined to the use of the

$K - K_j$ equations that constitute (13). The approach of d_j is preferable for large n, but not feasible when the sample is undersized.

5. Asymptotic Variances and Covariances

The asymptotic distribution of an estimator is typically used for two different purposes: as a substantially correct description of the sampling variability of the estimator when the sample is so large that there is virtually no difference between the actual and the asymptotic distributions, and as a crude (but one hopes not too bad) approximation of the actual sampling distribution when the sample is of medium size. It is appropriate to make this explicit distinction here because what follows has no real merits for the first purpose. The reason is that when n is sufficiently large, the problem discussed in this chapter does not exist. The analyst will then prefer the 2SLS estimator to our $d_j{}^*$.

To find the sampling error of $d_j{}^*$ we substitute $Z_j \delta_j + \epsilon_j$ for y_j in the right-hand side of (18), obtaining

$$\begin{bmatrix} Z_j'C_jZ_j\delta_j + Z_j'C_j\epsilon_j \\ X_j'Z_j\delta_j + X_j'\epsilon_j \end{bmatrix} = \begin{bmatrix} Z_j'C_jZ_j & Z_j'X_j \\ X_j'Z_j & 0 \end{bmatrix}\begin{bmatrix} \delta_j \\ 0 \end{bmatrix} + \begin{bmatrix} Z_j'C_j\epsilon_j \\ X_j'\epsilon_j \end{bmatrix},$$

which may be combined with (18) as follows:

$$\begin{bmatrix} Z_j'C_jZ_j & Z_j'X_j \\ X_j'Z_j & 0 \end{bmatrix}\begin{bmatrix} d_j{}^* - \delta_j \\ \lambda_j \end{bmatrix} = \begin{bmatrix} Z_j'C_j\epsilon_j \\ X_j'\epsilon_j \end{bmatrix}. \tag{22}$$

If we could regard the matrices Z_j, C_j, and X_j as all consisting of fixed elements, the right-hand vector in (22) would have zero mean and covariance matrix

$$\sigma_{jj}\begin{bmatrix} Z_j'C_j \\ X_j' \end{bmatrix}\begin{bmatrix} C_jZ_j & X_j \end{bmatrix} = \sigma_{jj}\begin{bmatrix} Z_j'C_j^2Z_j & Z_j'C_jX_j \\ X_j'C_jZ_j & X_j'X_j \end{bmatrix},$$

which would imply that the covariance matrix of $d_j{}^*$ is the leading $N_j \times N_j$ submatrix of

$$\sigma_{jj}\begin{bmatrix} Z_j'C_jZ_j & Z_j'X_j \\ X_j'Z_j & 0 \end{bmatrix}^{-1}\begin{bmatrix} Z_j'C_j^2Z_j & Z_j'C_jX_j \\ X_j'C_jZ_j & X_j'X_j \end{bmatrix}\begin{bmatrix} Z_j'C_jZ_j & Z_j'X_j \\ X_j'Z_j & 0 \end{bmatrix}^{-1}. \tag{23}$$

It is not true, however, that we can regard the elements of Z_j, C_j, and X_j as fixed, the reason being that Z_j contains Y_j as a submatrix, and Y_j consists of values taken by jointly dependent variables. But it is shown in the Appendix that the result stated here is at least asymptotically true under classical conditions, $d_j{}^* - \delta_j$ being asymptotically normal with zero mean vector and a covariance matrix equal to the leading $N_j \times N_j$ submatrix of (23). The disturbance variance σ_{jj} is then estimated consistently by the mean square of the corresponding residuals,

$$s_{jj} = (1/n)(y_j - Z_j d_j{}^*)' (y_j - Z_j d_j{}^*), \qquad (24)$$

so that (23) with σ_{jj} replaced by s_{jj} can be used straightforwardly for the computation of asymptotic standard errors.

For the derivation of the asymptotic covariances of coefficients of two different equations, say the jth and the lth, we assume $E(\epsilon_j \epsilon_l{}') = \sigma_{jl} I$, where σ_{jl} is the contemporaneous covariance of the disturbances of the two equations. An analogous derivation shows that the asymptotic covariance matrix of $d_j{}^*$ (column) and $d_l^{*\prime}$ (row) is the leading $N_j \times N_l$ submatrix of

$$\sigma_{jl} \begin{bmatrix} Z_j'C_jZ_j & Z_j'X_j \\ X_j'Z_j & 0 \end{bmatrix}^{-1} \begin{bmatrix} Z_j'C_jC_lZ_l & Z_j'C_jX_l \\ X_j'C_lZ_l & X_j'X_l \end{bmatrix} \begin{bmatrix} Z_l'C_lZ_l & Z_l'X_l \\ X_l'Z_l & 0 \end{bmatrix}^{-1}, \qquad (25)$$

and that σ_{jl} is estimated consistently by the mean product of the two sets of residuals,

$$s_{jl} = (1/n)(y_j - Z_j d_j{}^*)' (y_l - Z_l d_l{}^*). \qquad (26)$$

This result includes that of (23) and (24) as a special case for $j = l$.

6. A Numerical Illustration

The estimation procedure proposed in Section 4 is applied below to Klein's Model I. The sample underlying this model is not undersized ($n = 21$, $K = 8$), but this has the advantage that it is possible to make a numerical comparison with the 2SLS estimates. The model consists of three behavioral equations,

$$C_t = \beta_0 + \beta_1 P_t + \beta_2 P_{t-1} + \beta_3(W_t + W_t') + \epsilon_t \qquad (27)$$

$$I_t = \beta_0' + \beta_1' P_t + \beta_2' P_{t-1} + \beta_3' K_{t-1} + \epsilon_t' \qquad (28)$$

$$W_t = \beta_0'' + \beta_1'' X_t + \beta_2'' X_{t-1} + \beta_3''(t - 1931) + \epsilon_t'', \qquad (29)$$

where t is time measured in calendar years, C consumption, P profits, W the private wage bill, W' the government wage bill, I net investment, K

capital stock at the end of the year, and X the output of the private sector. There are six endogenous variables: C, P, W, I, K, and X; the model is completed by three definitional equations which need not concern us here. There are eight predetermined variables: W', T (business taxes), G (government nonwage expenditure), t (time), 1 (a constant), and three lagged endogenous variables (P_{-1}, K_{-1}, X_{-1}). For the estimation of the consumption function (27) we take $W + W'$ as one endogenous variable.

The estimation procedure requires exclusively sums of squares and products, which are given in Theil (1971, Sections 9.5 and 10.6). The point estimates of the coefficients can then be obtained from (18), those of the variances and contemporaneous covariances from (24) and (26), and the estimated asymptotic sampling variances and covariances from (23) and (25) after σ_{jj} and σ_{jl} are replaced by their estimates. The point estimates of the coefficients and their asymptotic standard errors are shown in Table 1, together with those of 2SLS. The corresponding

TABLE 1

Alternative Estimates of the Coefficients of Klein's Model I

Equation	Variable	Proposed estimator		2SLS	
(27)	1	16.13	(1.3)	16.55	(1.3)
	P	.09	(.17)	.02	(.12)
	P_{-1}	.15	(.14)	.22	(.11)
	$W + W'$	.82	(.04)	.81	(.04)
(28)	1	23.01	(10.7)	20.28	(7.5)
	P	.06	(.29)	.15	(.17)
	P_{-1}	.69	(.26)	.62	(.16)
	K_{-1}	−.17	(.05)	−.16	(.04)
(29)	1	1.51	(1.2)	1.50	(1.1)
	X	.44	(.08)	.44	(.04)
	X_{-1}	.15	(.08)	.15	(.04)
	$t − 1931$	.13	(.03)	.13	(.03)

point estimates are mostly close to each other, but the asymptotic standard errors of the proposed estimator tend to be larger, particularly those of coefficients belonging to the same variable in current and lagged form: P and P_{-1} in (27) and (28), and X and X_{-1} in (29). It is quite possible that the 2SLS standard errors present an overly optimistic picture of the reliability of such estimates, which may be argued as

124   HENRI THEIL

follows. These standard errors are obtained by multiplying the 2SLS
estimate of σ_{jj} by the inverse of

$$\begin{bmatrix} Y_j'Y_j - U_j'U_j & Y_j'X_j \\ X_j'Y_j & X_j'X_j \end{bmatrix},$$ (30)

and then taking square roots of the diagonal elements. In (30), U_j is
the matrix of residuals of the least-squares regressions of Y_j on X.
When there are only 21 observations, these regressions on eight variables
will tend to "overfit." The diagonal elements of $U_j'U_j$ will then be
too small relative to those that would be obtained if we had the true
reduced-form disturbances. This raises the diagonal elements in the
leading submatrix of (30), which in turn leads to smaller elements of
this matrix after inversion, and hence to standard errors that are
optimistically but not realistically small.

The estimates of the variances and contemporaneous covariances of
the disturbances are shown below, and the estimated asymptotic
covariance matrix is given in Table 2.

Proposed estimator   2SLS

$$\begin{bmatrix} .91 & .37 & -.39 \\ & 1.72 & .22 \\ & & .48 \end{bmatrix} \qquad \begin{bmatrix} 1.04 & .44 & -.39 \\ & 1.38 & .19 \\ & & .48 \end{bmatrix} \begin{matrix} (\epsilon) \\ (\epsilon') \\ (\epsilon'') \end{matrix}$$

Appendix

Our starting point is a set of assumptions and some convergence
results described by Theil (1971, Section 10.1). They involve an $n \times L$
random matrix Y consisting of values taken by L jointly dependent
variables. The equation system is written in the form

$$Y\Gamma + XB = E \qquad (A1)$$

where X is an $n \times K$ matrix of values taken by K predetermined
variables, E is an $n \times L$ matrix of disturbances, and Γ and B are
unknown parameter matrices of order $L \times L$ and $K \times L$, respectively.
It is assumed that Γ is nonsingular and that the n rows of E are
independent random drawings from an L-dimensional population with
zero mean vector, an unknown covariance matrix Σ, and finite moments
of every order.

TABLE 2

ESTIMATED ASYMPTOTIC COVARIANCE MATRIX OF THE PROPOSED COEFFICIENT ESTIMATES OF KLEIN'S MODEL I [a]

	Equation (27)				Equation (28)				Equation (29)			
	10	P	P_{-1}	$W+W'$	10	P	P_{-1}	K_{-1}	10	X	X_{-1}	$t-1931$
10	170.0	−60.7	287.5	−27.3	282.7	−63.5	37.2	−11.7	−52.2	−6.2	15.1	7.5
P		32.5	−210.7	−19.2	56.0	−1.5	2.3	−2.9	−25.7	29.7	−26.3	−6.8
P_{-1}			198.3	−.3	61.0	−28.2	35.4	−3.6	50.1	−19.4	11.5	14.0
$W+W'$				14.5	−114.6	27.1	−23.8	5.4	2.8	−2.9	2.5	−4.5
10					11343.7	−2532.4	2154.0	−528.0	48.9	−8.3	.3	−55.3
P						821.7	−705.7	114.7	−3.2	12.0	−11.9	12.2
P_{-1}							660.5	−101.9	−15.2	−10.5	13.5	−12.8
K_{-1}								25.0	−.9	.3	−.1	2.8
10									144.5	31.0	7.6	21.5
X										60.0	−55.7	−14.4
X_{-1}											56.4	11.2
$t-1931$												11.2

[a] All figures are to be multiplied by 10^{-4}. To obtain figures of the same order of magnitude, the constant terms are interpreted in this table as coefficients of a variable which equals 10 (rather than 1) for each observation. Thus, the variance estimate of the β_1 estimate is .02875, that of the β_0 estimate is 1.700, and their covariance estimate is −.0607.

To handle the lagged endogenous variables, we write the predetermined part of (A1) as

$$XB = X_0B_0 + \sum_{g=1}^{G} Y_{-g}B_g .$$ (A2)

Here G stands for the largest endogenous lag in the system and $Y_{-1},..., Y_{-G}$ for matrices of order $n \times L$ containing successive lagged values. The matrix Y_{-g} is shown below; note that the first index is a time subscript and that the second refers to the variable:

$$Y_{-g} = \begin{bmatrix} y_{1-g,1} & y_{1-g,2} & \cdots & y_{1-g,L} \\ y_{2-g,1} & y_{2-g,2} & \cdots & y_{2-g,L} \\ \vdots & \vdots & & \vdots \\ y_{n-g,1} & y_{n-g,2} & \cdots & y_{n-g,L} \end{bmatrix} \quad (g = 1,..., G).$$ (A3)

Furthermore, $X_0 = [x_{th}]$ is an $n \times (K - GL)$ matrix consisting of the nonstochastic values of all predetermined variables that are not endogenous. It is assumed that all GL roots of the determinantal equation

$$| z^G\Gamma + z^{G-1}B_1 + \cdots + B_G | = 0$$ (A4)

have absolute values less than unity. Finally, we need the following assumption when there are predetermined variables which are not lagged endogenous $(K > GL)$: for each $\eta = 0, 1,..., G$, the $(K - GL) \times (K - GL)$ matrix whose (h, k)th element is

$$\frac{1}{n - \eta} \sum_{t=1}^{n-\eta} x_{th}x_{t+\eta,k} \quad (h, k = 1,..., K - GL)$$ (A5)

converges to a finite matrix $\bar{Q}_n$ as $n \to \infty$, and the limit matrix $\bar{Q}_0$ is positive definite.

Presample values ($y_{0j},..., y_{1-G,j}$ for $j = 1,..., L$) will be treated as constants. Two important results on convergence as $n \to \infty$ can then be derived from the above assumptions. First, the second-order moment matrix of the predetermined variables, $n^{-1}X'X$, converges in probability to a symmetric positive definite limit, to be denoted by Q, and the moment matrix of all random variables of the system has the following probability limit:

$$\plim_{n\to\infty} \frac{1}{n} \begin{bmatrix} X' \\ Y' \\ E' \end{bmatrix} [X \quad Y \quad E] = \begin{bmatrix} Q & -QB\Gamma^{-1} & 0 \\ -(QB\Gamma^{-1})' & (\Gamma')^{-1}(B'QB + \Sigma)\Gamma^{-1} & (\Sigma\Gamma^{-1})' \\ 0 & \Sigma\Gamma^{-1} & \Sigma \end{bmatrix}.$$ (A6)

Second, if we write $\epsilon_1,\ldots,\epsilon_L$ for the successive columns of the disturbance matrix E, the KL-element vector

$$
n^{-1/2}\begin{bmatrix} X'\epsilon_1 \\ \vdots \\ X'\epsilon_L \end{bmatrix}
\tag{A7}
$$

has a normal limiting distribution with zero mean vector and covariance matrix $\Sigma \otimes Q$.

We proceed to write (22) in the following form, multiplying both sides by $1/n$:

$$
\begin{bmatrix} (n^{-1}Z_j'\bar{X}_j)(n^{-1}D_j)^{-1}(n^{-1}\bar{X}_j'Z_j) & n^{-1}Z_j'X_j \\ n^{-1}X_j'Z_j & 0 \end{bmatrix}\begin{bmatrix} d_j{}^* - \delta_j \\ \lambda_j \end{bmatrix}
$$

$$
= \begin{bmatrix} (n^{-1}Z_j'\bar{X}_j)(n^{-1}D_j)^{-1}(n^{-1}\bar{X}_j'\epsilon_j) \\ n^{-1}X_j'\epsilon_j \end{bmatrix}.
\tag{A8}
$$

Assuming that D_j is specified as the diagonal matrix whose diagonal coincides with that of $\bar{X}_j'\bar{X}_j$, we may conclude from (A6) that the left-hand square matrix in (A8) converges to a nonzero limit matrix. (The same result also holds under other specifications of D_j, but this will not be pursued here.) We proved at the end of Section 3 that the left-hand matrix in (A8) is nonsingular if $X'Z_j$ has full column rank; the above limit matrix will be nonsingular if $n^{-1}X'Z_j$ converges in probability to a matrix with full column rank (rank N_j), which is basically the identification condition of the jth equation. The vector in the right-hand side of (A8) converges in probability to a zero vector, because $n^{-1}\bar{X}_j'\epsilon_j$ and $n^{-1}X_j'\epsilon_j$ are submatrices of $n^{-1}X'E$, which has a zero probability limit according to (A6). This proves that $d_j{}^*$ is a consistent estimator of δ_j.

It also proves that the mean square (24) is a consistent estimator of σ_{jj}. For if $d_j{}^*$ converges in probability to δ_j, this mean square has asymptotically the same distribution as $n^{-1}\epsilon_j'\epsilon_j$, which is the average of the n random variables $\epsilon_{1j}^2,\ldots,\epsilon_{nj}^2$. Since these random variables are identically distributed with expectation σ_{jj}, we may use Khintchine's theorem to conclude that this average converges in probability to the expectation σ_{jj}.

To prove the asymptotic normality of $d_j{}^*$ we go back to (11), which may be written as

$$
X_j = X\begin{bmatrix} I \\ 0 \end{bmatrix} \quad \text{and} \quad \bar{X}_j = X\begin{bmatrix} 0 \\ I \end{bmatrix}
\tag{A9}
$$

with zero and unit matrices of appropriate order. We substitute (A9) in the right-hand vector of (A8) to obtain

$$\left[\begin{matrix} (n^{-1}Z_j'\bar{X}_j)(n^{-1}D_j)^{-1}\,[0\ \ I] \\ [I\ \ 0] \end{matrix}\right] (n^{-1}X'\epsilon_j) = H_j(n^{-1}X'\epsilon_j), \qquad (A10)$$

where H_j is the $(N_j + K_j) \times K$ matrix on the left. Write G_j for the square matrix in the left-hand side of (A8). Then, after premultiplying this equation by $n^{1/2}G_j^{-1}$, we obtain

$$\left[\begin{matrix} n^{1/2}(d_j{}^* - \delta_j) \\ n^{1/2}\lambda_j \end{matrix}\right] = G_j^{-1}H_j n^{-1/2}X'\epsilon_j . \qquad (A11)$$

Since G_j converges in probability to a nonsingular limit $\bar{G}_j$ and H_j to a limit $\bar{H}_j$, we may conclude that the limiting distribution of both sides of (A11) is identical with that of $\bar{G}_j^{-1}\bar{H}_j n^{1/2}X'\epsilon_j$, provided that the latter vector has a limiting distribution. But we know that the limiting distribution of the vector (A7) is normal with zero mean and covariance matrix $\Sigma \otimes Q$, so that $\bar{G}_j^{-1}\bar{H}_j n^{-1/2}X'\epsilon_j$ has a normal limiting distribution with zero mean and covariance matrix

$$\sigma_{jj}\bar{G}_j^{-1}\bar{H}_j Q\bar{H}_j'\bar{G}_j^{-1}. \qquad (A12)$$

The matrix $\bar{H}_j Q\bar{H}_j'$ is estimated consistently by $H_j(n^{-1}X'X)\,H_j'$, which can be evaluated as follows:

$$\left[\begin{matrix} (n^{-1}Z_j'\bar{X}_j)(n^{-1}D_j)^{-1}\,[0\ \ I] \\ [I\ \ 0] \end{matrix}\right] (n^{-1}X'X)\left[\begin{matrix} 0 \\ I \end{matrix}\right] (n^{-1}D_j)^{-1}\,(n^{-1}\bar{X}_j'Z_j)\ \left[\begin{matrix} I \\ 0 \end{matrix}\right]\right]$$

$$= \left[\begin{matrix} (n^{-1}Z_j'\bar{X}_j)(n^{-1}D_j)^{-1}\,(n^{-1}\bar{X}_j'X) \\ n^{-1}X_j'X \end{matrix}\right]\left[\begin{matrix} 0 \\ I \end{matrix}\right] (n^{-1}D_j)^{-1}\,(n^{-1}\bar{X}_j'Z_j)\ \left[\begin{matrix} I \\ 0 \end{matrix}\right]\right]$$

$$= \left[\begin{matrix} (n^{-1}Z_j'\bar{X}_j)(n^{-1}D_j)^{-1}\,(n^{-1}\bar{X}_j'\bar{X}_j)(n^{-1}D_j)^{-1}\,(n^{-1}\bar{X}_j Z_j) \\ (n^{-1}X_j'\bar{X}_j)(n^{-1}D_j)^{-1}\,(n^{-1}\bar{X}_j'Z_j) \end{matrix}\right.$$

$$\left. \begin{matrix} (n^{-1}Z_j'\bar{X}_j)(n^{-1}D_j)^{-1}\,(n^{-1}\bar{X}_j'X_j) \\ n^{-1}X_j'X_j \end{matrix}\right].$$

The last matrix is $1/n$ times the matrix in the middle of (23). Since the latter matrix is pre- and postmultiplied by the inverse of $n^{-1}G_j$, we may conclude from (A12) that the leading $N_j \times N_j$ submatrix of (23) is indeed an estimated asymptotic covariance matrix of $d_j{}^*$.

The consistency of the estimator (26) with respect to σ_{jl} and the covariance matrix (25) can be derived along exactly the same lines on the basis of the joint asymptotic distribution of $d_j{}^*$ and $d_l{}^*$.

Acknowledgments

Research supported in part by the National Science Foundation under grant GS2607. The author is indebted to John Paulus for programming the computations which are reported in Section 6.

7

Efficient Estimation in Overidentified Models: An Interpretive Analysis

ARTHUR S. GOLDBERGER

1. Introduction

If a structural equation is overidentified, there are alternative distinct estimators of its parameters. The notion that a sensible estimation procedure will, or should, average up the alternative estimators appears quite frequently. For example, Christ (1966, p. 411) and Malinvaud (1970, pp. 634–641) express the idea in the context of econometric simultaneous equation systems. Blalock (1968, p. 3), Boudon (1968, p. 213), Theil (1961, pp. 225–231), and Basmann (1960) are relevant as well.

In this paper, which is purely expository, we explore the theme that efficient estimation in overidentified models involves the construction of appropriately weighted averages of basic estimators. Overidentification being a very general concept—a point emphasized by Kmenta (1971, pp. 439–448)—our illustrations will refer to linear regression with linear constraints, multivariate regression, and path analysis, as well as to simultaneous equation models.

131

2. A Simple Example

Suppose that a classical regression model applies to

$$y = \beta_1 x_1 + \beta_2 x_2 + \epsilon.$$

Least-squares regression of y on x_1 and x_2 chooses estimates for β_1 and β_2 to minimize

$$\sum (y - \beta_1 x_1 - \beta_2 x_2)^2.$$

These estimates are the b_1 and b_2 which solve the normal equations

$$m_{11} b_1 + m_{12} b_2 = m_{1y}, \qquad m_{12} b_1 + m_{22} b_2 = m_{2y}, \qquad (1)$$

where the ms denote sample moments: $m_{12} = \Sigma x_1 x_2$, etc., and all variables have, from the start, been expressed as deviations about their sample means.

Suppose that we know that $\beta_1 = \beta_2$. Then b_1 and b_2 provide two distinct unbiased estimates of the common parameter, say β. This parameter is overidentified.

A restricted least-squares (RLS) procedure is used to estimate the model. It chooses estimates for β_1 and β_2 to minimize

$$\sum (y - \beta_1 x_1 - \beta_2 x_2)^2$$

subject to the constraint that $\beta_1 = \beta_2$. To implement this RLS procedure, write $y = \beta x^* + \epsilon$ where $x^* = x_1 + x_2$, and regress y on x^*. That is, choose the estimate of β to minimize

$$\sum (y - \beta x^*)^2.$$

This estimate is the solution to the normal equation

$$\sum x^{*2} b^* = \sum x^* y,$$

namely

$$b^* = \frac{\sum x^* y}{\sum x^{*2}} = \frac{\sum (x_1 + x_2) y}{\sum (x_1 + x_2)^2} = \frac{m_{1y} + m_{2y}}{m_{11} + 2m_{12} + m_{22}}. \qquad (2)$$

Inserting (1) into (2) we find that

$$b^* = \frac{(m_{11} b_1 + m_{12} b_2) + (m_{12} b_1 + m_{22} b_2)}{m_{11} + 2m_{12} + m_{22}} = \frac{(m_{11} + m_{12}) b_1 + (m_{12} + m_{22}) b_2}{m_{11} + 2m_{12} + m_{22}}$$

$$= w^* b_1 + (1 - w^*) b_2, \qquad (3)$$

say, where

$$w^* = (m_{11} + m_{12})/(m_{11} + 2m_{12} + m_{22}).$$

Thus, the RLS estimator b^* is a *weighted average* of the distinct estimators b_1 and b_2. The expression "weighted average" may be misleading since w^* and $1 - w^*$ can fall outside the range 0 to 1. Nevertheless, it seems to be instructive.

What can be said about b^* from the point of view of efficiency (i.e. minimum variance)? Given the two unbiased estimates b_1, b_2 of the single parameter β, consider any linear combination of them,

$$\hat{\beta} = w_1 b_1 + w_2 b_2.$$

For $\hat{\beta}$ to be unbiased we must have $w_1 + w_2 = 1$, since

$$E(w_1 b_1 + w_2 b_2) = w_1 E(b_1) + w_2 E(b_2) = w_1 \beta + w_2 \beta = (w_1 + w_2)\beta.$$

In that event we may simply write $w_1 = w$, $w_2 = (1 - w)$, and

$$\hat{\beta} = w b_1 + (1 - w) b_2.$$

The variance of $\hat{\beta}$ will be

$$V(\hat{\beta}) = w^2 V(b_1) + (1 - w)^2 V(b_2) + 2w(1 - w) C(b_1, b_2).$$

Now choose w, and thus $\hat{\beta}$, to minimize this variance. Differentiating, we have

$$dV(\hat{\beta})/dw = 2w V(b_1) - 2(1 - w) V(b_2) + 2(1 - 2w) C(b_1, b_2),$$

which when set at zero and solved for w yields

$$w = \frac{V(b_2) - C(b_1, b_2)}{V(b_1) + V(b_2) - 2C(b_1, b_2)}. \tag{4}$$

From classical least-squares regression theory, we know that

$$V(b_1) = \sigma^2 m^{11}, \qquad V(b_2) = \sigma^2 m^{22}, \qquad C(b_1, b_2) = \sigma^2 m^{12}.$$

Here $\sigma^2 = V(\epsilon)$ and the m^{jk} are elements of the matrix inverse to the regressor moment matrix:

$$\begin{pmatrix} m^{11} & m^{12} \\ m^{21} & m^{22} \end{pmatrix} = \begin{pmatrix} m_{11} & m_{12} \\ m_{21} & m_{22} \end{pmatrix}^{-1} = \frac{1}{m_{11}m_{22} - m_{12}^2} \begin{pmatrix} m_{22} & -m_{12} \\ -m_{12} & m_{11} \end{pmatrix}.$$

Inserting these values into (4), we find

$$w = (m_{11} + m_{12})/(m_{11} + 2m_{12} + m_{22}) = w^*.$$

Thus the RLS estimator b^* is the efficient weighted average of b_1 and b_2 in the sense that of all such averages it has minimum variance.

The minimum-variance argument can usefully be presented in a slightly different way. If we have two unbiased estimates b_1 and b_2 of the same parameter β, with variances σ_{11}, σ_{22}, and covariance σ_{12}, then Aitken's generalized least-squares principle proposes that they be combined as follows: choose as the estimate of β the value which minimizes the quantity

$$q = \sigma^{11}(b_1 - \beta)^2 + \sigma^{22}(b_2 - \beta)^2 + 2\sigma^{12}(b_1 - \beta)(b_2 - \beta),$$

where

$$\begin{pmatrix} \sigma^{11} & \sigma^{12} \\ \sigma^{21} & \sigma^{22} \end{pmatrix} = \begin{pmatrix} \sigma_{11} & \sigma_{12} \\ \sigma_{21} & \sigma_{22} \end{pmatrix}^{-1}.$$

Differentiating q gives

$$dq/d\beta = -2\sigma^{11}(b_1 - \beta) - 2\sigma^{22}(b_2 - \beta) + 2\sigma^{12}(b_1 + b_2 - 2\beta),$$

which when set at zero and solved for β yields b^*, since $\sigma_{ij} = \sigma^2 m^{ij}$. Thus the GLS principle produces the minimum-variance linear unbiased combination of the basic estimates b_1 and b_2.

Now let us approach the problem from yet another point of view. Having written $y = \beta(x_1 + x_2) + \epsilon$, one can still maintain that x_1 and x_2, being independent of ϵ, are available as separate instrumental variables. This leads to two distinct estimates of β, namely the $b(1)$ and $b(2)$ defined by

$$\sum x_1(x_1 + x_2)\, b(1) = \sum x_1 y, \qquad \sum x_2(x_1 + x_2)\, b(2) = \sum x_2 y,$$

that is, by

$$(m_{11} + m_{12})\, b(1) = m_{1y}, \qquad (m_{12} + m_{22})\, b(2) = m_{2y}. \tag{5}$$

These two estimates of the same parameter can be averaged into

$$\hat{\beta} = c\, b(1) + (1 - c)\, b(2).$$

If c is chosen to minimize $V(\hat{\beta})$ then

$$c = [V(b(2)) - C(b(1), b(2))]/[V(b(1)) + V(b(2)) - 2C(b(1), b(2))]. \tag{6}$$

From instrumental-variable theory, we know that

$$V(b(1)) = \sigma^2 m_{11}/(m_{11} + m_{12})^2, \qquad V(b(2)) = \sigma^2 m_{22}/(m_{22} + m_{12})^2,$$

$$C(b(1), b(2)) = \sigma^2 m_{12}/[(m_{11} + m_{12})(m_{22} + m_{12})].$$

When these values are inserted into (6), we find that $c = w^*$; taking this in conjunction with (5), we find that $\hat{\beta} = b^*$. Thus the RLS estimator b^* is also the efficient weighted average of the instrumental variable estimates $b(1)$ and $b(2)$.

We have emphasized the GLS principle for combining estimates but other averaging schemes are occasionally employed. For example, one could ignore the differential sampling variability of b_1 and b_2 and just split the difference, taking $\frac{1}{2}(b_1 + b_2)$ as an estimate of β. Or one could ignore the differential sampling variability of $b(1)$ and $b(2)$ and take $\frac{1}{2}(b(1) + b(2))$ instead. These estimates will, coincidences apart, differ from one another. They will differ from, and have larger variance than, b^*. Note that such "unweighted" averages are, in effect, obtained by an ordinary rather than "generalized" least squares criterion: e.g. $\frac{1}{2}(b_1 + b_2)$ is the value for β which minimizes the quantity $(b_1 - \beta)^2 + (b_2 - \beta)^2$.

Our simple example suggests several ideas which recur in the sequel. These are: (i) restricted estimates may be interpreted as weighted averages of unrestricted estimates; (ii) minimum-variance considerations dictate the choice of weights; (iii) an efficient estimator has an invariance property in that it can be obtained by application of a single principle to several different arrangements of the observed data.

3. The Generalized Least-Squares Principle

The generalized least-squares principle, to which we have referred, is most familiar in the context of linear regression with autocorrelated and/or heteroscedastic disturbances. But its scope is much broader than that. Let us consider the GLS principle as a general rule for combining estimators.

Suppose that $h(1)$ and $h(2)$ are two distinct unbiased estimators of the parameter vector θ, with covariance matrix

$$\begin{pmatrix} V(h(1)) & C(h(1), h(2)) \\ C(h(2), h(1)) & V(h(2)) \end{pmatrix} = \begin{pmatrix} \Sigma_{11} & \Sigma_{12} \\ \Sigma_{21} & \Sigma_{22} \end{pmatrix} = \Sigma.$$

The GLS principle calls for θ to be estimated as the value which minimizes the quantity

$$q = \text{tr}\left[\begin{pmatrix} h(1) - \theta \\ h(2) - \theta \end{pmatrix}' \Sigma^{-1} \begin{pmatrix} h(1) - \theta \\ h(2) - \theta \end{pmatrix}\right]$$

$$= (h(1) - \theta)' \Sigma^{11}(h(1) - \theta) + (h(2) - \theta)' \Sigma^{22}(h(2) - \theta)$$

$$+ (h(1) - \theta)' \Sigma^{12}(h(2) - \theta) + (h(2) - \theta)' \Sigma^{21}(h(1) - \theta),$$

where

$$\begin{pmatrix} \Sigma^{11} & \Sigma^{12} \\ \Sigma^{21} & \Sigma^{22} \end{pmatrix} = \Sigma^{-1}.$$

Differentiating q with respect to the vector θ, we find

$$-\tfrac{1}{2}\partial q/\partial\theta = \Sigma^{11}(h(1) - \theta) + \Sigma^{22}(h(2) - \theta) + \Sigma^{21}(h(1) - \theta) + \Sigma^{12}(h(2) - \theta)$$

$$= -(\Sigma^{11} + \Sigma^{22} + \Sigma^{21} + \Sigma^{12})\theta + (\Sigma^{11} + \Sigma^{21})\,h(1) + (\Sigma^{12} + \Sigma^{22})h(2).$$

Setting this at zero to locate the minimum of q yields

$$h = W^*h(1) + (I - W^*)\,h(2) \tag{7}$$

as the GLS estimator of θ, where

$$W^* = (\Sigma^{11} + \Sigma^{22} + \Sigma^{12} + \Sigma^{21})^{-1}\,(\Sigma^{11} + \Sigma^{21}). \tag{8}$$

Thus, the GLS estimator h appears as a weighted average of the two unbiased estimators $h(1)$ and $h(2)$. Once again the weighted average interpretation may be misleading; there is no assurance that an individual element of h will lie between the corresponding element in $h(1)$ and $h(2)$. But once again it is sufficiently suggestive that we adopt it.

An important property of the GLS estimator is that it has minimum variance among all linear combinations of $h(1)$ and $h(2)$ which are unbiased estimators of θ. Any such combination will be of the form

$$\hat{\theta} = Wh(1) + (I - W)\,h(2).$$

Defining $\Delta = W - W^*$, we can write

$$\hat{\theta} = (W^* + \Delta)\,h(1) + (I - W^* - \Delta)\,h(2) = h + \Delta(h(1) - h(2)),$$

whence

$$V(\hat{\theta}) = V(h) + \Delta V(h(1) - h(2))\,\Delta' + \Delta C(h(1) - h(2), h) + C(h, h(1) - h(2))\,\Delta'.$$

But

$$C(h, h(1) - h(2)) = C(W^*h(1) + (I - W^*) h(2), h(1) - h(2))$$
$$= W^*(\Sigma_{11} - \Sigma_{12}) + (I - W^*)(\Sigma_{21} - \Sigma_{22}) = 0,$$

using (8) and the fact that $\Sigma^{-1}\Sigma = I$. Consequently

$$C(h(1) - h(2), h) = 0$$

also, whence

$$V(\hat{\theta}) = V(h) + \Delta V(h(1) - h(2)) \Delta'. \tag{9}$$

Since the second matrix on the right is nonnegative definite and is zero if and only if $\Delta = 0$, we conclude that the minimum-variance choice is $W = W^*$, that is $\hat{\theta} = h$.

If $h(1)$ and $h(2)$ are independent, or simply uncorrelated, then $\Sigma_{12} = 0 = \Sigma_{21}'$, whence $\Sigma^{11} = \Sigma_{11}^{-1}$, $\Sigma^{22} = \Sigma_{22}^{-1}$, and $\Sigma^{12} = 0 = \Sigma^{21'}$. In that event, h reduces to

$$h = (\Sigma_{11}^{-1} + \Sigma_{22}^{-1})^{-1} (\Sigma_{11}^{-1} h(1) + \Sigma_{22}^{-1} h(2)),$$

and it is apparent that the weighting is inverse to the variances. A familiar example illustrates this. Suppose we have two independent random samples of sizes T_1 and T_2 from a population with mean μ and variance σ^2. The respective sample means m_1 and m_2 have variances σ^2/T_1 and σ^2/T_2, so that the GLS combination of them will be $(T_1 m_1 + T_2 m_2)/(T_1 + T_2)$, which is just the mean of the pooled sample.

Up to this point, we have implicitly assumed that Σ is nonsingular, but the contrary case will arise in the sequel. A full treatment of GLS with singular Σ would rest on the "generalized inverse" of Σ. For our purposes the following will suffice. The argument leading up to (9) showed that a sufficient condition for $\hat{\theta} = W h(1) + (I - W) h(2)$ to be the minimum-variance linear combination of $h(1)$ and $h(2)$ is that

$$W(\Sigma_{11} - \Sigma_{12}) + (I - W)(\Sigma_{21} - \Sigma_{22}) = 0. \tag{10}$$

This argument did not rest on nonsingularity of Σ. Consequently, given a proposed $\hat{\theta}$, one can check that it has minimum variance by showing that its W satisfies (10).

In practice, Σ may be unknown, so that the GLS principle may not be operational. However, if a consistent estimator of Σ, say $\hat{\Sigma}$, is available, then one can draw on a modified GLS principle, which uses $\hat{\Sigma}$ in place of Σ in constructing h. A general theorem is that the MGLS estimator will, at least asymptotically, have the same minimum-variance properties as the GLS estimator itself.

4. Univariate Regression with Linear Constraints

With this background in hand, we turn to consider some typical overidentified models. Suppose that a classical regression model applies to $y = X\beta + \epsilon$, where y is $T \times 1$, X is $T \times K$, β is $K \times 1$, and ϵ is $T \times 1$. Here, the nonstochastic matrix X has rank K, $E(\epsilon) = 0$, and $E(\epsilon\epsilon') = \sigma^2 I$. Suppose we know that $R\beta = 0$, where R is a known $J \times K$ matrix of rank J. That is, there are J independent linear constraints on the regression parameters in β. Without loss of generality, we suppose that the first J columns of R are linearly independent, and partition X, β, R as

$$X = (X_1 , X_2), \qquad \beta = \begin{pmatrix} \beta_1 \\ \beta_2 \end{pmatrix}, \qquad R = (R_1 , R_2).$$

Here X_1 is $T \times J$, X_2 is $T \times (K - J)$, β_1 is $J \times 1$, β_2 is $(K - J) \times 1$, R_1 is $J \times J$, and R_2 is $J \times (K - J)$. Then the equations of the model are

$$y = X_1\beta_1 + X_2\beta_2 + \epsilon, \qquad R_1\beta_1 + R_2\beta_2 = 0.$$

Since R_1 is nonsingular, the second of these can be solved for

$$\beta_1 = -R_1^{-1}R_2\beta_2 , \tag{11}$$

which is just another way of stating $R\beta = 0$.

Least-squares regression of y on X_1 and X_2 chooses estimates of β_1 and β_2 to minimize

$$(y - X_1\beta_1 - X_2\beta_2)' (y - X_1\beta_1 - X_2\beta_2).$$

These estimates are the b_1 and b_2 that solve the normal equations

$$M_{11}b_1 + M_{12}b_2 = M_{1y} , \qquad M_{21}b_1 + M_{22}b_2 = M_{2y} .$$

Here the Ms are the sample moment matrices: $M_{ij} = X_i'X_j$, etc. In view of (11), we find that we have two distinct unbiased estimators of β, namely

$$b_1(1) = b_1 \qquad \text{and} \qquad b_1(2) = -R_1^{-1}R_2b_2 .$$

The restricted least-squares procedure chooses estimates for β_1 and β_2 to minimize

$$(y - X_1\beta_1 - X_2\beta_2)' (y - X_1\beta_1 - X_2\beta_2)$$

subject to (11). To implement it, write

$$y = X_1(-R_1^{-1}R_2\beta_2) + X_2\beta_2 + \epsilon = (X_2 - X_1R_1^{-1}R_2)\beta_2 + \epsilon = X^*\beta_2 + \epsilon,$$

say. Regress y on X^* to estimate β_2 ; that is, choose the estimate of β_2 to minimize

$$(y - X^*\beta_2)'(y - X^*\beta_2).$$

Then insert this estimate of β_2 into (11) to produce the estimate of β_1. What results is

$$\binom{b_1{}^*}{b_2{}^*} = [I - (X'X)^{-1}R'(R(X'X)^{-1}R')^{-1}R]\binom{b_1}{b_2}.$$

Reading off the first J rows of this expression, we find that the RLS estimator of β_1 is

$$b_1{}^* = \left[(I, 0) - (M^{11}, M^{12})\binom{R_1'}{R_2'}(R(X'X)^{-1}R')^{-1}(R_1, R_2)\right]\binom{b_1}{b_2}$$

$$= Wb_1 + (I - W)(-R_1^{-1}R_2b_2) = Wb_1(1) + (I - W)b_1(2), \quad (12)$$

where

$$W = I - (M^{11}R_1' + M^{12}R_2')(R(X'X)^{-1}R')^{-1}R_1, \quad (13)$$

and

$$\begin{pmatrix} M^{11} & M^{12} \\ M^{21} & M^{22} \end{pmatrix} = (X'X)^{-1} = \begin{pmatrix} M_{11} & M_{12} \\ M_{21} & M_{22} \end{pmatrix}^{-1}.$$

In (12), $b_1{}^*$ is exhibited as a weighted average of the two unconstrained estimates of β_1, namely $b_1(1)$ and $b_1(2)$.

It is not hard to show that this weighting scheme gives the minimum variance. From classical regression theory we know that the covariance matrix of $b = \binom{b_1}{b_2}$ is $V(b) = \sigma^2(X'X)^{-1}$. Writing

$$\binom{b_1(1)}{b_1(2)} = \begin{pmatrix} I & 0 \\ 0 & -R_1^{-1}R_2 \end{pmatrix}\binom{b_1}{b_2},$$

it follows that

$$\Sigma = \begin{pmatrix} \Sigma_{11} & \Sigma_{12} \\ \Sigma_{21} & \Sigma_{22} \end{pmatrix} = \begin{pmatrix} V(b_1(1)) & C(b_1(1), b_1(2)) \\ C(b_1(2), b_1(1)) & V(b_1(2)) \end{pmatrix}$$

$$= \sigma^2 \begin{pmatrix} I & 0 \\ 0 & -R_1^{-1}R_2 \end{pmatrix}(X'X)^{-1}\begin{pmatrix} I & 0 \\ 0 & -R_2'R_1^{-1'} \end{pmatrix}$$

$$= \sigma^2 \begin{pmatrix} M^{11} & -M^{12}R_2'R_1^{-1'} \\ -R_1^{-1}R_2M^{21} & R_1^{-1}R_2M^{22}R_2'R_1^{-1'} \end{pmatrix}.$$

In general, i.e. when $K < 2J$, this Σ will be singular, so that (8) will not be defined. But a bit of algebra shows that the W of (13) satisfies $W(\Sigma_{11} - \Sigma_{12}) + (I - W)(\Sigma_{21} - \Sigma_{22})$. As noted in (10), this suffices to demonstrate that b_1^* is the minimum-variance combination of $b_1(1)$ and $b_1(2)$.

5. Multivariate Regression with Linear Constraints

Suppose that a classical multivariate regression model applies to $Y = X\Pi + \mathcal{E}$, where Y is $T \times M$, X is $T \times K$, Π is $K \times M$, and $\mathcal{E}$ is $T \times M$. Here, the nonstochastic matrix X has rank K, $E[\epsilon(t)] = 0$, and $E[\epsilon(t)\,\epsilon'(s)] = \Omega$ if $t = s$, and $= 0$ if $t \neq s$, where for $t = 1,...,T$, the $\epsilon'(t)$ denote the rows of $\mathcal{E}$. The $M \times M$ symmetric matrix Ω is assumed to be positive definite. Suppose further that we know that the elements of Π, namely the π_{km}, are subject to J independent linear constraints,

$$\sum_{k=1}^{K} \sum_{m=1}^{M} f_{km}^{j} \pi_{km} = f_0^{j}, \qquad (j = 1,..., J)$$

the fs being known constants. If we let F^j be the $K \times M$ matrix of the f_{km}^j, then these constraints can be written as

$$\mathrm{tr}(F^{j\prime}\Pi) = f_0^{j} \qquad (j = 1,..., J). \tag{14}$$

A generalized least-squares procedure is proposed for estimating the parameters of this model. It chooses the estimate for Π to minimize the quantity

$$\mathrm{tr}[\Omega^{-1}(Y - X\Pi)'\,(Y - X\Pi)] \tag{15}$$

subject to the constraints in (14).

For present purposes, we first show that this is equivalent to applying the GLS principle to unrestricted estimates of Π. These unrestricted estimates are

$$P = (X'X)^{-1} X'Y.$$

We know from classical multivariate regression theory that the covariance matrix of P is given by

$$V(P) = \Omega \otimes (X'X)^{-1}.$$

Applied to P, therefore, the GLS principle calls for the estimate of Π to be chosen to minimize the quantity

$$\text{tr}[\Omega^{-1}(P - \Pi)' X'X(P - \Pi)] \tag{16}$$

subject to (14). But

$$(Y - X\Pi)' (Y - X\Pi) = [(Y - XP) + X(P - \Pi)]' [(Y - XP) + X(P - \Pi)]$$
$$= TS + (P - \Pi)' X'X(P - \Pi),$$

where

$$S = (1/T)(Y - XP)' (Y - XP) = (1/T)(Y'Y - Y'X(X'X)^{-1} X'Y).$$

Thus

$$\text{tr}[\Omega^{-1}(Y - X\Pi)' (Y - X\Pi)] = T \text{ tr}(\Omega^{-1}S) + \text{tr}[\Omega^{-1}(P - \Pi)' X'X(P - \Pi)].$$

Since the quantity in (15) differs from the quantity in (16) only by $T \text{ tr}(\Omega^{-1}S)$ which is a constant independent of the choice of Π, it is apparent that minimizing (16) is equivalent to minimizing (15). Thus the GLS principle will lead to an invariant choice of Π whether it is applied to the model equations or directly to the unconstrained regression coefficient estimates.

At least in certain special cases, we can exhibit a weighted average interpretation for the GLS estimates.

For example, if the constraints can be written together as $\Pi R = 0$ where the $M \times N$ known matrix R has rank N, then the GLS estimator of Π is

$$P^* = P[I - R(R'\Omega R)^{-1} R'\Omega], \tag{17}$$

cf. Goldberger (1970b, pp. 31–37). Without essential loss of generality, suppose that the first N rows of R are linearly independent, and partition R as $\binom{R_1}{R_2}$ where R_1 is $N \times N$ and R_2 is $(M - N) \times N$. Then when the regression coefficient matrix is conformably partitioned as $\Pi = (\Pi_1, \Pi_2)$, the constraint $\Pi R = 0$ can be written as $\Pi_1 R_1 + \Pi_2 R_2 = 0$, which says that $\Pi_1 = -\Pi_2 R_2 R_1^{-1}$. Consequently, the unconstrained regression coefficient estimates in $P = (P_1, P_2)$ provide two unbiased estimates of Π_1, namely $P_1(1) = P_1$ and $P_1(2) = -P_2 R_2 R_1^{-1}$. The GLS estimator of Π_1, given by the first N columns of the P^* in (17), can now be read off as

$$P_1^* = P_1(1)W + P_1(2)(I - W), \tag{18}$$

where
$$W = I - R_1 (R' \Omega R)^{-1} (R_1' \Omega_{11} + R_2' \Omega_{21}), \tag{19}$$

and Ω has been conformably partitioned as

$$\Omega = \begin{pmatrix} \Omega_{11} & \Omega_{12} \\ \Omega_{21} & \Omega_{22} \end{pmatrix}. \tag{20}$$

Thus $P_1{}^*$ is displayed as a weighted average of the two unconstrained estimates of Π_1, namely $P_1(1)$ and $P_1(2)$.

Other examples which permit straightforward weighted-average interpretations for GLS estimates include the situations in which the linear constraints can be written together as $L\Pi = 0$ or as $L\Pi R = 0$; cf. Goldberger (1970b, pp. 27–31, 38–45). In other situations where the constraints do not fall into such simple patterns, it may be necessary to translate the multivariate model into a univariate model, following Zellner (1962), before proceeding to the weighted-average interpretation.

In practice Ω is unknown, so that the GLS principle is not operational. Let $\hat{\Omega}$ denote a consistent estimator of Ω, and consider the MGLS principle which calls for choosing the estimate of Π to minimize the quantity

$$\mathrm{tr}[\hat{\Omega}^{-1}(Y - X\Pi)' (Y - X\Pi)]$$

subject to the constraints in (14). Paralleling the argument above, we see this is equivalent to minimizing

$$\mathrm{tr}[\hat{\Omega}^{-1}(P - \Pi)' X'X(P - \Pi)]$$

subject to the same constraints. Since this has the same form as (16), it is apparent that any weighted-average interpretation obtainable for GLS estimators of Π will carry over to the MGLS estimators.

Alternative $\hat{\Omega}$s are available. One, proposed by Zellner (1962), is S. Another is the residual moment matrix which results from the restricted estimates of Π themselves. As discussed by Malinvaud (1970, pp. 338–340), use of the latter amounts to maximum-likelihood estimation when the disturbances are normally distributed.

6. Multivariate Regression with Nonlinear Constraints

6.1 An Unobservable Variable Model

Suppose that $y^* = \alpha' x$, where y^* is an unobservable scalar, $x = (x_1, ..., x_K)'$ is a $K \times 1$ vector of observable exogenous variables, and $\alpha = (\alpha_1, ..., \alpha_K)'$ is a $K \times 1$ vector of parameters. Suppose further that $y = \beta y^* + \epsilon$ where $y = (y_1, ..., y_M)'$ is an $M \times 1$ vector of observable endogenous variables, $\beta = (\beta_1, ..., \beta_M)'$ is an $M \times 1$ vector of parameters, and $\epsilon = (\epsilon_1, ..., \epsilon_M)'$ is an $M \times 1$ disturbance vector. Here ϵ is independent of x (and thus of y^*), $E(\epsilon) = 0$, and $E(\epsilon\epsilon') = \Omega$, with Ω being positive definite. Combining the structural equations gives the reduced-form relation between y and x:

$$y = \beta\alpha'x + \epsilon. \tag{21}$$

Given T independent observations on y', x', we have a multivariate regression model $Y = X\Pi + \mathcal{E}$ of the type considered in Section 5, except that the constraints on Π now take the nonlinear form

$$\Pi = \alpha\beta'. \tag{22}$$

Systems such as this, which incorporate unobservable variables, have appeared as components of path analysis models; see Duncan, Haller, & Portes (1968).

The force of (22) is that the $K \times M$ matrix Π has rank 1, being expressible as the product of a $K \times 1$ vector α and a $1 \times M$ vector β'. To eliminate an obvious indeterminancy in (22), we adopt the normalization rule

$$\alpha'X'X\alpha = 1. \tag{23}$$

Least-squares regression of Y on X will produce an unconstrained estimate of Π, namely

$$P = (X'X)^{-1}X'Y = (p_1, ..., p_m, ..., p_M).$$

Here $p_m = (X'X)^{-1}X'y_m$, and Y has been partitioned as

$$Y = (y_1, ..., y_m, ..., y_M).$$

If for the moment we suppose that a value for α is given, then we can develop K distinct estimates of each element of β. These estimates for β_m $(m = 1, ..., M)$ are given by

$$\beta_m(k) = p_{km}/\alpha_k \qquad (k = 1, ..., K), \tag{24}$$

where p_{km} is the element in the k, m slot of P, and we have drawn on the fact that p_{km} is an (unbiased) estimate of $\pi_{km} = \alpha_k\beta_m$. Alternatively, if for the moment we suppose that a value for β is given, then we can develop M distinct estimates of each element of α. These estimates for α_k $(k = 1, ..., K)$ are given by

$$\alpha_k(m) = p_{km}/\beta_m \qquad (m = 1, ..., M). \tag{25}$$

An MGLS procedure with S replacing Ω will choose unique estimates of α and β by minimizing the quantity

$$\mathrm{tr}[S^{-1}(\alpha\beta' - P)' \, X'X(\alpha\beta' - P)],$$

which, apart from an irrelevant constant, equals

$$q = (\alpha'X'X\alpha)(\beta'S^{-1}\beta) - 2\alpha'X'YS^{-1}\beta.$$

Here again $S = (1/T)(Y - XP)' \, (Y - XP)$. As shown by Hauser and Goldberger (1971), when the minimization is carried out subject to (23), the MGLS estimates of α and β, denoted by a and b respectively, are given by the solution to the following pair of equations:

$$a' = (b'S^{-1}b)^{-1} \, b'S^{-1}P', \tag{26}$$

$$b' = a'X'Y. \tag{27}$$

(Solving this pair of equations calls for b to be obtained as an appropriately normalized characteristic vector of $Y'XPS^{-1}$, but this is irrelevant for present purposes.) We write (27) as $b' = a'X'XP$, and read off its typical element as

$$b_m = a'X'Xp_m = \sum_{j=1}^{K}\sum_{k=1}^{K} a_j m_{jk} p_{km} = \sum_{j=1}^{K}\sum_{k=1}^{K} a_j m_{jk} a_k(p_{km}/a_k), \tag{28}$$

where m_{jk} denotes the element in the j, k slot of $X'X$. Noting that $\sum_{j=1}^{K}\sum_{k=1}^{K} a_j m_{jk} a_k = a'X'Xa = 1$, and that p_{km}/a_k has the form of (24), we can write

$$b_m = \sum_{k=1}^{K} w_k b_m(k), \tag{29}$$

where $w_k = a_k \sum_{j=1}^{K} a_j m_{jk}$, and $b_m(k) = p_{km}/a_k$. Since $\sum_{k=1}^{K} w_k = 1$, we see that the MGLS estimate of β_m is a weighted average of the K distinct estimates p_{km}/a_k. Similarly, we write the typical element of (26) as

$$a_k = (b'S^{-1}b)^{-1} \sum_{m=1}^{M}\sum_{n=1}^{M} b_n s^{nm} p_{km}$$

$$= (b'S^{-1}b)^{-1} \sum_{m=1}^{M}\sum_{n=1}^{M} b_n s^{nm} b_m(p_{km}/b_m)$$

$$= \sum_{m=1}^{M} w_m{}^* a_k(m),$$

where $w_m{}^* = (b'S^{-1}b)^{-1} b_m \sum_{n=1}^{M} b_n s^{nm}$, s^{nm} denotes the element in the n, m slot of S^{-1}, and $a_k(m) = p_{km}/b_m$. Since $\sum_{m=1}^{M} w_m{}^* = 1$, we see that the MGLS estimate of α_k is a weighted average of the M distinct estimates $a_k(m) = p_{km}/b_m$.

6.2 A Simultaneous Equation Model

A rather more general case arises in connection with a single over-identified structural equation in a conventional simultaneous equation model. Here the stochastic element arises from errors in the equations rather than from errors in the variables, but as remarked by Zellner (1970), the two sources are closely related. Suppose that

$$y_0 = Y\gamma + X_1\beta + u, \tag{30}$$

where y_0 is the $T \times 1$ vector of observations on a left-hand endogenous variable, Y is the $T \times (M - 1)$ matrix of observations on the other endogenous variables which appear in the equation, X_1 is the $T \times K_1$ matrix of observations on the exogenous variables that appear in the equation, u is the $T \times 1$ disturbance vector, and γ and β are parameter vectors of dimensions $(M - 1) \times 1$ and $K_1 \times 1$ respectively. In the full model there are also K_2 other exogenous variables whose observations are given in the $T \times K_2$ matrix X_2. The $T \times (K_1 + K_2)$ matrix $X = (X_1, X_2)$ has full column rank, and the usual assumptions are made on the disturbances.

The portion of the reduced form of the full model which concerns us is that which relates to $Y^* = (y_0, Y)$, the endogenous variables which appear in the structural equation (30). This portion of the reduced form we write variously as

$$Y^* = X\Pi^* + \mathcal{E}^*, \tag{31}$$

$$(y_0, Y) = X(\pi_0, \Pi) + (\epsilon_0, \mathcal{E}), \tag{32}$$

$$Y^* = (X_1, X_2) \begin{pmatrix} \Pi_1{}^* \\ \Pi_2{}^* \end{pmatrix} + \mathcal{E}^*, \tag{33}$$

and

$$(y_0, Y) = (X_1, X_2) \begin{pmatrix} \pi_1 & \Pi_1 \\ \pi_2 & \Pi_2 \end{pmatrix} + (\epsilon_0, \mathcal{E}). \tag{34}$$

Here $\mathcal{E}^* = (\epsilon_0, \mathcal{E})$ is the $T \times M$ matrix of reduced-form disturbances, in (32) the partitioning is by columns (left-hand versus right-hand endogenous variables), in (33) the partitioning is by rows (included vs. excluded exogenous variables), and in (34) the partitioning is by rows *and* columns.

Post-multiplication of (34) by the vector $\binom{1}{-\gamma}$ yields

$$y_0 = Y\gamma + X_1(\pi_1 - \Pi_1\gamma) + X_2(\pi_2 - \Pi_2\gamma) + (\epsilon_0 - \mathcal{E}\gamma). \qquad (35)$$

Identifying coefficients between (30) and (35), one finds the standard relations between structural and reduced-form coefficients:

$$\pi_1 - \Pi_1\gamma = \beta, \qquad \pi_2 - \Pi_2\gamma = 0. \qquad (36)$$

We suppose that the structural equation is overidentified, with $K_2 \geqslant M$, so that (36) constrains the reduced-form coefficient matrix.

Unconstrained least-squares regression of Y^* on X would estimate Π^* as $P^* = (X'X)^{-1} X'Y^*$, which means that it would estimate Π_2^* as

$$P_2^* = (X_2'N_1X_2)^{-1} X_2'N_1Y^*$$

where $N_1 = I - X_1(X_1'X_1)^{-1} X_1$. In more detail, this means that the unconstrained estimates of π_2 and Π_2 would be

$$p_2 = (X_2'N_1X_2)^{-1} X_2'N_1y_0 \quad \text{and} \quad P_2 = (X_2'N_1X_2)^{-1} X_2'N_1Y,$$

respectively. For given γ, it is clear from (36) that this would provide two distinct estimates of π_2, namely

$$p_2(1) = p_2 \quad \text{and} \quad p_2(2) = P_2\gamma.$$

The MGLS estimation procedure with S replacing Ω, would choose the value of Π^* to minimize, subject to (36), the quantity

$$\mathrm{tr}[S^{-1}(Y^* - X\Pi^*)' (Y^* - X\Pi^*)],$$

or equivalently the quantity

$$\mathrm{tr}[S^{-1}(P^* - \Pi^*)' X'X(P^* - \Pi^*)].$$

Here $S = (1/T)(Y^* - XP^*)' (Y^* - XP^*)$. The minimization leads to $\binom{1}{-\gamma}$ being estimated as $d = \binom{1}{-c}$, a suitably normalized characteristic vector of a certain matrix, and then to Π_2^* being estimated by

$$\Pi_2^* = P_2^* - (d'Sd)^{-1} P_2^*dd'S; \qquad (37)$$

cf. Goldberger & Olkin (1971). Inspecting (37) we find that its first column, which is the MGLS estimate of π_2, is

$$\hat{\pi}_2 = p_2 - (d'Sd)^{-1}(p_2, P_2)\begin{pmatrix} 1 \\ -c \end{pmatrix}d's_1,$$

$$= p_2 - (d'Sd)^{-1}(p_2 - P_2c)d's_1$$

where s_1 is the first column of S. We can rearrange this into

$$\hat{\pi}_2 = P_2cw + p_2(1 - w),$$

where $w = (d'Sd)^{-1}d's_1$. Thus we have exhibited the MGLS estimator $\hat{\pi}_2$ as a weighted average of p_2 and P_2c, which are the two distinct estimates of π_2 available when the value of γ is given by c.

7. Combining Estimating Equations and Combining Estimates

7.1 ALGEBRAIC ANALYSIS

Up to this point, we have focused on combining estimates. We now turn to the notion of combining estimating equations. To fix ideas we begin in purely algebraic terms. Consider an overdetermined system of linear equations

$$Ax = c, \tag{38}$$

where A is a given $m \times n$ matrix of rank $n < m$, x is the unknown $n \times 1$ vector, and c is a given $m \times 1$ vector. Suppose further that every $n \times n$ submatrix of A has rank n. Coincidences apart, no vector x will satisfy this system of m equations in n unknowns, but solutions to subsystems may be found. For example, let A_1 denote the submatrix of A obtained by deleting the last $m - n$ rows, and let c_1 denote the subvector of c obtained by deleting its last $m - n$ elements. The truncated system $A_1x = c_1$, which consists of the first n rows of $Ax = c$, can be solved for $A_1^{-1}c_1 = x(1)$, say. Proceeding in this fashion, one can generate $m!/(n!(m - n)!) = G$, say, distinct truncated systems

$$A_gx = c_g \qquad (g = 1,..., G), \tag{39}$$

since that is the number of different ways in which n rows can be selected out of m rows. Thus one can generate G "basic solutions"

$$x(g) = A_g^{-1}c_g \qquad (g = 1,..., G). \tag{40}$$

Coincidence apart, the basic solutions will all differ and none will be a solution to the full system $Ax = c$.

The transitions from (38) to (39) can be represented by matrix operations. For example, let $B_1 = (I_{n,n}, 0_{n,m-n})$; then $B_1 A = A_1$ and $B_1 c = c_1$. More generally, if the numbers of the rows retained in the gth truncated system were labeled $m_1(g),..., m_n(g)$, then $A_g = B_g A$ and $c_g = B_g c$, where B_g is the $n \times m$ matrix all of whose elements are zero except for those in the slots $(1, m_1(g)),..., (n, m_n(g))$. With this device the truncated systems and the solutions thereto may be written as

$$B_g Ax = B_g c \qquad (g = 1,..., G) \qquad (41)$$

and

$$x(g) = (B_g A)^{-1} B_g c \qquad (g = 1,..., G), \qquad (42)$$

respectively.

The transpose of each B_g is an $m \times n$ matrix B_g' which selects columns on postmultiplication in the same way that B_g selects rows on premultiplication. Each product $B_g' B_g$ is an $m \times m$ matrix all of whose elements are zero except for those in the diagonal slots

$$(m_1(g), m_1(g)),..., (m_n(g), m_n(g)).$$

Consequently, it is readily confirmed that

$$\sum_{g=1}^{G} B_g' B_g = GI \qquad (43)$$

where I is the $m \times m$ identity matrix.

Now let us return to the full system and combine its equations as follows. Let D be any $n \times m$ matrix of rank n. Multiplying $Ax = c$ through by D produces a system of n equations in n unknowns,

$$DAx = Dc, \qquad (44)$$

which, on the proviso that the rank of DA is n, will have the solution

$$x^* = (DA)^{-1} Dc. \qquad (45)$$

We wish to show how this solution to a system of combined equations can be depicted as a combination of the basic solutions $x(1),..., x(G)$. Equation (43) permits us to write

$$DA = (1/G) D(GI)A = (1/G) D \left(\sum_{g=1}^{G} B_g' B_g \right) A = (1/G) \sum_{g=1}^{G} (DB_g' B_g A)$$

and

$$Dc = (1/G) \sum_{g=1}^{G} (DB_g'B_gc).$$

The latter becomes

$$Dc = (1/G) \sum_{g=1}^{G} (DB_g'B_gAx(g))$$

by virtue of (42). Therefore from (45) we conclude that

$$x^* = \left[\sum_{h=1}^{G} (DB_h'B_hA) \right]^{-1} DB_g'B_gAx(g) = \sum_{g=1}^{G} W_gx(g) \qquad (46)$$

where

$$W_g = \left[\sum_{h=1}^{G} (DB_g'B_gA) \right]^{-1} DB_g'B_gA \qquad (g = 1,..., G).$$

Because $\sum_{g=1}^{G} W_g = I$, we say that (46) displays x^*, the solution to the combined system of equations, as a weighted average of the $x(g)$, the solutions to the truncated systems of equations. To be sure, while each $B_g'B_g$ lies between 0 and I in an obvious sense, there are no grounds for asserting that each W_g lies between 0 and I in the same sense. Nor is there any reason to expect that an individual element of x^* will lie between the maximum and minimum of the corresponding elements of the $x(g)$. Still, the term "weighted average" seems to be adequately descriptive to support our use of it.

7.2 Instrumental Variable Estimation

The analysis just developed finds its leading applications in the area of instrumental-variable estimation. Consider the structural equation $y = Z\beta + u$, where y is the $T \times 1$ vector of observations on an endogenous variable, Z is the $T \times (K - J)$ matrix of rank $(K - J)$ of observations on endogenous and exogenous variables, β is $(K - J) \times 1$, and u is $T \times 1$. This structural equation is embedded in a system for which X is the $T \times K$ matrix of rank K of observations on all the exogenous variables. The exogenous variables are assumed to be distributed independently of the disturbance vector u, which has $E(u) = 0$ and $E(uu') = \sigma^2I$.

Since the columns of X form a set of K legitimate instrumental variables, we multiply the structural equation through by X' and discard the error term to produce a set of K estimating equations for the $(K - J)$ elements of β, namely

$$X'Zb = X'y. \tag{47}$$

To proceed, we assume that every $(K - J) \times (K - J)$ submatrix of the $K \times (K - J)$ matrix $X'Z$ has rank $(K - J)$ and thus $X'Z$ itself has rank $(K - J)$. The set of estimating equations is overdetermined, reflecting the fact that the structural equation is overidentified.

The problem at hand is formally the same as that discussed in Section 7.1. Equation (47) has the form of (38), with the roles of A, x, c, m, and n being played by $X'Z$, b, $X'y$, K, and $(K - J)$, respectively. One may ignore certain overidentifying restrictions by discarding rows of $X'Z$. There are in fact $G = K!/[(K - J)! \, J!]$ different basic estimators of β, each corresponding to a retention of a certain $K - J$ exogenous variables as instruments. Each of the basic estimators $b(1),\ldots, b(G)$ will, under standard stochastic specifications, provide a consistent estimator of β. It is natural to combine these basic estimators in the interest of efficiency, or simply convenience, and the various procedures for estimation of individual overidentified structural equations that have appeared in the econometric and sociological literature amount to doing just that. To show that such a procedure does amount to averaging of the basic estimators, we need only show that the estimating equations it employs can be produced by multiplying (47) through by a $(K - J) \times K$ matrix D.

The two-stage least-squares procedure estimates β by b^*, the solution to

$$Z'X(X'X)^{-1} X'Zb^* = Z'X(X'X)^{-1} X'y, \tag{48}$$

cf. Theil (1971, pp. 451–454). Clearly, this is obtained when (47) is premultiplied by $Z'X(X'X)^{-1}$, so that b^* is a weighted average of the basic estimators $b(g)$, the weights being

$$W_g{}^* = \left(\sum_h Z'X(X'X)^{-1} B_h{}'B_h X'Z \right)^{-1} Z'X(X'X)^{-1} B_g{}'B_g X'Z$$

$$= (1/G)(Z'X(X'X)^{-1} X'Z)^{-1} Z'X(X'X)^{-1} B_g{}'B_g X'Z. \tag{49}$$

On this formulation of $b^* = \sum_g W_g{}^* b(g)$, the familiar formula for the covariance matrix of the two-stage least-squares estimator can be derived as

$$
\begin{aligned}
V(b^*) &= \sum_g \sum_h W_g^* C(b(g), b(h))\, W_h^{*\prime} \\
&= \sum_g \sum_h W_g^* (B_g X'Z)^{-1}\, B_g X' E(uu')\, X B_h (Z'XB_h')^{-1}\, W_h^{*\prime} \\
&= \sigma^2 (Z'X(X'X)^{-1} X'Z)^{-1}\, Z'X(X'X)^{-1}\, X'X(X'X)^{-1} \\
&\quad \times\, X'Z(Z'X(X'X)^{-1} X'Z)^{-1} \\
&= \sigma^2 (Z'X(X'X)^{-1} X'Z)^{-1},
\end{aligned}
$$

where we have used the facts that $\sum_g B_g' B_g X'X = G(X'X)$, etc.

In a related context, Boudon (1968, pp. 213–215) proposed that the conflict among the basic estimators be resolved in a simpler fashion. Specifically, Boudon proposes that the estimate of β be chosen as the value which minimizes the quantity

$$
(X'Z\beta - X'y)' \, (X'Z\beta - X'y),
$$

namely as the value b^{**} determined by

$$
Z'XX'Zb^{**} = Z'XX'y. \tag{50}
$$

Clearly, this is obtained when (47) is premultiplied by $Z'X$, so that b^{**} is a weighted average of the $b(g)$, the weights being

$$
W_g^{**} = \left(\sum_h Z'XB_h' B_h X'Z \right)^{-1} Z'XB_g' B_g X'Z.
$$

From this formulation of b^{**} as $\sum_g W_g^{**} b(g)$, the covariance matrix of Boudon's estimator can be derived as

$$
\begin{aligned}
V(b^{**}) &= \sum_g \sum_h W_g^{**} C(b(g), b(h))\, W_h^{**\prime} \\
&= \sigma^2 (Z'XX'Z)^{-1}\, Z'XX'XX'Z(Z'XX'Z)^{-1}.
\end{aligned}
$$

It is not hard to show that $V(b^{**}) - V(b^*)$ is nonnegative definite so that the 2SLS estimator has, asymptotically, smaller variance than Boudon's estimator. Indeed, it is well-known that the 2SLS estimator is as efficient as any other instrumental variable estimator in the present context, i.e., as any other combination of the basic estimators.

Our final example is taken from Duncan, Featherman, & Duncan, (1968, pp. 155–156), who, faced with an empirical problem in which

$K = 4$ and $K - J = 3$, decided on explicitly ad hoc grounds to add together the last two of the four estimating equations. This amounts to taking

$$\begin{pmatrix} 1 & 0 & 0 & 0 \\ 0 & 1 & 0 & 0 \\ 0 & 0 & 1 & 1 \end{pmatrix}$$

as the D-matrix. Equivalently, it amounts to using x_1, x_2, and $x_3 + x_4$ as the instrumental variables: in

$$b^{***} = (DX'Z)^{-1} DX'y,$$

the rows of DX' are x_1', x_2', $(x_3' + x_4')$, where x_1', x_2', x_3', x_4' are the rows of X'.

9. Conclusion

Starting with a simple example, we have attempted to exhibit efficient estimation procedures as devices for combining the conflicting pieces of information which are available in overidentified models. For the most part, we have worked directly with the conflicting estimates, but we have also sketched the relationship between the combining of estimating equations and the combining of estimates.

Acknowledgments

Work on this project was supported in part by grants from the Graduate School of the University of Wisconsin and the Social Science Research Council.

8

Cross-lagged and
Synchronous Common Factors in Panel Data

DAVID A. KENNY

1. Introduction

A correlation between two variables, e.g. reading ability and mathematical ability, can be explained in at least three different ways. One theorist might say that reading ability causes mathematical ability, while another might say reading causes mathematical ability. A third theorist, imbued in factor analysis, might say that both abilities are caused by some general ability factor. Or, at the very least, he would say that in the domain of educational tests, common factoredness must be disposed of first. A single correlation, of course, cannot rule out a common-factor explanation, but as we will show, panel data may.

Panel data involve at least two variables, say X and Y, that are measured at two different times, say 1 and 2, on the same set of subjects. With two-wave, two-variable (2W2V) panel data there are six correlations: two *synchronous correlations* $\rho_{X_1 Y_1}$ and $\rho_{X_2 Y_2}$, two *auto-correlations*, $\rho_{X_1 X_2}$ and $\rho_{Y_1 Y_2}$, and two *cross-lagged correlations*, $\rho_{X_1 Y_2}$ and $\rho_{X_2 Y_1}$.

The use of panel data for nonexperimental inference with continuous variables has been suggested by many authors. Campbell (1963) and Campbell & Stanley (1963) suggested the technique of "cross-lagged panel correlation," which involves a comparison of the cross-lagged

153

correlations. Rozelle & Campbell (1969) attempt to formulate some of the assumptions of this technique. They state that "third variable and 'co-symptom' effects over and beyond any mutual causal relations are assumed" (p. 77). They claim, but do not demonstrate, that unequal cross-lagged correlations imply that a common factor model is inadequate. Pelz & Andrews (1964) independently proposed a similar procedure. Rickard (1972) attempts to construct a general causal model and sketches a three-wave analysis. Duncan (1969a) and Heise (1970) elaborate a number of path models for panel data that generally involve direct causal paths between observables. Goldberger (1971) suggests the use of a regression model as a formalization of Campbell's cross-lagged panel correlation technique. Recently Duncan has written two papers (1972, 1973) that elaborate a number of models which contain unobservable common causes and measurement error. Werts & Linn (1970) and Blalock (1970) have shown that panel data may be used to test psychometric assumptions. A series of authors (Humphreys, 1960; Heise, 1969a; Wiley & Wiley, 1970; Werts, Jöreskog, & Linn, 1971) have suggested the use of panel data to infer the reliability and stability coefficients of variables.

This paper is an attempt to formalize Campbell's cross-lagged panel correlation technique. We will focus on testing competing models, not on the estimation of parameters. We will assume that the observables are caused by a set of factors. A factor is called *common* if it causes two or more observables; it is called *unique* if it causes only one observable. We construct two different types of factor models. In Model I we specify that the correlation between observables is due to a *synchronous* common factor—one which contemporaneously affects both observables. In Model II we specify that the correlation between the observables is due not only to a synchronous common factor but also to a common factor that affects the first variable (X) contemporaneously, and affects the second variable (Y) after some delay. We will call this second factor a *cross-lagged* common factor that *leads* from X to Y. Our objective is to find restrictions on the observable correlations that serve to discriminate between the two models.

The causal interpretation of a cross-lagged common factor is no simple matter. There is no automatic assumption that the verbal description of the factor is identical with that of the leading variable. Often, the leading variable will be multidimensional and any one of the dimensions could be the causally relevant one. This problem of verbal or substantive interpretation of a statistical result arises even in experimental research: manipulated independent variables are often multidimensional and a conventional significance test never by itself tells which dimension of the treatment affects the dependent variable. To test Model I against the more general Model II we will often need to constrain the way factor loadings change over time. We consider two types of proportionality constraints on the factor loadings: *between* and *within*. A *between-variable* proportionality constraint keeps the ratio of common factor loadings of *two observables* on the *same common factor* constant over time. A *within-variable* proportionality constraint keeps the ratio of loadings of the *same observable* on *two common factors* constant over time. Our experience with panel data of educational tests suggests that within-variable constraints are often plausible, while between-variable constraints rarely are.

Throughout this paper we employ standardized variables to take advantage of the simplicity of correlational algebra. This will mean some loss of generality, but in most cases our results can easily be extended to unstandardized variables.

2. Two-Wave, Two-Variable Models (2W2V)

2.1 Model I

Let X and Y be two standardized variables on which a number of subjects are measured at time 1 and again at time 2. Suppose that X and Y are contemporaneously caused by Z, an unmeasured factor. The remaining unobserved causes and errors of measurement of X are lumped into a residual or unique factor S, and those for Y into T. The set-up is

$$X_1 = a_1 Z_1 + S_1, \qquad Y_1 = b_1 Z_1 + T_1$$
$$X_2 = a_2 Z_2 + S_2, \qquad Y_2 = b_2 Z_2 + T_2.$$

The subscripts refer to time, subject subscripts are omitted. The lowercase letters are factor loadings, i.e. structural coefficients. The synchronous and lagged cross correlations of Z, S, and T are zero while their autocorrelations may be nonzero. Since X, Y, and Z are standardized, the variance of S_t equals $1 - a_t^2$ and the variance of T equals $1 - b_t^2$ ($t = 1, 2$). Denote the autocorrelation of Z_1 with Z_2 by j_{21}. The correlations of X and Y under Model I are given in Table 1. The autocorrelation of Z, j_{21}, is identified by

$$j_{21}^2 = \frac{(a_1 b_2 j_{21})(a_2 b_1 j_{21})}{(a_1 b_1)(a_2 b_2)} = \frac{\rho_{X_1 Y_2} \rho_{X_2 Y_1}}{\rho_{X_1 Y_1} \rho_{X_2 Y_2}}, \tag{1}$$

TABLE 1

2W2V CORRELATIONS FOR MODELS I AND II[a]

Synchronous correlations

$$\rho_{X_1 Y_1} = a_1 b_1 \quad [+g_1 h_1 p_{10}]$$
$$\rho_{X_2 Y_2} = a_2 b_2 \quad [+g_2 h_2 p_{21}]$$

Cross-lagged correlations

$$\rho_{X_1 Y_2} = a_1 b_2 j_{21} \quad [+g_1 h_2]$$
$$\rho_{X_2 Y_1} = a_2 b_1 j_{21} \quad [+g_2 h_1 p_{10} p_{21}]$$

Autocorrelations

$$\rho_{X_1 X_2} = a_1 a_2 j_{21} + \text{Cov}(S_1, S_2) \quad [+g_1 g_2 p_{21}]$$
$$\rho_{Y_1 Y_2} = b_1 b_2 j_{21} + \text{Cov}(T_1, T_2) \quad [+h_1 h_2 p_{10}]$$

[a] For Model I, ignore terms in brackets.

the product of cross-lagged correlations divided by the product of synchronous correlations. This identification has been shown by Werts & Linn (1970), Blalock (1970), and Duncan (1972). If j_{21}^2 is greater than unity, the synchronous common factor model is inappropriate. If j_{21}^2 is less than unity, the model is tenable. The remaining parameters cannot be identified, though if one is known a priori, the others are identified (Duncan, 1972).

Relying on $j_{21}^2 < 1$ to test a synchronous common factor model is extremely conservative on the side of accepting the model. Our experience indicates that the product of cross-lagged correlations rarely exceeds the product of synchronous correlations. To gain the possibility of a stronger test, the synchronous common factor model must be more sharply specified. Suppose, for example, that we add the between-variable proportionality constraint

$$a_1/a_2 = b_1/b_2 . \tag{2}$$

With $a_1 b_2 = a_2 b_1 = ab$, say, the two cross-lagged correlations both equal abj_{21}, and hence equal each other. Alternatively, suppose that we add the stronger requirement $a_1 = a_2$ and $b_1 = b_2$. Then not only must the cross-lagged correlations be equal but so must the synchronous correlations. [Note, however, that equality of synchronous correlations does not necessarily imply (2) since $\rho_{X_1 Y_1} = \rho_{X_2 Y_2}$ if $a_1 b_1 = a_2 b_2$, i.e. if $a_1/a_2 = b_2/b_1$.] Thus, equality of the cross-lagged correlations provides a test of the synchronous common factor model given that assumption (2) is made.

The autocorrelations may provide the researcher with another test of the model. If we know that the autocorrelations of the unique factors S and T are positive and that a and b do not change sign over time, then

$$\rho_{X_1 X_2} \rho_{Y_1 Y_2} \geqslant a_1 a_2 b_1 b_2 j_{21}^2 = \rho_{X_1 Y_2} \rho_{X_2 Y_1} .$$

2.2 MODEL II

If the researcher rejects a synchronous common factor model (Model I) he is forced to choose a different model. He might want to construct a model that includes both a synchronous and a cross-lagged common factor (Model II). Let U be a standardized unmeasured cross-lagged factor leading from X to Y. The set-up is

$$X_1 = a_1 Z_1 + g_1 U_1 + S_1 , \qquad Y_1 = b_1 Z_1 + h_1 U_0 + T_1$$

$$X_2 = a_2 Z_2 + g_2 U_2 + S_2 , \qquad Y_2 = b_2 Z_2 + h_2 U_1 + T_2 .$$

Again we assume that all the cross correlations of the unobservables are zero while their autocorrelations may be nonzero. We will also assume that U is first-order autoregressive, i.e.

$$U_1 = p_{10} U_0 + e_1 , \qquad U_2 = p_{21} U_1 + e_2 ,$$

where the disturbances e_1 and e_2 are mutually uncorrelated and are uncorrelated with prior values of U. Since U has a variance of unity, $p_{10} = \rho_{U_1 U_0}$ and $p_{21} = \rho_{U_1 U_2}$. The correlations of this model are presented in Table 1.

If we make the between-variable proportionality constraints of $a_1 b_2 = a_2 b_1 = ab$, say, and $g_1 h_2 = g_2 h_1 = gh$, say, we find that the difference between the cross-lagged correlations is

$$\rho_{X_1 Y_2} - \rho_{X_2 Y_1} = gh(1 - p_{10} p_{21}). \tag{3}$$

Since p_{10} and p_{21} are correlations, their product will be less than or equal to 1. Provided that both p_{10} and p_{21} are not unity, (3) will be nonzero. Thus, given between-variable proportionality constraints, Model I diverges from Model II in that it predicts equality of the cross-lagged correlations. If such between-variable proportionality constraints are not valid, Model I necessitates unequal cross-lagged correlations while Model II may still yield equal cross-lagged correlations.

Assuming that p_{10} and p_{21} have the same sign, the sign of (3) is the same as the sign of the product gh. As pointed out by Yee & Gage (1968) and by Rozelle &' Campbell (1969), there are four possible types of causal models in panel data. Put into the terminology of cross-lagged common factors, the relevant questions are: from what variable does the cross-lagged common factor lead, and with what signs do the variables load on the factor. If (3) is positive, then either the cross-lagged common factor leads from X and both loadings have the same sign, or it leads from Y and the loadings have different signs. If (3) is negative, then either the factor leads from X and the loadings have different signs, or it leads from Y and the loadings have the same sign. Thus if the researcher can specify from which variable the common factor leads, the data will indicate the sign of the product of the variables' loadings on the factor; if he can specify the sign of the product of loadings, the data will indicate from which variable the cross-lagged common factor leads.

3. Three-Wave, Two-Variable Models (3W2V)

3.1 MODEL I

With 2W2V data, between-variable proportionality constraints are needed if one is to discriminate between Models I and II. With the addition of a third wave such strong assumptions need not be made. The specification of our 3W2V Model I parallels that of our 2W2V Model I. The set-up is

$$X_t = a_t Z_t + S_t, \qquad Y_t = b_t Z_t + T_t \qquad (t = 1, 2, 3).$$

Again, X, Y, and Z are standardized, the variance of T_t equals $1 - a_t^2$, and the variance of S_t equals $1 - b_t^2$ ($t = 1, 2, 3$). The synchronous and cross-lagged correlations of the factors are zero while their auto-correlations may be nonzero. The common factor Z is assumed to be first-order autoregressive:

$$Z_t = j_{t,t-1} Z_{t-1} + e_t,$$

where the disturbance e_t is uncorrelated with prior values of Z.

TABLE 2

3W2V Correlations for Models I and II[a]

Synchronous correlations

$\rho_{X_1Y_1} = a_1b_1 \quad [+g_1h_1p_{10}]$
$\rho_{X_2Y_2} = a_2b_2 \quad [+g_2h_2p_{21}]$
$\rho_{X_3Y_3} = a_3b_3 \quad [+g_3h_3p_{32}]$

Cross-lagged correlations

$\rho_{X_1Y_2} = a_1b_2j_{21} \quad [+g_1h_2]$
$\rho_{X_2Y_3} = a_2b_3j_{32} \quad [+g_2h_3]$
$\rho_{X_1Y_3} = a_1b_3j_{21}j_{32} \quad [+g_1h_3p_{21}]$
$\rho_{X_2Y_1} = a_2b_1j_{21} \quad [+g_2h_1p_{10}p_{21}]$
$\rho_{X_3Y_2} = a_3b_2j_{32} \quad [+g_3h_2p_{21}p_{32}]$
$\rho_{X_3Y_1} = a_3b_1j_{21}j_{32} \quad [+g_3h_1p_{10}p_{21}p_{32}]$

Autocorrelations

$\rho_{X_1X_2} = a_1a_2j_{21} + \mathrm{Cov}(S_1, S_2) \quad [+g_1g_2p_{21}]$
$\rho_{X_2X_3} = a_2a_3j_{32} + \mathrm{Cov}(S_2, S_3) \quad [+g_2g_3p_{32}]$
$\rho_{X_1X_3} = a_1a_3j_{21}j_{32} + \mathrm{Cov}(S_1, S_3) \quad [+g_1g_3p_{21}p_{32}]$
$\rho_{Y_1Y_2} = b_1b_2j_{21} + \mathrm{Cov}(T_1, T_2) \quad [+h_1h_2p_{10}]$
$\rho_{Y_2Y_3} = b_2b_3j_{32} + \mathrm{Cov}(T_2, T_3) \quad [+h_2h_3p_{21}]$
$\rho_{Y_1Y_3} = b_1b_3j_{21}j_{32} + \mathrm{Cov}(T_1, T_3) \quad [+h_1h_3p_{10}p_{21}]$

---

[a] For Model I, ignore terms in brackets.

The correlations of X and Y are presented in Table 2. The first-order autocorrelations of Z, j_{21}, and j_{32}, are overidentified by

$$j_{21}^2 = \frac{(a_1b_2j_{21})(a_2b_1j_{21})}{(a_1b_1)(a_2b_2)} = \frac{\rho_{X_1Y_2}\rho_{X_2Y_1}}{\rho_{X_1Y_1}\rho_{X_2Y_2}} \tag{4}$$

$$= \frac{(a_1b_3j_{21}j_{32})(a_2b_1j_{21})}{(a_2b_3j_{32})(a_1b_1)} = \frac{\rho_{X_1Y_3}\rho_{X_2Y_1}}{\rho_{X_2Y_3}\rho_{X_1Y_1}} \tag{5}$$

$$= \frac{(a_3b_1j_{21}j_{32})(a_1b_2j_{21})}{(a_3b_2j_{32})(a_1b_1)} = \frac{\rho_{X_3Y_1}\rho_{X_1Y_2}}{\rho_{X_3Y_2}\rho_{X_1Y_1}}; \tag{6}$$

and

$$j_{32}^2 = \frac{(a_2b_3j_{32})(a_3b_2j_{32})}{(a_2b_2)(a_3b_3)} = \frac{\rho_{X_2Y_3}\rho_{X_3Y_2}}{\rho_{X_2Y_2}\rho_{X_3Y_3}} \tag{7}$$

$$= \frac{(a_1b_3j_{21}j_{32})(a_3b_2j_{32})}{(a_1b_2j_{21})(a_3b_3)} = \frac{\rho_{X_1Y_3}\rho_{X_3Y_2}}{\rho_{X_1Y_2}\rho_{X_3Y_3}} \tag{8}$$

$$= \frac{(a_3b_1j_{21}j_{32})(a_2b_3j_{32})}{(a_2b_1j_{21})(a_3b_3)} = \frac{\rho_{X_3Y_1}\rho_{X_2Y_3}}{\rho_{X_2Y_1}\rho_{X_3Y_3}}. \tag{9}$$

Equating (4) and (5), or (7) and (8), we find the following restriction on the observable correlations:

$$\rho_{X_1 Y_2} \rho_{X_2 Y_3} - \rho_{X_2 Y_2} \rho_{X_1 Y_3} = 0. \tag{10}$$

Similarily, equating (4) and (6), or (7) and (9), we find:

$$\rho_{X_2 Y_1} \rho_{X_3 Y_2} - \rho_{X_2 Y_2} \rho_{X_3 Y_1} = 0. \tag{11}$$

These two vanishing tetrads were first proposed in this context by Rickard (1972). Tetrad (10) involves the cross-lagged correlations where X is the earlier-measured variable, and tetrad (11) involves the cross-lagged correlations where Y is the earlier-measured variable. The remaining parameters or loadings are not identifiable but certain ratios and products of the parameters are.

3.2 MODEL II

Adding a cross-lagged common factor U that leads from X to Y we have our 3W2V Model II:

$$X_t = a_t Z_t + g_t U_t + S_t, \qquad Y_t = b_t Z_t + h_t U_{t-1} + T_t \qquad (t = 1, 2, 3).$$

Once again, cross correlations are assumed to be zero while the auto-correlations may be nonzero. Both Z and U are assumed to be first-order autoregressive with positive coefficients, $j_{t,t-1}$ and $p_{t,t-1}$, respectively. The correlations of this model are presented in Table 2. To obtain an overidentification we may make the following within-variable proportionality constraints:

$$a_1/g_1 = a_2/g_2 = a_3/g_3, \qquad b_1/h_1 = b_2/h_2 = b_3/h_3,$$

and also assume $j_{21} = p_{21}$ and $j_{32} = p_{32}$. Then tetrad (11) will be zero, but tetrad (10) will be nonzero in general (see Appendix for proof). If the cross-lagged common factor leads from Y to X, (10) would be zero while (11) would not. Thus tetrads (10) and (11) provide a basis for discriminating among a synchronous common factor model, a synchronous and cross-lagged common factor model with X leading, and a synchronous and cross-lagged common factor model with Y leading.

3.3 VIOLATION OF ASSUMPTIONS OF 3W2V MODEL I

Let us now examine the above conclusions in the event that one of the following two assumptions is not met: the absence of synchronous correlation between S and T, and Z being first-order autoregressive.

First, it is reasonable to expect test scores to be synchronously correlated for "irrelevant" reasons. In an educational setting, a person's attitude, health, the temperature of the room, etc. may affect his scores on both tests. Let us suppose that these errors of measurement are contemporaneously, but not serially, cross-correlated:

$$\text{Cov}(S_i, T_j) \neq 0 \quad \text{if} \quad i = j, \qquad \text{Cov}(S_i, T_j) = 0 \quad \text{if} \quad i \neq j.$$

This contemporaneously correlated measurement error would affect the synchronous correlations. Therefore any identification that involves a synchronous correlation may be incorrect. For instance, with 3W2V Model I, if a_t and b_t have the same sign, then $C(S_t, T_t) > 0$ will inflate the synchronous correlations. The autocorrelation of Z would be understated by (4) and (9), and the tetrads (10) and (11) would be negative. Still, the model is overidentified by

$$\frac{\rho_{X_1 Y_2} \rho_{X_2 Y_3}}{\rho_{X_1 Y_3}} = \frac{\rho_{X_2 Y_1} \rho_{X_3 Y_2}}{\rho_{X_3 Y_1}}$$

since they both equal $a_2 b_2$.

Second, the assumption that the common factor is first-order autoregressive may be unreasonable for many data sets. As an example, examine the case where there are two orthogonal common factors Z and V:

$$X_t = a_t Z_t + m_t V_t + S_t, \qquad Y_t = b_t Z_t + n_t V_t + T_t \qquad (t = 1, 2, 3).$$

Let us assume that Z and V are each first-order autoregressive with coefficients of $j_{t,t-1}$ and $k_{t,t-1}$ respectively. The tetrad in (10) will equal

$$(a_1 b_2 j_{21} + m_1 n_2 k_{21})(a_2 b_3 j_{32} + m_2 n_3 k_{32}) - (a_2 b_2 + m_2 n_2)(a_1 b_3 j_{21} j_{32} + m_1 n_3 k_{21} k_{32})$$

$$= a_1 b_2 m_2 n_3 j_{21} k_{32} + a_2 b_3 m_1 n_2 j_{32} k_{21} - a_2 b_2 m_1 n_3 k_{21} k_{32} - a_1 b_3 m_2 n_2 j_{21} j_{32}. \quad (12)$$

This expression will not necessarily equal zero. Even if $j_{21} = k_{21}$ and $j_{32} = k_{32}$, (12) will not equal zero unless we impose within-variable proportionality constraints on one of the variables. Alternatively, if $j_{21} = j_{32} \neq k_{21} = k_{32}$ and none of the loadings change over time, (12) will still not equal zero.

Clearly the presence of multiple synchronous common factors will make tetrads (10) and (11) fail to vanish even in the absence of a cross-lagged common factor. If the researcher suspects that certain observables affect both variables in the model, he should include such variables in the model. Such variables as social class, sex, ethnicity, school, and geographic region could easily bias any panel analysis if they were not controlled for.

4. Two-Wave, Multivariate Models (2WMV)

Most sets of panel data have only two waves but observe more than two variables. As we saw above, the presence of multiple common factors with different autoregressive coefficients creates problems in distinguishing between Models I and II in 3W2V data. With 2WMV data it is possible to distinguish the two models in the presence of multiple *orthogonal* common factors with different autocorrelations provided that within-variable proportionality constraints are imposed.

Let there be N variables and P orthogonal common factors. Let A_1 and A_2 be the $N \times P$ matrix of common factor loadings at times one and two, respectively:

$$A_1 = \begin{pmatrix} a_{11}^{(1)} & \cdots & a_{1P}^{(1)} \\ \vdots & a_{ip}^{(1)} & \vdots \\ a_{N1}^{(1)} & \cdots & a_{NP}^{(1)} \end{pmatrix} = \begin{pmatrix} a_{11}' \\ \vdots \\ a_{i1}' \\ \vdots \\ a_{N1}' \end{pmatrix}, \quad A_2 = \begin{pmatrix} a_{11}^{(2)} & \cdots & a_{1P}^{(2)} \\ \vdots & a_{ip}^{(2)} & \vdots \\ a_{N1}^{(2)} & \cdots & a_{NP}^{(2)} \end{pmatrix} = \begin{pmatrix} a_{12}' \\ \vdots \\ a_{i2}' \\ \vdots \\ a_{N2}' \end{pmatrix}.$$

Suppose that $A_1 = KA_2$ where K is an $N \times N$ diagonal matrix,

$$K = \begin{pmatrix} k_1 & & & \\ & \ddots & & 0 \\ & & k_i & \\ & 0 & & \ddots \\ & & & k_N \end{pmatrix}.$$

This captures the within-variable proportionality constraints, i.e., $a_{ip}^{(1)} = k_i a_{ip}^{(2)}$, so $a_{i1}^{(1)}/a_{i1}^{(2)} = \cdots = a_{iP}^{(1)}/a_{iP}^{(2)} = k_i$. The ith variable's communality at time one (h_{i1}^2) equals $a_{i1}'a_{i1}$ and its communality at time two (h_{i2}^2) equals $a_{i2}'a_{i2}$. Thus the ratio of its communalities equals k_i^2 since

$$h_{i1}^2/h_{i2}^2 = a_{i1}'a_{i1}/a_{i2}'a_{i2} = a_{i2}'k_ik_ia_{i2}/a_{i2}'a_{i2} = k_i^2.$$

The synchronous correlation of the variables i and j at time one $(\rho_{i_1 j_1})$ equals $a'_{i1} a_{j1} = k_i k_j a'_{i2} a_{j2}$, and at time two $(\rho_{i_2 j_2})$ equals $a'_{i2} a_{j2}$. Thus the ratio of the synchronous correlations,

$$q_{ij} = \rho_{i_1 j_1} / \rho_{i_2 j_2},$$

equals $k_i k_j$. Let Q be the $N \times N$ matrix of the q_{ij}. The matrix Q is single-factored in the sense that

$$\frac{q_{ij} q_{mj}}{q_{im}} = \frac{(a'_{i1} a_{j1})(a'_{j1} a_{m1})(a'_{i2} a_{m2})}{(a'_{i2} a_{j2})(a'_{j2} a_{m2})(a'_{i1} a_{m1})} = \frac{k_i k_j k_j k_m}{k_i k_m} = k_j{}^2.$$

Consequently, each k_i is just-identified if $N = 3$ and overidentified if $N > 3$. In the latter case, the K-matrix might be fitted by Spearman's two-factor solution (Harman, 1967). The adequacy with which a single factor reproduces Q can serve as a test of the within-variable proportionality constraints. Assuming that the test is passed, we can proceed as follows: Let C be the $N \times N$ matrix of cross-lagged correlations, and let J be the $P \times P$ diagonal matrix of the factor autocorrelations; then

$$C = A_1 J A_2'.$$

Let $K^{1/2}$ be the diagonal matrix whose diagonal elements are the $k_i^{1/2}$. Pre- and postmultiply C by $K^{-1/2}$ and $K^{1/2}$ respectively to find

$$K^{-1/2} C K^{1/2} = K^{-1/2} (A_1 J A_2') \, K^{1/2} = K^{1/2} A_2 J A_2' K^{1/2}$$
$$= (K^{1/2} A_2 J^{1/2})(K^{1/2} A_2 J^{1/2})',$$

where $J^{1/2}$ is a diagonal matrix whose diagonal elements are the square roots of the factor autocorrelations. Thus in the present model $K^{-1/2} C K^{1/2}$ is a symmetric matrix. Consequently, observed differences between its corresponding off-diagonal elements indicate a misspecification and suggest a cross-lagged common factor. The pattern of unequal off-diagonal elements may also suggest a verbal interpretation for the cross-lagged common factor; see Crano, Kenny, & Campbell (1972).

5. Conclusion

We have explored the possibility of testing for a synchronous common factor in panel data. With the 2W2V models, we needed to make an assumption about the proportionality of factor loadings between variables across time. Adding a third wave necessitates no assumption about factor loadings but requires an assumption of single factoredness. Our 2WMV model assumes multiple orthogonal common factors but requires the testable assumption of proportionality of factor loadings within a variable across time.

A common thread throughout this chapter has been the necessity of making assumptions to test between competing models. We have generally chosen proportionality assumptions. A synchronous common factor model can fit any body of data, *if* there are no constraints on the number of factors and the manner in which their loadings change over time. To gain the possibility of inferring the presence of a cross-lagged common factor we must make some assumptions. These should be testable, or at least reasonable. The reasonableness of the assumptions can be best examined by working with data in substantive areas. Further elaborations of testing factor models will only progress through the combined effort of the statistician and the researcher engaged in substantive problems.

We have ignored estimation and formal significance tests: A test for the equality of correlations whose arrays are intercorrelated is given in Peters & VanVoorhis (1940). A test of vanishing tetrads is given in Spearman & Holzinger (1924) and more recently reproduced by Duncan (1972). The estimation problem could possibly be simplified by adapting Jöreskog's (1970a) analyses of covariance structures. However, our 2WMV strategy does not limit the number of factors as Jöreskog does, but rather constrains the manner in which loadings change over time.

Appendix

The tetrad on the left-hand side of (10) is, in terms of the correlations given in Table 2:

$$\rho_{X_1Y_2}\rho_{X_2Y_3} - \rho_{X_2Y_2}\rho_{X_1Y_3} = (a_1b_2j_{21} + g_1h_2)(a_2b_3j_{32} + g_2h_3)$$
$$- (a_2b_2 + g_2h_2p_{21})(a_1b_3j_{21}j_{32} + g_1h_3p_{21})$$
$$= b_2h_3(a_1g_2j_{21} - a_2g_1p_{21}) + g_1g_2h_2h_3(1 - p_{21}^2)$$
$$+ b_3h_2j_{32}(a_2g_1 - a_1g_1j_{21}p_{21}).$$

If $a_1g_2 = a_2g_1$, $b_3h_2 = b_2h_3$, and $p_{21} = j_{21}$, then this reduces to

$$\rho_{X_1Y_2}\rho_{X_2Y_3} - \rho_{X_2Y_2}\rho_{X_1Y_3} = g_1g_2h_2h_3(1 - p_{21}^2) + b_2b_3j_{32}a_1g_2(1 - p_{21}^2)$$
$$= g_2h_2(1 - p_{21}^2)(g_1h_3 + a_1b_3j_{32})$$

which is nonzero in general.

The tetrad on the left-hand side of (11) is

$$\rho_{X_2 Y_1}\rho_{X_3 Y_2} - \rho_{X_2 Y_2}\rho_{X_3 Y_1} = (a_2 b_1 j_{21} + g_2 h_1 p_{10} p_{21})(a_3 b_2 j_{32} + g_3 h_2 p_{21} p_{32})$$
$$- (a_2 b_2 + g_2 h_2 p_{21})(a_3 b_1 j_{21} j_{32} + g_3 h_1 p_{10} p_{21} p_{32})$$
$$= a_2 g_3 p_{21} p_{32}(b_1 h_2 j_{21} - b_2 h_1 p_{10})$$
$$+ a_3 g_2 p_{21} j_{32}(b_2 h_1 p_{10} - b_1 h_2 j_{21}).$$

If $a_2 g_3 = a_3 g_2$, $b_1 h_2 = b_2 h_1$, and $j_{32} = p_{32}$, then this reduces to zero.

Acknowledgments

Work on this paper was supported in part by National Science Foundation grants GS1309X and GS30273X. Donald T. Campbell, principal investigator, provided the inspiration for this paper.

9

Diagnosing Indicator Ills in Multiple Indicator Models

HERBERT L. COSTNER AND RONALD SCHOENBERG

Measured variables, treated as surrogates for unmeasured constructs of theoretical interest, are commonly contaminated by sources of variation other than those which they are intended to reflect. In structural equation models such contamination of indicators may seriously distort parameter estimates and threaten the validity of the substantive conclusions that rest on them. A number of recent papers have examined the problem of indicator flaws in causal models (Blalock, 1963, 1969a; Blalock, Wells, & Carter, 1970; Costner, 1969; Hauser & Goldberger, 1971; Heise, 1969a; Land, 1970; Sullivan, 1971; Werts, Linn, & Jöreskog, 1971; Wiley & Wiley, 1970). While these papers identify clues that signal the existence of indicator flaws, they give little guidance in how to use these clues to isolate the precise nature of the indicator difficulties. The best safeguard against distortions due to indicator flaws undoubtedly lies in the development of better indicators, but such improvements may be facilitated by detailed knowledge of which indicators are most seriously contaminated and in what way. The analysis of indicator flaws is therefore relevant, not only to the achievement of more accurate parameter estimates, but also to the improvement of indicators and potentially to the development of increased clarity in theoretical concepts.

In this paper we explore a strategy for analyzing indicator flaws in overidentified multiple indicator models. Our strategy rests on the detailed examination of the goodness of fit and patterns of residuals for

167

"submodels" drawn systematically from the full set of indicators. The application of this strategy may suggest a selective addition of paths to the initial model in order to incorporate the indicator contamination as an aspect of the model itself, or it may suggest the necessity of discarding certain heavily contaminated indicators. Under certain circumstances, it may also suggest a reconceptualization of the theoretical dimensions and a corresponding reshuffling of the indicators. The ultimate utility of any such modification depends not only on the achievement of a more satisfactory fit between the model and the data, but also on the increased understanding of the basic theory and of the measured variables that serve to tie theoretical formulations to observed variations.

1. An Illustrative Problem

In the discussion to follow, we will use a model and data pertaining to the industrial and political development of nations. The data are among those previously analyzed by Olsen (1968), who drew the original data for the industrial development indicators from United Nations sources and the original data for the political development indicators from Banks & Textor (1963) and from Cutright (1963).

The three industrial development indicators are:

1. GNP: logarithm of gross national product per capita in dollars.
2. Energy: logarithm of total energy consumption in megawatt hours per capita.
3. Labor Diversity: a labor force diversification index based on the similarity of the actual distribution of the labor force of a nation over nine major sectors of the economy with a standard distribution representing the approximate current distribution in a highly industrialized society, the United States.

Each of the six political development indicators listed below is based on a combination of different items of information. For the first four listed, these component variables were subjectively coded by Banks and Textor into three or four levels using available published materials and frequent consultations with area specialists; the component variables were then combined by Olsen to constitute the indicator.

4. Executive Functioning: (a) functional effectiveness of the governmental bureaucracy, (b) interest aggregation by the executive, and (c) degree of governmental stability.
5. Legislative Functioning: (a) functional effectiveness of the

legislature, (b) interest aggregation by the legislature, and (c) extent of civilian control of politics.

6. Party Organization: (a) number of political parties (two or more versus no party, one party, and "one-and-a-half-party" systems), (b) interest aggregation by political parties, and (c) stability of political parties.

7. Power Diversification: (a) constitutionality of the government, (b) number of autonomous governmental branches, and (c) nonrestrictive recruitment of political leaders.

8. Citizen Influence: (a) electoral representation in politics, (b) freedom of group opposition, and (c) freedom of the press.

9. Cutright Index: an index of political representation based on parliamentary functioning, multiparty systems, and popular election of the executive (Cutright, 1963).

In Olsen's analysis the sum of a nation's scores on indicators 4, 5, 6, 7, and 8 was used as a seventh indicator of political development. However, because such a sum would necessarily have correlated errors with the indicators contributing to it, this composite indicator has been eliminated here to simplify the analysis.

The correlation matrix for these nine variables is given in Table 1.

TABLE 1

CORRELATIONS BETWEEN SELECTED INDICATORS OF THE INDUSTRIAL AND
POLITICAL DEVELOPMENT OF NATIONS, CIRCA 1960[a]

	Industrial development			Political development					
	GNP	Energy	Labor divers.	Exec. funct.	Legis. funct.	Party org.	Power divers.	Citizen infl.	Cutright index
	1	2	3	4	5	6	7	8	9
1	1.00	.95	.83	.66	.60	.56	.45	.51	.67
2		1.00	.83	.70	.54	.54	.38	.38	.66
3			1.00	.62	.62	.54	.38	.43	.61
4				1.00	.63	.47	.45	.48	.60
5					1.00	.76	.89	.89	.75
6						1.00	.64	.72	.64
7							1.00	.94	.67
8								1.00	.71
9									1.00

[a] Adapted from Olsen (1968), Tables 2 and 4, and supplemented by rs among indicators of political development by Professor Olsen. The total sample consists of the 115 independent nations listed in Banks and Textor (1963). Because of missing data, the n for any one correlation is less than the total sample.

The highest correlation between an indicator of industrial development and an indicator of political development is the .70 correlation between Energy and Executive Functioning. We might be tempted to conclude that these are the "best" indicators of industrial and political development respectively, arguing that the other correlations have been more heavily attenuated by measurement error. Stated so flatly, the conclusion appears naïve; but the selection of indicators that yield the highest correlations is actually quite common in the social sciences.

We begin our analysis with the simple model of Fig. 1, in which industrial development is viewed as the cause of political development. Clearly, we must interpret the causal parameter with considerable caution. In our model, it represents the effect of industrial development on political development, but this role cannot be distinguished from a mere correlation, nor from a mixture of the two effects in a feedback relationship, nor from some combination of these. It should be further noted that the model of Fig. 1 is a gross oversimplification and that a more complete model should include additional constructs related to both industrial and political development. Figure 1 does not represent either Olsen's model of economic and political development or our own; rather it represents a simplified model useful as a methodological illustration.

All of our variables are standardized to have zero mean and unit standard deviation. In algebraic form our model is

$$y = Bx + e,$$

where y is the vector of indicators, B the matrix of "loadings" or "epistemic coefficients" (the coefficients for the paths from the constructs to their indicators), x the vector of dimensions, and e the vector of error terms. Assuming that x and e are independent, it follows that

$$\Sigma = B\Phi B' + \Theta,$$

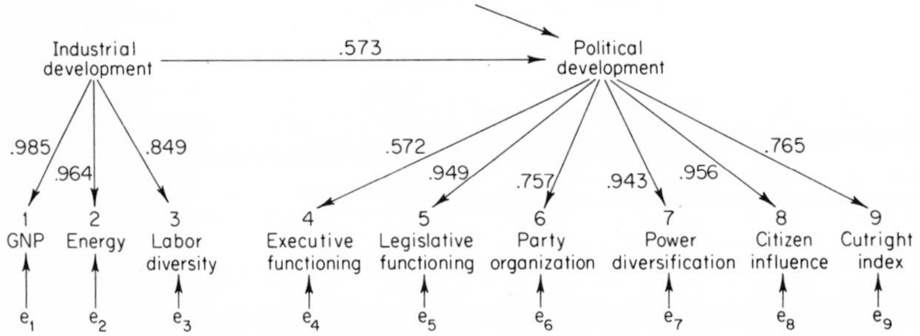

Figure 1.   Estimated causal model for indicators of industrial and political development.

where Σ is the population correlation matrix of the indicators, Φ is the population correlation matrix of the constructs, and Θ is a diagonal matrix containing the error variances. Given R, a sample correlation matrix of the indicators, we choose values for $\hat{B}$, $\hat{\Phi}$, $\hat{\Theta}$ to minimize

$$F = \log | \Sigma | + \text{tr}(R\Sigma^{-1}).$$

These values are maximum-likelihood estimates under the assumption that x and e are normally distributed; see Jöreskog (1969). The procedure in effect minimizes a scalar function of the difference between R and $\hat{\Sigma} = \hat{B}\hat{\Phi}\hat{B}' + \hat{\Theta}$, i.e., between the sample correlation matrix and the correlation matrix implied by the parameter estimates.

Applying this estimation procedure, we obtain the ten parameter estimates shown in Fig. 1. Table 2 shows the residuals matrix $R - \hat{\Sigma}$ from this estimation, i.e., the discrepancies between the observed correlations (Table 1) and the correlations reconstructed from the path estimates. The "goodness of fit" between the model and the data is indicated by the chi-square value and the corresponding probability level shown in Table 2.[†] The relatively large chi-square value in this instance indicates a disappointingly poor fit, suggesting that there is some

TABLE 2

Residuals between Observed Correlations (Table 1) and Correlations Implied by the Path Estimates (Fig. 1)[a]

	GNP 1	Energy 2	Labor divers. 3	Exec. funct. 4	Legis. funct. 5	Party org. 6	Power divers. 7	Citizen infl. 8	Cutright index 9
1	—	.000	−.006	.337	.065	.133	−.082	−.029	.238
2		—	.012	.384	.016	.122	−.140	−.148	.238
3			—	.342	.159	.172	−.078	−.035	.238
4				—	.087	.037	−.089	−.067	.163
5					—	.042	−.005	−.018	.024
6						—	−.073	−.003	.061
7							—	.038	−.051
8								—	−.022
9									—

[a] $\chi^2 = 365.5$; 26 degrees of freedom; $p < .001$.

[†] The degrees of freedom are calculated by subtracting the number of parameters estimated in the model from the number of observed correlations; therefore in this case we have 26 degrees of freedom.

misspecification in the model. This sets the stage for the basic problem to which this chapter is addressed, namely how to isolate the specific indicator or conceptual flaws responsible for the poor fit.

2. Intuitive Inferences from the Pattern of Residuals

A large discrepancy between the observed and implied correlation for any given pair of variables (i.e., a large entry in the residuals matrix) suggests that between those two variables there are sources of covariation that have been omitted from the initial model. This, in turn, suggests an examination of the residuals matrix to locate the largest discrepancies, a redesign of the model to provide for additional paths, and an estimate and "goodness of fit" test for the redesigned model. But this approach can be very misleading. The clues provided by the residuals matrix are highly fallible clues under certain circumstances.

This can best be illustrated by an examination of some sets of hypothetical data generated from arbitrarily selected parameter values. Since sampling variation would only detract from our illustrations of the consequences of specification errors, we will confine our attention to population correlations. For computing test statistics, we let $n = 1000$.

Consider the model with parameters specified as in Fig. 2a. This is the "true" model, i.e., the model used in generating the "observed" correlations. Suppose further that an investigator assumes that the model of Fig. 2b applies. We anticipate then that the residuals matrix would show a reasonably good fit for all pairs of variables except the two having correlated error, and that this residual would be relatively large and positive (i.e., the observed correlation should be larger than the implied correlation). The residuals matrix (Table 3) does indeed show this pattern, i.e., there is one very large discrepancy and it is precisely as anticipated, a positive discrepancy in the correlation between variables 3 and 4. The presence of nonzero residuals for each of the other pairs of variables clearly shows that all of the estimates have been biased by this one specification error. The estimation procedure, seeking to reconcile the investigator's model with the data that were actually generated by a slightly different model, does not limit the ramifications of a specification error to its exact locale. Nevertheless in this instance the pattern in the residuals serves as an excellent clue to the nature of the specification error.

But now let the "true" model be that in Fig. 3a, with estimates derived by the model of Fig. 3b. The intuitive expectation is for positive

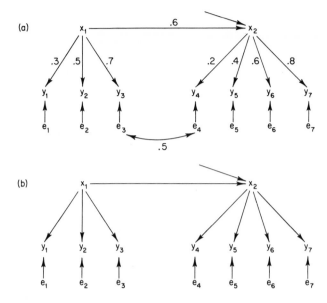

Figure 2.   Illustrative true model (a) and estimating model (b).

TABLE 3

RESIDUALS MATRIX PRODUCED FROM THE ESTIMATION OF THE MODEL IN FIG. 2b
USING CORRELATIONS GENERATED BY THE MODEL OF FIG. 2a

	y_1	y_2	y_3	y_4	y_5	y_6	y_7
y_1	—	.024	−.005	−.034	−.005	−.007	.006
y_2		—	−.001	−.055	−.006	−.008	.014
y_3			—	*.388*	−.047	−.068	−.050
y_4				—	−.063	−.094	−.098
y_5					—	.006	.038
y_6						—	.060
y_7							—

residuals for variables 4 and 5, 5 and 6, and 4 and 6, with other residuals
small. The actual pattern of discrepancies shown in Table 4 does not
correspond to this expectation. The residuals expected to be large and
positive are italicized. Contrary to our intuition, two of the three are
actually negative and the other is small (only three of the 21 discrepancies
are smaller). Even the largest of the discrepancies expected to be large
is smaller than other discrepancies that were expected to be small.
Having obtained the residuals matrix of Table 4, an investigator might

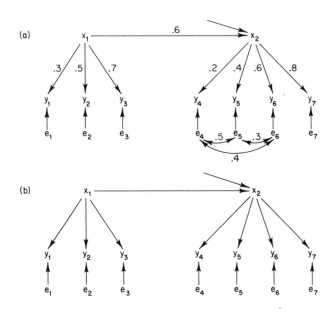

Figure 3.   Illustrative true model (a) and estimating model (b).

TABLE 4

RESIDUALS MATRIX PRODUCED FROM THE ESTIMATION OF THE MODEL IN FIG. 3b
USING CORRELATIONS GENERATED BY THE MODEL OF FIG. 3a[a]

	y_1	y_2	y_3	y_4	y_5	y_6	y_7
y_1	—	.000	.000	−.045	−.017	.009	.083
y_2		—	.000	−.074	−.028	.016	.138
y_3			—	−.104	−.039	.022	.193
y_4				—	*.108*	−*.005*	−.167
y_5					—	−*.037*	−.040
y_6						—	.080
y_7							—

[a] $\chi^2 = 221.8$; 13 degrees of freedom; $p < .001$.

reformulate his model as in Fig. 4; that is, he might put in paths between all pairs of indicators that had large residuals. But this has little in common with the model that actually generated the data. If the investigator then proceeded to derive estimates on the basis of the revised model, he would find that he had achieved a noteworthy improvement in fit (Table 5). This illustrates the well-known fact that two or more

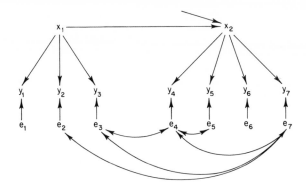

Figure 4.   Reformulation of estimating model 3b on the basis of the residuals matrix (Table 4).

TABLE 5

RESIDUALS MATRIX PRODUCED FROM THE ESTIMATION OF THE MODEL IN FIG. 4
USING CORRELATIONS GENERATED BY THE MODEL OF FIG. 3a[a]

	y_1	y_2	y_3	y_4	y_5	y_6	y_7
y_1	.000	.011	.016	−.030	.003	.004	.083
y_2		.003[b]	.011	−.055	.000	−.001	.019
y_3			.009[b]	−.019	.001	−.001	.017
y_4				.000	.000	.003	−.006
y_5					.000	.000	.001
y_6						.000	.003
y_7							.002[b]

[a] $\chi^2 = 14.1$; 8 degrees of freedom; $p = .079$.
[b] All values in the diagonal should be zero. Nonzero entries are apparently a consequence of rounding error in the iteration.

models may fit the same set of data reasonably well, but it does not help in reconstructing the model that generated the data. The investigator would have achieved a close fit, but he would draw incorrect conclusions about the nature of his indicator flaws and hence be led to employ inappropriate strategies in attempting to remedy them.

We now consider another illustration. Let the true model be given by Fig. 5a and suppose that our investigator specifies the model of Fig. 5b. Our intuition is that the path between X_1 and X_2, or the path between X_1 and X_3, or both, would be poorly estimated. Thus we might expect large residuals between pairs of indicators crossing these two pairs of constructs, i.e., between the indicators of X_1 on the one hand and the

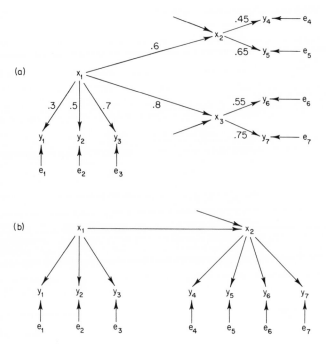

Figure 5. Illustrative true model (a) and estimating model (b).

indicators of X_2 on the other, or between indicators of X_1 and X_3. The actual pattern of residuals (Table 6) does not conform to this pattern at all. All the residuals involving indicators 1, 2, and 3 are small; the largest residual is between indicators 4 and 5, which are, in the true

TABLE 6

Residuals Matrix Produced from the Estimation of the Model in Fig. 5b
Using Correlations Generated by the Model of Fig. 5a[a]

	y_1	y_2	y_3	y_4	y_5	y_6	y_7
y_1	—	.000	.000	.002	.011	−.008	.000
y_2		—	.000	.003	.018	−.014	.000
y_3			—	.004	.025	−.019	.000
y_4				—	.171	−.042	−.044
y_5					—	−.045	−.043
y_6						—	.047
y_7							—

[a] $\chi^2 = 58.6$; 13 degrees of freedom; $p < .001$.

model, indicators of the same construct. One could reason that correlated errors between a subset of indicators of a given construct simply indicates that the indicators in that subset "behave" differently from the remaining indicators and thus can reasonably be called indicators of a different construct. But one might require other evidence before drawing such a conclusion. In any case, if we modify the estimating model to include correlation between the error terms of indicators 4 and 5, we arrive at the residuals in Table 7. The fit is relatively good, but the model is not the one used to generate the correlations.

TABLE 7

RESIDUALS MATRIX PRODUCED FROM THE ESTIMATION OF THE MODEL IN FIG. 5b MODIFIED BY THE INCLUSION OF A CORRELATED ERROR BETWEEN INDICATORS 4 AND 5, USING CORRELATIONS GENERATED BY THE MODEL OF FIG. 5a[a]

	y_1	y_2	y_3	y_4	y_5	y_6	y_7
y_1	—	.000	.000	.014	.021	−.009	−.003
y_2		—	.000	.024	.035	−.015	−.005
y_3			—	.034	.048	−.021	−.007
y_4				—	.000	−.021	−.019
y_5					—	−.030	−.028
y_6						—	.030
y_7							—

[a] $\chi^2 = 14.2$; 12 degrees of freedom; $p = .286$.

The general conclusion to be drawn from these illustrations is that the respecification suggested by an intuitive appraisal of the pattern of residuals may be grossly misleading, unless the specification error was very simple (and sometimes even then). Such respecification may lead to a significant improvement in fit even though the respecified model does not resemble the model that has generated the data. These hazards in turn suggest considerable caution in drawing substantive conclusions from the pattern of residuals. But they further indicate the need for other kinds of diagnostic clues in the analysis of indicator flaws.

3. Two-Indicator Submodels

We turn attention now to "submodels" formed by taking subsets of the indicators in an original model. For example, each of the illustrative models above, with three indicators for X_1 and four indicators for X_2, contains eighteen different submodels formed by taking pairs of indicators for X_1 and pairs of indicators for X_2. Furthermore, each contains an additional four submodels formed by taking triplets of indicators for each of the unmeasured constructs. We shall see that certain features of these submodels provide diagnostic clues which were not available in the residuals matrix for the model as a whole.

Consider the two-indicator models shown in Figs. 6a, 6b, 6c, and 6d. Assume that the model of Fig. 6a is the model used in estimating, while

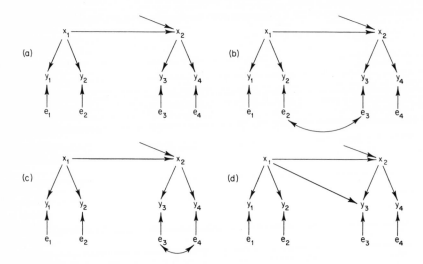

Figure 6. Illustrative two-indicator models.

any of the four models shown may be the true model, i.e., the model that generates the observed correlations. As shown in Costner (1969), two estimates may be made for each parameter in the model of Fig. 6a and the two estimates for each parameter will be identical to each other if the true model is that of Fig. 6a or Figs. 6c or 6d. But the two estimates will not be identical to each other if the true model is that of Fig. 6b (where there is correlated error between indicators of different unmeasured constructs). Translated into the terms of the present discussion, this means that the fit will be perfect (since we are ignoring sampling variability) if the true model is that of Figs. 6a, 6c, or 6d, but imperfect if the true model is that of Fig. 6b. This specificity in the sensitivity of two-indicator models to correlated error between indicators of different constructs allows the use of two-indicator submodels to generate clues to a specific kind of indicator flaw. A satisfactory fit in a two-indicator submodel suggests that correlation of the error terms of indicators of different constructs is absent for the four indicators involved. An unsatisfactory fit in a two-indicator submodel suggests that such correlation is present. The precise location of the correlation may be detected by considering the complete set of two-indicator submodels. In this manner, we may begin to rule out, or rule in, certain specific kinds of correlated errors and thus move closer to a good approximation of the true model.

As an illustration we return to Fig. 2. Consider each of the two-indicator submodels contained in the model of Fig. 2b, where the data are generated by the true model of Fig. 2a. Table 8 reports the goodness of fit test for all 18 two-indicator submodels. All fits are perfect except those including both variable 3 and variable 4, thus effectively

TABLE 8

"Fit" (χ^2) for All Possible Two-Indicator Submodels Contained in the Model of Fig. 2b, Utilizing Data Generated by the Model of Fig. 2a

Indicators of X_2	Indicators of X_1					
	1, 2		1, 3		2, 3	
	χ^2	p	χ^2	p	χ^2	p
4, 5	.00	—	13.26	<.001	40.68	<.001
4, 6	.00	—	14.98	<.001	46.04	<.001
4, 7	.00	—	17.63	<.001	54.33	<.001
5, 6	.00	—	.00	—	.00	—
5, 7	.00	—	.00	—	.00	—
6, 7	.00	—	.00	—	.00	—

pinpointing the specification error. In real sample data, the results will typically be much less clear, of course, and it will be useful to summarize the fits of the two-indicator submodels as in Table 9, showing the proportion of two-indicator submodels that are poor fits by an arbitrary criterion ($p < .001$) for each pair of cross-construct indicators. Again, the location of the specification error is indicated: all submodels that include indicators 3 and 4 fit poorly, while a much smaller proportion of other cross-construct pairs of indicators have been included in models with poor fits (i.e., only when indicators 3 and 4 appear in the submodel with them).

Another illustration is presented in Table 10. The fit for all of the two-indicator submodels contained in the model of Fig. 3b is essentially perfect when using the data generated by the true model of Fig. 3a,

TABLE 9

SUMMARY OF TABLE 8 SHOWING PROPORTION OF TWO-INDICATOR SUBMODELS
HAVING p VALUES OF .001 OR LESS FOR EACH CROSS-CONSTRUCT PAIR OF INDICATORS

Indicators of X_2	Indicators of X_1		
	1	2	3
4	3/6	3/6	6/6
5	1/6	1/6	2/6
6	1/6	1/6	2/6
7	1/6	1/6	2/6

TABLE 10

"FIT" (χ^2) FOR ALL POSSIBLE TWO-INDICATOR SUBMODELS CONTAINED IN THE MODEL OF
FIG. 3b, UTILIZING DATA GENERATED BY THE MODEL OF FIG. 3a

Indicators of X_2	Indicators of X_1					
	1, 2		1, 3		2, 3	
	χ^2	p	χ^2	p	χ^2	p
4, 5	.17	.680	.29	.587	.32	.569
4, 6	1.94	.163	3.41	.065	3.77	.052
4, 7	.00	—	.00	—	.00	—
5, 6	.00	—	.00	—	.00	—
5, 7	.00	—	.00	—	.00	—
6, 7	.00	—	.00	—	.00	—

since there are no correlated errors between indicators of different
dimensions in this model.[†] In this case the specification errors have not
been located by considering the fit of the two-indicator submodels, but

---

[†] The fits are not exactly perfect because of a boundary problem with respect to the
indicator error terms. If a negative error variance were allowed, the maximum-likelihood
procedure would have made estimates of the parameters that would have fit perfectly.
This situation with regard to the error terms will occasionally introduce discrepancies
between observed and implied correlations where none would otherwise exist. This
feature of the estimating procedure (we have used a computer program described in
Jöreskog et al., 1970) was not realized by the present authors initially and the result
shown in Table 10 was unexpected. The illustration has been retained though this complication could have been avoided by assigning different values to the parameters of the
hypothetical model.

certain possibilities—namely correlated errors between indicators of different constructs—have been ruled out. Note that some of these possibilities were seriously considered when we appraised the full residuals matrix in Fig. 4.

Disregarding sampling variation, the fit of two-indicator submodels yields necessary and sufficient evidence of the existence or nonexistence of extra correlations between error terms of indicators of different constructs. A good fit for the model as a whole is necessary but not sufficient evidence for the nonexistence of such extra connections: we found that including the extra connections in the model where there were large residuals produced an improvement in fit in spite of the fact that the revised model did not coincide with the true model (see Table 5).

The two-indicator submodels of the third set of hypothetical data (Fig. 5) were also analyzed and the fits found to be all perfect. This was the expected result since there are no correlated errors between indicators of different constructs. Needless to say, real sample data cannot be expected to yield perfect fits as is the case with these hypothetical population data. But two-indicator submodels using real data may yield a fit so close as to suggest that such correlated errors are not major contributors to the poor fit of the model as a whole.

We now return from illustrations using hypothetical data to our real data described earlier pertaining to the economic and political development of nations. From the original model (Fig. 1) we may constitute 45 two-indicator submodels. For these 45 submodels, the chi-square values for fit are shown in Table 11. With such a large number of submodels it is difficult to discern any pattern with the outcomes displayed as in Table 11, and a summary table analogous to Table 9, will help locate the probable correlated errors. Each of the nine cross-indicator pairs occurs ten times in Table 11. Table 12 gives the proportion of those times in which the p value of a two-indicator submodel that contained that pair of indicators was .001 or less.

The outcome for these real data is evidently not so clear as for the hypothetical data. For no pair of cross-construct indicators shown in Table 12 do all two-indicator submodels have a poor fit by the criterion used. However, for certain pairs of cross-construct indicators, the fit is frequently poor even if not always so. Indicator 8 (Citizen Influence) appears to have correlated errors with indicator 1 (GNP) and indicator 2 (Energy). Also, indicator 5 (Legislative Functioning) seems to have correlated errors with indicator 2 (Energy) and indicator 3 (Labor Diversity). Unfortunately, when the correlated errors suggested by the two-indicator submodel analysis were entered into the full model, the information matrix failed to invert, implying some difficulty with

TABLE 11

"FIT" (χ^2) FOR ALL POSSIBLE TWO-INDICATOR SUBMODELS CONTAINED IN THE MODEL OF FIG. 1, BASED ON DATA IN TABLE 1

Indicators of political development	Indicators of industrial development					
	1, 2		1, 3		2, 3	
	χ^2	p	χ^2	p	χ^2	p
4, 5	16.5	<.001	1.6	.204	11.9	.001
4, 6	3.5	.061	0.1	.786	1.6	.209
4, 7	12.9	<.001	0.8	.381	0.8	.357
4, 8	41.4	<.001	1.0	.314	4.1	.042
4, 9	3.5	.060	0.2	.685	0.3	.579
5, 6	4.0	.047	1.1	.294	4.1	.043
5, 7	9.9	.002	34.6	<.001	33.2	<.001
5, 8	42.7	<.001	23.6	<.001	14.1	<.001
5, 9	6.8	.009	4.2	.040	12.0	.001
6, 7	5.7	.017	1.7	.196	0.0	—
6, 8	35.2	<.001	2.7	.103	1.8	.186
6, 9	0.3	.617	0.5	.473	1.0	.330
7, 8	59.4	<.001	1.1	.284	6.6	.010
7, 9	8.9	.003	0.6	.442	1.7	.198
8, 9	41.7	<.001	0.9	.356	6.5	.011

TABLE 12

SUMMARY OF TABLE 11 SHOWING PROPORTION OF TWO-INDICATOR SUBMODELS HAVING p VALUES OF .001 OR LESS FOR EACH CROSS-CONSTRUCT PAIR OF INDICATORS

Indicators of political development	Indicators of industrial development		
	1	2	3
4	3/10	4/10	1/10
5	4/10	6/10	6/10
6	1/10	1/10	0/10
7	3/10	3/10	2/10
8	6/10	6/10	2/10
9	1/10	2/10	1/10

regard to the identifiability of the model.[†] The same difficulty was encountered when correlated errors involving indicator 5 but not 8, or involving indicator 8 but not 5, were incorporated into the model. To have a well-defined model, therefore, it is necessary either to disregard these correlated errors (and thus confound the subsequent analysis) or to discard both indicators 5 and 8. We have chosen the latter alternative.

The substantive meaning of the cross-construct correlated errors suggested by the two-indicator submodels may be as important as the knowledge of their existence. A substantive interpretation of cross-construct correlated errors may take any of three rather different forms. We might, for example, presume that there is a feedback effect on certain aspects of industrial development from certain manifestations of (i.e., indicators of) political development, but not from other manifestations. Thus Citizen Influence may not only be affected by the level of economic development but may, in turn, further affect GNP, while Party Organization may be affected by the level of industrial development but not have feedback effects on GNP. Similarly, one might hypothesize a feedback relationship between Legislative Functioning and Energy, even though certain other manifestations of political development which are affected by industrial development do not, in turn, have further effects on Energy.

But a substantive interpretation of the correlated errors does not require that one focus on the possibility of differential feedback effects. A second kind of possibility is that several processes are involved in the connection between industrial development and political development. For example, an increase in the level of industrial development may stimulate the development of the organizational basis for institutional political opposition (e.g., Party Organization) but the rise in the general standard of living resulting from increased industrial development may also stimulate segments of the population who were formerly politically apathetic to demand a greater voice in government and thus stimulate the institution of certain democratic forms (e.g., Citizen Influence). If one of these effects of increasing industrial development appears rapidly and the other much more slowly, this would give rise to the appearance of correlated errors of the kind suggested by the two-indicator submodels, but such correlated errors should be diminished by introducing an appropriate lag for the indicator representing the delayed effect.

[†] A failure to invert implies either negative variances, in which case the model is not well defined, or infinite variances (or very large ones) indicating nonidentification.

184   HERBERT L. COSTNER AND RONALD SCHOENBERG

Finally, there is the possibility that the correlated errors are a result of indicator flaws in the more commonly understood meaning of that term, i.e., that they arise from biases introduced in the process of selecting and recording data. Since the assigned values of all of the indicators of political development used in the present illustration depend heavily on the subjective judgment of specialists acquainted with a number of different aspects of a given nation-state, it is likely that factors other than those named have influenced those judgments. For example, the specialists may upgrade the rating of a given nation's degree of citizen influence if the GNP (and hence the general standard of living) is relatively high, and correspondingly downgrade the ratings contributing to citizen influence when the GNP is low. Thus correlated errors need not be assumed to be in the nature of the phenomenon being investigated but may arise from invalid measurement. When measurement procedures are as shaky as those for political development used here, it is probably wise to assume that the correlated errors arise from faulty measurements rather than proposing an elaboration of the basic theory. It is clearly desirable to have alternative attempts to measure Citizen Influence and Legislative Functioning that would be free of the correlated errors suggested in the analysis of the present data.

4. Three-Indicator Submodels

The insensitivity of two-indicator submodels to specification errors of certain types suggests that we should look for additional clues to locate such specification errors. Three-indicator submodels provide one source of additional clues.

Turning back to our hypothetical data to illustrate our procedure, we first consider the four three-indicator submodels contained in Fig. 3b and the corresponding submodels contained in the true model (Fig. 3a). The four three-indicator submodels contained in the true model are shown in Fig. 7 along with a general form of the estimating model. It is evident that the complex pattern of correlated errors has, in three of these submodels, been transformed into a very simple pattern, i.e., only one correlated error per submodel (see Figs. 7b, 7c, and 7d). We might then suppose that the correct correlated errors would be clearly indicated by the patterns of residuals for these three submodels. The residuals are presented in Table 13. Unfortunately, in none of the four sets of residuals are there large residuals for the correlations between indicators 4 and 5, or for 5 and 6, or for 4 and 6, the pairs of indicators

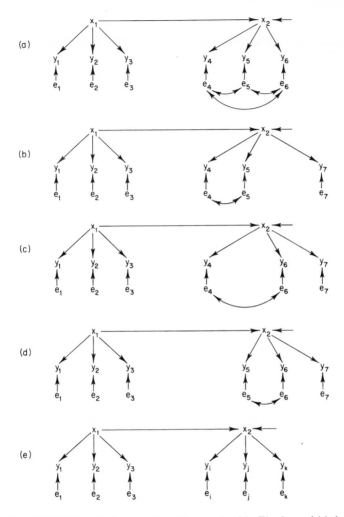

Figure 7. (a)–(d) Three-indicator submodels contained in Fig. 3a, and (e) the general estimating submodel.

having correlated errors. In Tables 13b, 13c, and 13d the largest residuals are for the correlations between indicators 1 and 7, 2 and 7, and 3 and 7. These are cross-construct pairs of indicators, and the analysis of the two-indicator submodels has already suggested that correlated errors between indicators of different constructs do not exist (see Table 10). We must therefore consider alternative patterns that would give rise to this particular pattern of correlated errors. One possibility would be a causal connection between X_1 and indicator 7, a pattern to which the two-indicator submodels would not have been sensitive. This possibility is plausible on the basis of the residuals of Tables 13b, 13c, and 13d because, in each of these sets of residuals, indicator 7 has large residuals with each of the indicators of X_1. But an examination of the residuals shown in Table 13a makes this possibility less plausible. If a causal connection between X_1 and indicator 7 were

TABLE 13

RESIDUALS FOR THE FOUR THREE-INDICATOR SUBMODELS SHOWN IN FIG. 7[a]

13a	(The model of Fig. 7a is the true model; Fig. 7a is a three-indicator submodel of Fig. 3a which is the whole true model.)			13b	(The model of Fig. 7b is the true model; Fig. 7b is a three-indicator submodel of Fig. 3a which is the whole true model.)		
	y_4	y_5	y_6		y_4	y_5	y_7
y_1	−.034	−.002	.040	y_1	−.013	−.004	.117
y_2	−.057	−.004	.067	y_2	−.021	−.006	.195
y_3	−.079	−.005	.093	y_3	−.029	−.008	.273
y_4	—	.012	−.001	y_4	—	.003	−.047
y_5		—	−.012	y_5		—	−.002

$\chi^2 = 41.6$
8 degrees of freedom
$p < .001$

$\chi^2 = 115.4$
8 degrees of freedom
$p < .001$

13c	(The model of Fig. 7c is the true model; Fig. 7c is a three-indicator submodel of Fig. 3a which is the whole true model.)			13d	(The model of Fig. 7d is the true model; Fig. 7d is a three-indicator submodel of Fig. 3a which is the whole true model.)		
	y_4	y_6	y_7		y_5	y_6	y_7
y_1	−.020	.000	.092	y_1	−.018	−.013	.060
y_2	−.034	.000	.154	y_2	−.029	−.021	.100
y_3	−.047	.000	.215	y_3	−.041	−.029	.140
y_4	—	.000	−.090	y_5	—	.020	−.042
y_6		—	.000	y_6		—	−.008

$\chi^2 = 95.6$
8 degrees of freedom
$p < .001$

$\chi^2 = 54.2$
8 degrees of freedom
$p < .001$

[a] Residuals for y_1, y_2, for y_1, y_3, and for y_2, y_3 were .000 in each instance and have been omitted here to conserve space.

the only omission from the estimating model, then the three-indicator submodel including indicators 4, 5, and 6 (but omitting 7) should yield a good fit. But such is not the case, as shown in Table 13a. There may be multiple specification errors, one of which is a causal connection between X_1 and indicator 7. Still, we should consider alternative possibilities before settling on this one.

The large positive residuals between indicator 7 and each of the indicators of X_1 could arise from a pattern of correlated error that led to an underestimate of the loading of indicator 7 on X_2. For, if this loading is underestimated, the correlation between indicator 7 and each of the X_1 indicators would be underestimated, and we should then expect the large residuals found in Tables 13b, 13c, and 13d. In a three-indicator model, if two of the three indicators of a single construct have correlated error, this will lead to an overestimate of their loadings on that construct and a corresponding underestimate of the loading of the third indicator. Hence, from Table 13b we would surmise that indicators 4 and 5 may have correlated error, from Table 13c that indicators 4 and 6 may have correlated error, and from Table 13d that indicators 5 and 6 may have correlated error. If this were the case we should then expect the lack of fit that is in fact exhibited when indicators 4, 5, and 6 are included in the three-indicator submodel (Table 13a).

We retain both of the above described possibilities as separate tentative hypotheses (described graphically in Fig. 8). Upon making estimates based on both possibilities for each of the three indicator models, we would, of course, find a better fit for the submodels based on Fig. 8b; i.e., the fit in the submodels would be perfect since that is the model that generated the correlations. As a final check we may recompose the complete model in accord with the best-fitting modifications for the three-indicator submodels and test the fit for the model as a whole. In this instance again the reconstituted whole model would fit perfectly. This illustration suggests that three-indicator submodels can be used to locate a "good" model even though the simplest reading of the pattern of residuals for a given three-indicator submodel may be misleading.

We consider a second set of hypothetical data, generated by the model shown in Fig. 5a. The four three-indicator submodels contained in this true model are shown in Fig. 9 along with a general form of the estimating model for the three-indicator submodels. The residuals are presented in Table 14. These residuals in Table 14a indicate a rather poor fit, with the largest residual being for the correlation between indicators 4 and 5. In accord with the discussion above pertaining to the residuals for three-indicator submodels, this suggests two possibilities: a correlated

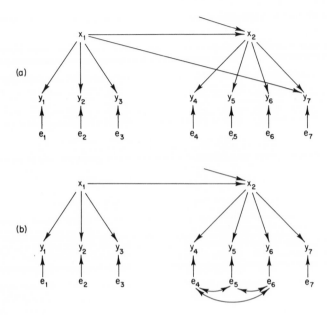

Figure 8.   Tentative respecifications of the estimating model of Fig. 3 on the basis of possibilities suggested by the patterns of residuals for the three-indicator submodels (Table 13).

error for indicators 4 and 5, or a path from X_1 to indicator 6. Smaller but still relatively large residuals also appear for the correlations between indicators 4 and 6, 5 and 6, and 3 and 6 but these smaller residuals do not, as a set, immediately suggest a tentative hypothesis. The residuals in Table 14b again show a rather poor fit, with the largest residual between indicators 4 and 5. This, then, suggests two possibilities: a correlated error between indicators 4 and 5 (the same as suggested in Table 14a) or a path from X_1 to indicator 7. The other smaller residuals in this table do not immediately suggest a tentative hypothesis. The residuals shown in Table 14c show a good fit, and since indicator 5 has been omitted in this three-indicator submodel it is reasonable to conclude that indicator 5 is in some way contaminated, e.g., by the correlated error with indicator 4. In Table 14d (in which indicator 4 has been omitted) the fit is again relatively good, further strengthening the plausibility of a correlated error between indicators 4 and 5. Thus, a correlated error between indicators 4 and 5 is implied by the pattern of residuals in both three-indicator submodels where indicators 4 and 5 appear together, and by the relatively good fit when one or the other of these two is omitted. Recall that a modification in the original model

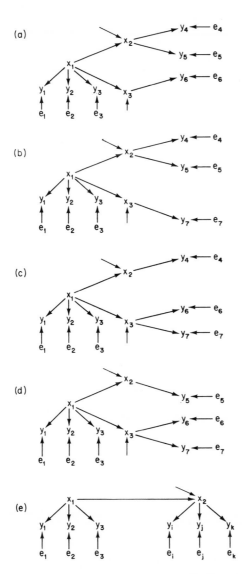

Figure 9.   (a)–(d) Three-indicator submodels contained in Fig. 5a, and (e) the general estimating submodel from Fig. 5b.

(Fig. 5b) to account for correlated error between indicators 4 and 5 has been tried on the basis of an intuitive inspection of the original residuals matrix (Table 6) and the fit was found to be relatively good

TABLE 14

RESIDUALS FOR THE FOUR THREE-INDICATOR SUBMODELS SHOWN IN FIG. 9

14a (The model of Fig. 9a is the true model; Fig. 9a is a three-indicator submodel of Fig. 5a which is the whole true model.)

	y_4	y_5	y_6
y_1	−.015	−.007	.020
y_2	−.024	−.012	.033
y_3	−.034	−.016	.046
y_4	—	.105	−.051
y_5		—	−.049

$\chi^2 = 31.9$
8 degrees of freedom
$p < .001$

14b (The model of Fig. 9b is the true model; Fig. 9b is a three-indicator submodel of Fig. 5a which is the whole true model.)

	y_4	y_5	y_7
y_1	−.012	−.006	.008
y_2	−.020	−.011	.014
y_3	−.027	−.015	.019
y_4	—	.149	−.037
y_5		—	−.031

$\chi^2 = 38.7$
8 degrees of freedom
$p < .001$

14c (The model of Fig. 9c is the true model; Fig. 9c is a three-indicator submodel of Fig. 5c which is the whole true model.)

	y_4	y_6	y_7
y_1	.019	−.004	−.001
y_2	.031	−.007	−.002
y_3	.043	−.010	−.002
y_4	—	−.020	−.022
y_6		—	.001

$\chi^2 = 6.2$
8 degrees of freedom
$p = .622$

14d (The model of Fig. 9d is the true model; Fig. 9d is a three-indicator submodel of Fig. 5d which is the whole true model.)

	y_5	y_6	y_7
y_1	.022	−.008	.002
y_2	.037	−.013	−.004
y_3	.052	−.018	−.006
y_5	—	−.030	−.029
y_6		—	.025

$\chi^2 = 12.4$
8 degrees of freedom
$p = .136$

(see Table 7). Hence there is relatively strong evidence supporting this respecification.

An alternative suggestion emerging from the analysis of three-indicator submodels is that indicators 4 and 5 do not "behave" in the same way in this model as do indicators 6 and 7. Such a grouping of indicators initially treated as reflecting the same underlying construct suggests a reconceptualization of the underlying construct to make substantive sense of the separate groupings of indicators and the construction of a new model based on this reconceptualization. The plausible reconceptualization and regrouping of indicators is, of course, to treat indicators 4 and 5 as reflecting one construct and indicators 6 and 7 as reflecting another, with both being affected by X_1. But this is precisely the nature of the model that generated the data and with such a respecification the fit would, of course, be perfect. This illustration suggests that the analysis of indicators may lead to a reconceptualization of the underlying construct and this, rather than any addition of paths to incorporate correlated errors, may be the useful way of respecifying a model.

5. Summary of Strategy

At this point we shall summarize the steps in the strategy we have developed:

1. Consider all two-indicator submodels. Since two-indicator submodels are sensitive to correlated errors between indicators of different constructs—and only to such correlated errors—the fit for the two-indicator submodels should suggest rather clearly which, if any, pairs of cross-construct indicators have correlated errors.

2. Incorporate the correlated errors across constructs suggested in step 1 into a respecified model.

3. Estimate the respecified model, provided it is identifiable. If it is not identifiable with the inclusion of the correlated errors added in step 2, discard the most heavily contaminated indicators in order to achieve identification.

4. Consider all three-indicator submodels of the respecified model. The fit of three-indicator submodels will be sensitive to correlated errors across constructs, to correlated errors between indicators of the same construct, and to omitted paths between constructs and indicators. Since the analysis of two-indicator submodels will have already led to the addition of all cross-construct correlated errors, we use the three-indicator submodels with those cross-construct correlated errors included, to provide clues to the other two kinds of specification error. The basic problem is to locate them when at least some of the three-indicator submodels fail to fit satisfactorily.

5. Formulate tentative hypotheses as to the nature of the specification errors on the basis of the patterns of residuals of all or some selected subset of the three-indicator submodels. In doing so one considers the possibilities that

a. a pattern of relatively large residuals between a single indicator of one construct and each of the indicators of the other construct may arise from either

    i. an omitted path from the construct with all three indicators involved in this pattern to the single indicator of the other construct involved, or

    ii. a correlated error between the two indicators that are not implicated in this pattern; and

b. a large residual between two indicators of a single construct may arise from either

    i. an omitted correlated error between those two indicators, or

    ii. an omitted path from another construct to the third indicator in the set where two have a large residual.[†]

6. When the tentative hypotheses of step 5 have been formulated, combinations of these may be incorporated into the previously respecified model (step 3) to see if the indicators of any construct "group" themselves (i.e., have nonoverlapping sets of correlated errors and/or have similar suggested "loadings" on another construct). If so, reconceptualize that construct into two (or more) unmeasured variables, each with its own distinct set of indicators. If not, the tentative hypotheses of step 5 may be incorporated into each of the three-indicator submodels and new estimates derived. If the fit in all of the respecified three-indicator submodels is still not satisfactory, additional tentative hypotheses may be formulated as above (step 5) and again incorporated into a new specification of the three-indicator submodels.

7. Respecify the whole model by incorporating the changes suggested by step 6. Unless additional changes are suggested by the pattern of residuals for this new estimating model, it may be treated as the "final" model for deriving parameter estimates and interpreting the indicator flaws substantively.

6. Applying the Three-Indicator Submodel Procedure to Real Data

We now return to our real data described earlier pertaining to the economic and political development of nations. Recall that the analysis

---

[†] These "rules of thumb" have been formulated inductively from an examination of residuals for hypothetical data in which the specification errors were known; we were not able to deduce them.

of two-indicator submodels (i.e., steps 1–3 in the above outline) already has led us to discard indicators 5 and 8. The model, which now consists of three indicators of Industrial Development and four remaining indicators of Political Development, is presented in Fig. 10. The residuals for the model of Fig. 10 are shown in Table 15. The pattern

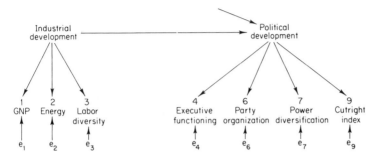

Figure 10. Revision of Fig. 1, omitting indicators with cross-construct correlated errors.

TABLE 15

RESIDUALS FOR THE MODEL OF FIG. 10[a]

	1	2	3	4	6	7	9
1	—	.000	−.004	.121	−.007	−.097	.001
2		—	.002	.164	−.023	−.164	−.005
3			—	.150	.046	−.097	.026
4				—	−.057	−.059	−.023
6					—	.105	−.015
7						—	.038
9							—

[a] $\chi^2 = 52.1$; 13 degrees of freedom; $p < .001$.

of these residuals suggests adding paths from Industrial Development to indicators 4 and 7. However, intuitive inferences from residuals are potentially misleading as we have discovered from our hypothetical data.

In accord with step 4 in the outline above, we consider each of the three-indicator submodels in the model of Fig. 10. The residuals for each of these three-indicator submodels are presented in Table 16.

Proceeding to step 5 we formulate a set of tentative hypotheses about the specification errors. The large residuals in Table 16a are relatively

TABLE 16

RESIDUALS FOR EACH OF THE THREE-INDICATOR SUBMODELS CONTAINED IN THE MODEL OF FIG. 10

a[a]	1	2	3	4	6	7
1	—	.000	−.003	.041	−.015	−.056
2		—	.000	.083	−.033	−.124
3			—	.079	.038	−.062
4				—	−.080	−.034
6					—	.190

b[b]	1	2	3	4	6	9
1	—	.001	−.001	.021	−.019	−.014
2		—	−.003	.060	−.040	−.026
3			—	.060	.032	.010
4				—	−.057	−.023
6					—	.075

c[c]	1	2	3	4	7	9
1	—	.000	−.003	.088	−.075	−.011
2		—	.001	.130	−.143	−.018
3			—	.120	−.078	.016
4				—	−.047	−.045
7					—	.078

d[d]	1	2	3	6	7	9
1	—	.000	−.004	.019	−.082	.034
2		—	.004	.004	−.146	.030
3			—	.069	−.083	.056
6				—	.076	−.035
7					—	.006

[a] $\chi^2 = 441$; 3 degrees of freedom; $p < .001$.
[b] $\chi^2 = 15.4$; 8 degrees of freedom; $p = .052$.
[c] $\chi^2 = 39.1$; 8 degrees of freedom; $p < .001$.
[d] $\chi^2 = 26.3$; 8 degrees of freedom; $p = .001$.

numerous but fall into relatively clear patterns suggesting either an added path from Industrial Development to indicator 4 or a correlated error between indicators 6 and 7, *and* either an added path from Industrial Development to indicator 7 or a correlated error between indicators 4 and 6. The other residuals matrices in which indicator 4 appears (i.e., Tables 16b and 16c) each suggest an added path from

Industrial Development to indicator 4 also. And the other residuals matrices in which indicator 7 appears (i.e., Tables 16c and 16d) each suggest an added path from Industrial Development to indicator 7 also. It is true that the same pattern of residuals might have suggested correlated errors between indicators of a given construct (e.g., indicators 6 and 7 and indicators 4 and 6 in Table 16a, indicators 6 and 9 in Table 16b, indicators 4 and 9 and indicators 7 and 9 in Table 16c, and indicators 6 and 9 again in Table 16d), but there is no consistency in these suggested correlated errors over the several tables. There is indeed a notable inconsistency: a positive correlated error is suggested between indicators 6 and 9 in Table 16b whereas a negative correlated error is suggested between the same two indicators in Table 16d. Such lack of clear pattern and a notable inconsistency leads to the implication that the apparent correlated errors are actually attributable to the omitted paths involving indicators 4 and 7.

Turning to step 6, we respecify the three-indicator submodels on the basis of the tentative hypotheses of step 5, obtaining Fig. 11. The residuals for these new models are shown in Table 17. The fit for none of these models is especially bad (for none of them is $p < .009$), and for two of them (Tables 17b and 17d) the fit is reasonably good. We conclude that we should incorporate these additional paths into the whole model.

Since both indicator 4 and indicator 7 appear to have an added path from Industrial Development, it might seem useful to reconceptualize Political Development into two separate constructs, with indicators 4 and 7 as indicators of one and indicators 6 and 9 as indicators of the other. But an examination of the signs of the residuals indicates that this would be inappropriate: after all, the residuals suggest that the added path to indicator 4 is positive while the added path to indicator 7 is negative. In fact, regrouping the indicators of Political Development into these two sets yields a very poor fit ($\chi^2 = 49$, degrees of freedom $= 11$, $p < .001$) and also yields a correlation in excess of 1.0 for the two subconstructs of Political Development, clearly indicating that such a regrouping is inappropriate.

We now proceed to reconstitute the whole model (step 7) incorporating the added paths tentatively substantiated in step 6. The new model is shown in Fig. 12 in which the parameter estimates are also given. The residuals based on this estimating model are presented in Table 18. The fit is reasonably good and is a notable improvement over the fit obtained using the model of Fig. 10.

With Fig. 12 as our final model, it is intriguing to consider now the possible substantive meaning of the added positive path from Industrial Development to indicator 4 (Executive Functioning) and the added

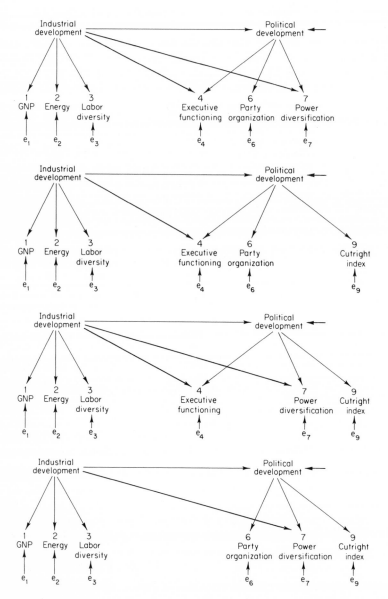

Figure 11. Tentative respecifications of the three-indicator submodels contained in Fig. 10 on the basis of patterns of residuals for the original three-indicator submodels contained in Fig. 10.

TABLE 17

Residuals for Each of the Three-Indicator Submodels Shown in Fig. 11

aᵃ	1	2	3	4	6	7
1	—	.001	.003	−.021	.011	.043
2		—	−.005	.012	−.015	−.031
3			—	.021	.057	.022
4				—	−.004	.000
6					—	.000

bᵇ	1	2	3	4	6	9
1	—	.001	.001	−.022	.016	.003
2		—	−.004	.014	−.008	−.011
3			—	.021	.062	.024
4				—	−.015	.006
6					—	.000

cᶜ	1	2	3	4	7	9
1	—	.000	.005	−.021	.045	.009
2		—	−.005	.010	−.030	−.009
3			—	.021	.024	.029
4				—	.000	.000
7					—	.000

dᵈ	1	2	3	6	7	9
1	—	.001	−.002	−.023	.033	.020
2		—	−.001	−.042	−.036	.010
3			—	.030	.015	.040
6				—	.026	.000
7					—	−.016

^{a} $\chi^2 = 17.0$; 6 degrees of freedom; $p = .009$.
^{b} $\chi^2 = 7.5$; 7 degrees of freedom; $p = .382$.
^{c} $\chi^2 = 15.5$; 6 degrees of freedom; $p = .016$.
^{d} $\chi^2 = 12.5$; 7 degrees of freedom; $p = .086$.

negative path from Industrial Development to indicator 7 (Power Diversification). It is probably wise with data such as these to assume faulty measurement as the source of added paths rather than moving directly to theoretical interpretations of them. We are inclined to suppose that the ratings and judgments contributing to the Executive Functioning variable have been biased in favor of highly industrialized nations while the ratings and judgments contributing to the Power

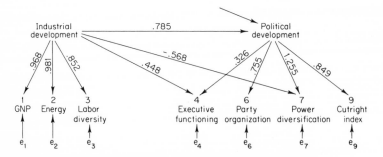

Figure 12.   Final respecification of the industrial–political model.

TABLE 18

RESIDUALS FOR THE MODEL OF FIG. 12[a]

	1	2	3	4	6	7	9
1	—	.001	.005	−.021	−.014	.045	.025
2		—	−.006	.010	−.041	−.030	.006
3			—	.020	.035	.024	.042
4				—	−.041	−.001	.025
6					—	.029	−.001
7						—	−.017

[a] $\chi^2 = 19.5$; 11 degrees of freedom; $p = .053$.

Diversification variable have been biased in favor of the less industrialized nations. Thus, the specialists making ratings may have been inclined to overestimate the degree of "functional effectiveness of the governmental bureaucracy" (a contributor to Executive Functioning) because of a "halo effect" from the relatively efficient industrial enterprise, while simultaneously underestimating the "functional effectiveness of the governmental bureaucracy" in less industrialized societies. In the same vein, the specialists supplying the ratings may have been inclined, for highly industrialized societies, to overestimate the degree to which the recruitment of political leaders was restrictive (thus deflating the overall measure of Power Diversification for such societies) because of the concentrated power of the industrial managerial cadre and the presumption that it would influence political processes in a restrictive way.

Alternatively, a theoretical interpretation is possible. Bureaucratic effectiveness in the industrial enterprise may actually stimulate an increase in the "functional effectiveness of the governmental bureaucracy" instead of simply affecting *ratings* of such functional effectiveness through a "halo effect." And industrial development may increase Power Diversification by one process (e.g., by stimulating educational progress and hence increasing the pool from which political leadership may be drawn) while simultaneously suppressing increases in Power Diversification by another process (e.g., by facilitating the development of a "power elite"). If there were other measures, less subject to potentially biased judgment, which would suggest the existence of additional paths between Industrial Development and indicators of Political Development similar to Executive Functioning and Power Diversification, then substantive possibilities such as these would be given more plausibility.

7. Conclusion

Our major concerns in this paper have been to point out the potentially misleading inferences that are readily drawn from an intuitive interpretation of the residuals matrix for a path model, and to illustrate an alternative strategy for diagnosing specification errors. Our strategy, relying on an examination of the fit and residuals for two- and three-indicator submodels, suggests respecifications that are not always obvious from an examination of the residuals for the model as a whole. It can be, unfortunately, a rather tedious procedure for models with many indicators, but it provides a more reliable guide for the analysis of indicator flaws than does the residuals matrix or a random search for a better-fitting model.

Substantive knowledge of indicator characteristics may also provide valuable leads to correlated errors among indicators. There is no intent here to propose that such substantive leads be disregarded. Rather, our search has been for a general, codifiable procedure that may be used to supplement such substantive leads or to provide independent support for their plausibility.

10

Ratio Variables and Path Models

KARL SCHUESSLER

1. Introduction

This chapter discusses complications in path analysis consequent upon the peculiarities of ratio variables. To unfold these peculiarities, we retrace the work of Karl Pearson on ratio variables and extensions of that work by later investigators; and to exhibit complications arising from ratio variables, we consider sociological examples of path analysis and of related correlational analyses in which such variables are present. A major point is that refinements in theory (perhaps in the form of structural equations) may be achieved by allocating the moments of a ratio to the moments of its components. For example, it may be theoretically suggestive as well as empirically interesting to partition a covariance of ratios into the covariances of the components making up those ratios.

A ratio variable is one variable divided by another, while a variable divided into a constant is an inversion of that variable. For example, where X, Y, and Z are component variables,

$$U = X/Z \quad \text{and} \quad V = Y/Z$$

are ratio variables, but $W = 1/Z$ is the reciprocal of Z. The meaning of these symbols will be maintained throughout, unless there is an indication to the contrary. In sociology, the deflation of one variable by another (e.g., births by population) is usually undertaken to facilitate comparisons among units (e.g., counties); whereas a nonlinear transformation of a given variable (e.g., division of a variable into unity) is usually undertaken to meet the assumptions of a statistical procedure (e.g., the analysis of variance).

Since U is determined by X and Z, its variance will generally differ from the variance of X. For essentially the same reason, the correlation of U and V will differ from the correlation of X and Y. Likewise, the correlation of U and another variable F will generally differ from the correlation of X and F, since that correlation (r_{uf}) is determined by the joint relation of X, Z, and F. These matters are not themselves problematical, but, when they go unrecognized, they may create problems and flaws in substantive interpretation. For example, one may spuriously conclude that anomia (as measured) produces political extremism (as measured) if one norms both measures on general intelligence before calculating the relation between them. Of course, it is not the empirical correlation of ratio variables that is spurious, but rather the false inference drawn from that correlation.

To be more concrete, let us consider a sample of persons who have held the Ph.D. degree in sociology for just five years. Let us suppose that grades in graduate school (X), number of post-doctoral publications (Y), and aptitude for graduate work (Z) are uncorrelated in this sample, but that these facts are unknown to the investigator. He has in mind the hypothesis that grades in graduate school affect a person's publication record. However, before testing that hypothesis, he divides both grades (X) and number of publications (Y) by aptitude (Z) to remove the influence of this latter variable. The correlation between the deflated variables (U and V) could be substantial, notwithstanding the absence of correlations among the component variables, and he might carelessly draw the erroneous conclusion that grades have an effect on publication. In this case, the correlation of U and V itself is not spurious, but rather the faulty claim that grades (X) have an effect on later productivity (Y).

As our second example, let us suppose that the investigator is interested in the relation between the suicide rate (V) and the percent over 65 years of age (U) for large cities at a specific point in time. In line with this interest, it would be natural to regress the suicide rate on the percent over 65 years of age. But before doing that, let us suppose that the investigator statistically "weights" each rate (U and V) by its population base (Z), presumably to correct for differences in population size. The resulting correlation between ZU and ZV could diverge appreciably from zero, notwithstanding the absence of a correlation between the two ratio variables. In this situation, it would be a mistake to conclude in favor of a relation between the suicide rate and the percent over 65 years, although one might carelessly do that. Here, the inference about the dependency of V on U is false, but not the correlation of $ZU = X$ and $ZV = Y$.

Since path analysis culminates in coefficients that measure causal effects, and since coefficients based on ratio variables will generally differ from coefficients based on component variables, it is hazardous to draw conclusions about the latter from the former and vice versa. In guarding against those hazards, and paraphrasing Yule's (1910) advice, a rudimental procedure is to state in advance whether the hypothesis to be tested pertains to component variables (e.g., X and Y) or ratio variables (e.g., U and V).

However, whatever his hypothesis, the investigator may still find it instructive to analyze ratio variables in terms of their components, and vice versa. For example, where the dependence of a ratio variable U on a causal variable C is in question, it may be revealing to measure the effect of C on U via components X and Z.

This possibility may be represented by a path model if we take the liberty of transforming ratios into logarithms. Under these simplified conditions, we obtain the linear relations

$$U' = X' - Z', \qquad W' = -Z',$$

where $U' = \log U$, $X' = \log X$, $Z' = \log Z$. Reducing U' and W' to standard form, denoted by lowercase letters, we get each variable as the sum of its weighted parts:

$$u' = p_{u'x'}x' + p_{u'z'}z', \qquad w' = p_{w'z'}z', \tag{1}$$

where $p_{u'x'}$ is the path coefficient of U' on X', etc. If X' and Z' are determined by a causal variable C, except for random disturbances, we may express each as the sum of its weighted parts:

$$x' = p_{x'c}c + p_{x'e}e_{x'}, \qquad z' = p_{z'c}c + p_{z'e}e_{z'}, \tag{2}$$

with the understanding that c, $e_{x'}$, and $e_{z'}$ are also in standard form. Substituting (2) into (1), we obtain u' and w' in terms of the causal factor C and the random disturbances $e_{x'}$ and $e_{z'}$:

$$
\begin{aligned}
u' &= p_{u'x'}(p_{x'c}c + p_{x'e}e_{x'}) + p_{u'z'}(p_{z'c}c + p_{z'e}e_{z'}) \\
w' &= p_{w'z'}(p_{z'c}c + p_{z'e}e_{z'}).
\end{aligned}
\tag{3}
$$

Such a decomposition may be especially illuminating in sociology, where ratio variables generally carry no theoretical justification (unlike, say, density in physics) and where few empirical interrelations are without some interest.

In developing these matters, we first give some statistical formulas for ratio variables, based largely on the work of Pearson; secondly, we consider applications of path analysis and of related correlational analysis in sociology in the light of these formulas; lastly, in a short conclusion, we note some points that might be pursued.

2. Early Work

Pearson's (1897) work answered to the problem: express the correlation between $U = X/Z$ and $V = Y/Z$ in terms of statistical moments of X, Y, and Z. His first step was to approximate the mean of U in moments of X and Z, and the mean of V in moments of Y and Z, as follows:

$$\bar{U} = (1/N)\sum(X/Z) = (1/N)(\bar{X}/\bar{Z})\sum(1 + x/\bar{X})(1 + z/\bar{Z})^{-1},$$

where $x = X - \bar{X}$, $z = Z - \bar{Z}$. Carrying out the required operations and neglecting terms of order higher than the second, he obtained the approximation

$$\bar{U} \doteq (\bar{X}/\bar{Z})(1 + V_z^2 - V_{xz}), \tag{4}$$

where $V_z^2 = \sigma_z^2/\bar{Z}^2$ is the rel-variance of Z, and $V_{xz} = \sigma_{xz}/\bar{X}\bar{Z}$ is the rel-covariance of X and Z. Similarly,

$$\bar{V} \doteq (\bar{Y}/\bar{Z})(1 + V_z^2 - V_{yz}).$$

His next step was to approximate the variance of U in moments of X and Z, and the variance of V in moments of Y and Z as follows:

$$\sigma_u^2 = (1/N)\sum(X/Z)^2 - \bar{U}^2$$
$$= [(1/N)(\bar{X}/\bar{Z})^2\sum(1 + x/\bar{X})^2(1 + z/\bar{Z})^{-2}] - \bar{U}^2.$$

Multiplying, summing, and dividing by N, and ignoring terms of order higher than the second, one gets the approximation

$$\sigma_u^2 \doteq (\bar{X}/\bar{Z})^2(V_x^2 + V_z^2 - 2V_{xz}). \tag{5}$$

By the same argument,

$$\sigma_v^2 \doteq (\bar{Y}/\bar{Z})^2(V_y^2 + V_z^2 - 2V_{yz}).$$

The same method was then used to find the approximate covariance of U and V, as follows:

$$\sigma_{uv} = [(1/N)\sum (UV)] - \overline{U}\overline{V}$$
$$= [(1/N)(\overline{X}\overline{Y}/\overline{Z}^2)\sum (1 + x/\overline{X})(1 + y/\overline{Y})(1 + z/\overline{Z})^{-2}] - \overline{U}\overline{V}.$$

Performing the required operations, and neglecting terms of order higher than the second, we get an approximation to the covariance:

$$\sigma_{uv} \doteq (\overline{X}\overline{Y}/\overline{Z}^2)(V_{xy} - V_{xz} - V_{yz} + V_z^2). \tag{6}$$

Note that (6) reduces to (5) when $V = U$.

Upon dividing both sides of (6) by the product of the standard deviations of U and V, as given by (5), one obtains the approximate correlation coefficient:

$$r_{uv} = \frac{V_{xy} - V_{xz} - V_{yz} + V_z^2}{(V_x^2 + V_z^2 - 2V_{xz})^{1/2} (V_y^2 + V_z^2 - 2V_{yz})^{1/2}}. \tag{7}$$

This yields a good approximation to the correlation of U and V, provided that higher-order moments in the series expansion are negligible.

Pearson was especially concerned with the possibility that r_{uv} might be large when $r_{xy} = r_{xz} = r_{yz} = 0$. To evaluate this possibility, one sets correlations among X, Y, and Z equal to zero, whereupon (7) reduces to

$$r_{uv} \doteq \frac{V_z^2}{[(V_x^2 + V_z^2)(V_y^2 + V_z^2)]^{1/2}}. \tag{8}$$

This is Pearson's well-known formula for spurious correlation, the name he applied to r_{uv} on condition that X, Y, and Z are mutually uncorrelated.

Some years later, in a study of death rates, Pearson, Lee, & Elderton (1910) suggested that the correlation of deaths from different diseases (e.g., cancer and diabetes) for constant population ($r_{xy.z}$) might be used in place of the correlation of ratios, since this partial was presumably free of spurious elements. He wrote: "the discovery of possible inter-relations between diseases by an examination of their death rates ... has not been without fascination for more than one investigator. Personally, I have considered the problem more than once, but always failed to make progress owing to existence of spurious correlations which I did not see how to meet." Continuing, he suggested that it would be possible to get over this difficulty by correlating deaths (or death rates) from different diseases for population constant. That procedure would give the desired result, he maintained, provided that the number of deaths by cause (e.g., cancer) in a given population was not unduly inflated (or deflated) by such extraneous factors as age. In the ensuing discussion he remarked, somewhat casually, that either $r_{xy.z}$ or $r_{uv.z}$ might be used to measure the relation between death rates, since they are generally the same. But this identity requires that zero-order correlations between U and V, U and Z, and V and Z, respectively, be calculated by (7).

Checking and elaborating this point several years later, Brown, Greenwood, & Wood (1914) concluded that, contrary to Pearson, $r_{xy.z}$ and $r_{uv.z}$ are seldom if ever the same, for the reason that the relation of Z to X and Y will generally differ from the relation of Z to U and V. They worked out a number of examples in support of this conclusion, excerpts from which are given in Table 1, and undertook to account statistically for the divergence of $r_{xy.z}$ and $r_{uv.z}$ in specific cases. Noting the close correspondence between r_{uv} and $r_{uv.z}$ for their series, they suggested that r_{uv} might be used to approximate $r_{uv.z}$ when the latter was required but not easily available. But they supplied no theoretical basis for this suggestion.

TABLE 1

CORRELATIONS BETWEEN DEATHS FROM CANCER (X) AND FROM DIABETES (Y) FOR CONSTANT POPULATION (Z), BETWEEN DEATH RATES $(U$ AND $V)$, AND BETWEEN DEATH RATES FOR CONSTANT POPULATION[a]

Series	$r_{xy.z}$	r_{uv}	$r_{uv.z}$
118 English Towns	.39	.36	.36
41 English Counties	−.28	.43	.41
69 Italian Provinces	.16	.19	.22
40 American Cities	.69	.38	.38

[a] From Brown et al. (1914).

STATISTICAL DIGRESSION[†]

Formulas (4)–(8) may be obtained by the method of expanding a function in a Taylor series and taking the statistical expectation of that expansion. To illustrate, we first expand the function $u = f(x, z)$ in a Taylor series at the point (x_0, z_0):

$$u = f(x_0, z_0) + f_x(x - x_0) + f_z(z - z_0)$$
$$+ \tfrac{1}{2}[f_{xx}(x - x_0)^2 + f_{zz}(z - z_0)^2 + 2f_{xz}(x - x_0)(z - z_0)]$$
$$+ \cdots \tag{9}$$

[†] This section is based on notes provided by Arthur Goldberger.

where f_x and f_z, and f_{xx}, f_{zz}, and f_{xz} are first and second derivatives, respectively, of the function f, evaluated at the point x_0, z_0. (In this section variables are symbolized by lowercase letters.)

With $u = x/z$, the terms are

$$f(x_0, z_0) = x_0/z_0 \qquad f_x = 1/z_0 \qquad f_z = -x_0/z_0^2$$
$$f_{xx} = 0 \qquad f_{zz} = 2x_0/z_0^3 \qquad f_{xz} = -1/z_0^2.$$

Substituting these results in (9), and dropping terms of order higher than second, we get the approximation:

$$u = x/z \doteq x_0/z_0 + (1/z_0)(x - x_0) + (-x_0/z_0^2)(z - z_0)$$
$$+ \tfrac{1}{2}[2(x_0/z_0^3)(z - z_0)^2 + 2(-1/z_0^2)(x - x_0)(z - z_0)]. \qquad (10)$$

To express the mean of $u = f(x, z)$ in terms of moments of x and z, the procedure is to expand the function at the point $E(x)$, $E(z)$, and to take the statistical expectation of the expansion. Carrying out these operations, and dropping terms of order higher than the second, one gets the approximation:

$$E(u) \doteq f[E(x), E(z)] + \tfrac{1}{2}[f_{xx}V(x) + f_{zz}V(z) + 2f_{xz}C(x, z)], \qquad (11)$$

where $E(\cdot)$ denotes expectation, and

$$V(x) = E[x - E(x)]^2, \; V(z) = E[z - E(z)]^2, \; C(x, z) = E[x - E(x)][z - E(z)].$$

Applying (11) to the ratio function $u = x/z$, we obtain

$$E(u) \doteq E(x)/E(z) + [E(x)/E^3(z)] V(z) - [1/E^2(z)] C(x, z)$$
$$= [E(x)/E(z)]\{1 + V(z)/E^2(z) - C(x, z)/(E(x) E(z))\}. \qquad (12)$$

This is the same as (4) except for differences in symbols.

Proceeding to second moments, we restrict ourselves to first-order terms from the outset, inasmuch as higher terms are eventually dropped. For $u = f(x, z)$ at the point $E(x)$, $E(z)$, we then have

$$u = f[E(x), E(z)] + f_x[x - E(x)] + f_z[z - E(z)].$$

Since $f[E(x), E(z)]$ is a first-order approximation to the mean $E(u)$, by subtracting it from both sides of (12), we obtain the approximate deviation from the mean:

$$u - E(u) \doteq f_x[x - E(x)] + f_z[z - E(z)]. \qquad (13)$$

Squaring (13) and taking expectations, one gets

$$V(u) = f_x^2 V(x) + f_z^2 V(z) + 2f_x f_z C(x, z).$$

Specializing to case of $u = x/z$, we find

$$
\begin{aligned}
V(u) = V(x/z) &\doteq [1/E(z)]^2 \, V(x) + [-E(x)/E^2(z)]^2 \, V(z) \\
&\quad + 2[1/E(z)][-E(x)/E^2(z)] \, C(x, z) \\
&= [E^2(x)/E^2(z)]\{V(x)/E^2(x) + V(z)/E^2(z) \\
&\quad - 2C(x, z)/(E(x) \, E(z))\},
\end{aligned}
\tag{14}
$$

which is (5) apart from notational differences.

For the covariance of $u = f(x, z)$ and $v = g(y, z)$, we find the product of $u - E(u)$, as given by (13), and the approximate deviation

$$v - E(v) \doteq g_y[y - E(y)] + g_z[z - E(z)],$$

and take the expectation of that product:

$$C(u, v) = f_z g_z V(z) + f_x g_y C(x, y) + f_x g_z C(x, z) + f_z g_y C(y, z). \tag{15}$$

Upon setting $u = x/z$ and $v = y/z$, we get the derivatives

$$f_x = 1/E(z) \qquad f_z = -E(x)/E^2(z)$$

$$g_y = 1/E(z) \qquad g_z = -E(y)/E^2(z),$$

whereupon (15) becomes

$$
\begin{aligned}
C(u, v) &= \frac{E(x) \, E(y)}{E^4(y)} \, V(z) + \frac{1}{E^2(z)} \, C(x, y) - \frac{E(y)}{E^3(z)} \, C(x, z) - \frac{E(x)}{E^3(z)} \, C(y, z) \\
&= \frac{E(x) \, E(y)}{E^2(z)} \left[\frac{V(z)}{E^2(z)} + \frac{C(x, y)}{E(x) \, E(y)} - \frac{C(x, z)}{E(x) \, E(z)} - \frac{C(y, z)}{E(y) \, E(z)} \right],
\end{aligned}
\tag{16}
$$

which is (6) couched in different notation. Dividing the covariance of u and v, as given by (16), by the geometric mean of their variances, each given by (14), we obtain the approximate correlation of (7). The Taylor-series approach extends readily to functions of more variables; see Kendall & Stuart (1958, pp. 231–232).

3. Later Work

Although Pearson's work together with that of his contemporaries has not issued in a vast literature on ratio variables, it has been extended from time to time in response to specific issues. Since these studies have some bearing on the application of path analysis and the like to ratio variables, we briefly review them here.

In a study of economic indexes, Neifeld (1927) sought to explicate statistically the generally positive relation between ratios with a common denominator, U and V, and the generally negative relation between "chain relatives," U and V^{-1}. He gave a number of examples, several of which are reproduced in Table 2. His study has relevance for sociologists today, since they are occasionally involved in the analysis of chain relatives, where the numerator in one ratio is the denominator in the other.

TABLE 2

Correlations Between Ratios
Based on Income (X), Automobile
Registration (Y), and Population
(Z), by States[a]

X/Z and Y/Z	.733
X/Z and Z/Y	−.796
Z/X and Y/Z	−.785
Z/X and Z/Y	.844

[a] From Neifeld (1927).

In a somewhat similar study, Douglass & Huffaker (1929) undertook to show that the generally negative correlation of intelligence (IQ) and accomplishment (AQ)—the latter defined as the educational quotient (EQ) divided by the intelligence quotient (IQ)—was dictated by the nature of the component variables and did not supply a demonstration that intelligence tends to retard accomplishment. They took as their point of departure Pearson's (1897) formula for approximating the correlation of $U = X_1/X_3$ and $V = X_2/X_4$:

$$r_{uv} \doteq \frac{V_{12} - V_{14} - V_{23} + V_{34}}{(V_1{}^2 + V_3{}^2 - 2V_{13})^{1/2}(V_2{}^2 + V_4{}^2 - 2V_{24})^{1/2}} . \tag{17}$$

(This formula may also be derived by the method of the previous section.) With $X_3 = 1$ and $X_4 = X_1$, (17) reduces to

$$r_{uv} \doteq \frac{r_{12}V_2 - V_1}{(V_1{}^2 + V_2{}^2 - 2V_{12})^{1/2}} . \tag{18}$$

Taking X_1 to be IQ, and X_2 to be EQ, (18) gives the correlation between IQ and EQ/IQ = AQ. They noted that, since EQ generally has a smaller coefficient of variation than IQ, the correlation of IQ and AQ is generally negative.

More recently, Kuh & Meyer (1955) undertook to establish the conditions under which r_{uv} might be used to estimate $r_{xy.z}$, much as Brown et al. (1914) had considered the relation of $r_{uv.z}$ to r_{uv}. Kuh and Meyer's analysis culminated in the demonstration that r_{uv}, as given by (7), is equal to $r_{xy.z}$ if $V_z = r_{xz}V_x = r_{yz}V_y$, which condition in turn requires that both X and Y have homogeneous linear regressions on Z. They went on to indicate that in this situation the regression coefficient b_{uv} in the sample might be used to estimate the regression coefficient B_{yx} in the population, when the error variance in Y increases as the square of the deflating variable.

Almost a decade later, Madansky (1964) pointed out that the Kuh–Meyer result and the interpretation sometimes placed on it are strictly justified if and only if the deflating variable Z is a known constant. He went on to show, in particular, that when the covariance of X and Y is zero, and when the deflator is a random variable (as might be true for economic time series), the regression of V on U may diverge from zero, even when both X and Y have homogeneous linear regressions on Z.

In a quite recent note for statisticians, Rangarajan & Chatterjee (1969) have reiterated that the sign of r_{uv} may be either positive or negative, and even oppose the sign of r_{xy}, when X and Y are correlated with one another but not with Z. (Their formulas contain some oddities but their general conclusion stands.) Their comment reinforces Pearson's original point that the correlation of U and V generally differs from the correlation of X and Y.

In an even more recent note, Fleiss & Tanur (1971) have considered the relation of $r_{uv.z}$ to $r_{uv.w}$ where $W = 1/Z$. To illustrate that relation, they took the case where X, Y, and Z are uniformly and independently distributed on the integers 1 to 100, and found $r_{uv} = .719$. Next, they calculated $r_{uv.z}$ by the product-moment formula

$$r_{uv.z} = \frac{r_{uv} - r_{uz}r_{vz}}{(1 - r_{uz}^2)^{1/2}(1 - r_{vz}^2)^{1/2}} . \tag{19}$$

Although they anticipated a small value from this "technically improper application," they obtained a surprisingly (to them) large value of .663. But upon calculating $r_{uv.w}$, they got a value of zero, as is necessarily the case when X and Y are uncorrelated and the conditional expectations of U and V are linear. From their analysis, they drew the conclusion, presented primarily as a reminder to users of statistics, that the product-moment formula (19) is "totally inappropriate" unless the expectations of X and Y conditional on Z are linear. This reinforces the general point that linear methods will not do justice to nonlinear data.

FORMULAS FOR PRODUCTS

As one may have surmised, it is not possible to obtain general formulas for the exact mean and variance of a ratio variable, and the covariance of two such variables, from the moments of the components of those variables. However, these results have recently been worked out for the products of random variables (Goodman, 1960; Bohrnstedt & Goldberger, 1969); their relevance to the present problem is that if the moments of X, Y and $W = 1/Z$ are known, the exact second moments of $U = XW$ and $V = YW$ may be computed.

4. Guidelines for Research

From the foregoing review, it is possible to discern some of the pitfalls of ratio variables and ways of guarding against them. These latter methods, here summarized in the form of three working rules, may be regarded as either guidelines for carrying out research, or as criteria for evaluating it.

The first rule holds that the composition of variables whose relations are in question be unambiguously specified. If we ignore this rule, we run the risk of appealing to evidence that is immaterial to our hypothesis. The relations among component variables, X, Y, and Z, cannot be settled by an appeal to results based on the manipulation of ratios U and V. For example, a correct decision about the significance of the regression of Y on X may be purely fortuitous, as implied by Kuh & Meyer (1955), if we base that decision on the regression of V on U. The first principle insists that our statistical procedure have a direct bearing on the hypothesis to be tested.

The second cautions against the indiscriminate use of approximate formulas for the correlation of ratios. The approximations are reliable only if terms beyond the second in the expansions are small. Since this is generally in doubt, it is less risky to calculate the correlation of U and V directly from those variables, rather than rely on an approximation in terms of the moments of X, Y, and Z.

The third rule stipulates that the terms in a compound quantity (e.g., ratio or product) be statistically analyzed for their respective contributions to the variation of that quantity itself. Thus, we may analyze X and Y for their contributions to the variation of U, or we may analyze U and Z for their contributions to X. Similarly, we may analyze X, Y, and Z for their individual and joint contributions to the covariation of U and V.

The foregoing precepts hold equally for path coefficients on ratio variables, since these coefficients depend (in a mathematical sense) on moments of component variables. To show this dependency, let us start with a simple path model:

$$X_2 = p_{21}X_1 + p_{2u}U_2, \qquad X_3 = p_{31}X_1 + p_{32}X_2 + p_{3u}U_3, \qquad (20)$$

where X_1, X_2, and X_3 are ratio variables in standard form. Upon minimizing sums of squared residuals one gets

$$p_{21} = r_{12} \qquad\qquad p_{31} = (r_{31} - r_{32}r_{12})/(1 - r_{12}^2)$$

$$p_{2u} = (1 - r_{12}^2)^{1/2} \qquad p_{32} = (r_{32} - r_{31}r_{21})/(1 - r_{12}^2) \qquad (21)$$

$$p_{3u} = (1 - R_{3.21}^2)^{1/2}.$$

From these results, and from the reducibility of correlations of ratio variables to moments of component variables, it follows that path coefficients for ratios are expressible to a first approximation in terms of moments of component variables. In other words, the path coefficient of one ratio variable on another may be partitioned into terms consisting of moments of component variables.

An implication is that path coefficients on ratio variables will be subject to more refined interpretation when the makeup of those variables is taken into account. To indicate illustratively what such an accounting might entail, in the ensuing discussion we consider socio-logical applications of path analysis and of related correlational analyses to ratio variables. Our intent is not to criticize what was done in a particular study, but rather to exemplify an approach when ratio variables are present and one is leery of their effects.

5. Selected Examples

5.1 Population Categories

Our first example is based on Blalock's (1961) study of racial discrimination in the South. For an understanding of that process, he initially turned to selected characteristics of counties, the correlations among which are given in Table 3.

TABLE 3

Correlations among Selected Characteristics of Counties[a]

Variable	X_1	X_2	X_3	X_4	X_5
X_1 Percent of population urban or rural nonfarm	1.00	−.39	.67	.26	.74
X_2 Percent population nonwhite		1.00	.07	−.53	−.44
X_3 Percent white families with incomes $1,500+			1.00	.04	.60
X_4 Percent black males, 25 and over, more than six years of schooling				1.00	.39
X_5 Percent black families with incomes $1,500+					1.00

[a] From Blalock (1961).

Applying Simon's (1954) method of causal analysis, he compared observed correlations with those arising from specific causal equations. Among other possibilities, he considered the following recursive relations, expressed here as a path model:

$$X_4 = p_{42}X_2 + p_{4u}U_4, \qquad X_5 = p_{51}X_1 + p_{52}X_2 + p_{54}X_4 + p_{5u}U_5.$$

Upon calculating path coefficients by ordinary least squares one gets these results:

$$p_{42} = -.53 \qquad p_{4u} = .85$$

$$p_{51} = .66 \qquad p_{52} = -.09 \qquad p_{54} = .17 \qquad p_{5u} = .63.$$

Our present concern is not with the validity of these equations (in the sense of no errors of specification) but rather with the question of whether the inquiry pertains to deflated variables. From Blalock's writing it is clear that the theory pertains to deflated variables, and that, since inferences are not extended to component variables, the problem of spurious effects (in Pearson's sense) does not arise. For example, county differences in urbanization (X_1) are regarded as causing county differences in discrimination (X_5).

Having disposed of the question of spurious effects, we move next to the task of allocating coefficients for ratio variables to coefficients for component variables, on the assumption that this is a useful exercise. We limit our analysis to the finding that an increase in X_2 produces a decrease in X_4, as registered by the path coefficient of $-.53$. It is possible only to speculate on this matter, since the calculations required for a numerical analysis are not available.

It is pertinent that, in this problem, component variables are over-lapping categories within the same population. The total population includes the nonwhite population; the nonwhite population includes males over 25; and, of this latter category, some have had more than six years of schooling. Categories may thus be arranged from most to least inclusive as follows: total population (T), nonwhite population (B), nonwhite male population over 25 (M), and nonwhite males over 25 with six years of schooling (E). With such a setup, the correlation across counties between a larger and smaller category (e.g., B and E) will depend on whether the latter is a relatively constant proportion of the former from one county to another. For example, the correlation of all blacks (B) and black males over 25 (M) will tend to unity, if the number of black males over 25 is a relatively constant proportion of all blacks, while that correlation will tend to diverge from unity if that proportion varies from county to county.

The effect of such tendencies on the covariance of X_2 and X_4 may be judged by considering their presence in the numerator of (17), reproduced here with appropriate subscripts:

$$(V_{be} + V_{tm}) - (V_{bm} + V_{te}),$$

on the assumption that it is a reliable approximation. Although many different combinations of rel-covariances may give rise to the same covariance of ratios, in the present case it is our guess that the rel-covariance of B and M is large relative to the others, and that its weight (relative to the smaller terms) accounts for the negative covariance (and path coefficient). It is tenable that the number of black males over 25 years bears some fixed relation to all black males, while, owing to the uneven distribution of social and economic opportunities, both the proportion of black males over 25 with six years of schooling in the black population, and the proportion of black males over 25 in the general population show appreciably less constancy. In the face of these tendencies, admittedly conjectural, a positive covariance of X_2 and X_4 is virtually precluded.

The significance of all this consists not merely in allocating a covariance of percentages to its constituent covariances, but also in pointing to possible refinements in analysis. For example, when population categories are arbitrary and subject to manipulation, one may wish to compare results for several or more categories which presumably measure the same thing. Results for males over 30 with at least eight years of schooling may differ from those for males over 25 with at least six years of schooling. Instead of taking the proportion having more than some fixed number of years of schooling, one may wish to take number of years of schooling completed by some fixed proportion (e.g., 50%).

Also by way of extending the analysis, one may introduce causally antecedent variables to account for the variation of a given component and thus for the ratios into which it enters. County populations are affected by technological factors and these might be introduced for their direct bearing on population size and indirect bearing on economic discrimination (as measured).

5.2 Decomposition of Dependent Variable

Our second example draws on Duncan's (1966) use of path analysis to reflect the weight of each of three factors in the product which they form. As his point of departure, he took

$$\frac{P}{A} = \frac{P}{D} \times \frac{D}{S} \times \frac{S}{A},$$

where P is the population, A the area, D the number of dwelling units, and S the number of structures. In logarithmic form, this is

$$K_0 = K_1 + K_2 + K_3,$$

where $K_0 = \log(P/A)$, $K_1 = \log(P/D)$, etc. He proceeded to calculate path coefficients and correlation coefficients (given in Table 4) for these transformed variables. Since these results are based on ratio variables, they may be examined for spurious effects, and for the manner in which they depend on component variables.

On the question of spurious effects, Duncan's problem supplies its own answer: given the product of three ratios, find the relative contribution of each ratio to the product ratio. Since he was concerned with the statistical effect of one ratio on another, the question of spurious effects does not arise.

216 KARL SCHUESSLER

TABLE 4

CORRELATIONS AND PATH COEFFICIENTS FOR LOGARITHMS OF DENSITY AND ITS
COMPONENTS, CHICAGO COMMUNITY AREAS, 1940[a]

Variable	K_0	K_1	K_2	K_3	p_{0K}
K_0 log density	1.000	−.419	.636	.923	
K_1 log persons per dwelling unit		1.000	−.625	−.315	.132
K_2 log dwelling units per structure			1.000	.305	.468
K_3 log structures per acre				1.000	.821

[a] From Duncan (1966).

But possible restrictions on the range of coefficients arising from common terms in the ratio variables invite discussion. In antilogarithmic form, variables K_0 and K_1 have population as their common numerator, while K_0 and K_3 have area as a common denominator; the number of dwelling units appears as the denominator in K_1, and as the numerator in K_2; while the number of structures appears as the denominator in K_2 and the numerator in K_3. Our interest lies in the statistical effect of these common terms on relations between pairs of ratios, and, in consequence, on path coefficients.

It is instructive to compare the relation of K_1 and K_2, with the relation of K_2 and K_3, since they are alike in form but different in sign. Measuring variables from their means, one obtains

$$k_1 = p - d, \qquad k_2 = d - s, \qquad k_3 = s - a,$$

where $k_1 = K_1 - \overline{K}_1$, $p = \log P - \overline{\log P}$, $d = \log D - \overline{\log D}$, etc.

Summing cross-products ($k_1 k_2 = pd - d^2 - ps + ds$), and reducing sums to means, one gets the covariance of K_1 and K_2 as

$$\sigma_{12} = (\sigma_{pd} + \sigma_{ds}) - (\sigma_d^2 + \sigma_{ps}).$$

Similarly, one gets the covariance of K_2 and K_3 in terms of component covariances as

$$\sigma_{23} = (\sigma_{ds} + \sigma_{sa}) - (\sigma_s^2 + \sigma_{da}).$$

(Comparing these expressions with (6), we find that the approximate rel-covariance of two variables has the same form as the covariance of their logs. The explanation lies in the log transformation which changes equal ratios between antilogs to equal intervals between logs.)

With the covariance in expanded form, it is possible to gauge the statistical weights of the constituent covariances in the covariance of ratios (as logs). As with the previous example, it is possible only to speculate on the combination of results producing the negative covariance of K_1 and K_2, and the combination producing the positive covariance of K_2 and K_3.

It is plausible (to me) that components vary directly as one another, so that covariances among components are uniformly positive. For example, as population increases, the number of dwelling units increases, etc. In that event, the quantity $(\sigma_d{}^2 + \sigma_{ps})$ must be greater than the quantity $(\sigma_{pd} + \sigma_{ds})$, since the covariance of K_1 and K_2 is negative. By the same token, the quantity $(\sigma_s{}^2 + \sigma_{da})$ must be smaller than the quantity $(\sigma_{ds} + \sigma_{sa})$ since the covariance of K_2 and K_3 is positive.

In accounting for this difference in signs, our conjecture is that it is produced by the difference between the variances of the common terms, $\sigma_d{}^2$ and $\sigma_s{}^2$. We surmise that the variance of dwelling units is large relative to the covariances, whereas the variance of structures is small relative to the other terms. This reasoning suggests that in a given problem the sign of the covariance of ratios may be largely determined by the weight of the variance of the common term.

5.3 Causal Relation Between Components

As our third example, consider prison admissions per capita for states as the product of prison admissions per crime and crimes per capita:

$$\frac{A}{P} = \frac{A}{C} \times \frac{C}{P},$$

where A gives the admissions to prison, P the population, and C the number of crimes.

In contrast to the preceding example, we treat the variables on the right as constituting a causal system with one variable dependent on the other. In this analysis, and in studies of the deterrent effects of punishment on crime generally (cf. Logan, 1971), the hypothesis to be tested is that the crime rate (C/P) decreases as the admission rate (A/C) increases.

The question of spurious effects does not arise, since the hypothesis under test pertains to the ratio variables themselves rather than to their components. Nevertheless, the nature of the inverse relation between A/C and C/P bears some investigation.

Transforming to logarithms and expressing the variables as deviations from the mean, $k_1 = a - c$, $k_2 = c - p$, we obtain the covariance of K_1 and K_2 as the sum of the covariances:

$$\sigma_{12} = (\sigma_{ac} + \sigma_{cp}) - (\sigma_c{}^2 + \sigma_{ap}).$$

If the variances of $\log A$, $\log C$, and $\log P$ are approximately equal, and their covariances are positive and equal, the difference between $(\sigma_{ac} + \sigma_{cp})$ and $(\sigma_c^2 + \sigma_{ap})$ will be negative, since the common variance will generally exceed the common covariance. (If $\sigma_x^2 = \sigma_y^2 = \sigma^2$, then $\sigma_{yx} = r_{yx}\sigma^2$. When $|r| = 1$, $|\sigma_{yx}| = \sigma^2$; when $|r| < 1$, $|\sigma_{yx}| < \sigma^2$). Such a combination of results may account for the negative correlation between the admission rate and the crime rate.

To broach this possibility, I ran the following analysis: First, admissions, crimes, and populations for states in 1966 were grouped into class intervals and their means and standard deviations calculated. From these results, given in Table 5, it is evident that distributions are skewed to the right and that the standard deviation tends to exceed the mean, although the rate of excess is not constant. Second, measures were converted to logs, and variances and covariances calculated for these converted measures, anticipating that variances would be stabilized by this transformation. These results, shown in Table 6, are roughly in line with our speculations, although there are discrepancies: (a) covariances are approximately equal, but variances show less homogeneity, with the variance of $\log P$ appreciably smaller than the other two variances; (b) variances tend to exceed covariances, but the variance

TABLE 5

FREQUENCY (f) DISTRIBUTIONS FOR STATE POPULATIONS, CRIMES, AND PRISON ADMISSIONS, 1966[a]

Population (in millions)	f	Crimes (in ten thousands)	f	Admissions (in thousands)	f
0–1	20	0–2	20	0.0–0.9	19
2–3	13	3–5	16	1.0–1.9	14
4–5	8	6–8	4	2.0–2.9	7
6–7	1	9–11	2	3.0–3.9	2
8–9	1	12–14	2	4.0–4.9	3
10–11	4	15–20	3	5.0–6.9	3
12 and over	2	21 and over	2	7.0 and over	1
	49		49		49
Mean	3.81	6.60		2.11	
Variance	17.93	101.07		8.22	
SD	4.23	10.05		2.82	
SD/Mean	1.11	1.59		1.33	

[a] From Uniform Crime Reports 1967, U. S. Government Printing Office; National Prisoner Statistics 1966, U. S. Department of Justice.

TABLE 6

Variance–Covariance Matrix for Logarithms of State Crime Data

	$\log A$	$\log C$	$\log P$
$\log A$	.26	.24	.21
$\log C$		.28	.22
$\log P$			.20

of $\log A$ is smaller than its covariances. Nevertheless, the findings are generally in accord with the idea that the negative covariance of K_1 and K_2 is attributable to approximately equal covariances between components, coupled with a larger variance. To corroborate this point, we calculated

$$\sigma_{12} = (\sigma_{ac} + \sigma_{cp}) - (\sigma_c{}^2 + \sigma_{ap}) = (.24 + .22) - (.28 + .21) = -.03,$$

which finding reflects the weight of the variance (.28) relative to the approximately equal covariances. An implication is that a positive relation between the admission rate and the crime rate is unlikely in the absence of a weak relation between the number of admissions and the population. Such a relation could occur, but it is not very probable.

6. Related Correlational Analyses

As may be deduced from the foregoing, ratio variables will create complications not only in path analysis, but also in factor analysis, the analysis of covariance, and for that matter in all ordinary correlational analyses.

6.1 Factor Analysis

In applied factor analysis, one eventually obtains $m < n$ factors which account for the observed intercorrelations among the n observed variables. The factor model is

$$U_i = X_i/Z_i = a_{i1}F_1 + \cdots + a_{ij}F_j + \cdots + a_{im}F_m + b_iS_i, \qquad (22)$$

where a_{ij} is the coefficient of the ith variable on the jth common factor, and b_i is the coefficient of the ith variable on its specific factor S_i.

When variables are ratios, the question arises as to whether the extracted factors should be construed as ratios. One possible answer is this: since factors by definition are components in variables, they may be presumed to take the same form as the variables they constitute. An implication is that one gets loadings on factors in the form of ratios upon factoring correlations among ratio variables. A looser interpretation of factors would do violence to the main idea of factor analysis that an observed variable is the sum of its weighted parts. The conclusion that factors in ratio variables are themselves ratio variables might be relaxed if factors were construed as causes of the observed variables whose correlations were factored. But in that case, we regard the observed variables as measures of their own causes and thereby encounter logical difficulties. Admittedly, these are matters for speculation, since extracted factors are never observed.

6.2 ANALYSIS OF COVARIANCE

Since the analysis of covariance and path analysis rest on essentially the same linear model, they are equally subject to the complications of ratio variables. In covariance analysis, each measure is regarded as consisting of (a) one element common to its subgroup, (b) elements attributable to regression on the covariates, and (c) one element caused by random forces. In the case of a single classification and two covariates, the population model is

$$Y_{ij} = B_{ya}A_i + B_{yx}X_{ij} + B_{yz}Z_{ij} + e_{ij}, \tag{23}$$

where Y_{ij} is the jth measure in the ith subgroup, A_i is the intercept for the ith subgroup, $B_{ya} = 1.00$ is the coefficient of Y on A_i. It is assumed that the e_{ij} are randomly and independently distributed with mean zero and common variance.

Upon transforming all variables into standard form, one gets the path model:

$$y = p_a a + p_x x + p_z z + p_e e, \tag{24}$$

where p_a is the path coefficient of Y on A, etc. Squaring both sides, summing and reducing sums to means, we get the total variance (unity) on the left as a function of path coefficients and correlations among predictor variables on the right:

$$1.00 = (p_e^2 + p_a^2 + p_x^2 + p_z^2) + 2(p_a p_x r_{ax} + p_a p_z r_{az} + p_x p_z r_{xz}). \tag{25}$$

Transposing $p_e{}^2$ from right to left, we get the explained variance, or squared multiple correlation (R^2), which permits us to appraise the direct and joint contributions of each component to the dependent variable:

$$1.00 - p_e{}^2 = R^2 = (p_a{}^2 + p_x{}^2 + p_z{}^2) + 2(p_a p_x r_{ax} + p_a p_z r_{az} + p_x p_z r_{xz}). \quad (26)$$

Our interest lies not in this algebraic decomposition, but rather in possible restrictions on path coefficients by reason that calculations are based on ratio variables.

To probe this point, consider Burnham & Sprague's (1970) analysis of voting behavior between and within counties in New Jersey. In their study, they sought (somewhat incidentally) to determine whether the combined effect of percentage professional and managers in the male labor force (X) and percentage skilled and semiskilled workers (Z) on the percentage George Wallace vote (Y) was the same from one county to another. (Caution: X, Y, and Z stand for ratio variables in this analysis.) For evidence on this point, they calculated correlation and regression coefficients for civil divisions within counties and for all counties combined. From these results, given in Table 7, they drew the conclusion that the relationship between the Wallace vote (Y) and the

TABLE 7

ZERO-ORDER CORRELATIONS, STANDARDIZED PARTIAL REGRESSION COEFFICIENTS, AND SQUARED MULTIPLE CORRELATION COEFFICIENTS FOR COUNTIES, AND FOR ALL COUNTIES COMBINED[a,b]

County	Election districts	r_{xy}	r_{yz}	r_{xz}	$B_{yx.z}$	$B_{yz.x}$	$R^2_{y.xz}$
Bergen	61	−.868	+.907	−.945	−.103	+.810	.824
Camden	33	−.825	+.821	−.934	−.455	−.396	.701
Hudson[c]	12	−.624	+.331	−.572	+.076	+.522	.391
Passaic	16	−.513	+.483	−.648	−.346	+.258	.302
Four New Jersey counties	122	−.665	+.766	−.801	−.146	+.649	.594

[a] From Burnham & Sprague (1970).
[b] Y = percent Wallace vote in 1968 presidential election, X = percent professional and managerial in 1960 male labor force, Z = percent skilled and semiskilled in 1960 male labor force.
[c] For Hudson County, Burnham and Sprague give $B_{yz.z} = -.647$ and $B_{yz.x} = -.040$. Our recalculated values are consistent with both zero-order correlations and the multiple correlations.

composition of the labor force (as indexed by X and Z) differed from county to county (although they ran no significance test).

Since their inquiry pertains to differences between group means adjusted for regression, it may be brought within the framework of the analysis of covariance or path analysis. Within the framework of path analysis, the population model is given by (24). Our interest lies mainly in the pattern of covariances for absolute numbers which together give approximately the covariance of ratios.

In considering this matter, it eventually became necessary to carry out all calculations on the original data, since only the roughest estimates could be obtained from the entries in Table 7. (The data were very generously supplied by Burnham and Sprague.) We proceeded as follows:

1. Calculated regression coefficients (apart from $B_a = 1.00$) from within-group moments:

$$B_{yx} = -.0503, \qquad B_{yz} = .1929.$$

2. Calculated the value of A for each subgroup by

$$A_i = \bar{Y}_i - (B_{yx}\bar{X}_i - B_{yz}\bar{Z}_i),$$

which yielded

$$A_1 = 6.3740, \qquad A_2 = 1.2886, \qquad A_3 = .3415, \qquad A_4 = 1.4353.$$

3. Converted regression coefficients to path coefficients (standardized partial regression coefficients) by the standard conversion formula:

$$p_{ij} = (\sigma_j/\sigma_i)(B_{ij}),$$

which yielded

$$p_{ya} = .5114, \qquad p_{yx} = -.1231, \qquad p_{yz} = .4764.$$

The direct contribution of A (regarded as a dummy variable) to the total variance is a little more than 25%:

$$p_{ya}^2 = (.5114)^2 = .2615.$$

From this result, we conclude that county differences in the composition of work force do not account for county differences in the Wallace vote, and that differences between adjusted means will reach the level of statistical significance.

Our concern is with the connection between path coefficients on ratio variables and the various components from which those ratios were formed. By the way of example, we may wonder whether p_{yz} and p_{yx} differ in sign because X and Z have a common base, or whether that common base is of negligible statistical importance.

In framing an answer to this question, we suppose that workers are occupationally similar within the civil divisions, and occupationally dissimilar between divisions. Therefore, the number of professionals will not be some fixed proportion of the labor force from one division to another, but rather will vary according to the aforesaid tendency toward occupational homogeneity within divisions. We hypothesize that, in divisions where skilled and semiskilled workers are a substantial majority, professionals will be a relatively insubstantial minority. In consequence of these tendencies, the correlation between such broad occupational groups as professionals and managers (X) and skilled and semiskilled (Z), will tend to its lower limit of -1.00. Furthermore, their correlations with a third variable will necessarily differ in sign, as will their path coefficients on that variable. (The correlation between occupational categories close to each other in prestige may of course be positive.)

Although the explanation of these tendencies (we surmise) lies not in the composition of X and Z (which have a common denominator) but rather in the occupational similarity of civil divisions, it may be instructive to find the approximate correlation of X and Z in terms of their components. To do this, we compute rel-variances and rel-covariances for number of males classified as professionals and managers (P), number of males classified as skilled and semiskilled (S), and total number of males in the work force (T), with these results:

$$V_p{}^2 = 1.547 \qquad V_{ps} = 1.867 \qquad V_{pt} = 1.911$$

$$V_s{}^2 = 3.253 \qquad V_{st} = 3.066$$

$$V_t{}^2 = 2.965.$$

Substituting these quantities for corresponding terms in (7), we obtain the approximate correlation between X and Z:

$$r_{xz} \doteq \frac{1.867 - 1.911 - 3.066 + 2.965}{[1.547 + 2.965 - (2)(1.911)]^{1/2}\,[3.253 + 2.965 - (2)(3.066)]^{1/2}}$$

$$\doteq \frac{-.145}{(.690)^{1/2}\,(.086)^{1/2}} \doteq -.595.$$

From this result, we conclude that the negative correlation between percent males classified as professionals and managers (X) and percent classified as skilled and semiskilled (Z) is attributable to the positive covariances of P with T, and of S with T. Although both P and S increase as T increases, they increase at very different rates, and thereby cause the ratios P/T and S/T to be negatively correlated. (Note that the approximate value of r_{xy} ($-.595$) is appreciably smaller than the exact value of $-.801$. This simply means that cubic and higher terms in the series expansion cannot be safely neglected for these data.)

6.3 Social Indicators

In analyzing multiple indicators, we may regard (as an opening hypothesis) each one as a compound of a factor common to all and a factor specific to that particular measure:

$$Y_i = F + E_i, \tag{27}$$

where the Y_i are indicators, F is common to all Y_i, and E_i is specific to Y_i. When error terms are uncorrelated with one another and with the common factor, the correlation between Y_i and Y_j is

$$r_{ij} = (\sigma_f/\sigma_i)(\sigma_f/\sigma_j), \tag{28}$$

the product of the weight of F in Y_i and the weight of F in Y_j. Thus, the correlation between two measures will simply reflect the weights of the common factor when each is of the form $Y_i = F + E_i$.

However, when one measure is present in another, the correlation between them will reflect not only the common factor, but also the contaminating presence of the one variable in the other. For example, if $Y_j' = Y_i + Y_j$, the correlation between Y_i and Y_j' will be

$$r_{ij'} = \frac{2\sigma_f^2 + \sigma_{e_i}^2}{\sigma_i(\sigma_i^2 + \sigma_j^2 + 2\sigma_{ij})^{1/2}} \tag{29}$$

which will generally differ from r_{ij}. Clearly, one indicator should not be permitted to intrude in another, if we intend that the correlation between them be attributable solely to a single common factor.

This problem may arise with ratio variables that purport to measure different aspects of the same thing. Gibbs' (1966) measure of urbanization, as analyzed by Jones (1967), supplies an example. (The example may be a trifle forced, since Gibbs makes no claim that his measures are of the form $Y = F + E$.)

TABLE 8

<small>Urban Population and Total Population in Selected Intervals, Yugoslavia, 1961[a]</small>

Number	Size of localities	X Proportion of urban population	Y Proportion of total population	XY Product of proportions
1	2000+	1.000	.412	.412
2	5000+	.709	.292	.207
3	10,000+	.555	.229	.127
4	20,000+	.483	.187	.090
5	50,000+	.285	.118	.034
6	100,000+	.218	.090	.020
7	500,000+	.077	.032	.002
				Sum .892

[a] From Gibbs (1966).

Table 8 shows the proportion of the urban population in seven cumulated intervals, and the proportion of the total population in the same seven intervals, for Yugoslavia. The table shows, for example, that 70.9% of the urban population live in places of 5000 population or more, and 29.2% of the total population live in places of that size. Gibbs noted that the total urban population, expressed as a proportion of the total population, is conventionally used as a measure of degree of urbanization. This is $Y_1 = .412$ of Table 8, symbolized DU for "degree of urbanization." After reviewing some of the limitations of this measure, he suggested, with supporting reasons, that the sum of the products of columns 3 and 4 (given in column 5) might be used as a supplementary index. In symbols,

$$\text{SU} = \sum_1^7 X_i Y_i,\tag{30}$$

where SU symbolizes "scale of urbanization."

Subsequently, Jones (1967) pointed out that, since $X_i = (1/Y_1)\, Y_i$, SU may be expressed entirely in terms of the Y:

$$\text{SU} = Y_1 + \frac{\sum_2^7 Y_i^2}{Y_1}.\tag{31}$$

Replacing Y_1 by DU and $\sum_2^7 Y_i^2$ by S, we may write this as

$$\text{SU} = \text{DU} + (S/\text{DU}),\tag{32}$$

which makes explicit that DU—the conventional measure of urbanization—has intruded itself into SU—the proposed supplementary measure. An implication is that the correlation between DU and SU will reflect not only the common factor of urbanization, but also the presumably unwanted presence of DU in SU. Consequently, that correlation should not be factored to obtain the weight of the common factor in each of the measures. This principle, which applies to the correlation between any two overlapping variables, may be easily overlooked with ratio variables.

7. Concluding Discussion

Since ratios and their components are mathematically related, it is possible to express one in terms of the other. Such expressions would not be sought for their own sake, but rather to test a hypothesis (perhaps in the form of a structural equation), or to clarify a network of puzzling relationships. In any event, the decomposition of moments of ratios into moments of components does not carry the implication that components are the cause of ratios, or vice versa. This point is deserving of emphasis because of the preoccupation in this chapter with the resolution of a covariance of ratios into the covariances of its components. That resolution does not provide a demonstration that components cause ratios, although it may suggest, in a given problem, that causal variables have a differential effect on components.

The point that an algebraic partitioning may be used to explore a set of relationships is also deserving of iteration. When employed in that manner, the partitioning may suggest that components mediate between causal variables and ratios, or the reverse, that ratios mediate between causal variables and components. Moreover, an exploratory decomposition may stimulate inquiry into the makeup of categories and into the possibility that conclusions hold only for those categories.

The allocation of ratios to their components is of additional interest because of its bearing on a number of recurrent problems in sociological research. We mention several.

7.1 DISTRIBUTION OF RATES

Ratio variables such as birth rates are a convenience in social research in that they satisfy the requirements of an additive scale with absolute zero and, hence, are subject to all ordinary statistical calculations.

However, such variables suffer the disadvantage that their distribution is contingent on the makeup of the base population which is liable to arbitrary determination. For example, the distribution of death rates for states will differ from the distribution of death rates for counties. In general, the same events (e.g., deaths, births) will give rise to different statistical patterns according to the method of classifying them. Although this notion is commonplace in social statistics, it should be borne in mind in analyzing rates; otherwise one may overlook the conditional nature of his results and conclusions.

7.2 Ecological Fallacy and Spurious Relations

One may make a spurious attribution of relationship in Pearson's sense, and commit the ecological fallacy in Robinson's (1950) sense, from the same calculations. Therefore, it is necessary to keep both pitfalls in mind. For example, after calculating the relation across states of percent blacks and percent with less than six years of schooling, one may draw the inference that schooling for individuals is causally dependent on color. Such an inference from the relation of group measures to the relation of individual measures has come to be known as the ecological fallacy, even though it may be factually correct. One might use the same coefficient of relation to estimate the relation between the absolute number of blacks in the state and the absolute number of persons with less than six years of schooling. In this case, we commit the fallacy of treating the correlation between numbers per capita as equal to the correlation of the absolute numbers themselves. This distinction between pitfalls is noteworthy, as it is possible to avoid one and fall into the other. Thus, one may state that his hypothesis pertains unmistakably to ratios rather than actual numbers, and he still may mistakenly extend his conclusions to relations between individual characteristics.

7.3 Level of Measurement

It is clear from (4) and (5) that the mean and standard deviation of a ratio variable will change as the coefficients of variation of the components change, and vice versa. Statisticians warn research workers that the coefficient of variation should be avoided except for scales with an absolute zero. With scales having an arbitrary origin, one may inflate (or deflate) that coefficient by shifting the arbitrary origin. An implication is that such methods as path analysis not be applied to ratio variables formed from one or more merely interval scales, since the characteristics of such composite variables will depend on the origin of the interval scale which is (by definition) arbitrary in location.

7.4 Measurement Error

Since ratio variables may be based on counts, and since counts are subject to error, it is necessary to take into account such errors in stating one's conclusions. For example, if $X = X^* + e_x$ and $Z = Z^* + e_z$, where X^* and Z^* are hypothetical true values, and e_x and e_z are random measurement errors, then the ratio of sums

$$U = (X^* + e_x)/(Z^* + e_z)$$

will generally differ from the true value $U^* = X^*/Z^*$. Essentially the same problem arises in statistical estimation, except that in the foregoing expression X^* and Z^* would be regarded as parameters and e_x and e_z as sampling errors. The effect of measurement errors on the correlation of ratios has been studied by Briggs (1962); the problem of estimating ratios and their standard errors is discussed in most textbooks on sampling (e.g., Cochran, 1963).

11

Psychological and Cultural Factors in the Process of Occupational Achievement

OTIS DUDLEY DUNCAN AND DAVID L. FEATHERMAN

1. The Problem

Social and behavioral scientists have suggested that several distinct kinds of variables play important roles in the process of social stratification. But progress toward a comprehensive model of stratification, incorporating all of these variables, has been uneven. We do have rather firm estimates of the correlations between socioeconomic status of the family of orientation and adult achievement as measured by educational attainment, occupational level, and income (Blau & Duncan, 1967; Duncan, Featherman, & Duncan, 1968). Several bodies of relatively reliable data have documented differentials in achievement—not entirely attributable to concomitant variation in socioeconomic background—among ethnic and religious groups (Duncan & Duncan, 1968; Goldstein, 1969; Gockel, 1969; Warren, 1970). It is also rather well established that psychometric tests of ability correlate substantially with both socioeconomic background and educational attainment (Sewell & Shah, 1967). The specific contribution of ability to occupational achievement is, however, somewhat difficult to estimate (Duncan, 1968; Griliches & Mason, this volume). Even more uncertain is our knowledge about the social psychological variables identified variously as motives, aspirations, value orientations, and so forth (Kahl, 1965; Stacey, 1965; Crockett, 1966). Efforts to include such variables in models

229

of the achievement process (e.g., Duncan, 1969b) have served to highlight the difficult problems of measurement and inference that are encountered as soon as one attempts to achieve any degree of rigor in this area.

One problem has been the difficulty in assembling for a single representative sample a set of measurements on each of the variables mentioned. Kahl (1965, p. 678), for example, had occasion to remark, "I am still waiting for a study that combines both intelligence and motivation within the context of social structure." Rosen (1959) produced evidence of differences among ethnic and religious groups in achievement orientations, but we must turn to other bodies of data, such as those cited above, for evidence of actual differences in achievement. Comparability between such different bodies of data is always in question. Lenski (1963) was in a somewhat more favorable position; he was able to put together information from one cross-section sample on socio-religious group membership, socioeconomic origins, occupational achievement, and attitudes and values concerning work. He did not, however, make use of a well-specified model of socioeconomic achievement; nor did he attempt to cope explicitly with the problem of reciprocal causation as between his psychological variables and his measure of achievement. Despite these deficiencies, Lenski's research poses our problem in an especially clear way. Moreover, the attempt to replicate aspects of Lenski's study (Schuman, 1971) led to the creation of the body of data we shall employ here.

The most nearly satisfactory research design developed thus far appears in Featherman's (1971) investigation of social and psychological explanations of religion–ethnic subgroup differences in achievement. A particular advantage of his study was the availability of panel data, including three indexes of motivational orientations measured at an early stage of the socioeconomic career along with subsequent measures of achievement six to ten years later. The study provided, at best, modest support for the notion that motives and other personality dimensions function as "key" (Crockett, 1966) intervening variables in the process of achievement.

No doubt it is premature to draw any firm conclusions in this area. A critic might easily find fault with the particular indexes of achievement orientation that Featherman had available; his study included no estimate of the respondent's intellectual ability; and one might wish to entertain models specified somewhat differently from his. The present study likewise must be seen as yet another effort to wrest some intelligence from less than ideal information and to cope with intrinsically refractory problems of conceptualization and model specification.

TABLE 1

Correlation Matrix for Selected Variables in DAS Data for Native White Men Living in Detroit Metropolitan Area: 1966
[Based on 887 men reporting all variables]

Variable[a]	y_1	y_2	y_3	y_4	y_5	y_f	y_g	y_h	x_6	x_7	x_8	Mean	S.D.
Protestant ethic y_1	1.000	.098	.196	.252	.242	.338	.219	.262	.232	.134	.184	0.460	0.397
Occupational aspiration y_2		1.000	.302	.329	.363	.306	.386	.366	.249	.163	.143	46.9	19.0
Social class y_3			1.000	.467	.445	.414	.401	.540	.309	.258	.242	3.45	1.15
Respondent's occupation y_4				1.000	.601	.746	.548	.864	.431	.303	.286	45.9	24.2
Respondent's education y_5					1.000	.625	.893	.825	.569	.336	.337	5.07	1.58
y_f						1.000	.565	.736	.687	.399	.545	—	0.13
y_g							1.000	.743	.499	.297	.294	—	5.58
y_h								1.000	.544	.478	.387	—	0.62
Intelligence x_6									1.000	.278	.262	14.0	5.3
Father's occupation x_7										1.000	.469	34.0	23.6
Father's education x_8											1.000	3.36	1.80

[a] Definitions:

y_1 Tau measure of conformity of responses to questions 49–52 to order implied by "Protestant" orientation to work.

y_2 Occupational aspiration scale.

y_3 Subjective social class identification.

y_4 Respondent's current (1966) occupation scored on Duncan socioeconomic index.

y_5 Years of school completed by respondent, transformed scale, with score of 2 for 0–8 grades, 4 for 9–11 grades, 5 for 12 grades, 6 for some college, 7 for college graduate, 8 for one or more years of graduate training.

y_f, y_g, y_h Unmeasured variables (see text). Variables $\hat{y}_f$, $\hat{y}_g$, and $\hat{y}_h$ were estimated for each respondent, using the regression coefficients in Table 3; the correlations reported here were computed directly from these estimated scores.

x_6 Score on Similarities subtest of Wechsler test of adult intelligence.

x_7 Father's occupation scored on Duncan socioeconomic index.

x_8 Years of school completed by father, transformed scale as in variable y_5.

We have data from Project 938 of the Detroit Area Study (DAS). This involved a cross-sectional sample of native white men 21–64 years old living in metropolitan Detroit in 1966. The response rate of 80% produced 985 interviews, of which 28 were double-weighted to take account of subsampling introduced in the final stage of the field work (Schuman, 1971). Of the 1013 weighted cases, 887 are available for the present analysis, since they provide information on all the variables investigated here. (See Tables 1 and 2 for list of variables.)

Using these variables (described in detail in Section 2), we propose (in Section 3) a model in which cultural differences among ethnic and

TABLE 2

MEAN SCORES ON MEASURED VARIABLES BY RELIGION–ETHNIC CATEGORIES, FOR SAMPLE OF 887 MEN IN 1966 DAS SAMPLE REPORTING ALL VARIABLES [DEVIATIONS FROM GRAND MEANS, TABLE 1]

| | Religion–Ethnic | | Variable[a] | | | | | | | |
j	Category	n_j	y_1	y_2	y_3	y_4	y_5	x_6	x_7	x_8
1	Jewish	21	.045	10.3	1.03	19.1	1.60	2.5	21.2	.93
2	Irish Catholic	60	−.046	−0.5	.20	4.3	.28	1.1	6.7	.49
3	German Catholic	68	.046	0.8	−.20	1.2	.14	0.6	2.2	.33
4	French Catholic	49	−.072	−3.6	−.25	−3.3	−.03	0.0	−0.3	−.15
5	Polish Catholic	93	−.036	−3.3	−.21	−6.3	−.36	−1.4	−9.3	−.52
6	Italian Catholic	36	−.110	3.6	−.09	2.3	.16	0.0	−5.6	.03
7	Catholic, other N.W. European and N. American	32	.034	−0.3	−.04	−4.7	−.50	−1.6	5.1	.52
8	Other Catholic and Orthodox	54	−.004	0.8	−.12	0.3	.01	−0.5	−5.5	−.41
9	German Lutheran	49	.059	1.7	.16	5.1	.22	0.8	−2.3	−.11
10	Other Lutheran	48	−.047	−6.1	.11	−7.7	−.23	−1.1	−1.2	.04
11	Presbyterian	72	.104	2.5	.22	10.0	.75	1.9	11.3	.39
12	Episcopalian	31	.089	2.5	.71	10.5	.68	2.8	18.5	1.55
13	Methodist	71	.098	1.4	.11	0.3	.02	1.0	0.4	−.19
14	Baptist	91	−.090	0.4	−.41	−9.2	−.69	−2.2	−9.2	−.41
15	Protestant, nondenominational	32	−.078	−5.8	−.07	−0.9	−.72	−0.2	−4.0	−.23
16	"Fundamentalist"	26	.064	−7.0	−.80	−17.9	−.91	−3.5	−15.6	−.70
17	No religion	28	−.060	−0.5	.23	4.3	−.07	0.5	1.2	−.50
18	Residual	26	.056	10.7	.67	11.9	.78	2.0	12.1	.26
	Correlation ratio	—	.177	.198	.294	.307	.328	.285	.357	.271

[a] See Table 1 for full identification. y_1 = Protestant ethic, y_2 = occupational aspiration, y_3 = social class, y_4 = respondent's occupation, y_5 = respondent's education, x_6 = intelligence, x_7 = father's occupation, x_8 = father's education.

religious groups give rise to differences in psychological dispositions; while the latter, in turn, influence occupational achievement, whether directly or via educational attainment. We consider (in Section 4) some alternative specifications of the model, selecting one as most relevant for the purpose at hand. Estimates obtained on this specification are presented and discussed in terms of the light they may shed on the problem of assessing the role of psychological factors in the process of achievement.

2. Description of Variables

In the DAS data we have measures of family background (father's occupation and education) and socioeconomic achievement (respondent's education and occupation) much like those used in other work on occupational achievement (Duncan, Featherman, & Duncan, 1968). Indeed, special pains were taken to ensure that the coding of the occupation items followed the procedures used by the Bureau of the Census, so that rather strict comparability to the occupational data in the study of Blau & Duncan (1967) can be assumed. The DAS data also include a measure of intelligence, the respondent's score on the 13-item Similarities Subscale of the Wechsler Adult Intelligence Scale. Wechsler (1955, pp. 13–17) reports an odd–even reliability of .85 for this subscale and indicates that it correlates about .80 with the full scale score (based on eleven subtests, including Similarities). We would have preferred to have a more comprehensive intelligence test score obtained around age 12, i.e., at a point in the life-cycle clearly prior to the completion of schooling and entry into an occupational career. This information is not available, and we have merely adopted the expedient of treating the WAIS Similarities score, as obtained, as if it were such a measure. No doubt we thereby incur error, although it is not clear that measurement error with respect to this variable is more serious than it is with respect to father's occupation or education. In any event, it has been shown (Duncan, Featherman, & Duncan, 1968, Section 6.5) that the expedient followed here produces estimates very similar to those yielded by a much more elaborate and (presumably) better-justified procedure used with another set of data (Duncan, 1968).

Despite the modest sample size, we have used a fairly elaborate composite classification of religious preferences and ethnic group affiliations. Jewish respondents, irrespective of national origins, are treated as a single category. Five main nationalities are distinguished

among Catholics, and two additional categories account for the remainder
of the Catholics. German Lutherans are distinguished from other
Lutherans. For the remaining religious groups, nationality is ignored.
In point of fact, heavy majorities in the several major Protestant
denominations report northwest European origins. We distinguish
four such denominations in addition to the Lutherans. Non-
denominational "Protestants," members of any of the several
"Fundamentalist" groups, and respondents having no religious
preference account for three more categories. The residual consists of
a miscellany of "other" religions, and "other" denominations, the
largest single one being Congregational. Altogether, then, we have 18
categories (listed in Table 2) in our religion–ethnic classification. They
are represented by as few as 21 respondents (Jewish) or as many as 93
(Polish Catholic). Naturally, mean scores on socioeconomic and attitude
variables estimated for such small samples are subject to a good deal
of sampling error, so that we are well advised to avoid the temptation
to interpret differences between specific denominational or ethnic
groups. Moreover, we do not assume that there are in the population
substantial differences in socioeconomic background or achievement
for all such pairs of groups. The reason for retaining this much detail
in the classification, therefore, is simply to allow the religion–ethnic
variable to produce as much variation as it can. If we must err, we
prefer in the present context to err on the side of over- rather than
under-estimating this variation. In this connection, we have been
influenced by Warren's (1970) argument that "Protestant" is not a
socioeconomically homogeneous category and by the growing appreciation that significant ethnic differentiation persists among Catholics,
even in the "triple melting pot" (Lenski, 1963, p. 362).

The measure of "Protestant" work values was adapted from the
research of Lenski (1963). Our score was derived from responses to
this series of questions:

Three items in the DAS questionnaire were selected as indicators of
psychological dispositions (motives or orientations): (1) a measure of
the degree to which the respondent's work values conform to the
"Protestant Ethic"; (2) a measure of occupational aspiration; and (3)
the respondent's subjective social class identification. Some description
and comments on these are in order.

> Q. 49.   Now I'd like to ask you some more questions about your
> own interests and ideas. Would you please look at this
> card, and tell me which thing on this list you would most
> prefer in a job.

1. High income
2. No danger of being fired
3. Short working hours, lots of free time
4. Chances for improvement
5. The work is important and gives a feeling of accomplishment

Q. 50. Which comes next?
Q. 51. Which is third most important?
Q. 52. Which is *least* important?

The wording of the alternatives is the same as that used by Lenski, except that in the fourth alternative the word "improvement" was used where Lenski's question read "advancement." Note that the series of questions has the effect of requiring the respondent to make a complete ranking of the five alternatives. To use all the information in this ranking, we need some assumptions about the relationship of the alternatives to the "Protestant" norm. We followed Lenski's (1963, p. 89) interpretation of the meaning of the alternatives:

> Each of these, we believed, represented a separate and distinct basis for evaluating jobs and careers. The last alternative is closest to the Protestant Ethic as conceived by Weber; it stresses both the worth of the work and the personal satisfactions it can afford. The first alternative, in contrast, stresses only the extrinsic satisfactions linked with work—the paycheck. In much of the current literature on the Protestant Ethic, this, together with a desire for advancement, is conceived to be the essence of the Protestant Ethic. While it is undoubtedly futile at this late date to try to "purify" sociological usage, it may at least prove worthwhile to call attention to these two divergent conceptions of the Protestant Ethic. Of our five alternatives, the fifth best expresses the classical Weberian understanding of the term, the first the current popular understanding, while the fourth occupies the middle ground between them. A concern for chances for advancement is consistent with both the classical and current usages.
>
> The third alternative on our list was designed to express a view completely in opposition to any conception of the Protestant Ethic. The second was designed with the same purpose, but in retrospect it seems somewhat less in conflict with the Weberian definition than it seemed at first, since it does express a desire to work.

On the basis of this discussion, we placed the five alternatives in Q. 49 in the following rank order according to the degree to which they approach the "Protestant" norm of a structure of work values: 5–4–1–2–3, in which the first choice is alternative 5 and the last choice 3. A respondent who placed the alternatives in just this order would be considered to conform perfectly to the Protestant Ethic in terms of his work values.

To score the responses to this series of questions we constructed for each respondent the implicit rank order of the five alternatives. We then computed Kendall's tau-statistic between the respondent's rank order and the standard or normative order. A value of tau of $+1.0$ represents perfect agreement of the respondent with the "Protestant" norm, while a value of -1.0 represents a perfect disagreement. The following distribution of respondents according to values of tau was obtained:

tau:	1.0	0.8	0.6	0.4	0.2	0.0	-0.2	-0.4	-0.6	-0.8	-1.0	NA	Total
f:	102	220	208	199	119	68	38	21	15	10	2	11	1013

As Lenski notes, there is a high degree of endorsement of the Protestant Ethic in the general population. Only a small minority of men present a ranking that leads to a negative value of tau. In using the value of tau as a measure of the degree to which the respondent's orientation conforms to the Protestant Ethic, therefore, we are producing something like Allport's (1934) J-curve of conformity to a social norm, although conformity is here measured in ideological rather than behavioral terms.

The second indicator is a variable that purports to measure the respondent's achievement orientation to occupations. It is based on responses to this question:

Q. 56.   Now suppose you were starting out in life and had to choose a job (occupation) for the first time. Would you look at this list please and tell me whether you would be *satisfied* or *dissatisfied* about the prospect (idea) of entering each of these lines of work?

		Satisfied	Dissatisfied
a.	Clerk in a store	—	—
b.	Carpenter	—	—
c.	Lawyer	—	—
d.	Bookkeeper	—	—
e.	Construction laborer	—	—
f.	Public school teacher	—	—
g.	Truck driver	—	—
h.	Garage mechanic	—	—

A rationale for interpretation of data derived in this way has been offered by Morgan, David, Cohen, & Brazer (1962, Appendix C). They suggest that the need for achievement is a "supposedly enduring personality trait—a disposition to strive for success." From the literature on achievement motivation, Morgan and his collaborators deduced that "An index of achievement motivation should ... be provided by the extent to which an individual places high values on succeeding in the difficult, high prestige occupations, and low values on succeeding in the easy occupations." These investigators used a procedure resembling the one employed here; however, there are differences in the list of occupations, the phrasing of the question, and the scoring of the responses.

Our procedure was to assign to each of the eight occupations in Q. 56 its score on Duncan's socioeconomic index (Reiss *et al.*, 1961). Then, for each respondent, we took the mean score of those occupations that he deemed "satisfactory" to be his score on an occupational aspiration scale. This method of scoring resembles that used for attitude scales constructed by Thurstone's method of equal-appearing intervals (Schuessler, 1971, p. 320). In our DAS sample, the occupational aspiration score has a mean of 46.9 and a standard deviation of 19.0. As Table 1 shows, the mean is quite comparable to the mean of current occupational status scores (45.9; standard deviation 24.2) in this population; but it is substantially higher than the actual status scores of the first jobs held by DAS respondents (33.7; standard deviation 22.7; not shown in the table). Some emphasis can be given to the form in which the question was worded: It called for a *hypothetical* orientation that the respondent would have in beginning his work career, not for a report on what his motivational state actually was when he did commence working. It seems likely that occupational aspiration, measured in this way, will reflect the respondent's actual level of achievement to date as well as his initial motivation. This possibility is taken into account in our model, as noted subsequently.

The third indicator, social class identification, is based on responses to the following DAS questions:

Q. 76. There's quite a bit of talk these days about social class. If you were asked to use one of these four names for your social class, which would you say you belong in: middle class, lower class, working class, or upper class?

Q. 77. Would you say you are in the average part of the _____ [class named in Q. 76] or in the upper part?

Numerical scores were assigned to responses as follows:

1. Lower class
2. Working class
3. Upper working class
4. Middle class
5. Upper middle class
6. Upper class

The sample mean was 2.45 and the standard deviation was 1.15; thus, both "working class" and "middle class" identifications were chosen by large numbers of respondents.

The first of these questions on class identification used in DAS (Q. 76) resembles the one proposed by the psychologist Richard Centers (1949). In Centers' work the responses are taken to indicate the "class consciousness" that emerges from the interplay of economic self-interest and the forces of economic circumstances encountered by the individual. Limitations of this point of view were suggested by Hodge & Treiman (1968), who pointed out that class identification correlates with the socioeconomic status of friends, neighbors, and relatives, independently of the respondent's own education, occupation, and income. We venture an interpretation of the question that differs considerably from those of previous investigators, to wit, that "class identification" is really, in part, a projective question that taps the respondent's desires or inclinations as well as (if not instead of) his estimate of his objective standing in society. With the DAS data we cannot, of course, put these alternative interpretations to any kind of rigorous test. But results obtained with our model seem consistent with the assumption that the response to this question, like those on work values and occupational aspiration, is an indicator of an unmeasured motivational factor which plays a role as an intervening variable in the process of achievement.

Some further notes on scoring procedures appear with Table 1, which shows the means, standard deviations, and intercorrelations of the variables (including three unmeasured variables still to be described) considered in the study, other than the religion–ethnic classification. The mean scores on the measured variables for the 18 groups in that classification appear in Table 2. The last line of this table provides a descriptive statistic, the correlation ratio of each measured variable on the religion–ethnic classification, which reflects the degree to which these groups differ from each other. The classification, by itself, is seen to account for about 3% of the variation in the Protestant Ethic question (y_1) but nearly 13% of the variation in father's occupation (x_7), with the other variables falling between these extremes.

3. The Model

While it is only moderately difficult to rationalize a model once it is formulated, it is often difficult to say where all the ideas came from that get translated into a model. The present model has evolved over a long period and undergone some major transformations. Featherman's first unpublished memorandum dates from December 1966. Further work resulted in the version presented by Duncan, Featherman, & Duncan (1968, Section 7.6) and revised slightly for the Madison conference. Partly as a consequence of lessons derived from that conference and partly under the stimulation of Schuman's (1971) partial replication of Lenski's (1963) work, we enlarged the list of exogenous variables to include the religion–ethnic classification, took a different approach to the definition of unobserved variables, and improved our strategy of statistical estimation.

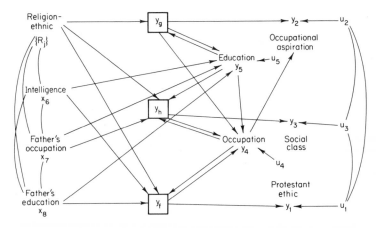

Figure 1. Path diagram representing the model given by Eqs. (1)–(8).

The model is presented in Fig. 1 in the form of a path diagram. Straight lines with arrows at one end represent coefficients measuring the dependence of endogenous variables upon other endogenous variables, exogenous variables, or disturbances. Curved lines represent correlations between exogenous variables (taken as given in the sample) or between disturbances, where not specified to be zero in the population. Unmeasured variables have letter subscripts and appear on the diagram in boxes to distinguish them from observed variables and disturbances. The ys are endogenous variables, the us are disturbances, and the xs and $\{R_j\}$ are exogenous. The symbol R_j ($j = 1,..., 18$) represents a dummy variable for the jth religion–ethnic category. Hence, an arrow leading from $\{R_j\}$ refers to a vector of structural coefficients, and a curve terminating at $\{R_j\}$ to a vector of correlations. We have, with minor modifications, followed Sewall Wright's (1934) conventions for path diagrams, and we find the diagrammatic representation indispensable in thinking through the conceptual problems of model construction. However, we have not followed Wright's convention of expressing variables in standard form nor relied on path analysis algorithms in estimating coefficients.

The model consists of the following eight equations:

$$y_1 = y_f + u_1 \tag{1}$$

$$y_2 = y_g + b_{24}y_4 + u_2 \tag{2}$$

$$y_3 = y_h + u_3 \tag{3}$$

$$y_4 = b_{4f}y_f + b_{4g}y_g + b_{4h}y_h + b_{45}y_5 + u_4 \tag{4}$$

$$y_5 = b_{5g}y_g + b_{56}x_6 + b_{57}x_7 + b_{58}x_8 + u_5 \tag{5}$$

$$y_f = b_{f4}y_4 + b_{f6}x_6 + b_{f8}x_8 + \sum_j b_{fj}R_j \qquad (j = 1,..., 18) \tag{6}$$

$$y_g = b_{g5}y_5 + \sum_j b_{gj}R_j \qquad (j = 1,..., 18) \tag{7}$$

$$y_h = b_{h4}y_4 + b_{h5}y_5 + b_{h7}x_7 + \sum_j b_{hj}R_j \qquad (j = 1,..., 18). \tag{8}$$

To avoid singularity, we constrain the coefficient of R_{18} in each equation to be zero. All variables are expressed as deviations from their means. It will be noted that there are no disturbance terms in Eqs. (6)–(8) for the unmeasured factors, while those factors appear with unit coefficients in Eqs. (1)–(3) for their respective indicators.

In common with other models of the Blau–Duncan type, we take father's education and occupation as exogenous; and we treat our measure of intelligence in the same way. Similarly, we treat respondent's religious–ethnic classification as exogenous, despite the fact that it refers to current religious preference rather than preference at the outset of the occupational career or preference in the family of orientation. We know that some men change religious preference in the course of the life-cycle and suspect that at least some of them do so to effect an adjustment to the degree of socioeconomic success or failure they have enjoyed (Warren, 1970). Here, as with the other exogenous variables, we forego any attempt to evaluate the effect of measurement errors, which, we suspect, may engender small, albeit not necessarily predictable, biases in our coefficient estimates.

Disturbances are specified to be uncorrelated with exogenous variables. Moreover, we treat y_5 as predetermined with respect to y_4, and both y_5 and y_4 as predetermined with respect to y_1, y_2, and y_3. Hence, u_4 and u_5 are uncorrelated with each other and with u_1, u_2, and u_3 although the latter are allowed to be correlated with each other. We are, therefore, retaining the basic recursive feature of the Blau–Duncan model, although simultaneity comes into the picture presently.

In our formulation, y_1, y_2, and y_3 are fallible indicators of the psychological dispositions that really influence achievement, y_f, y_g, and y_h. We reason that they are measured contemporaneously with the level of achievement that the dispositions presumably help to explain. For this reason, we do not assign any causal role to y_1, y_2, and y_3 themselves, but rather to their unobserved counterparts y_f, y_g, and y_h. We are prepared to find rather high values of the disturbance variances in the first three equations.

If psychological dispositions are sociogenic as well as (or, perhaps, instead of) psychogenic, then we must reckon with the possibility that a disposition that is reflected in an indicator at a given time may have arisen in part as a consequence of the very activity that it tends to instigate. Thus, a man who has enjoyed economic security throughout his career may indeed find that his occupational decisions turn upon the degree to which the work gives a sense of accomplishment, whereas the man who has had to struggle for employment and a decent wage will understandably give priority to monetary return or job security. Hence, work values, as they develop in the course of the life-cycle, may as well be caused by occupational achievement as be causes thereof. By the same token, although we presume that in reporting himself as "middle" or "upper" class a respondent is partially voicing an ambition or revealing a tendency to strive for status, we must acknowledge that his class identification may also be a consequence of the objective status attained. Similarly, the question designed to tap occupational aspiration cannot plausibly be assumed to be free of the effects of occupational level at the time of interview. Moreover, our impression is that the preferences for different kinds of work elicited by this question could well be modified as the individual attains successively higher levels of schooling, even though occupational ambition may be a significant spur to the pursuit of an education.

In short, we feel that the kinds of disposition reflected in the questions we are working with must realistically be conceived as interacting with the social roles incumbency of which they tend to encourage or discourage. Thus the model represents y_4 as being implicated in reciprocal causal relationships with both y_h and y_f; and y_5 is involved with y_g in the same way. Moreover, we allow a direct influence of occupation (y_4) on the measured value of occupational aspiration (y_2). Not only y_f and y_h but also y_g appear in the set of influences on occupational achievement.

We have not, however, allowed y_f and y_h to serve as causes of educational attainment (y_5). To do so would have broken down the recursive structure that we wished to carry over from earlier stratification models. This particular recursive feature seems to us rather basic in the general class of stratification models with which we are working. Moreover, it does not seem to have been challenged in any careful criticism of these models. The specification that the disturbances in the education and occupation equations are uncorrelated does, of course, put some strain on the assumption that we have identified and included all common causes of these two forms of achievement. In any given model this condition is not likely to be met literally. Yet most of the obvious "omitted variables" can be shown to be somewhat highly correlated with one or another of our exogenous variables and/or to have significant direct effects only upon education or upon occupation but not both. Hence, our specification is thought to incur relatively minor biases.

Although it appeared desirable to set up the model in such a way as to preclude indirect feedback from occupation to education, the particular arrangement of the three unmeasured variables that we propose to accomplish this is, admittedly, somewhat arbitrary. (One might argue that y_f belongs where we have y_g and vice versa, for example.) The only "test" of our arrangement that we can think of consists of eyeballing the coefficient estimates for reasonableness. Perhaps an exceptionally energetic critic will wish to estimate a set of equations differently specified from ours in this important respect.

Particular attention is drawn to the main "engine" that "drives" this model: we have a priori excluded from the occupation (y_4) and education (y_5) equations the religion–ethnic variable. Some such exclusion is essential for identification. More important is the sense in which it expresses the particular theoretical bias we wish to impart to the model. We want to interpret all effects of religion–ethnic affiliation on achievement as working via the (unobserved) psychological dispositions, to put forward the best possible statistical case for the kind of argument made by Rosen (1959) and Lenski (1963). This strategy, obviously, does not result in a *test* of their kind of theory. We do not actually pit the cultural–psychological hypothesis against some alternative hypothesis and choose between them on the basis of a crucial statistic. We can in no sense "prove" the cultural–psychological argument. The nearest we could come to "disproving" it would be to show that the effects it posits do not appear, even when the model is biased in favor of bringing them to light. The reader must understand, therefore, that we are not proposing what we think of as a "true" model, but rather we are attempting to represent as well as possible with the data at hand one line of argument about the process of stratification—not necessarily the line that we ourselves find most plausible.

It is worth noting that the situation with this model is a particularly favorable one for our strategy in that we have as indicators of our unobserved dispositions not only some subjective questions which may be taken as psychological "reflections" of the dispositions, but also an antecedent variable, the religion–ethnic classification, which is taken to be an important source of the dispositions. Thus the dispositions are approached from both sides, and we are able to skirt completely the typical hazard of circular argument in motivational interpretations, i.e., that the motives may only be recognizable in the very behaviors that they are taken to explain.

4. Estimation and Results

Since each of Eqs. (1)–(8) contains one or more unobserved variables, none of them can be estimated as it stands. We proceed to derive new equations by straightforward substitutions. Equations (6), (7), and (8), respectively, are substituted into (1), (2), and (3) to obtain the following:

$$y_1 = b_{f4}y_4 + b_{f6}x_6 + b_{f8}x_8 + \sum_j b_{fj}R_j + u_1 \tag{1a}$$

$$y_2 = b_{24}y_4 + b_{g5}y_5 + \sum_j b_{gj}R_j + u_2 \tag{2a}$$

$$y_3 = b_{h4}y_4 + b_{h5}y_5 + b_{h7}x_7 + \sum_j b_{hj}R_j + u_3 , \tag{3a}$$

where $j = 1,..., 18$, but the coefficients for R_{18} are set at zero. Recalling that y_4 and y_5 , while endogenous in the model, are predetermined with respect to y_1 , y_2 , and y_3 , we see that each of these equations contains in effect only one endogenous variable, and so it may be estimated by ordinary least squares (OLS). The same would be true of equations of the same form containing any or all of the exogenous variables.

Indeed, we first estimated versions of (1a)–(3a) containing all the predetermined variables. In the first version of (1a), the coefficient for x_7 had the "wrong" sign and a ratio of only -0.14 to its standard error; the coefficient for y_5 had a t-ratio of 1.41. Both of these variables were dropped from the equation. Estimating the initial version of (2a) we obtained a coefficient for x_8 that had the wrong sign and a ratio of $-.07$ to its standard error; x_7 had a coefficient only 0.78 times as large as its standard error; and the coefficient for x_6 had a t-ratio of 1.17. All of these variables were dropped. In the initial version of (3a), we found that x_6 had a coefficient 0.63 times as large as its standard error, while x_7 and x_8 had coefficients respectively 1.23 and 1.35 times as large as the standard error. It was deemed advisable to retain one of these in the model, and x_7 seemed conceptually more central. In the final version the estimated coefficient for this variable has a t-ratio of 1.91.

Although we relied heavily on significance tests with regard to the variables mentioned, in deciding to retain the religion–ethnic classification in each of these equations we were guided much more strongly by our conceptualization of the model. In view of the size of our sample, we are not surprised if a classification with 17 degrees of freedom does not always test out statistically significant. We do note that inclusion of the classification in each of the equations results in a substantively nontrivial increment to explained sums of squares. If we delete terms in $\{R_j\}$ from (1a)–(3a) and compute R^2s, we obtain the following ("without") in comparison with the R^2s for those equations as written:

	without	with $\{R_j\}$
(1a)	.092	.114
(2a)	.151	.168
(3a)	.267	.292.

These results are taken to be consistent with the hypothesis that religious and ethnic factors give rise to differences in psychological dispositions.

The OLS estimates of coefficients in Eqs. (1a)–(3a) appear in Table 3, except that we have transformed the coefficients of the dummy variables to make them comparable to the deviations of variables y_1, y_2, and y_3 from the grand means in Table 2. It is of interest that these three equations produce distinct "profiles" of coefficients. No two of them include the same array of explanatory variables. Moreover, the religion–ethnic groups do not have the same patterns of coefficients on the three indicators. "Fundamentalists," for example, come out high on "Protestant Ethic" but low on social class. As noted earlier, however, it is probably best not to emphasize specific comparisons among these groups in view of the small numbers in most of them in our sample.

Proceeding to the occupation equation, we now solve (1), (2), and (3) respectively for y_f, y_g, and y_h, and substitute these solutions into (4). The result is

$$y_4 = a_{41}y_1 + a_{42}y_2 + a_{43}y_3 + a_{45}y_5 + v_4, \tag{4a}$$

where

$$a_{41} = b_{4f}/(1 + b_{24}b_{4g})$$
$$a_{42} = b_{4g}/(1 + b_{24}b_{4g})$$
$$a_{43} = b_{4h}/(1 + b_{24}b_{4g}) \tag{9}$$
$$a_{45} = b_{45}/(1 + b_{24}b_{4g})$$
$$v_4 = (u_4 - b_{4f}u_1 - b_{4g}u_2 - b_{4h}u_3)/(1 + b_{24}b_{4g}).$$

TABLE 3

OLS Estimates of Coefficients in Eqs. (1a)–(3a)[a]

Independent variable	Eq. (1a) Protestant ethic (y_1)	Eq. (2a) Occupational aspiration (y_2)	Eq. (3a) Social class (y_3)
y_4 Occupation	.0028	.132	.014
	(.0006)	(.031)	(.002)
y_5 Education	—	3.11	.168
	—	(0.48)	(.027)
x_6 Intelligence	.0099	—	—
	(.0027)	—	—
x_7 Father's occupation	—	—	.0030
	—	—	(.0016)
x_8 Father's education	.023	—	—
	(.008)	—	—
Religion–Ethnic, j =			
1 Jewish	−.055	2.8	.43
2 Irish Catholic	−.081	−1.9	.07
3 German Catholic	.029	0.2	−.25
4 French Catholic	−.059	−3.1	−.20
5 Polish Catholic	.007	−1.3	−.04
6 Italian Catholic	−.117	2.8	−.13
7 Catholic, other N.W. European, and North American	.052	1.9	.09
8 Other Catholic and Orthodox	.010	0.7	−.11
9 German Lutheran	.039	0.3	.06
10 Other Lutheran	−.016	−4.4	.26
11 Presbyterian	.048	−1.2	−.08
12 Episcopalian	−.004	−1.0	.40
13 Methodist	.091	1.3	.10
14 Baptist	−.033	3.8	−.14
15 Protestant, nondenominational	−.068	−3.5	.07
16 "Fundamentalist"	.164	−1.8	−.35
17 No religion	−.065	−0.9	.18
18 Residual	−.003	6.7	.34
R^2	.114	.168	.292

[a] Values in parentheses are standard errors. For comparison with Table 2, the coefficients for dummy variables have been transformed so that their weighted mean, using n_j from Table 2 as the weight, is zero.

We see that three of the right-hand variables in (4a) are correlated with the disturbance, so that OLS is not a consistent method of estimation. But we have y_5 and the twenty exogenous variables as predetermined variables, so that the equation is overidentified. We proceed, therefore, to estimate (4a) by two-stage least-squares (2SLS) with y_5, x_6, x_7, x_8, and R_1 ,..., R_{17} as predetermined variables.

Actually, the specification of (4a) and (4) was arrived at only after trying various alternative versions of (4a). The results of estimating these by 2SLS are reported in Table 4. Equation (4a) itself is not

TABLE 4

2SLS ESTIMATES OF COEFFICIENTS IN VARIOUS VERSIONS OF EQ. (4a)[a]

Independent variable	Alternative version of Eq. (4a)					
	(4a)	(4b)	(4c)	(4d)	(4e)	(4f)
y_1 Protestant ethic	10.7	12.2	9.91	8.51	3.64	—
	(8.9)	(10.8)	(8.65)	(9.89)	(9.68)	—
y_2 Occupational aspiration	0.450	0.815	0.417	0.460	0.367	0.374
	(0.256)	(0.246)	(0.250)	(0.254)	(0.251)	(0.252)
y_3 Social class	10.9	14.0	9.5	10.3	10.3	10.5
	(3.0)	(3.2)	(3.2)	(3.2)	(2.9)	(2.9)
y_5 Education	3.03	—	3.51	3.21	3.45	3.53
	(1.30)	—	(1.35)	(1.33)	(1.27)	(1.26)
x_6 Intelligence	—	—	—	—	0.296	0.329
	—	—	—	—	(0.189)	(0.168)
x_7 Father's occupation	—	—	0.035	—	—	—
	—	—	(0.036)	—	—	—
x_8 Father's education	—	—	—	0.254	—	—
	—	—	—	(0.509)	—	—
R^2	.260	−.086	.311	.278	.321	.312

[a] Values in parentheses are estimated standard errors. R^2 is defined as $1 - \text{Var}(\hat{v}_4)/\text{Var}(y_4)$.

entirely satisfactory, since the coefficient for neither y_f nor y_g is as large as two standard errors. Equation (4b), dropping education (y_5), remedies this situation for y_g though not for y_f. Nevertheless, Eq. (4b) seems highly questionable, both conceptually and statistically. The remaining versions, (4c)–(4f), were run to investigate the advisability of including one or another of the exogenous variables in the occupation equation. On the basis of the standard errors as well as the numerical magnitudes of the coefficients, there is little reason to include father's education (x_8) or father's occupation (x_7). The latter result is of some conceptual interest, for it is usual in Blau–Duncan models to find that father's occupation has a small but significant path even when respondent's education and various exogenous variables are in the equation (see the y_4 equation in Table 5). The finding that it may be dropped from Eq. (4) can be interpreted as an indication that the psychological variables adequately pick up what had hitherto looked like a direct effect of father's occupation.

Version (4e) is more perplexing. When intelligence (x_6) is in the equation, it turns up with a coefficient that has a t-ratio of 1.57; at the same time the coefficient for y_f (the unobserved variable corresponding to the Protestant Ethic) drops to a negligible size. One could argue that what we have in y_f is a rather clumsy proxy for intelligence, rather than a variable that is distinctively motivational in nature. At any rate, there is presented for the analyst's consideration a kind of trade-off: if he wants to argue for a direct effect of intelligence on occupational achievement (in addition to its indirect effect via education), he must give up any emphasis on a Protestant Ethic sort of motivational variable; but if the motivational variable is retained, the effect of intelligence is in doubt. To be consistent with our strategy of emphasizing the motivational variables where the situation is ambiguous, we have adopted the latter resolution of the dilemma. In opting for Eq. (4a), therefore, we discard the intelligence variable whose significance is on the borderline but retain the two motivation variables, y_f and y_g, whose significance is at least equally questionable. For the benefit of readers who may prefer the alternative resolution of the dilemma, we provide estimates for version (4f), which eliminates y_f from the equation but retains x_6. In that event, the t-ratio for $\hat{a}_{46}$ rises to 1.96. We are not, therefore, taking issue with an argument placing greater stress on intelligence but simply reiterate that the rhetorical strategy of this paper was to give the benefit of any doubt to the motivational variables.

Having decided to adopt (4a), we obtain estimates of the coefficients in (4) by solving for the bs in (9). That is, we take the $\hat{a}$s estimated for Eq. (4a) and $\hat{b}_{24}$ as estimated for Eq. (2a) and compute the remaining bs from the following formulas:

$$\hat{b}_{4g} = \hat{a}_{42}/(1 - \hat{a}_{42}\hat{b}_{24}), \qquad \hat{b}_{4f} = \hat{a}_{41}(1 + \hat{b}_{24}\hat{b}_{4g})$$

$$\hat{b}_{4h} = \hat{a}_{43}(1 + \hat{b}_{24}\hat{b}_{4g}), \qquad \hat{b}_{45} = \hat{a}_{45}(1 + \hat{b}_{24}\hat{b}_{4g}).$$

With $\hat{b}_{24} = 0.132$, the bs do not differ greatly from the corresponding $\hat{a}$s. We obtain the following estimate for Eq. (4):

$$y_4 = 11.4y_f + 0.478y_g + 11.6y_h + 3.23y_5 + \hat{u}_4 \qquad (R^2 = .588).$$

Proceeding to the education equation, we substitute the expression for y_g obtained from Eq. (2) into Eq. (5) and obtain

$$y_5 = b_{5g}(y_2 - b_{24}y_4) + b_{56}x_6 + b_{57}x_7 + b_{58}x_8 + v_5, \qquad (5a)$$

where $v_5 = u_5 - b_{5g}u_2$. A full-information approach would use (2a) and (5a) jointly to estimate all parameters. We adopt a simpler expedient, in the spirit of 2SLS, to handle the problem posed by the first term on the right. We substitute $\hat{b}_{24}$ (previously obtained) for b_{24}, create a new variable, $y_2 - \hat{b}_{24}y_4$, and proceed with 2SLS estimation of parameters in (5a), using the exogenous variables as instruments. We obtain the following estimates for Eq. (5), with the standard errors in parentheses:

$$y_5 = 0.0384y_g + 0.126x_6 + 0.00702x_7 + 0.116x_8 + \hat{u}_5$$
$$ (0.016) \quad\;\; (0.012) \quad (0.0022) \quad\;\; (0.028) \qquad\qquad (R^2 = .514).$$

All the coefficients are clearly significant, so that we are not tempted to consider any alternative specification of this equation. The significance of coefficients for x_7 and x_8 is of some substantive interest for anyone who believes that ostensible direct effects of these variables in a Blau–Duncan model primarily represent the impact of family socialization on the formation of status ambitions. If our model is correct, something more than this—perhaps mere economic strength—seems to be at stake.

It may be noted in passing that although we specify that the disturbances in (4) and (5) are uncorrelated, this does not carry over to (4a) and (5a). In fact, the correlation of sample residuals $\hat{v}_4$ and $\hat{v}_5$ is .21.

In evaluating the model, it is helpful to examine the results obtained when the unmeasured variables are omitted. In Table 5 we present estimates for the two main equations of the model with the motivational variables solved out. The "derived" estimates work backward from the structural equations, substituting Eqs. (6), (7), and (8) into Eqs. (4) and (5); this yields

$$y_4 = b'_{45}y_5 + b'_{46}x_6 + b'_{47}x_7 + b'_{48}x_8 + \sum_j b'_{4j}R_j + u_4', \qquad (4')$$

where

$$b'_{45} = (b_{45} + b_{4g}b_{g5} + b_{4h}b_{h5})/K$$
$$b'_{46} = b_{4f}b_{f6}/K$$
$$b'_{47} = b_{4h}b_{h7}/K$$
$$b'_{48} = b_{4f}b_{f8}/K$$
$$b'_{4j} = (b_{4f}b_{fj} + b_{4g}b_{gj} + b_{4h}b_{hj})/K$$
$$u_4' = u_4/K$$
$$K = 1 - b_{4f}b_{f4} - b_{4h}b_{h4},$$

TABLE 5

Regression Coefficients in Semi-Reduced Form of the Occupation Equation and Reduced Form of the Education Equation, as Derived from Estimated Structural Coefficients and as Directly Estimated by OLS[a]

Independent variable	Occupation (y_4)		Education (y_5)	
	Derived	OLS	Derived	OLS
y_5 Education	8.22	7.32[b]	—	—
x_6 Intelligence	.139	.460[b]	.143	.141[b]
x_7 Father's occupation	.043	.065[b]	.0080	.0069[b]
x_8 Father's education	.324	.765[c]	.132	.130[b]
Religion–Ethnic, $j =$				
1 Jewish	7.1	4.2	.12	.98
2 Irish Catholic	−1.2	0.9	−.08	.03
3 German Catholic	−3.0	−0.4	.01	.00
4 French Catholic	−5.4	−3.0	−.13	−.01
5 Polish Catholic	−1.3	−2.0	−.06	−.03
6 Italian Catholic	−1.9	1.5	.12	.19
7 Catholic, other N.W. European, and North American	3.1	−1.0	.08	−.38
8 Other Catholic and Orthodox	−0.9	1.2	.03	.17
9 German Lutheran	1.6	3.4	.01	.13
10 Other Lutheran	0.9	−5.4	−.19	−.08
11 Presbyterian	−1.1	2.5	−.05	.35
12 Episcopalian	5.1	1.9	−.04	−.04
13 Methodist	3.6	−0.2	.06	−.11
14 Baptist	−0.2	−2.2	.16	−.26
15 Protestant, nondenominational	−2.0	4.9	−.15	−.63
16 "Fundamentalist"	−3.8	−8.1	−.08	−.23
17 No religion	1.1	4.8	−.04	−.09
18 Residual	8.8	4.3	.29	.39
R^2		.373	.399	.374	.402
R^2 for equation omitting religion–ethnic dummies	—	.384	—	.374

[a] For comparison with Table 2, the coefficients for dummy variables have been transformed so that their weighted mean, using n_j from Table 2 as the weight, is zero.

[b] Ratio to standard error exceeds 2.0.

[c] Ratio to standard error is between 1.0 and 2.0.

and

$$y_5 = b'_{56}x_6 + b'_{57}x_7 + b'_{58}x_8 + \sum_j b'_{5j}R_j + u_5', \qquad (5')$$

where

$$b'_{56} = b_{56}/L \qquad\qquad b'_{57} = b_{57}/L$$

$$b'_{58} = b_{58}/L \qquad\qquad b'_{5j} = b_{5g}b_{gj}/L$$

$$u_5' = u_5/L \qquad\qquad L = 1 - b_{5g}b_{g5}.$$

"Derived" estimates of the b' coefficients are computed by inserting into each of these formulas the estimate $\hat{b}$ corresponding to the structural coefficient b. OLS estimates are obtained by OLS applied directly to Eqs. (4') and (5').

In the case of the education equation (5') the OLS and derived coefficients agree fairly closely as far as x_6, x_7, and x_8 are concerned. The two sets of coefficients for the religion–ethnic groups are, however, only broadly similar. The reason for the differences is clear. The OLS estimates are obtained by regressing education itself on religion–ethnic categories (along with the other exogenous variables), whereas the derived coefficient for the jth religious–ethnic group is obtained from the calculation

$$\hat{b}_{5g}\hat{b}_{gj}/(1 - \hat{b}_{5g}\hat{b}_{g5}) = .0435\hat{b}_{gj}.$$

Hence, roughly speaking, the derived education coefficients for the religion–ethnic groups are merely transformations of the group differences in occupational aspiration (y_2), which is our indicator of y_g. Thus, a close correlation between the derived coefficients for education in Table 5 and the mean scores on y_2 in Table 2 is evident. The discrepancies between the two sets of education coefficients in Table 5, therefore, essentially reflect the imperfect between-group correlation of occupational aspiration and educational attainment, inasmuch as our model allows religious–ethnic classification to affect education only via y_g. It is possible that the "fit" of derived to OLS coefficients would be improved if we were to allow some religion–ethnic groups to have direct effects on education; but the specification of which ones to treat in this fashion would be quite arbitrary from a substantive viewpoint.

In the case of the occupation equation (4') the OLS and derived estimates are fairly different for all coefficients. If the model is correct, presumably the latter are preferred estimates. However, it is somewhat disconcerting that the coefficient for y_5 (education) is substantially larger while the coefficients for x_6, x_7, and x_8 are smaller in the derived set than in the OLS set. Discrepancies like these suggest the desirability of performing a statistical test of the overidentifying restrictions of the model. However, we have not attempted to carry out such a test. Clearly, some question remains about the specification of this equation, in view of this result and the equivocal outcome of significance tests on the structural coefficients.

In any event, the "Protestant Ethic" thesis certainly receives no strong support—recall the low t-ratio for y_1 in Eq. (4a) and the debatable outcome of the comparison between (4a) and (4e). On the other hand, one of the major consequences of including the other two psychological variables is to reduce sharply the estimated direct effect of educational attainment on occupational achievement. Whereas that effect is estimated at 7.3 in Table 5 by OLS in a model excluding psychological variables, it drops to 3.0 in Eq. (4a) [or 3.5 in Eqs. (4c) and (4f)] in Table 4. Now, it may well be that education influences occupation primarily by giving rise to motives that instigate occupational ambition and performance; but in most discussions this causal path has not received an emphasis commensurate with these estimates. We must point out, therefore, that the argument for motives as key factors in achievement seems to entail a correlative deemphasis of the cognitive and instrumental functions of education for allocation to occupational roles.

Readers acquainted with psychometric techniques may wonder why we have allowed unobserved factors to proliferate in our model to the extent of having three of them corresponding to an equal number of indicators. Would it not have made more sense to posit a single common factor (or two at most), estimate the factor loadings, and use these results to devise a composite motivational variable for inclusion in the model? Some of the issues raised by such a procedure are discussed in Hauser's paper in this volume. For our part, we wanted to entertain a somewhat more complicated hypothesis than is expressed by the conventional factor models. In particular, we thought it necessary to allow at least one of our indicators to be directly "contaminated" by another measured variable in the model.

Similarities and differences between our procedure and the usual psychometric one are suggested by the path diagrams in Fig. 2. The upper one extracts Eqs. (1)–(3) from the model and treats them as a self-contained block in which the predetermined variables (y_f, y_g, y_h) are merely intercorrelated, without regard to the causal structure producing those correlations. The lower diagram represents the model of a single common factor, symbolized by a "grey box." Standardized path coefficients are posted on the straight lines with arrows at one end;

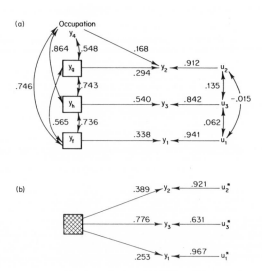

Figure 2. Correlations among social-psychological indicators accounted for (a) by the model in this chapter and (b) by a single common factor.

and correlations are posted on the curved lines with arrows at both ends, following Wright's (1934) convention. In the lower diagram, the path coefficients for arrows leading from the grey box are factor loadings; if one squares the values of the residual paths, one obtains the respective unique variances of the indicators. With only three indicators, of course, the common factor solution is trivial; barring the "Heywood case," it is guaranteed completely to account for the intercorrelations of the indicators. In our model, such correlations are accounted for, not by a single (unobserved) common factor, but by a set of (observed and unobserved) causes, which are themselves intercorrelated. But there is no constraint in our model requiring that it fully account for the correlations among the indicators. Thus, it is of substantive interest that the residuals for y_1 and y_2 correlate virtually nil, while both have slight positive correlations with the residual for y_3. It seems that there is some modest amount of nonunique variance in the social class item that we are not taking into account in the model. Nevertheless, social class has the smallest residual variance of the three indicators in our model just as it has the least uniqueness in the factor analysis model. In both diagrams, actually, all the indicators have a great deal of variance not accounted for.

In the upper diagram one can read off the correlation between the indicators and the corresponding unobserved factors. Thus

$r_{1f} = p_{1f} = .338$ and $r_{3h} = p_{3h} = .540$. But since y_2 is determined not only by an unmeasured factor but also by y_4 we have $r_{2g} = p_{2g} + p_{24}r_{4g} = .294 + .092 = .386$. All these correlations point to the rather low level of validity of the indicators. *If our model is correct, however, our estimates of the structural coefficients for the unmeasured factors are not biased by this low validity.* On the other hand, if the critic insists that we have substantially underestimated the validity of the indicators he will have to concede that we have somehow specified the model in such a way as to *exaggerate* the correlation of the unmeasured factors with occupation. Given r_{14} (for example), if we raise p_{1f} we must lower r_{4f}.

It does not appear that we could have greatly improved our results from this critic's point of view by using a factor-weighted, or other, composite of our three indicators. Such a variable, it is clear from the lower diagram, would be dominated by the one indicator, social class identification. But we already have a pretty good idea of how this variable works in the context of our kind of model. In any event, we do not feel uncomfortable with the notion that y_f, y_g, and y_h comprise a dispositional "syndrome" without being merely different measures of the "same thing." Indeed, we suspect that in a context where a multiplicity of motivational indicators is available, one will find that these three will have their highest loadings on different factors.

We do not suggest that the foregoing observations dispose of the problem of validity. It may be that indicators quite different in content from those we had available are required to come to grips with the issues posed by the psychological theories of achievement. It may be, too, that some relevant social psychological factors are not only different in content from those we tapped but are also uncorrelated with intelligence, socioeconomic background, and religion–ethnic affiliation. In that event their effects are captured only in the disturbance terms of our equations.

Acknowledgments

We are grateful to Professors Edward O. Laumann and Howard Schuman, Directors of the 1966 Detroit Area Study, for permission to use data collected in that project. A preliminary version of this paper appeared in the report by Duncan *et al.* (1968, Section 7.6) submitted to the U. S. Office of Education. Additional work was completed in connection with NSF project GS 2707, "Causal Models in Social Research." J. Michael Coble prepared the programs used in computation; and Eugene Won assisted with the calculations.

12

Disaggregating a Social-Psychological Model of Educational Attainment

ROBERT M. HAUSER

1. Introduction

One effort to integrate measurement and model construction in sociology has been the exploration of problems of identification, estimation, and inference in linear models with multiple indicators of each of several theoretical variables (Siegel & Hodge, 1968; Costner, 1969, 1971, this volume; Blalock, 1969a, 1970, 1971a; Althauser & Heberlein, 1970; Althauser, Heberlein, & Scott, 1971). These models, where measured variables appear only as effects (reflections or indicators) of theoretical constructs, may be treated within the framework of confirmatory factor analysis (Hauser & Goldberger, 1971). In the sociological literature less attention has been paid to the equally interesting cases where measured variables appear as causes (components) of theoretical variables, or as both causes and effects (Blalock, 1969a, pp. 270-271; Land, 1970; Hauser, 1971, pp. 71-77, 113-127). Hauser & Goldberger (1971, pp. 95-114) have considered the estimation of a model containing several causes and several effects of a single theoretical construct. They show that when disturbances of the effects of the construct are allowed to be correlated freely with one another, estimation can be carried out by canonical correlation analysis (also see

Blalock, 1969b, pp. 42–43). Some less restrictive models of this last type may be treated using Jöreskog's (1970a) general model for the analysis of covariance structures.

This chapter is an extended empirical treatment of the estimation and interpretation of a block-recursive model of socioeconomic achievement which treats measured variables as both causes and effects of theoretical variables. This essay serves two major purposes: it draws attention to the substantive distinction between the interpretation of measures as effects and as causes of the concepts which they represent, and it illustrates the advantages of disaggregating the components of composite variables.

Recent sociological treatments of measurement have been too quick to rely on the factor-analysis model for specification of the measurements; in many instances our measures are best regarded as causes, rather than effects, of theoretical constructs of interest. For example, population change is measured as the summed effects of natality, mortality, and migration, and the labor force is measured as the sum of employment and unemployment. Likewise, we will ordinarily think of resources as determinants of potential production, rather than as reflections of it. In other cases, where we think there is random reporting error, or where the theoretical construct is an underlying mental trait, personality disposition, or attitude, the factor-analysis model will be appropriate. In no case can the choice between representing measures as causes or effects of theoretical constructs be made without reference to a subject matter. This choice will usually affect the number of overidentifying restrictions imposed by a causal model (Hauser & Goldberger, 1971), since the factor model constrains the pattern of covariation among indicator disturbances, and the other model does not constrain the correlations among components. The choice between models will also affect the values of structural coefficients.

While formal treatments of social measurement draw heavily on the factor-analysis model, in practice one often finds theoretical constructs represented by indexes that are weighted composites of observed variables. Unless a reliability correction is applied, this is equivalent to postulating a measurement model in which components cause the theoretical construct. Index construction is often separated from other facets of the analysis and interpretation of data, and this may lead to the loss of information which could be obtained from index components. That is, measures are selected and entered into weighted linear composites which are said to represent variables of theoretical interest, and only the composites enter subsequent analyses of the data. For example, this is the fashion in which many indexes of socioeconomic status, personality characteristics, attitudes, and values are developed and applied.

Where equal or otherwise arbitrary weights are assigned to the components of a composite, little interest attaches to the explicit representation of the weights in the context of a larger model. On the other hand, when they are chosen to reproduce the effects of the components as closely as possible, the weights may be informative. Moreover, when there is more than one criterion variable, the possibility arises that the relative weights of components will differ from one criterion to another. This possibility—and the information implicit in it—is ignored when components are arbitrarily weighted in a composite. When the components of a composite variable are represented explicitly in a model, it is possible to interpret differences in the effects of antecedent variables on the several components. This information, too, is lost if components are ignored after they have been entered into a composite.

In the present example we shall also apply these ideas in the construction and interpretation of a composite variable whose components are weighted to represent the net effects of the components on subsequent variables after other variables have been taken into account. We shall see that this requires an extension of estimation procedures discussed by Hauser & Goldberger (1971). Rather than treating any of these issues formally at this point, we shall discuss them as they arise in the course of our analysis.

2. The Initial Model

In two recent papers W. H. Sewell and his associates have presented a social-psychological model of post-high school educational attainment and occupational achievement in a cohort of Wisconsin high school graduates (Sewell, Haller, & Portes, 1969; Sewell, Haller, & Ohlendorf, 1970). The portion of the model dealing with educational attainment is depicted by the path diagram in Fig. 1. The diagram shows only those direct effects said to be different from zero by Sewell et al. (1970, p. 1023, Fig. 2). Following Wright's (1934) practice we denote causal influence by straight unidirectional arrows from cause to effect and denote correlations not analyzed in causal terms by curved two-headed arrows. A high school senior's grades (G) are taken to depend directly upon academic ability (Q). The student's perception of the expectations which others hold for his future educational attainment (O) depends upon his socio-

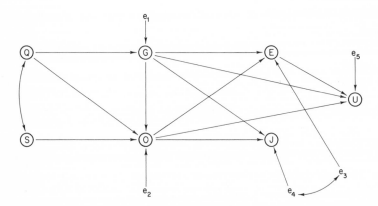

Figure 1.   A social-psychological model of educational attainment. Q = mental ability, S = socioeconomic status, G = high school grades, O = perceived expectations of
significant others, E = college plans, J = occupational aspiration, U = educational
attainment.

economic background (S), and also on his ability and grades. His post-
high school educational plans (E) and occupational aspirations (J)
depend directly on his grades and on the expectations of significant
others, but are presumed to be affected only indirectly by ability and
socioeconomic background. No assumption is made as to the causal
priority of educational plans and occupational aspirations. Finally,
the student's educational attainment (U) is directly influenced by
grades, significant others' expectations, and educational plans, but not
by background, ability, or occupational aspiration. Thus, the model
proposes that the effects of socioeconomic background and academic
ability on post-high school educational attainment are entirely mediated
by intervening school achievements, perceived social supports, and
aspirations. The rationale for these assumptions is spelled out in greater
detail in the papers just cited.

Using the notation of path analysis, where p_{ij} denotes the direct effect
of variable j on variable i, and all variables are expressed in standardized
form, the model equations may be written as

$$G = p_{GQ}Q + p_{G1}e_1 \tag{1}$$

$$O = p_{OS}S + p_{OQ}Q + p_{OG}G + p_{O2}e_2 \tag{2}$$

$$E = p_{EG}G + p_{EO}O + p_{E3}e_3 \tag{3}$$

$$J = p_{JG}G + p_{JO}O + p_{J4}e_4 \tag{4}$$

$$U = p_{UG}G + p_{UO}O + p_{UE}E + p_{U5}e_5 \,, \tag{5}$$

where the disturbances e_j are taken as mutually uncorrelated (except for the correlation of e_3 with e_4) and uncorrelated with the regressors in their own and preceding equations. We use p_{Aj} as an abbreviation for p_{Ae_j} and r_{jk} for $r_{e_j e_k}$. As shown in Fig. 1, no assumption was made about the source of the correlation between the two predetermined variables S and Q, nor was there an attempt to account for the residual correlation (r_{34}) between college plans (E) and occupational aspirations (J). Given measurements of S, Q, G, O, E, J, and U, it would be appropriate to estimate the coefficients of the model by ordinary least squares applied to each equation.

In fact these seven theoretical variables were not each directly measured, for there were multiple measures of socioeconomic status (S) and of perceived others' expectations (O). In Sewell, Haller, & Portes and Sewell, Haller, & Ohlendorf, weighted linear composites of these measures were constructed to represent S and O, but the weights were not chosen in the context of the larger model, and only the composites were used in estimating and evaluating the model. Using the same Wisconsin data, we shall first estimate a disaggregated version of the model in which each measure of S and O appears separately. Then, we shall attempt to produce a more parsimonious set of estimates in which the constructs S and O are treated explicitly, but important results of the disaggregated model are retained.

3. Description of Sample and Variables

Relevant data were collected on the achievements of a sample of ten thousand Wisconsin high school graduates during the period 1957–1964. The estimates presented here pertain to the 3427 males who were alive in 1964 and for whom all data were ascertained. A variety of coding and metric conventions were applied in earlier analyses of these data, and some new variations have been tried in the course of the present effort. On the whole these variations produce negligible changes in the intercorrelations.

There are four measurements of the socioeconomic status of the family of orientation. Father's educational attainment (V) and mother's educational attainment (M) were reported by the student in a questionnaire administered in school during the spring of 1957, his senior year. The following levels of parental education were ascertained and assigned the values shown: 8 or fewer years of school (7 years), some high school (10 years), high school graduate (12 years), some college (14 years), college graduate (16 years), some or completed graduate work (18 years). Father's occupational status (X), coded in the Duncan (1961) socio-economic index for occupations, and average parental (gross adjusted) income, 1957–1960 (I) were ascertained by a match to Wisconsin state income tax returns. (The average was taken in order to secure a stable measure of the family's economic level.) Academic ability (Q) is represented by the student's score on the Henmon–Nelson test, which was administered during the eleventh grade and ascertained from the Wisconsin State Testing Service. High school percentile rank (G) was ascertained from the high school and transformed to produce an approximately normal distribution.

There are three measures of the student's perceptions of the expectations of significant others, ascertained from the following items in the 1957 questionnaire:

24. My teachers in high school have:
     —encouraged me to go to college
     —discouraged me from going to college
     —have had no effect on my decision
25. My parents:
     —want me to go to college   —do not care whether I go
     —do not want me to go   —will not let me go
26. Most of my friends are:
     —going to college   —going into military service
     —getting jobs   —other _____ .

We shall refer to these items as teachers' encouragement (T), parental encouragement (P), and friends' plans (F). Each of the items was dichotomized to distinguish the college level response from all others. College plans (E) and occupational aspiration (J) were also ascertained from the 1957 questionnaire. College plans is a dichotomy that distinguishes the student who had definite plans to attend college in the fall of 1957 from all others, while occupational aspiration is represented by the Duncan score for the type of occupation the student "hope[s] eventually to enter." In most cases only a major occupation category was chosen by the student from a checklist, but a substantial minority of students volunteered a specific occupation title.

Educational attainment in 1964 (U) was ascertained from the student's parents in a 1964 post-card survey in which the overall response rate was over 87%, including 96% of those for whom addresses were located. More attrition occurred because of failure to ascertain family income, high school rank, and occupational aspiration than because of nonresponse in 1964. Educational attainment is coded in terms of the

TABLE 1

CORRELATIONS, MEANS, AND STANDARD DEVIATIONS OF VARIABLES IN SOCIAL-PSYCHOLOGICAL MODEL OF POST-HIGH SCHOOL EDUCATIONAL ATTAINMENT: MALE WISCONSIN HIGH SCHOOL GRADUATES OF 1957 ALIVE IN 1964 WITH ALL DATA PRESENT ($N = 3427$)[a]

	V	M	X	I	Q	G	T	P	F	E	J	U
V	1.000											
M	.505	1.000										
X	.494	.318	1.000									
I	.389	.291	.523	1.000								
Q	.244	.230	.212	.203	1.000							
G	.151	.149	.127	.116	.586	1.000						
T	.159	.141	.144	.146	.352	.439	1.000					
P	.299	.269	.290	.288	.369	.335	.424	1.000				
F	.278	.256	.284	.288	.318	.321	.327	.418	1.000			
E	.306	.269	.299	.304	.435	.469	.438	.542	.496	1.000		
J	.287	.246	.301	.288	.455	.466	.413	.507	.474	.766	1.000	
U	.334	.292	.325	.319	.481	.545	.405	.489	.491	.659	.594	1.000
Mean	10.16	10.50	31.09	59.42	101.6	46.78	.4724	.6037	.3697	.4006	48.81	13.62
S.D.	3.145	2.981	22.49	33.26	14.94	18.18	.4993	.4892	.4828	.4901	27.58	1.995

[a] V = father's education, M = mother's education, X = father's occupation, I = average parental income ($100), Q = mental ability, G = high school grades, T = teachers' encouragement, P = parental encouragement, F = friends' plans, E = college plans, J = occupational aspiration, U = educational attainment.

number of years of schooling completed by the respondent, but some exceptions were made. For example, a college graduate received a code of 16 years, no matter how long he took to earn a degree, but in some cases where no degree was obtained, it was necessary to code school years attended (up to 15). Also, up to a year's credit was given for extended vocational training.

4. Unconstrained Estimates of the Disaggregated Model

In their earlier analyses of these data Sewell and his associates constructed composite measures of socioeconomic background from V, M, X, and I and of significant others' expectations from T, P, and F using factor loadings in some cases and equal weights in others. Here we begin by entering each indicator in the model separately and then go on to see what information is lost or gained in aggregation. Also, rather than prejudging the existence of each direct path, we estimate all paths implied by our ordering of the variables under unidirectional causation. Finally, we make a modest change in the specification of the model by regressing mental ability on the measures of socioeconomic background. Our estimates of the effects of background on ability will be biased upward by virtue of the dependence of both background and ability on other phenotypic and genotypic traits of parents. However, this specification is useful because it coincides with the assumptions of social class bias in mental tests and of environmental influence on mental development which are made by many sociologists, and it serves to emphasize the modest relationship between socioeconomic background and ability.

The correlations among the measured variables are shown in Table 1, along with their means and standard deviations. Table 2 presents the structural coefficients of the model consisting of Eqs. (6)–(13), given below, as estimated by ordinary least squares:

$$Q = p_{QV}V + p_{QM}M + p_{QX}X + p_{QI}I + p_{Q1}e_1 \tag{6}$$

$$G = p_{GV}V + p_{GM}M + p_{GX}X + p_{GI}I + p_{GQ}Q + p_{G2}e_2 \tag{7}$$

$$T = p_{TV}V + p_{TM}M + p_{TX}X + p_{TI}I + p_{TQ}Q + p_{TG}G + p_{T3}e_3 \tag{8}$$

$$P = p_{PV}V + p_{PM}M + p_{PX}X + p_{PI}I + p_{PQ}Q + p_{PG}G + p_{P4}e_4 \tag{9}$$

$$F = p_{FV}V + p_{FM}M + p_{FX}X + p_{FI}I + p_{FQ}Q + p_{FG}G + p_{F5}e_5 \tag{10}$$

$$E = p_{EV}V + p_{EM}M + p_{EX}X + p_{EI}I + p_{EQ}Q + p_{EG}G + p_{ET}T$$
$$+ p_{EP}P + p_{EF}F + p_{E6}e_6 \tag{11}$$

$$J = p_{JV}V + p_{JM}M + p_{JX}X + p_{JI}I + p_{JQ}Q + p_{JG}G + p_{JT}T$$
$$+ p_{JP}P + p_{JF}F + p_{J7}e_7 \tag{12}$$
$$U = p_{UV}V + p_{UM}M + p_{UX}X + p_{UI}I + p_{UQ}Q + p_{UG}G + p_{UT}T$$
$$+ p_{UP}P + p_{UF}F + p_{UE}E + p_{UJ}J + p_{U8}e_8 . \tag{13}$$

TABLE 2

Unconstrained Coefficients for a Social-Psychological Model of Post-High School Educational Attainment

Predetermined variables	Dependent variables							
	Q	G	T	P	F	E	J	U
	Path coefficients (standardized regression coefficients)[a]							
V	.111	(.005)	(.034)	.089	.072	.042	(.028)	.050
M	.126	(.015)	(.022)	.092	.093	(.028)	(.012)	.033
X	.073	(.001)	(.026)	.093	.099	.040	.068	.047
I	.085	(−.010)	.049	.121	.136	.068	.054	.053
Q		.583	.116	.178	.111	.079	.129	.067
G			.354	.178	.203	.191	.186	.236
T						.122	.102	(.018)
P						.257	.224	.075
F						.213	.201	.123
E								.307
J								.062
Residual path	.954	.810	.885	.872	.888	.724	.746	.660
	Regression coefficients[a]							
V	52.7	(3.05)	(.540)	1.39	1.10	.653	(24.1)	3.19
M	63.2	(9.02)	(.376)	1.51	1.50	(.463)	(11.0)	2.22
X	4.84	(.051)	(.057)	.202	.213	.088	8.34	.420
I	3.82	(−.519)	.073	.178	.197	.099	4.46	.320
Q		71.0	.387	.584	.360	.259	23.8	.891
G			.973	.478	.540	.515	28.2	2.59
T						11.9	561.	(7.38)
P						25.7	1262.	30.4
F						21.6	1150.	50.9
E								125.0
J								.451
Constant	85.9	−26.3	−.531	−.681	−.701	−.596	−11.9	9.50
Coefficient of determination	.089	.344	.216	.239	.212	.475	.443	.564

[a] Coefficients enclosed in parentheses are not significantly different from zero at the .05 level. Regression coefficients are multiplied by 100 for convenience in presentation.

By sociological standards, at least, the model is fairly powerful. It accounts for at least 20% of the variance in each of the several dependent variables (Q excepted), and it accounts for more than half of the variance in post-high school educational attainment.

We shall not attempt to interpret the model fully at this point, but only make a few observations that are relevant to the aggregation of component variables. No one of the four socioeconomic status variables (V, M, X, I) has remarkably larger effects on subsequent variables (Q, G, T, P, F, E, J, U) than any other, and the relative weights (standardized) of the four variables appear to be similar across equations. This regularity comes out clearly in Table 3, which shows the total effects of V, M, X, and I on each of the subsequent variables. The total effects are coefficients in the reduced-form regressions of each endogenous variable on V, M, X, and I. The effect of parental income is generally largest, though not by a great margin. The greater weight of income may be attributable to our averaging over years, which may have made it more reliable than the other three status variables. Overall, one is left with the impression

TABLE 3

UNCONSTRAINED REGRESSIONS OF ACHIEVEMENT VARIABLES
ON SOCIOECONOMIC BACKGROUND VARIABLES

Socioeconomic variables	Dependent variables							
	Q	G	T	P	F	E	J	U
	Path coefficients (standardized regression coefficients)							
V	.111	.070	.072	.122	.098	.125	.109	.142
M	.126	.088	.068	.130	.125	.123	.106	.133
X	.073	.043	.049	.114	.116	.114	.139	.130
I	.085	.040	.073	.144	.153	.160	.142	.158
Residual path	.954	.983	.980	.924	.930	.920	.927	.906
	Regression coefficients[a]							
V	52.7	40.4	1.14	1.89	1.50	1.94	95.6	9.00
M	63.2	53.9	1.14	2.13	2.02	2.03	97.8	8.92
X	4.84	3.49	.109	.247	.249	.249	17.1	1.15
I	3.82	2.19	.109	.211	.222	.236	11.8	.945
Constant	85.9	34.6	.138	−.0147	−.205	−.228	16.5	10.8
Coefficient of determination	.089	.034	.039	.146	.136	.154	.140	.179

[a] Regression coefficients are multiplied by 100 for convenience in presentation.

that little information would be lost if the four status measures were entered into a composite in which parental income were given slightly more weight than the other three components. Still, had we not disaggregated the components of background, we could not have been sure that the relative effects of the components on each subsequent variable were similar.

When we look at the standardized effects of the three perceived expectations of significant others $(T, P,$ and $F)$ on the subsequent variables—plans, aspirations, and attainment (E, J, U)—we also find a rough proportionality of effects. This comes out clearly in Table 4, which shows the total effects of $T, P,$ and F on $E, J,$ and U after the effects of antecedent variables (V, M, X, I, Q, G) have been taken into account. In the case of educational plans and occupational aspirations, the effects of parental encouragement and friends' plans are each about twice as large as those of teachers' encouragement. In the case of educational attainment the coefficients do not follow this neat pattern, but the larger effects of parental encouragement and friends' plans are

TABLE 4

UNCONSTRAINED REGRESSIONS OF COLLEGE PLANS (E), OCCUPATIONAL ASPIRATION (J), AND ATTAINMENT (U), ON SOCIOECONOMIC BACKGROUND VARIABLES (V, M, X, I), MENTAL ABILITY (Q), GRADES (G), TEACHERS' AND PARENTAL ENCOURAGEMENT $(T$ AND $P)$, AND FRIENDS' PLANS (F)

Predetermined variables	Dependent variables			Predetermined variables	Dependent variables		
	E	J	U		E	J	U
	Path coefficients[a]				Regression coefficients[a]		
V	.042	(.028)	.065	V	.653	(24.1)	4.12
M	(.028)	(.012)	.043	M	(.463)	(11.0)	2.85
X	.040	.068	.064	X	.088	8.34	.568
I	.068	.054	.077	I	.099	4.46	.464
Q	.079	.129	.099	Q	.259	23.8	1.32
G	.191	.186	.306	G	.515	28.2	3.36
T	.122	.102	.062	T	11.9	561.	24.8
P	.257	.224	.168	P	25.7	1262.	68.3
F	.213	.201	.201	F	21.6	1150.	83.2
				Constant	−.596	−11.9	8.70
Residual path	.724	.746	.707	Coefficient of determination	.475	.443	.500

[a] Coefficients enclosed in parentheses are not significantly different from zero at the .05 level. Regression coefficients are multiplied by 100 for convenience in presentation.

still evident. Here, as in the case of the socioeconomic background variables, the proportionality of effects suggests that little information would be lost in an appropriately weighted composite of the perceived expectation variables. However, it is more evident here than in the first instance that we should want to assign unequal weights to the component variables. Also, it is pertinent that the pattern which appears in the effects of T, P, and F on E, J, and U net of V, M, X, I, Q, and G is not the same as the pattern of their gross effects. That is, if we regress E, J, and U only on T, P, and F, we find the coefficients of T are each two-thirds rather than one-half as large as those of P or F in the same equation.

While the measures of perceived others' expectations have roughly proportional effects on later variables, there is significant variability in the effects of background, ability, and grades on those measures. In Table 2 we see that parental encouragement and friends' plans depend more on each measure of socioeconomic background than does teachers' encouragement, while the last variable is affected more by high school grades than are parental encouragement or friends' plans. Thus, there is a significant reversal in the sources of perceived encouragement from teachers in comparison with parents or friends, and this would go undetected if we did not look separately at the determination of each of the components of others' expectations. The greater effect of academic achievement relative to social origins on perceived teachers' encouragement suggests that teachers tend to reward and encourage high achievers irrespective of background, rather than to pursue a course of overt or covert status discrimination. There is other evidence supporting this interpretation in the model, notably the absence of significant direct effects of socioeconomic background variables on grades. At the same time the role of teachers in freeing students from the influence of their social origins is mitigated insofar as teachers' encouragement has less influence on aspirations and attainments than do parental encouragement or friends' plans. This finding, too, would have escaped us if we had not disaggregated the components of perceived others' expectations.

5. Constrained Estimates

Having argued by example the merits of disaggregation, we now attempt to produce a new set of estimates for the attainment model which will be as informative, but more parsimonious than those just described. We postulate the existence of two theoretical constructs. One (S) is a composite of the socioeconomic background variables (V, M, X, I), and the other (O) is a composite of the perceived expectations of teachers, parents, and friends (T, P, F) from which the effects of socioeconomic background, ability, and grades have been eliminated. In each case we are forming a rather strong hypothesis that need not be consistent with the sample data, though we already have reason to believe they will be.

In the first instance, we postulate that the several aspects of the social and economic position of the family of origin do not affect a son's achievements except by virtue of their contribution to an overall level of socioeconomic standing enjoyed by the family. This conception is presumably implied by the casual references to "socioeconomic status" which have become commonplace in both academic and semipopular writing. We view the relationship between socioeconomic status and our measures of it as productive, rather than reflective. That is, the social achievements of parents give rise to an overall level of social standing; they are not merely reflections of an underlying status position. Our measurement model would permit a causal analysis of parental achievements that is consistent with our causal interpretation of sons' achievements. The reflective model does not permit such an analysis because it says that socioeconomic status is the only variable which causes parental achievements (compare Hauser, 1970, pp. 120–124). The intuitive appeal of the concept of socioeconomic status is tempered by consideration of the disparate family resources one might associate with education, occupation, and income and of the differing susceptibility of those components to outside intervention. In a recent discussion, Hodge (1970) argued forcefully that the construction of status composites is misleading because the several aspects of social standing have different effects on different variables.

In the second case, we argue that students integrate their perceptions of what significant others expect of them into a unitary level of perceived expectation which operates as a motivational force on their subsequent aspirations and achievements. The alternative is to suppose that support from different quarters is required for different modes of achievement. For example, young men might value the expectations of teachers more than those of parents in deciding how long to attend school, but reverse the relative weight given those expectations in thinking about occupational goals. As we have seen, this is not generally the case. As in the case of socioeconomic status, we view the relationship between O and its measures as productive. Perceptions from each source give rise to a general level of perceived others' expectations and are not merely

consequences of a preexisting perception of others' expectations (compare
Hauser, 1970, pp. 120–124).

The revised model is depicted by the path diagram in Fig. 2. Note
that both S and O are represented as completely determined by their
components. Further, the model specifies that each component affects
subsequent variables only by way of the construct to which it contributes.
Beyond forming the composites, we alter the structure of the model

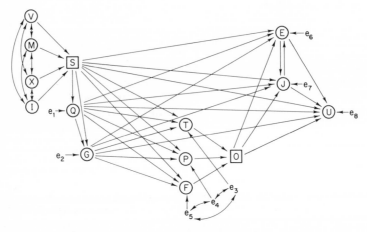

Figure 2.   A model of educational attainment with composites representing socioeconomic status and perceived expectations of significant others. S = socioeconomic
status, O = perceived expectations of significant others.

in one other detail by allowing educational plans (E) and occupational
aspirations (J) to affect one another directly. In keeping with sociological
discussions of this point we propose that the amount of schooling a
youth wants to obtain may be affected by his holding a vocational goal
with specific educational prerequisites. On the other hand, a youth may
aspire to a level of occupational achievement whose range is determined
by the amount of schooling he expects to complete. Our treatment of
this issue can hardly be decisive; given the rest of our model, we do not
have enough instruments to identify the equations for E and J. We
obtain estimates of the coefficients of those two equations by the artifice
of assuming equal reciprocal effects, i.e., $p_{EJ} = p_{JE}$, and uncorrelated
error, i.e., $r_{67} = 0$. The path diagram in Fig. 2 represents the following
system of equations:

$$S = p_{SV}V + p_{SM}M + p_{SX}X + p_{SI}I \tag{14}$$

$$Q = p_{QS}S + p_{Q1}e_1 \tag{15}$$

$$G = p_{GS}S + p_{GQ}Q + p_{G2}e_2 \tag{16}$$

$$T = p_{TS}S + p_{TQ}Q + p_{TG}G + p_{T3}e_3 \tag{17}$$

$$P = p_{PS}S + p_{PQ}Q + p_{PG}G + p_{P4}e_4 \tag{18}$$

$$F = p_{FS}S + p_{FQ}Q + p_{FG}G + p_{F5}e_5 \tag{19}$$

$$O = p_{OT}T + p_{OP}P + p_{OF}F \tag{20}$$

$$E = p_{ES}S + p_{EQ}Q + p_{PG}G + p_{EO}O + p_{EJ}J + p_{E6}e_6 \tag{21}$$

$$J = p_{JS}S + p_{JQ}Q + p_{JG}G + p_{JO}O + p_{JE}E + p_{J7}e_7 \tag{22}$$

$$U = p_{US}S + p_{UQ}Q + p_{UG}G + p_{UO}O + p_{UE}E + p_{UJ}J + p_{U8}e_8 . \tag{23}$$

The ten equations and 34 distinct coefficients (excluding those of the disturbances, $e_1, ..., e_8$, and the correlations among e_3, e_4, and e_5) of this system are far simpler than the system of eight equations and 56 coefficients for which estimates were presented above. Our estimates for the present overidentified model are displayed in Table 5. A quick comparison of Table 2 and Table 5 suggests that the data fit the revised model rather well. For example, in the unconstrained model the coefficients of determination are never more than .003 larger than those in the overidentified model. In short, while one might still wish to argue that S and O are not homogeneous constructs as described above, it is not easy to support that argument with these data.

To produce the estimates in Table 5 we first generated an adjusted correlation matrix which met the constraints imposed by our postulation of the constructs S and O. Then we used that matrix to estimate the structural coefficients for each equation in the model. The hypothetical constructs S and O introduce constraints of proportionality on the effects of their measured components. For example, by substituting Eq. (14) into (15) we can write the coefficients of V, M, X, and I in the reduced-form regression of Q on V, M, X, I as

$$\begin{array}{ll} p_{QV} = p_{QS}p_{SV} & p_{QX} = p_{QS}p_{SX} \\ p_{QM} = p_{QS}p_{SM} & p_{QI} = p_{QS}p_{SI} . \end{array} \tag{24}$$

Similarly, in the regression of G on V, M, X, I, and Q the coefficients are

$$\begin{array}{ll} p_{GV} = (p_{GS} + p_{GQ}p_{QS})p_{SV} & p_{GX} = (p_{GS} + p_{GQ}p_{QS})p_{SX} \\ p_{GM} = (p_{GS} + p_{GQ}p_{QS})p_{SM} & p_{GI} = (p_{GS} + p_{GQ}p_{QS})p_{SI} . \end{array} \tag{25}$$

TABLE 5

ESTIMATED COEFFICIENTS IN AN OVERIDENTIFIED STRUCTURAL MODEL OF POST-HIGH SCHOOL
EDUCATIONAL ATTAINMENT

Predeter-mined variables	Dependent variables									
	S	Q	G	T	P	F	O	E	J	U
Path coefficients (standardized structural coefficients)[a]										
V	.310									
M	.317									
X	.313									
I	.390									
S		.294	.007	.099	.297	.300		.094	.081	.142
Q			.584	.116	.177	.111		.039	.103	.065
G				.353	.178	.202		.136	.124	.231
T							.238			
P							.533			
F							.501			
O								.333	.269	.176
E									.313	.305
J								.313		.063
Residual path	.000	.956	.810	.886	.873	.888	.000	.727	.747	.662
Structural coefficients[a]										
V	19.7									
M	21.2									
X	2.78									
I	2.34									
S		220.	6.4	2.48	7.28	7.26		2.31	112.	14.2
Q			71.0	.387	.581	.360		.128	19.0	.868
G				.971	.479	.537		.367	18.8	2.53
T							94.9			
P							218.			
F							207.			
O								8.18	372.	17.6
E									1762.	124.
J								.556		.458
Coefficient of deter-mination	1.000	.087	.343	.215	.238	.211	1.000	.472	.442	.562

[a] Structural coefficients are multiplied by 100 for convenience in presentation. Standard deviations of S and O are arbitrarily set at 1.995, the standard deviation of U.

Consequently, we find that

$$\frac{p_{QV}}{p_{GV}} = \frac{p_{QM}}{p_{GM}} = \frac{p_{QX}}{p_{GX}} = \frac{p_{QI}}{p_{GI}} = \left(\frac{p_{QS}}{p_{GS} + p_{GQ}p_{QS}}\right), \qquad (26)$$

so there are three constraints connecting coefficients of the socioeconomic components in the two regressions of Q on V, M, X, and I and of G on V, M, X, I, and Q. Constraints like these are imposed on the effects of V, M, X, and I across all of the equations in the revised model.

The proportionality constraints apply to the total effects of S, e.g., $p_{GS} + p_{GQ}p_{QS}$ is the total effect of S in the regression of G on S and Q. Thus, in generating constrained correlations we may ignore the causal structure imposed on variables subsequent to S and simply regress them on S with freely correlated error. With this in mind we used the scheme pictured in Fig. 3 to estimate the weights and correlations involving S. Following Hauser & Goldberger (1971, pp. 95–114), a pair of first canonical variates were extracted from two groups of variables, where V, M, X, and I were in the first group and Q, G, T, P, F, E, J, and U were in the second. The first canonical correlation was .516. The second canonical correlation was .071, a value for which Wilks' lambda rounded to unity and was clearly nonsignificant (Cooley & Lohnes, 1962, p. 37). In Fig. 3 we define S as the first canonical variate in V, M, X, and I. Then the correlations between S and the variables in the second group gave us the total effects that we wished to estimate. In effect, we absorbed the first canonical variate in Q, G, T,

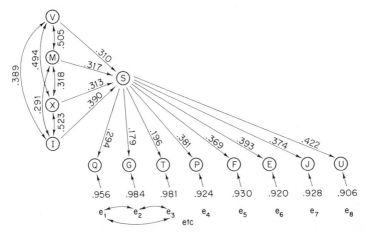

Figure 3. Construction of a socioeconomic background composite. Numbers are correlation coefficients or standardized regression coefficients.

P, F, E, J, and U into the paths leading from S to each of those variables in Fig. 3, so the desired correlations were given by products of the first canonical correlation (.516) with correlations between the variate in Q, G, T, P, F, E, J, and U and each of its components.

Further insight into the goodness of fit of the revised model may be obtained by comparing the regressions of Q, G, T, P, F, E, J, and U on V, M, X, and I in Table 3 with those on S. In Table 6 the latter have been displayed in the form of constrained reduced-form coefficients of

TABLE 6

CONSTRAINED REGRESSIONS OF ACHIEVEMENT VARIABLES ON SOCIOECONOMIC BACKGROUND VARIABLES

Socioeconomic variables	Dependent variables							
	Q	G	T	P	F	E	J	U
	Path coefficients (standardized regression coefficients)							
V	.091	.056	.061	.118	.114	.122	.116	.131
M	.093	.057	.062	.121	.117	.125	.119	.134
X	.092	.056	.061	.119	.115	.123	.117	.132
I	.115	.070	.077	.149	.144	.153	.146	.165
Residual path	.956	.984	.981	.924	.930	.920	.928	.906
	Regression coefficients[a]							
V	43.4	32.1	.966	1.84	1.76	1.90	102.	8.32
M	46.8	34.7	1.04	1.99	1.89	2.05	110.	8.97
X	6.12	4.54	.136	.260	.248	.268	14.3	1.17
I	5.16	3.82	.115	.219	.209	.226	12.1	.989
Constant	87.3	36.2	.154	−.0026	−.209	−.225	15.3	10.9
Coefficient of determination	.087	.032	.038	.145	.136	.154	.140	.179

[a] Regression coefficients are multiplied by 100 for convenience in presentation.

V, M, X, and I. One is tempted to interpret the differences between constrained and unconstrained reduced-form coefficients. For example, the positive deviations in the effects of V and M on Q and G suggest that educational background takes on special importance in cognitive development and performance. However, recalling that the fit of data and model is very good, such intuitions should not be taken too seriously.

A similar procedure was used to estimate weights and correlations involving O, but there is an additional complication here. Substituting Eq. (20) for O in Eqs. (21), (22), and (23), we have

$$E = p_{ES}S + p_{EO}Q + p_{EG}G + p_{EO}p_{OT}T + p_{EO}p_{OP}P$$
$$+ p_{EO}p_{OF}F + p_{EJ}J + p_{E6}e_6 \tag{27}$$

$$J = p_{JS}S + p_{JO}Q + p_{JG}G + p_{JO}p_{OT}T + p_{JO}p_{OP}P$$
$$+ p_{JO}p_{OF}F + p_{JE}E + p_{J7}e_7 \tag{28}$$

and

$$U = p_{US}S + p_{UO}Q + p_{UG}G + p_{UO}p_{OT}T + p_{UO}p_{OP}P$$
$$+ p_{UO}p_{OF}F + p_{UE}E + p_{UJ}J + p_{U8}e_8 . \tag{29}$$

Denoting the effects of T, P, and F in (27) by p_{ET}, p_{EP}, and p_{EF}, and likewise in Eq. (28), we see that

$$p_{ET}/p_{JT} = p_{EP}/p_{JP} = p_{EF}/p_{JF} \quad (= p_{EO}/p_{JO}), \tag{30}$$

so there are two constraints linking the coefficients of T, P, and F in the structural equations for E and J. Similar constraints apply to the effects of T, P, and F when we compare Eq. (27) with (29), and (28) with (29). While the type of constraint expressed by (30) is obviously similar to that in (26), the present situation differs because Eqs. (27)–(29) include variables (S, Q, G) that are causally prior to T, P, and F and whose effects are not constrained in those equations. Recalling that the relative effects of T, P, and F on E, J, and U would change if we did not take S, Q, and G into account, it is clear that we cannot ignore S, Q, and G in estimating the constrained effects of T, P, and F on E, J, and U. At the same time the model does not impose any constraints on the effects of S, Q, and G in the equations for E, J, and U.

In the appendix to this paper we show that the Hauser–Goldberger canonical correlation procedure can be adapted to this case. In effect, we apply the canonical correlation procedure to the matrix of partial correlations that is formed by regressing the variables in the two groups of interest on the variables whose effects are not constrained. Thus, we carried out a canonical correlation analysis of the partial correlations between T, P, and F in the first group and E, J, and U in the second, where the partialling operation was carried out with respect to Q, G, and the four components of S. The first canonical correlation was .508, while the second was .064, for which Wilks' lambda rounded to unity. The matrix of constrained partial correlations was obtained by manipulating the canonical correlation output as we did in the case of S, and the (partly) constrained zero-order correlations were calculated by substituting the constrained partial correlations back into the original expressions for the partial correlations.

In Table 7 we present the coefficients of the constrained regressions of E, J, and U on V, M, X, I, Q, G, T, P, and F which were subjected

TABLE 7

CONSTRAINED REGRESSIONS OF COLLEGE PLANS (E), OCCUPATIONAL ASPIRATION (J), AND ATTAINMENT (U), ON SOCIOECONOMIC BACKGROUND VARIABLES (V, M, X, I), MENTAL ABILITY (Q), GRADES (G), TEACHERS' AND PARENTAL ENCOURAGEMENT (T AND P), AND FRIENDS' PLANS (F)

Predetermined variables	Dependent variables			Predetermined variables	Dependent variables		
	E	J	U		E	J	U
	Path coefficients				Regression coefficients[a]		
V	.041	.038	.059	V	.645	33.4	3.75
M	.042	.039	.060	M	.696	36.1	4.05
X	.042	.038	.060	X	.091	4.72	.529
I	.052	.048	.074	I	.077	3.98	.446
Q	.079	.128	.097	Q	.258	23.7	1.30
G	.194	.185	.301	G	.522	28.1	3.31
T	.110	.098	.082	T	10.8	541.	32.6
P	.247	.221	.183	P	24.8	1250.	74.8
F	.232	.207	.172	F	23.5	1180.	71.0
				Constant	−.606	−13.9	8.65
Residual path	.725	.747	.708	Coefficient of determination	.474	.441	.499

[a] Regression coefficients are multiplied by 100 for convenience in presentation.

to both sets of constraints, i.e., those on V, M, X, and I as well as those on T, P, and F. For the sake of clarity, we have temporarily ignored the complications arising from simultaneity in E and J and the appearance of E and J in the structural equation for U. Thus, the estimates in Table 7 may be compared directly with corresponding unconstrained estimates in Table 4. Again, the fit is quite good. Coefficients of determination differ by no more than .002 between the two sets of estimates, and the largest single difference between constrained and unconstrained standardized reduced-form coefficients of T, P, or F is only .03.

The constrained correlation matrix, including entries for S and O, is presented in Table 8. For purposes of presentation, we arbitrarily

TABLE 8

Constrained Correlations, Means, and Standard Deviations of Variables in Social-Psychological Model of Post-High School Educational Attainment: 1957 Male Wisconsin High School Graduates Alive in 1964 with All Data Present (N = 3427)[a]

	V	M	X	I	S	Q	G	T	P	F	O	E	J	U
V	1.0000	.5050	.4940	.3890	.7770[b]	.2287[b]	.1392[b]	.1524[b]	.2963[b]	.2866[b]	.3377[b]	.3050[b]	.2904[b]	.3183[b]
M		1.0000	.3180	.2910	.6871[b]	.2022[b]	.1231[b]	.1348[b]	.2620[b]	.2524[b]	.2981[b]	.2697[b]	.2568[b]	.2903[b]
X			1.0000	.5230	.7713[b]	.2270[b]	.1382[b]	.1513[b]	.2941[b]	.2845[b]	.3352[b]	.3028[b]	.2883[b]	.3259[b]
I				1.0000	.7671[b]	.2258[b]	.1374[b]	.1505[b]	.2925[b]	.2829[b]	.3334[b]	.3011[b]	.2867[b]	.3241[b]
S					1.0000	.2943[b]	.1792[b]	.1961[b]	.3813[b]	.3688[b]	.4346[b]	.3926[b]	.3737[b]	.4225[b]
Q						1.0000	.5860	.3520	.3690	.3180	.4397	.4350	.4550	.4810
G							1.0000	.4390	.3350	.3210	.4437	.4690	.4660	.5450
T								1.0000	.4240	.3270	.6275[b]	.4291[b]	.4100[b]	.4195[b]
P									1.0000	.4180	.8434[b]	.5354[b]	.5053[b]	.4993[b]
F										1.0000	.8013[b]	.5073[b]	.4772[b]	.4731[b]
O											1.0000	.6415[b]	.6058[b]	.6028[b]
E												1.0000	.7660	.6590
J													1.0000	.5940
U														1.0000
Mean	10.16	10.50	31.09	59.42	13.62	101.6	46.78	.4724	.6037	.3697	13.62	.4006	48.81	13.62
S.D.	3.145	2.981	22.49	33.26	1.995	14.94	18.18	.4993	.4892	.4828	1.995	.4901	27.58	1.995

[a] S = socioeconomic status, O = perception of significant others.
[b] Constrained correlations.

gave S and O the same mean and standard deviation as U. Thus, in Table 5 the standardized and unstandardized regressions of U on S and O are the same. Given the matrix in Table 8, preparation of the estimates in Table 5 was straightforward. Coefficients in all of the structural equations except those of E and J were estimated by ordinary least squares.

Under our assumptions ($p_{EJ} = p_{JE}$ and $r_{67} = 0$) the equations for E and J are just-identified. Substituting Eq. (22) in (21) and vice versa and solving the resultant expressions for E and J, respectively, we obtain

$$E = \left[\frac{p_{ES} + p_{EJ}p_{JS}}{1 - p_{EJ}p_{JE}}\right] S + \left[\frac{p_{EQ} + p_{EJ}p_{JQ}}{1 - p_{EJ}p_{JE}}\right] Q + \left[\frac{p_{EG} + p_{EJ}p_{JG}}{1 - p_{EJ}p_{JE}}\right] G$$
$$+ \left[\frac{p_{EO} + p_{EJ}p_{JO}}{1 - p_{EJ}p_{JE}}\right] O + \left[\frac{p_{E6}e_6 + p_{EJ}p_{J7}e_7}{1 - p_{EJ}p_{JE}}\right] \tag{31}$$

and

$$J = \left[\frac{p_{JS} + p_{JE}p_{ES}}{1 - p_{EJ}p_{JE}}\right] S + \left[\frac{p_{JQ} + p_{JE}p_{EQ}}{1 - p_{EJ}p_{JE}}\right] Q + \left[\frac{p_{JG} + p_{JE}p_{EG}}{1 - p_{EJ}p_{JE}}\right] G$$
$$+ \left[\frac{p_{JO} + p_{JE}p_{EO}}{1 - p_{EJ}p_{JE}}\right] O + \left[\frac{p_{E7}e_7 + p_{JE}p_{J6}e_6}{1 - p_{EJ}p_{JE}}\right]. \tag{32}$$

Since the errors in (31) and (32) are uncorrelated with the regressors, we estimated these reduced-form equations by ordinary least squares. Denoting the coefficients of (31) and (32) by q_{jk}, and using the assumption $p_{JE} = p_{EJ}$, we obtained simple expressions for the structural coefficients in terms of the reduced-form coefficients and p_{EJ}:

$$
\begin{array}{ll}
p_{ES} = q_{ES} - q_{JS}p_{EJ} & p_{JS} = q_{JS} - q_{ES}p_{EJ} \\
p_{EQ} = q_{EQ} - q_{JQ}p_{EJ} & p_{JQ} = q_{JQ} - q_{EQ}p_{EJ} \\
p_{EG} = q_{EG} - q_{JG}p_{EJ} & p_{JG} = q_{JG} - q_{EG}p_{EJ} \\
p_{EO} = q_{EO} - q_{JO}p_{EJ} & p_{JO} = q_{JO} - q_{EO}p_{EJ}.
\end{array}
\tag{33}
$$

Applying the basic theorem of path analysis (Duncan, 1966, p. 5) to Eqs. (21) and (22), we find

$$r_{EJ} = p_{ES}r_{SJ} + p_{EQ}r_{QJ} + p_{EG}r_{GJ} + p_{EO}r_{OJ} + p_{EJ} + p_{E6}r_{6J}, \tag{34}$$

and, recalling that $r_{67} = 0$ and $p_{EJ} = p_{JE}$,

$$r_{6J} = p_{JE}r_{E6} = p_{EJ}r_{E6}, \tag{35}$$

so

$$p_{E6}p_{EJ}r_{E6} = r_{EJ} - (p_{ES}r_{SJ} + p_{EQ}r_{QJ} + p_{EG}r_{GJ} + p_{EO}r_{OJ} + p_{EJ}). \qquad (36)$$

Also, we can write

$$r_{EE} = 1 = p_{ES}r_{SE} + p_{EQ}r_{QE} + p_{EG}r_{GE} + p_{EO}r_{OE} + p_{EJ}r_{JE} + p_{E6}r_{6E}, \qquad (37)$$

so

$$p_{E6}r_{6E} = 1 - (p_{ES}r_{SE} + p_{EQ}r_{QE} + p_{EG}r_{GE} + p_{EO}r_{OE} + p_{EJ}r_{JE}). \qquad (38)$$

Dividing Eq. (36) by (38), we obtain

$$p_{EJ} = \frac{r_{EJ} - (p_{ES}r_{SJ} + p_{EQ}r_{QJ} + p_{EG}r_{GJ} + p_{EO}r_{OJ} + p_{EJ})}{1 - (p_{ES}r_{SE} + p_{EQ}r_{QE} + p_{EG}r_{GE} + p_{EO}r_{OE} + p_{EJ}r_{JE})}. \qquad (39)$$

Substituting from expressions (33) for p_{ES}, p_{EQ}, p_{EG}, and p_{EO} and rearranging terms, we obtained a quadratic equation in p_{EJ}, namely,

$$(r_{EJ} - r'_{EJ})p_{EJ}^2 - [(1 - R_{E.SQGO}^2) + (1 - R_{J.SQGO}^2)]p_{EJ} + (r_{EJ} - r'_{EJ}) = 0. \qquad (40)$$

Here

$$r'_{EJ} = q_{ES}r_{SJ} + q_{EQ}r_{QJ} + q_{EG}r_{GJ} + q_{EO}r_{OJ} \qquad (41)$$

is the correlation between E and J implied by S, Q, G, and O in the reduced-form Eqs. (31) and (32). The roots of Eq. (40) were $p_{EJ} = 3.192$ and $p_{EJ} = .313$. We chose to complete the solution only with the latter root because the former implies implausible negative values for other structural coefficients. The remaining structural coefficients were obtained by substitution in Eqs. (33), and residual paths were computed in the usual fashion (Hauser, 1971, p. 79).

In preparing the constrained estimates in Table 5, we allowed correlations among e_3, e_4, and e_5, the disturbances affecting T, P, and F, but not among any other disturbances. Now that we have disaggregated the composite, the possibility arises of positing a causal scheme to account for the correlations among the components of perceived others' expectations. We do not offer such an interpretation, however, because we think it plausible that there are positively correlated errors of measurement in those variables or that some unmeasured common causes of them, like the actual expectations of significant others, have been omitted from the model. The correlations among the disturbances are simply partial correlations of the form $r_{ij.SQG}$. In the case of our constrained estimates, S, Q, and G account for about half the correlations among T, P, and F, and the estimated disturbance correlations are $r_{34} = .291$, $r_{35} = .178$, and $r_{45} = .252$.

6. Discussion

Because we have represented the components of socioeconomic background and perceived others' expectations in the revised model, we have obtained insights that were lost when only the composites were entered into the model. At the same time the revised model is more parsimonious than the completely disaggregated model. That is, we have formally tested the overidentifying restrictions that are implicit in the construction of the two composites; we have estimated the relative weights of the components of the composites; and we have estimated the effects of antecedent variables on each component of perceived others' expectations.

Looking at the first column of Table 5, we see that the standardized weights of V, M, and X in S are virtually equal, while that of I is about 25% greater. Keeping in mind the fact that I represents a four-year average income, while V, M, and X are each based on single reports, two of which were made by proxy respondents, we are more impressed with the similarity of the weights than with the differences among them. Thus, the data offer little support for the argument that the achievement process is dominated by a single aspect of social inequality, whether it be income (Schiller, 1970), mother's education (Ellis & Lane, 1963; Krauss, 1964), or some feature of occupations (Bowles, 1972).

While the canonically determined weights of the socioeconomic components rather closely reproduce their effects on subsequent variables in our data, the preceding exposition shows that the relative weights of the components and the goodness of fit obtained when such weights have been chosen are both empirical matters. For example, in the Wisconsin data the rough equality of background effects breaks down when we introduce additional measures of achievement. Of the four background variables, only father's occupational status affects son's occupational status directly, and only parental income affects son's earnings directly (Hauser, Lutterman, & Sewell, 1971). Thus, the concept of socioeconomic status as a composite of status characteristics has at most a heuristic or expository value relative to the set of criterion measures on which its components have proportional effects. In the trivial case of a single criterion, the appropriate weights are given by multiple regression, for which other weighting schemes may serve as cheap substitutes (Wang & Stanley, 1970). Where proportionality of effects does not obtain, but one uses a composite anyway, the result is what Duncan (1955, p. 84) called "a single dimension with a two-way stretch."

Our estimates of relative weights of the components of perceived others' expectations, shown in the seventh column of Table 5, also fit the data very well. While this result supports the hypothesis that young men integrate perceived expectations from various sources into a general notion of what achievements others expect of them, it is subject to the same limits on generality that we have applied to our findings about socioeconomic status. The estimated weights of T, P, and F suggest that the perceived expectations of teachers have only about half the impact on aspirations and educational attainment which is exercised by perceived expectations of parents and friends. Since T, P, and F are in the same (dichotomous) metric, this comes out in the raw regression coefficients as well as in the standardized coefficients.

The lesser influence of perceived teachers' expectations is all the more interesting in light of the differential effects of socioeconomic status (S), mental ability (Q), and grades (G) on each component of perceived expectation, which are shown in the fourth through sixth columns of Table 5. The effects (raw or standardized) of socioeconomic status on parental encouragement (P) and friends' plans (F) are each about three times larger than its effect on teachers' encouragement. However, perceived teachers' encouragement depends more heavily on grades than do the other two components. Each component depends to about the same degree on mental ability net of socioeconomic status and grades. The effect of mental ability on perceived parental encouragement may be larger than its effects on the other two components, which suggests that parents may rely more on manifestations of ability outside the school setting than do teachers or peers.

Combining our observations about the causes and effects of the components of perceived others' expectations, we conclude that the expectations created by teachers may be an egalitarian force in the achievement process insofar as they depend more on academic ability and performance than on socioeconomic background. The perceived expectations of parents and friends are a more conservative force because they reflect socioeconomic origins to a greater degree. From an egalitarian point of view we would want the perceptions of teachers' expectations to have greater influence on later aspirations and achievements than those of parents' or peers' expectations, but this possibility is not realized because the latter two components of perceived others' expectations turn out to have more influence.

An observation about specification of the measurement model follows from our finding that S, Q, and G have nonproportional effects on T, P, and F, while T, P, and F have proportional effects on later variables. This finding is consistent with the representation of T, P, and F as components of O, but it is not consistent with the representation of O in a factor model as a cause of T, P, and F. The factor model of measurement introduces constraints on the relationships between indicators of a construct and both the causes and effects of the construct (Hauser & Goldberger, 1971, pp. 87–90; Blalock, 1970, pp. 106–109), while our model constrains only the relationships of measures with effects of the construct. Had we represented O as a factor of T, P, and F, we would either have had to reject the factor model or to attribute the observed nonproportional effects of S, Q, and G on T, P, and F to sampling error (compare Hauser, 1970, pp. 120–124).

It is instructive to interpret other features of the estimates in Table 5 in light of the causal scheme in Fig. 1 which was proposed by Sewell, Haller, & Ohlendorf. Disregarding the weights of the composites, the separate effects of S, Q, and G on T, P, and F, the correlation between Q and S, and the mutual effects of E and J, we have estimated eight path coefficients which were postulated to be zero in the population by Sewell, Haller, & Ohlendorf: p_{GS}, p_{ES}, p_{EQ}, p_{JS}, p_{JQ}, p_{US}, p_{UQ}, and p_{UJ}. While our estimate of each of these (standardized) coefficients is smaller than the value of .15 which Sewell $et\ al.$ (1970, p. 1020) regarded as of "no interpretable importance," their criterion seems too lax. There are five other estimated coefficients (p_{TS}, p_{TQ}, p_{FQ}, p_{EG}, p_{JG}) in Table 5 whose values lie below that cut-off point, and two of these coefficients (p_{EG}, p_{JG}) were hypothesized to be greater than zero in Sewell, Haller, & Ohlendorf (though not in Sewell, Haller, & Portes, 1969, p. 85). Moreover, since the model purports to explain the effects of socioeconomic background on educational attainment, the choice of .15 as a criterion of "interpretable importance" seems questionable when we recall (from Table 3) that three of the four estimated total effects of socioeconomic background components on educational attainment fall below that value.

Our sample is so large ($N = 3427$) that even very small path coefficients will not be attributed to chance fluctuations from zero population values at any conventional probability level. In this situation it is helpful to pose the question of which paths to delete in terms of the ability of the model to account for the effects of variables whose direct effects might be deleted. For example, our estimate of $p_{US} = .142$ represents about a third of the total effect ($r_{SU} = .422$) of socioeconomic background on educational attainment. In Table 9 we present similar calculations based on our estimates of each of the coefficients which were said to be zero by Sewell, Haller, & Portes. Disregarding the case of $p_{UJ} = .063$, where the direct and total effects are the same by assumption, in four of the remaining seven cases the direct effects account for more than 20% of the total effects in question, and in only one case does the direct effect represent less than 10% of the total effect.

TABLE 9

Selected Direct Effects and Total Effects (Sum of Direct and Indirect Effects) in Revised Model of Educational Attainment

	Direct effect (1)	Total effect (2)	(1)/(2)
$p_{GS} = .007$		.179	.039
$p_{ES} = .094$		.393	.239
$p_{EQ} = .039$		.350	.111
$p_{JS} = .081$		.374	.217
$p_{JQ} = .103$		.378	.272
$p_{US} = .142$		.422	.336
$p_{UQ} = .065$		.390	.167
$p_{UJ} = .063$		.063	1.000

Without attempting to specify exactly the point at which an effect becomes "unimportant" we conclude that our estimates do not fully support the hypotheses suggested by the causal scheme in Fig. 1. The reader should bear in mind that our conclusion is based on an interpretation of the model, not on our having estimated larger values of the eight coefficients in question than Sewell, Haller, & Ohlendorf. Indeed, in six of the eight cases our estimated (standardized) coefficients are numerically smaller than those in Sewell $et\ al.$ (1970, p. 1021). They do not estimate p_{UJ}, and our estimate of $p_{US} = .142$ compares with their $p_{27} = .128$.

We do not wish to argue too strongly on behalf of the present estimates. On the contrary, we have drawn attention to the possible inconsistencies between our estimates and the theoretical scheme in Fig. 1 in order to suggest the possibility that our specification of the revised model in Fig. 3 may be incorrect.

For example, one might suppose there were random measurement error in one or more of the intervening variables in Fig. 3; corrections for attenuation in such variables would reduce estimates of the direct effects of variables which precede the error-ridden variable on those that follow it. Alternatively, one or both of the composite variables might be incompletely specified. Our assumption that S and O are each exact functions of their measured causes amounts to a claim that we have exhausted their measured causes. One might respond to a critic of the assumption by introducing a stochastic disturbance into each of the composite variables, but this would not in itself yield alternative estimates unless one were prepared to make additional identifying assumptions.

In light of these and other possibilities we have experimented with several modifications of the revised model in an attempt to generate a set of estimates that would satisfy the overidentifying restrictions of the scheme in Fig. 1. To date we have not been able to come up with a specification that satisfies those restrictions and does not lead to implausible results elsewhere in the model. However, we are not prepared to dismiss the possibility that such a specification exists.

Appendix

Hauser and Goldberger (1971) considered a set-up in which multiple causes and multiple indicators of a single unobservable variable are observed. Their model, in slightly revised notation, was

$$y^* = \alpha' x_2 \tag{42}$$

$$y = \beta y^* + v. \tag{43}$$

Here y^* is the unobservable variable, x_2 is the $K_2 \times 1$ vector of its observable causes, y is the $M \times 1$ vector of observable indicators, and v is the $M \times 1$ vector of unobservable disturbances. It is assumed that v is distributed independently of x_2 with $E(v) = 0$ and $E(vv') = \Omega$. In spelling out the procedure for efficient estimation of the parameters of this overidentified model, they developed the following points: (i) The force of the model is to place constraints on the entire matrix of coefficients in the reduced form relating the y to x_2. (ii) The constraints are of a type which arise in econometric simultaneous equation models. (iii) The modified generalized least-squares procedure (which uses S, the unconstrained estimate of Ω, in place of Ω) is equivalent to the maximum-likelihood procedure, under normality. (iv) The crux of the estimation involves running a canonical correlation between y and x_2.

Here we extend the analysis to cover the situation where additional causal variables directly affect the indicators, that is where (43) is replaced by

$$y = \beta y^* + \Pi_1' x_1 + v. \tag{44}$$

Here x_1 is a $K_1 \times 1$ vector, which like x_2, is independent of v.

The reduced form, which relates the indicators to *all* of the observable causes, is

$$y = \Pi_1'x_1 + \beta(\alpha'x_2) + v = (\Pi_1', \Pi_2')\binom{x_1}{x_2} + v = \Pi'x + v, \qquad (45)$$

say, where $\Pi_2 = \alpha\beta'$ is $K_2 \times M$, $\Pi = \binom{\Pi_1}{\Pi_2}$ is $K \times M$ (with $K = K_1 + K_2$) and $x = \binom{x_1}{x_2}$ is $K \times 1$.

The situation clearly resembles that considered by Hauser and Goldberger, but now only a *portion* of the reduced-form coefficient matrix, namely Π_2, is constrained.

Given a sample of T joint observations from the extended model, the modified generalized least-squares procedure calls for choosing the estimate of Π to minimize the quantity

$$\text{tr}[S^{-1}(P - \Pi)' X'X(P - \Pi)]. \qquad (46)$$

Here $P = (X'X)^{-1} X'Y$, $S = (Y - XP)' (Y - XP)$, X is the $T \times K$ matrix of standardized observations on x, and Y is the $T \times M$ matrix of standardized observations on y. The minimization is to be carried out subject to the constraint $\Pi_2 = \alpha\beta'$.

Partitioning $X = (X_1, X_2)$ and $P = \binom{P_1}{P_2}$ like $\Pi = \binom{\Pi_1}{\Pi_2}$ in conformity with the partitioning of x, we define

$$X_{2.1} = (I - X_1(X_1'X_1)^{-1} X_1') X_2,$$

which is the matrix of residuals in the "auxiliary regressions" of X_2 on X_1, and

$$P_1^* = P_1 + (X_1'X_1)^{-1} X_1'X_2P_2 = (X_1'X_1)^{-1} X_1'Y,$$

which is the matrix of coefficients in the regressions of Y on X_1. The last equality follows from writing the normal equations

$$\begin{pmatrix} X_1'X_1 & X_1'X_2 \\ X_2'X_1 & X_2'X_2 \end{pmatrix}\begin{pmatrix} P_1 \\ P_2 \end{pmatrix} = \begin{pmatrix} X_1'Y \\ X_2'Y \end{pmatrix}$$

and premultiplying the first row by $(X_1'X_1)^{-1}$.

We can now write

$$XP = X_1P_1 + X_2P_2 = X_1P_1^* + X_{2.1}P_2.$$

Similarly,

$$X\Pi = X_1\Pi_1 + X_2\Pi_2 = X_1\Pi_1^* + X_{2.1}\Pi_2,$$

where

$$\Pi_1^* = \Pi_1 + (X_1'X_1)^{-1} X_1'X_2\Pi_2.$$

Then

$$X(P - \Pi) = X_1(P_1{}^* - \Pi_1{}^*) + X_{2.1}(P_2 - \Pi_2),$$

whence

$$(P - \Pi)' X'X(P - \Pi) = (P_1{}^* - \Pi_1{}^*)' X_1'X_1(P_1{}^* - \Pi_1{}^*)$$

$$+ (P_2 - \Pi_2)' X_{2.1}'X_{2.1}(P_2 - \Pi_2),$$

since $X_1'X_{2.1} = 0$ by construction.

Thus (46), the quantity to be minimized, is

$$\mathrm{tr}[S^{-1}(P_1{}^* - \Pi_1{}^*)' X_1'X_1(P_1{}^* - \Pi_1{}^*)]$$

$$+ \mathrm{tr}[S^{-1}(P_2 - \Pi_2)' X_{2.1}'X_{2.1}(P_2 - \Pi_2)]. \tag{47}$$

The constraint applies only to the second term, on which we now focus. Define

$$Y_{.1} = (I - X_1(X_1'X_1)^{-1} X_1')Y = Y - X_1P_1{}^*,$$

the matrix of residuals in the regressions of Y on X_1. If we regress $Y_{.1}$ on $X_{2.1}$, the coefficient matrix is P_2 and the residual moment matrix is S. To justify these assertions, simply note that the normal equations above imply that

$$X_{2.1}'X_{2.1}P_2 = X_{2.1}'Y_{.1},$$

and then that

$$Y_{.1} - X_{2.1}P_2 = (Y - X_1P_1{}^*) - X_{2.1}P_2 = Y - (X_1P_1{}^* + X_{2.1}P_2) = Y - XP.$$

Consequently, the second term in (47) and its constraint have exactly the form of the quantity considered by Hauser and Goldberger. Applying their analysis, we learn that, subject to the constraint $\Pi_2 = \alpha\beta'$, the second term in (47) is minimized by $\hat{\alpha}$ and $\hat{\beta}$ computed from the canonical correlation of $Y_{.1}$ on $X_{2.1}$. Thus the partial correlations between the ys and x_2s (controlling on x_1) form the basic inputs for $\hat{\Pi}_2 = \hat{\alpha}\hat{\beta}'$.

Acknowledgments

Work on the paper was supported in part by the National Institutes of Health, U. S. Public Health Service (M-6275) and by the Social and Rehabilitation Service, U. S. Department of Health, Education, and Welfare (CRD-314). Computations were carried out at the University of Wisconsin Madison Academic Computing Center with the assistance of Victor Jesudason, Taissa S. Hauser, and Peter Dickinson.

13

Education, Income, and Ability

ZVI GRILICHES AND WILLIAM M. MASON

1. Introduction

Current estimates of the contribution of education to economic growth have been questioned because they ignore the correlation of education with ability. Whether the neglect of ability differences results in estimates of the contribution of education to income that are too high was considered in an earlier paper by one of the authors (Griliches, 1970) and a negative answer was conjectured. In this chapter, we pursue this question a bit further, using a new and larger body of data. A definitive answer to this question remains elusive because of the vagueness and elasticity of "education" and "ability" as analytical concepts and because of the lack of data on early (preschooling) intelligence.

The data examined in this paper are based on a 1964 sample of U.S. military veterans. The variables measured include scores on a mental ability test, indicators of parental status, region of residence while growing up, school years completed before service, and school years completed during or after service. This allows us to inquire into the separate effects of parental background, intelligence, and schooling.

The basic problems and analytical framework can be set out very simply. Let income (or its logarithm) be a linear function of education and ability:

$$Y = \beta_1 E + \beta_2 G + u,$$

where Y is income, E is education, G is ability, u represents other factors affecting income, assumed to be random and uncorrelated with E and G, and we have suppressed the constant term for notational convenience. The relation is presumed to hold true for cross-sectional data. If education and ability are positively associated, then a measure of the contribution of education to income that ignores the ability variable (most commonly, the simple regression coefficient of Y on E) will be biased upward from β_1 by the amount $\beta_2 b_{GE}$, where b_{GE} is the regression coefficient of ability on education in the sample. The first substantive section of this paper (Section 3) investigates the magnitude of this bias, via the estimation of income equations which contain measures of both education and ability.[†]

In our data the output of the educational process is measured by the number of school grades completed in the formal education system, while ability is measured by the performance on a test at an age when most of the schooling has already been completed. Both of these measures are far from ideal for our purposes. Consider the education variable: What we would like to have is a measure of education achieved (E); what we actually have is years of schooling completed (S), without reference to the conditions under which individuals obtained their formal schooling and the kinds of schooling pursued. We write $E = S + Q$, where the discrepancy Q ($=$ quality of schooling) is assumed to be uncorrelated with the quantity of schooling (S).[‡] The quality of schooling is likely to be correlated with ability, because there is some correlation between socioeconomic status and ability, because more able students are more likely to get into better schools, and because performance on intelligence tests taken at age 18 or so also reflects in part differences in both the quantity and quality of education.

Allowing for differences in the quality of education makes the assessment of the bias somewhat more complicated. The true income-generating equation becomes

$$Y = \beta_1 E + \beta_2 G + u = \beta_1 S + \beta_1 Q + \beta_2 G + u.$$

[†] Concern with the accuracy of the education estimate due to the omission of ability may, of course, be readily extended to other factors associated with educational attainment and known to contribute to the determination of socioeconomic outcomes. Denison (1964), for instance, notes the salience of race, inherited wealth, family position, and diligence, and the list can easily be lengthened. In the present analysis we control for these factors to a considerable degree.

[‡] This is not too unreasonable an assumption, since there is a wide variation in quality of education at all levels of schooling. It is possible, however, that children going to better schools are also more likely to accumulate more years of schooling. If that is the case, we define Q to be that part of the "quality" distribution which is uncorrelated with "quantity." The rest follows in a similar manner.

In this framework, ignoring not only G but also Q leads to the same result as before, namely $b_{YS} = \beta_1 + \beta_2 b_{GS}$, since b_{QS} (the regression coefficient of quality on quantity of schooling) is zero by assumption. But when Y is regressed on S and G, the estimated education coefficient becomes

$$b_{YS.G} = \beta_1 + \beta_1 b_{QS.G},$$

where $b_{QS.G}$ is the partial regression coefficient of quality on quantity of schooling holding ability constant.[†] Given our assumptions it can be shown (see the Appendix) that

$$b_{QS.G} = -b_{QG} \cdot b_{GS}/(1 - r_{GS}^2),$$

where r_{GS}^2 is the squared correlation coefficient between the quantity of schooling and ability. Since we expect both b_{QG} (the regression coefficient of educational quality on ability) and b_{GS} (the regression coefficient of ability on educational quantity) to be positive, $b_{QS.G}$ will be negative. Substituting this expression for $b_{QS.G}$ back into the expression for $b_{YS.G}$ gives

$$b_{YS.G} = \beta_1 - \beta_1 b_{QG} \cdot b_{GS}/(1 - r_{GS}^2).$$

Comparing this with

$$b_{YS} = \beta_1 + \beta_2 b_{GS},$$

it is clear that by going from b_{YS} to $b_{YS.G}$ we reduce the coefficient of schooling for two reasons: First, we eliminate the upward bias due to the earlier omission of ability. Second, however, we *introduce* another bias due to the correlation of ability with the omitted quality variable. This new bias is partly a function of the correlation between ability and quantity of schooling.

In this chapter we solve the problem of the second bias by concentrating our attention on that part of schooling which occurred during or after military service. This "schooling increment" (SI) turns out to be virtually uncorrelated with our measure of ability (implying $b_{G(SI)} \doteq 0$) and hence is not subject to this type of bias.

The schooling increment variable helps us also to solve another vexing problem—how to disentangle causality when the available measure of ability may itself be in part the result of schooling. Since the

---

[†] These formulas hold as computational identities between least-squares coefficients. They can also be interpreted as expectations of computed least-squares coefficients from random samples from a population satisfying our assumptions.

intelligence test reported in our data is administered prior to entering service, performance on it cannot be affected by the schooling increment. Thus, because our measure of ability is causally prior to SI, and because using SI reduces the bias problem in estimating the effects of education on income, we shall put most of the stress on the results obtained for only a *part* of schooling, namely SI.

We have already noted that our ability measure is not ideal, because it is obtained after much of the formal schooling has already been completed. What we would like is a measure of ability obtained before the major effects of the school system have been felt. Although it is possible using data such as ours to construct models that incorporate estimates of the effects of *early* ability (see Duncan, 1968; Bowles, 1972), we have chosen to work exclusively with our measure of *late* ability. Even so, our ability variable is still not ideal for our purposes. It is possible that our measure of ability, *taken as a measure of late ability*, still has errors in it. To the extent that the errors are random, a direct application of least squares in their presence may understate the effect of ability on income and consequently bias the estimated education coefficient upward. To circumvent this, we devise, in Section 4, a model of income determination that contains an unobserved ability variable in place of measured ability. Manipulation of this model permits an estimate of the effect of ability freed of random errors.

The last part of the paper, Section 5, summarizes our results and compares them to previous work in this field.

2. The Sample and the Variables

Our analysis is based on a sample of post-World War II veterans of the U.S. military, contacted in a 1964 Current Population Survey (CPS) of the Bureau of the Census. The population consisted of men who were then in the age range 16 to 34, essentially the ages of draft eligibility. The sample includes about 3000 veterans, for whom supplementary information from individual military records was collated with the CPS questionnaire responses.[†] For a substantial proportion of the veterans, their military records contain individual scores on the Armed Forces Qualification Test (AFQT), which we use here in lieu of standard civilian mental ability (IQ) tests.

The men who serve in the United States military do not represent any

---

† See Klassen (1966) and Rivera (1965) for a description of the sample. These data have also been used by Duncan (1968), Mason (1968, 1970) and others.

recent cohort of draft-age men, since those at either extreme of the
ability and socioeconomic distributions are less likely to serve than those
in the middle.[†] Thus, conclusions based on our analysis of these data
apply only to the veterans population. But, since this population is

TABLE 1

MEANS AND STANDARD DEVIATIONS OF VARIABLES FOR VETERANS
AGE 21–34 IN THE 1964 CPS[a]

Variable	Mean or proportion	Standard deviation	Symbol in subsequent tables	Group label
Personal Background:				
Age (years)	29.0	3.5	AGE	
Color (white)	0.96	0.20	COLOR	
Schooling before service (years)	11.5	2.3	SB	
Schooling increment (years)	0.8	1.4	SI	
Total schooling (years)	12.3	2.5	ST	
AFQT (percentile)	54.6	24.8	AFQT	
Length of active military service (months)	30.7	16.9	AMS	
Father's schooling (years)	8.7	3.2	FS	Fa. Stat.
Father's occupational SES	29.0	20.6	FO	
Grew up in South	0.29	0.45	ROS	
Grew up in large city	0.22	0.42	POC	Reg. Bef.
Grew up in suburb of large city	0.05	0.22	POS	
Current Location:				
Now living in the South	0.27	0.44	RNS	
Now living in the West	0.15	0.35	RNW	Reg. Now
Now living in an SMSA	0.68	0.47	SMSA	
Current Achievement:				
Length of time in current job (months)	54.3	42.8	LCJ	Curr. Exp.
Never married	0.14	0.35	NM	
Current Occupational SES	39.2	22.7	—	
Log current occupational SES	3.47	0.68	LOSES	
Income (weekly, dollars)	122.5	52.4	—	
Log income	4.73	0.40	LINC	

[a] $N = 1454$, for this and subsequent tables based on the 1964 CPS.

[†] Educational deferments have channeled substantial numbers of young men into
entirely civilian careers, and a low score on the AFQT reduces the probability of being
drafted. For a general discussion of this aspect of the Selective Service System see U.S.
President's Task Force on Manpower Conservation (1964). For an overview of Selective
Service, see Davis & Dolbeare (1968).

sizable, the data are of interest despite their obvious limitation. Moreover, this is one of the few relatively large sets of data combining information on income, education, demographic characteristics, mental test scores, and socioeconomic background, the latter three being important as controls in estimating the income–education relationship.

Within the veterans sample, the individuals on whom we base our conclusions are 1454 men who were employed full-time when contacted by the CPS, who were between the ages of 21 and 34, not then enrolled in school, who were either white or black, who provided complete information about their current occupation, income, education, family background, and for whom AFQT scores were available.

The major characteristics of our sample and the variables we use are summarized in Table 1. The definition and measurement of most of the variables are standard and we shall comment here only on a few of the more important ones.

Income is gross weekly earnings in dollars. It is an answer to the question: "Give your usual earnings on this job before taxes and other deductions." The data also provide another concept of income: "earnings expected from all jobs in 1964." We experimented at some length with both concepts of income, getting somewhat better (more stable) results for the actual income measure. Since the major results were similar, we shall report here only those for the actual income measure. We also experimented a bit with functional form before settling on the semilog form for the "income-generating" function, leading to the use of the logarithm of income (LINC) as our main dependent variable.

Education is measured in years of school (highest grade) completed and is recorded at two points in time: before entry into military service and at the time of the survey. Taking the difference between total grades of school completed (ST) and grades of school completed before military service (SB) gives us a measure of the increment in schooling (SI) acquired during or after military service.[†] The minimum value of this variable is zero (no increment in schooling) and the maximum is six grades. This measure of incremental education is central to our analysis both because it occurs after the time at which ability was measured and because it is so little correlated with our measure of ability.

[†] Each of the education measures is based on eight categories of school years completed and is scored as follows: Less than eight years = 4, eight years = 8, 9 to 11 years but not high school graduate = 10, high school graduate = 12, some college but less than two years = 13.5, two or more years of college but no degree = 15, B.A. = 16, graduate study beyond the B.A. = 18. As a matter of convenience we shall hereafter refer to SI as postservice schooling, ignoring the possibility that some of the increment may have occurred while the man was in service.

Performance on the AFQT is scaled as a percentile score estimated from eight grouped categories.[†] This test includes questions on vocabulary, arithmetic, and spatial relations, but also contains a section on tool knowledge. The AFQT has been treated by other investigators (e.g., Duncan, 1968; Jensen, 1969) as an intelligence test, so that we are following in the footsteps of others in this regard.[‡]

It is clear that *some* error may arise from using the AFQT as an intelligence test, in addition to the kinds of errors which could be present in using one of the standard civilian IQ tests.[§] Another difficulty with the use of the AFQT in our analysis, a difficulty which is inherent in the use of *any* global IQ test for purposes such as ours, is that IQ by definition is an aggregation of several different traits (e.g., verbal ability, mathematical ability) sampled from some larger population of traits. The weights used in combining these traits to obtain a global IQ score are not necessarily those that would maximize the contribution of each trait to some other variable (e.g., income). Therefore, the use of AFQT instead of the separate traits which comprise it, and the use of only those traits, may lead to attenuation in our estimate of the effect of ability on income. This explains our interest in the errors-in-variables approach to be taken up in Section 4.

The long list of other variables considered can be divided, somewhat imperfectly, into personal background, and current location and achievement variables. Among the first group, we have the usual variables for

---

[†] The percentile scores are the midpoints of each of the eight categories provided in the data. For a number of individuals in the sample, there were records of results for mental tests other than the AFQT. Prior to our acquisition of the data these scores were converted to AFQT equivalents following instructions provided by the Department of Defense. Despite the use of the AFQT to select individuals into the armed forces, all levels of performance on the AFQT are represented in our sample.

[‡] Our review of the literature on intelligence tests turned up nothing about the reliability of the AFQT or about correlations between it and civilian IQ tests. The only articles we have found which discuss the AFQT are those of Karpinos (1966, 1967), which are concerned not so much with the characteristics of the test as they are with the characteristics of those who fail it. We have seen fragmentary evidence about the AGCT, which is a predecessor of the AFQT. But extrapolation from experiences with the AGCT to the AFQT would merely be speculative. Nonetheless, we feel reasonably confident in using the AFQT as a measure of IQ, because of its face validity and because Duncan, Featherman & Duncan (1968, pp. 80–119) present evidence which may be interpreted as suggesting that several different mental ability tests, including the AFQT, have about the same relationships with socioeconomic variables.

[§] If the AFQT is not virtually interchangeable with the standard civilian IQ tests, then Jensen (1969) could well be wrong in assuming that the heritability of the AFQT is the same as for the standard civilian tests. Griliches (1970, pp. 92–104) suggests that the heritability of the AFQT may be quite low, and pursues related issues.

age (in years), color (dummy: white = 1, black = 0), and region and place of origin dummies (these are in terms of places "you lived most until age 15") which record growing up in the South, in a large city (over 100,000 in population), or in a suburb of such a city. In addition to these, we have also two measures of parental status: father's schooling (in years of school completed) and father's occupation (coded according to Duncan's 1961 SES scale).[†]

The usual rationale for including an age variable is that older men are likely to have had more training on the job and more opportunity to find the better jobs that are appropriate to their training. This, however, is probably measured better not by calendar time but by the actual time spent in the civilian labor force accumulating work "experience."[‡] We can estimate this roughly by defining:

$$\text{Potential experience} = \text{age} - 18 - (\text{education before service} - 12)$$

$$- \text{education after service}$$

$$- (\text{total months in service})/12.$$

Since this measure is a linear function of variables that we include anyway (age and schooling), there is no need to compute it explicitly. It does provide, however, an interpretation for the role of time spent in military service (AMS), when the latter variable is introduced separately.[§]

The "current location" and "current achievement" variables are represented by regional dummy variables for current location in the South and West (RNS and RNW), a dummy variable for current residence in a Standard Metropolitan Statistical Area (SMSA), a measure of the length of time on current job (LCJ), a dummy variable for never married (NM), and a measure of the socioeconomic status of the individual's current occupation (LOSES, the logarithm of Duncan's occupational SES index).

[†] These are of course only incomplete measures of the family's socioeconomic status, and are subject moreover to the possibility of recall error and misperception on the part of the respondents (sons), from whom this information was elicited. Blau & Duncan (1967, Appendices D and E) take up the issue of recall error for these two variables in their OCG sample. Conclusions drawn from their discussion should apply here, since the OCG sample is comparable to ours in the same age group. For evidence on this see Duncan (1968), who reports virtually identical correlations between father's education and occupation for the OCG and the CPS sample from which we draw.

[‡] The use of such a measure was suggested to us by Jacob Mincer.

[§] There is scant reason (Mason, 1970) to believe that military service conveys an advantage in subsequent experience in the civilian labor force. Thus, we expect the AMS variable to have a negative coefficient in the income-generating equation.

In our model, each of these current location and achievement factors intervenes between education and income, and helps to explain the relationship between those two variables. For example, more education may lead to greater interpersonal competence and other socially desirable characteristics, which in turn may lead to a greater likelihood of being married. Married individuals may be expected to have the incentive of responsibility for others, and this may in turn lead to higher income. Although we present some results that take into account factors intervening between education and income, they are not of central interest to us. We shall, therefore, concentrate on the contribution to income of education and ability in the presence of background factors alone.

Table 1 presents means and standard deviations for the variables to be used. Note that this group of veterans is young, and hence will not exhibit differentials in income by education as large as those occurring in later, peak-earning, years. Also, because the number of blacks is quite small, white–black income differences will be characterized only by the coefficient for the color dummy variable. Although there are interactions between the color dummy variable and some of the other variables in the income-generating equation (Duncan, 1969c), there are too few blacks in our sample to estimate the coefficients of the interaction terms reliably.

Observe, finally, that the average increment in schooling for our sample is nearly one complete grade (0.8). Actually, 68% of the group did not return to school after service, so that those with additional schooling must have completed on average more than one additional grade. Since the grades completed range from high school to graduate school, the incremental schooling variable is not limited to a particular range of schooling, and its coefficient may thus be taken as representing the general effect of additional schooling.

In Table 2 we list the simple correlation coefficients among the major variables of our sample. Note that there is very little correlation between the increment in schooling and various personal background variables such as color, father's schooling and occupation, and the respondent's AFQT score. We have in this variable something as close to a well-designed experimental situation as we are likely to get in social science statistics.

3. Direct Results

The causal model we use to guide our assessment of the relationships between income, education, ability, and other variables at our disposal can be stated as follows, using the variable labels given in Table 1:

$$SB = F(\text{Fa. Stat., Reg. Bef., COLOR}) \tag{1}$$

$$AFQT = G(\text{Fa. Stat., Reg. Bef., COLOR, SB}) \tag{2}$$

$$AMS = H(\text{Fa. Stat., Reg. Bef., COLOR, AGE, SB, AFQT}) \tag{3}$$

$$SI = J(\text{Fa. Stat., Reg. Bef., COLOR, AGE, SB, AFQT, AMS}) \tag{4}$$

$$LINC = K(\text{Fa. Stat., Reg. Bef., COLOR, AGE, SB, AFQT, AMS, SI}), \tag{5}$$

where each of these functions is a linear structural equation. Figure 1 provides a slightly more globally stated graphical equivalent to (1)–(5). As it stands, the model is given by a set of recursive equations. Including other functional relationships linking current achievement and location variables to income and other factors would complicate the model unnecessarily for our purposes. Thus, since we are primarily interested in the *total* effects of schooling and ability *net* of potential labor force experience and background factors, we will not report on all the structural equations that inclusion of occupational SES, marital status, and other variables would entail. For the same reason, we concentrate in this section on the income equation, using the actual estimates for the rest of the causal model only to obtain a few secondary results.

TABLE 2

CORRELATIONS BETWEEN SELECTED VARIABLES IN THE 1964 CPS SUBSAMPLE

Variables	(1)	(2)	(3)	(4)	(5)	(6)	(7)	(8)	(9)	(10)
(1) AGE	1.000	−.055	−.010	.109	.052	−.056	−.093	−.004	.120	.216
(2) COLOR		1.000	.011	−.028	−.006	.174	.004	.089	.031	.116
(3) SB			1.000	−.170	.832	.469	.283	.307	.397	.264
(4) SI				1.000	.405	.098	.103	.085	.216	.149
(5) ST					1.000	.490	.321	.333	.490	.329
(6) AFQT						1.000	.229	.242	.311	.235
(7) FS							1.000	.431	.250	.114
(8) FO								1.000	.266	.229
(9) LOSES									1.000	.338
(10) LINC										1.000

The organization for the rest of this section is as follows. First we describe the sensitivity of the education coefficients in Eq. (5) to inclusion of ability and personal background characteristics. We also appraise the contribution of education to income more generally. Next we describe

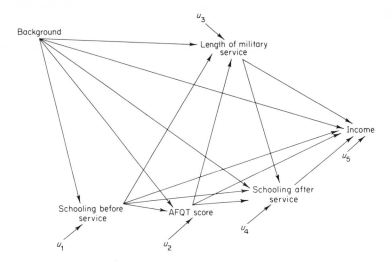

Figure 1. Basic causal model for income determination (random disturbances are denoted by the u values).

the contribution of the other explanatory variables in Eq. (5), and to some extent their contributions in the model taken as a whole. Finally, we summarize some of the relationships among variables other than income.

A. EDUCATION

There are several ways of measuring the bias in the education coefficient due to omission of ability. The bias can be assessed before, or after, the inclusion of personal background factors. Also, we use two schooling variables, so that there are two schooling coefficients to examine for each assessment of bias. We derive the needed bias figures by regressing the logarithm of income on (1) education, (2) education and ability, (3) education and personal background factors, (4) education, personal background factors, and ability. Comparisons made among these four regressions provide the necessary figures for assessing bias.

Table 3 presents a number of regression results relating the logarithm of income to selected variables. All of the regressions include age, length of military service, and color, so that the education, ability, and background effects are all net of color and the potential experience variable defined earlier. Regressions 1–4 use the two schooling variables separately; regressions 5–8 use total schooling instead.

Regression 1 provides the baseline estimates of the two schooling coefficients, estimates that do not allow for the effects of ability, father's

TABLE 3

Regression Equations with Log Income as Dependent Variable

Reg. No.	Coefficient of COLOR	SB	SI	ST	AFQT	Other sets of variables in equation	R^2
		(Standard error in parentheses)					
1	.2548 (.0472)	.0520 (.0042)	.0528 (.0070)			AGE, AMS	.1666
2	.2225 (.0479)	.0418 (.0049)	.0475 (.0072)		.00154 (.00045)	AGE, AMS	.1732
3	.1904 (.0473)	.0379 (.0045)	.0496 (.0070)			AGE, AMS, Fa. Stat., Reg. Bef.	.2129
4	.1714 (.0479)	.0328 (.0050)	.0462 (.0071)		.00105 (.00045)	AGE, AMS, Fa, Stat., Reg. Bef.	.2159
5	.2544 (.0471)			.0508 (.0039)		AGE, AMS	.1665
6	.2224 (.0479)			.0433 (.0044)	.00150 (.00045)	AGE, AMS	.1729
7	.1907 (.0473)			.0408 (.0041)		AGE, AMS, Fa. Stat., Reg. Bef.	.2115
8	.1732 (.0479)			.0365 (.0046)	.00097 (.00044)	AGE, AMS, Fa. Stat., Reg. Bef.	.2141
9	.1335 (.0487)				.00252 (.00041)	AGE, AMS, Fa. Stat., Reg. Bef.	.1794
10	.1742 (.0488)					AGE, AMS, Fa. Stat., Reg. Bef.	.1578
11	.2052 (.0456)	.0320 (.0048)	.0445 (.0068)		.00115 (.00045)	AGE, AMS, Fa. Stat., Reg. Bef., Curr. Exp.	.2979
12	.2240 (.0449)	.0372 (.0046)	.0468 (.0068)		.00129 (.00043)	AGE, AMS, Reg. Now, Curr. Exp.	.2851
13	.1970 (.0452)	.0244 (.0050)	.0352 (.0100)		.00095 (.00042)	AGE, AMS, Fa. Stat., Reg. Bef., Curr. Exp., LOSES	.3114
14						AGE, AMS, Reg. Bef.	.1178
15	.1994 (.0494)					AGE, AMS, Reg. Bef.	.1277
16	.1335 (.0486)				.00252 (.00041)	AGE, AMS, Fa. Stat., Reg. Bef.	.1794

status, and region of origin. Regressions 2 and 3, respectively, add AFQT and personal background factors to the baseline regression. Regression 4 includes both AFQT and personal background factors. Using these results, an estimate of the proportional bias in the schooling coefficients due to the omission of a relevant variable can be computed as one minus the ratio of the schooling coefficient after the inclusion of the relevant variable to the corresponding schooling coefficient in the equation that excludes this variable. Table 4 presents estimates, based on regressions 1–4 and 5–8 in Table 3, of the proportional bias in the schooling coefficients due to the exclusion of AFQT and personal background variables.

TABLE 4

Estimates of Proportional Bias in Schooling Coefficients
Due to Omission of Ability and Background Factors

Proportional bias in the coefficient of

SB	SI	ST	Variables omitted
.17	.10	.15	AFQT (Compare regressions 1 and 2, 5 and 6)
.25	.06	.20	Fa. Stat., Reg. Bef. (Compare regressions 1 and 3, 5 and 7)
.35	.12	.28	AFQT, Fa. Stat., Reg. Bef. (Compare regressions 1 and 4, 5 and 8)
.13	.07	.11	AFQT omitted; Fa. Stat., Reg. Bef. included (Compare regressions 3 and 4, 7 and 8)
.22	.03	.16	Fa. Stat., Reg. Bef. omitted; AFQT included (Compare regressions 2 and 4, 6 and 8)

Looking first at the figures for SB and SI, AFQT accounts for a drop of 7–10% in the coefficient of SI, and 13–17% in the coefficient of SB. On the other hand, when the personal background factors are included, the drop in the SB coefficient (22–25%) is much greater than in the SI coefficient (3–6%). Moreover, the decline in the SB coefficient when both AFQT and personal background variables are included is nearly three times (35%) the decline in the SI coefficient (12%). These results were to be expected. Education before service is more highly correlated than education after service to personal background factors and ability, and more likely to be biased downward because of the absence of a measure of school quality.[†] This is why we prefer the coefficient of SI as an estimate of the potential effects of changes in schooling levels. But even using Total Schooling, the decline (28%) is not all that great. Of the total decline in the coefficient for ST, 11–15% can be attributed to the introduction of the AFQT variable, the rest being due to parental background and region and size of city of origin, variables that are likely to be closely related to the omitted school quality dimension.

For analyses of the contribution of education to economic growth, the most appropriate estimate is that given by the coefficient of incremental schooling in regression 4, a regression which includes background and ability measures, but does not contain any later current experience and success variables. The value of this coefficient is .0462, and we have already observed that this is only 12% lower than the .0528 given by the first regression, which includes no background or ability measures. Thus, while the usual estimates of the contribution of education may be biased upward due to the omission of such variables, this bias does not appear to be large, and is much smaller than the 40% originally suggested by Denison (1962).

In regression 9 both schooling variables are excluded. Comparing the results of this equation with those of regression 4, we can see that education does in fact provide a significant independent contribution to the explanation of income. Comparison of regressions 4 and 8 indicates that even though the two schooling variables are acquired at different times and under different circumstances, their effects on income are similar. In fact, the difference between the two schooling coefficients in regression 4 is not statistically significant at the conventional 5% level, although this difference is significant at about the 8% level (which the computed $F = 3.2$ satisfies). We would expect the difference to be more highly significant with a larger sample, and we would also expect the inclusion of a school quality measure to eliminate it completely.

[†] The argument concerning the effects of the left-out variable of schooling quality is slightly more complicated than that outlined in the introduction because of the presence of *two* schooling variables. Considering only differences in the quality of schooling before military service and assuming that they are uncorrelated with both SB and SI, leads to the conclusion that the introduction of the AFQT variable will bias the estimated SB coefficient downward (due to the assumed positive correlation of quality of schooling Q with AFQT and the observed positive correlation of AFQT with SB). The estimated coefficient of SI would remain unbiased provided that it really was uncorrelated with SB, AFQT, and the unobserved Q. The correlation of SI with AFQT is effectively zero but it does have a nonnegligible negative correlation with SB. This leads also to a downward but smaller bias in the coefficient of SI, the ratio of the two biases (in the coefficient of SI relative to the bias in the coefficient of SB) being equal to $b_{SB.SI}$, which is about 0.3 in our data. See the Appendix for further details.

B. AFQT

The performance of AFQT is more modest than we anticipated, in view of the current emphasis on the role of intelligence in the achievement process, and the common use of the AFQT as a measure of IQ. While AFQT is relatively highly intercorrelated with schooling before military service and with the other personal background variables, its own *net* contribution to the explanation of the variance in the income of individuals is very small. For example, introducing AFQT into regression 2 increases the R^2 by only .007 relative to regression 1; introducing it into regression 4 increases the R^2 by .003 relative to regression 3. Even if one attributed all of the joint schooling–intelligence effects (including schooling before service and hence before the date of these tests) to the AFQT variable, one would raise its contribution to the R^2 to only .022 (regression 9 versus 10).

Another way to look at the relation between income and AFQT is to decompose the correlation between them into components using path coefficients. Doing so is equivalent to a repeated application of the excluded-variables formula, with all the variables scaled to have mean zero and a unit standard deviation. The advantage of such a decomposition is that it is additive, whereas a decomposition in terms of changes in R^2 is not.

The path-coefficient decomposition presupposes a causal ordering, which our model supplies. Labeling and grouping our variables into AFQT (T), SI (S), AMS (M), and Other (O), calling income Y, and using the excluded-variables formula repeatedly, we get the path-coefficient decomposition of:

$$r_{YT} = \beta_{YT.MSO} + \beta_{YM.SOT} \cdot \beta_{MT.O} + \beta_{YS.TOM}(\beta_{ST.MO} + \beta_{SM.OT} \cdot \beta_{MT.O})$$

$$+ r_{OT}[\beta_{YO.TSM} + \beta_{YS.TOM}(\beta_{SO.TM} + \beta_{SM.TO} \cdot \beta_{MO.T})$$

$$+ \beta_{YM.SOT} \cdot \beta_{MO.T}],$$

where the betas are the standardized partial regression coefficients and $\beta_{ij} = r_{ij}$. The first term on the right-hand side is the net effect of T on Y, the second and third terms together give the effect of T via M and S, and the last term gives the effect of T which is "due to" or "joint with" the other variables O.

The decomposition of r_{YT} via path coefficients yields the conclusion that more than half of the observed simple correlation between income and AFQT is "due to" or "joint with" the logically prior variables of Color, Fa. Stat., Reg. Bef., SB, and Age. The estimates for Eqs. (1)–(5) of our model imply that $r_{\text{LINC,AFQT}} = .2355 = (.0657 \text{ net}) + (.0361$ through SI and AMS) $+ (.1337$ joint with, or due to, other factors) $=$ (.102 attributable to AFQT net of prior factors) $+ (.133$ attributable to correlations between AFQT and prior factors).

In terms of the model used here, over half of the initial correlation between income and AFQT is explained by factors in the model that are prior to AFQT. And, even if schooling before service and the background variables were not taken as predetermined with respect to AFQT, it would still be the case that over half of the zero-order correlation would be allocated to *joint* influence with these other independent variables. Note, moreover, that for $r = .1$ (the approximate role of AFQT net of prior factors), $r^2 = .01$. The fraction of the variance in income accounted for by this component of AFQT is minute.

The literature on the residual factor in economic growth (e.g., Denison, 1964) has frequently adjusted, rather arbitrarily, the observed income distributions for variation presumed to be due to differences in the unobserved genetic endowment of individuals. Relevant variation in this latent variable is usually held to be measured best by variation in performances on intelligence tests, and to some extent by variation in parental social status. Since in this paper we have measures of these variables, we are in a position to question how much they contribute to the explanation of income differences. With our data, adding AFQT and Fa. Stat. to a regression of income on Age, AMS, Color, and Reg. Bef. increases the R^2 by only .052 (compare regressions 15 and 16 in Table 3). Adding Color, AFQT, and Fa. Stat. to a regression of income on Age, AMS, and Reg. Bef. increases the R^2 by only .061 (compare regressions 14 and 16 in Table 3). The increment in explained variance due to these "heredity"-associated variables is thus only about a fifth of the total "explainable" variance in income (the maximal R^2 in predicting income is given by regression 13 as .31). And, this calculation makes no allowance for the effects of quality of schooling and discrimination that are confounded with color, regional origin, and parental status variables.

Thus, the measurable effects of genetic diversity on income appear to be much smaller than is usually implied in debates on this subject. It follows, therefore, that since most of the effects of heredity are indirect, there is little bias in an estimate of a schooling coefficient which does not take heredity into account. Heredity will affect the distribution of schooling attained, but the estimated schooling coefficient measures its contribution to income correctly whatever the source of a change in schooling.

C. ADDITIONAL DETAILS AND RELATIONSHIPS

In Table 5 we display all the coefficients of regression 13. This regression includes almost all of the variables available to us, and accounts for about a third of the observed variance in logarithmic income. It is clear that the bulk of the variance in individual income is not accounted for by our equations, even when using a rather long list of variables, a result that is common to most other similar studies based on observations on individuals (e.g., see Hanoch, 1967).

TABLE 5

REGRESSION OF LOG INCOME ON ALL AVAILABLE RELEVANT VARIABLES

Variable	Coefficient	t-ratio
AGE	.0126	(4.3)
COLOR	.1970	(4.4)
FO	.0016	(3.2)
FS	−.0038	(−1.2)
POC	.0325	(1.4)
POS	.0971	(2.4)
ROS	−.0238	(−0.7)
SB	.0244	(4.9)
AFQT	.00095	(2.2)
SI	.0352	(4.8)
RNS	−.0751	(−2.3)
RNW	.1173	(4.5)
SMSA	.1365	(6.7)
LCJ	.0013	(5.7)
NM	−.1496	(−5.7)
LOSES	.0804	(5.3)
AMS	−.0011	(2.0)
Constant	3.6483	
R^2	.3114	

The regression coefficients displayed in Table 5 provide some more information on our results. Since the dependent variable is the logarithm of income, these coefficients (times 100) give the percentage effect on income of a unit change in the explanatory variables. The more interesting findings here are: (1) The nonsignificance of the father's schooling variable in the presence of father's occupational SES score. This is true also in most of the other regressions. (2) The relative importance of current location (being in an SMSA and in the West). (3) The rather surprising strong negative effect of never having married. (4) The negative effect of time spent in the military and the implied positive effect of potential experience in the labor force on income.[†]

In Table 6 we gather some auxiliary results on regressions relating other variables in our model. Among the more interesting of these are the highly significant (and rather large) effects of region, color, and schooling before service on AFQT, and the barely significant (and minor) effects of the parental status variables on it. The other interesting fact is that using occupational status rather than income as the dependent variable gives similar results: significance for the schooling variables and only marginal importance for parental status and AFQT.

4. Errors in the AFQT Variable and Other Extensions

We now consider the possibility that the AFQT is an erroneous measure of the "true ability" which is actually relevant for income determination. Since we have no direct knowledge of the errors in the AFQT, the discussion which follows is an essay: We assume the AFQT measures adult ability with random errors and specify a model for the explanation of earnings which takes these errors into account.[‡]

The sources of random error in the AFQT are presumed to be grouping, unreliability, aggregation, and left-out components of ability. Grouping, the use of midpoints of score intervals rather than the individual scores themselves, creates random errors if the actual scores

---

[†] Since (apart from irrelevant constants) potential experience = age − SB − SI − AMS/12, in a regression that contains separately Age, SB, SI, and AMS, its coefficient is given by *either* the coefficient of Age or by 12 times the negative of the coefficient of AMS. The latter yields .0132 = (−12)(−.0011) while the coefficient for Age is .0126. The two are thus quite consistent and support the interpretation that both calendar age and time spent in military service influence income via their effect on "experience." Another way of testing this is to constrain the coefficient of Age to equal 12 times minus the coefficient of AMS. The computed F-statistics for such constrained versions of regressions 1 and 4 are 3.7 and 2.8 respectively, indicating that the data are consistent with the constraint at the conventional 5% significance level (the critical F is 3.8). For regression 4, the constrained version implies that a year of experience is worth a 2.3% increase in income on the average, and that holding "experience" (but not age) constant leads to estimated 7.3 and 7.8% increases in income per year of schooling, for pre- and postservice schooling respectively.

[‡] Ideally we would like to correct all of our variables for random errors. But although it is possible to adjust some others besides ability for random errors (Siegel and Hodge, 1968), we do not have enough information to adjust all of the variables. And, since our major interest is with changes in the education coefficient due to the inclusion of the ability measure, it is the errors in the latter that are most crucial to our analysis.

TABLE 6

AUXILIARY REGRESSIONS RELATING DETERMINANTS OF INCOME

Dependent variable	Independent variables											R^2
	COLOR	FO	FS	POC	POS	ROS	SB	SI	AFQT	AGE	AMS	
					(Entries are t-ratios)							
SB	a	8	6	4	a	5						.152
SB	-4	6	4	3	a	3			17			.289
AFQT	5	5	5	2	a	6						.139
AFQT	6	2	3	a	a	4	17					.271
AMS	a	a	2	4	a	a	5					.083
SI	a	3	4	a	a	3	-11		8	4	4	.130
NM	a	-2	a	a	a	-3	a	a	a	-9	a	.073
LCJ	a	a	a	a	a	2	3	3	a	18	4	.208
RNS	3	a	a	a	a	46	a	a	a	a	a	.625
RNW	a	a	a	-4	a	-5	3	2	a	a	3	.051
SMSA	-3	a	a	12	6	-4	2	3	a	a	2	.145
LOSES	a	2	3	5	a	a	12	10	3	5	a	.290

a In the equation but estimated t-ratio less than 2.

are distributed evenly within intervals. Reliability errors, though doubtless present, are probably minor because of the grouping procedure. Aggregation, in the sense of using a global index instead of its separate components, could create random differences between the ability index which maximally predicts income and the AFQT index. Left-out components of ability could also differ randomly from the AFQT.

The AFQT may also be subject to nonrandom errors, such as those contributed by test-wiseness and motivation. In this paper we make no adjustments for nonrandom errors in the AFQT.

Our revised model is presented in Table 7 and in Fig. 2. The time subscripts 0, 1, 2 represent measurements taken before the start of formal schooling (approximately age 6), before entering military service (approximately age 18), and at the time of the survey (1964), respectively. Random disturbances appear only in equations with observable dependent variables. Basically we have an unobservable ability (or potential achievement, or human capital) variable (G) which is augmented by schooling, and which is estimable (subject to error) via test scores (T). We assume in this model that all of the influence of class (B) and heredity (H) are indirect, via the early ability variable (G_0).

We further assume that the contribution (γ) of a unit change in SI $(S_2 - S_1)$ to ability is the same as that of a unit change in S_1 (SB), and that the schooling increment is uncorrelated with the error in

TABLE 7

SCHEMATIC CAUSAL MODEL OF INCOME DETERMINATION[a]

(1)	$G_0 = a_1B + a_2H$
(2)	$T_0 = G_0 + t_0$
(3)	$S_1 = b_1B + b_2H + e$
(4)	$G_1 = G_0 + \gamma S_1$
(5)	$T_1 = G_1 + t_1$
(6)	$S_2 - S_1 = c_1S_1 + c_2B + w$
(7)	$G_2 = G_1 + \gamma(S_2 - S_1)$
(8)	$I_2 = \beta G_2 + u$

[a] Variables:
G potential achievement or ability to earn income (unobservable).
B background factors including social class of parents (Fa. Stat.) and location of adolescence (Reg. Bef.).
H heredity or genotype (unobservable).
T test score $(T_1 = \text{AFQT})$.
S schooling $(S_1 = \text{SB}, S_2 = \text{ST}, S_2 - S_1 = \text{SI})$.
I income (LINC).
e, t, w, u random disturbances.

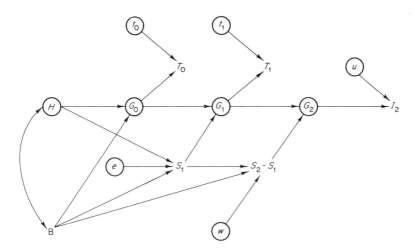

Figure 2. Revised causal model of income determination (circles denote unobservables).

observed test scores (t_1) and also with that part of heredity which is not
already reflected in S_1 or correlated with B. The various random
disturbance terms (e, t, w, and u) are assumed to be uncorrelated with
each other and with the causally prior variables of the system. These
assumptions are the important identifying restrictions in our model.

The present data are not sufficient to estimate this model in its
entirety. We have no measures of G, T_0, or H. Yet, we can mesh our
data with this model in a way which may allow us to identify the effect
of errors in AFQT and estimate the contribution of $S_2 - S_1$. Substituting Eqs. (4) and (1) into (5) gives

$$T_1 = \gamma S_1 + a_1 B + a_2 H + t_1 , \qquad (9)$$

and substituting (7) and (5) into (8) results in

$$I_2 = \beta[\gamma(S_2 - S_1) + (T_1 - t_1)] + u = \beta\gamma(S_2 - S_1) + \beta T_1 + (u - \beta t_1). \quad (10)$$

In Eq. (10) we have an errors-in-variables problem, or equivalently, a
simultaneity problem, in that T_1 is correlated with the disturbance
$u - \beta t_1$. To handle this problem, we can use the observable predetermined variables (S_1 and B) not appearing in Eq. (10), in a two-stage
procedure. In the first stage, we estimate (9), ignoring the unavailable H
variable, and get a predicted value of T_1, denoted by $\hat{T}_1$ (AFQT Hat).

This predicted value replaces T_1 in (10). In the second stage, we regress I_2 (LINC) on $S_2 - S_1$ (SI) and $\hat{T}_1$ to estimate $\beta\gamma$ and β.

This procedure solves the problem of error in T_1, assuming that our model is correctly specified, but does little about the effect of the omitted variable H (except for its influence via S_1). Here we have to count on the presumed relative independence of the increment in schooling from H, net of their joint relationship with S_1 and the variables contained in B.

The model we actually use is even more complicated than the one outlined above because it includes as additional variables Color, Age, AMS, Reg. Now, and Curr. Exp. variables. All of these are assumed to have an independent effect on income (not only via G) in Eq. (8) while Color is also assumed to enter in the previous equations for G and S [(1), (3), and (6)]. To carry all this along explicitly in Table 7, Fig. 2, and Eqs. (1)–(10) would only have obscured the basic logic of our procedure.

The first part of Table 8 reports our estimates of the revised model. Regressions 17 and 18 both use the constructed AFQT Hat variable and exclude the Fa. Stat., Reg. Bef., and SB variables assumed to affect income only via the unobservable G variable. The difference between these two regressions is that regression 18 includes the Reg. Now and Curr. Exp. variables. Regression 19 is comparable to 18 but uses the actual AFQT values instead of the estimated AFQT Hat. Comparing regressions 17 and 18 with 4, 11, and 13 in Table 3, we observe that the coefficient of incremental schooling does not decrease when we switch to the AFQT Hat variable and eliminate the direct influence of personal background variables (except for Color, Age, and AMS) and preservice schooling.

Constraining the model as we have done here so that background factors and schooling before service work through the unobserved ability variable results in almost the same estimates for the coefficients of the remaining schooling variable as in the earlier, unconstrained regressions. Allowing for direct effects of measured AFQT, schooling before service, and social background improves the fit only marginally (regression 4 versus 17, or 11 versus 18). Thus, the approach taken here suggests that our initial estimate of the schooling effect on income is robust with respect to the presence of random measurment errors in AFQT. Moreover, the comparable levels of fit in the error model and the unconstrained regressions support the model outlined in Table 7.

Considering next the AFQT Hat variable, note that its coefficient in regressions 17 and 18 is much larger and more highly significant than those for the original AFQT measure (Table 3). The estimated β implies that an increase of a percentile in the "true ability" score adds about 1 %

TABLE 8

TWO-STAGE REGRESSIONS FOR LOG INCOME AND LOG OCCUPATIONAL SES

Reg. No.	Coefficient of				Other variables in equation	R^2
	COLOR	SI	AFQT Hat[a]	AFQT		
	(Standard errors in parentheses)					

				Dependent variable is log income		
17	.0351 (.0494)	.0504 (.0069)	.01051 (.00078)		AGE, AMS	.1876
18	.0730 (.0468)	.0483 (.0065)	.00889 (.00078)		AGE, AMS, Reg. Now, Curr. Exp.	.2855
19	.1982 (.0458)	.0331 (.0067)		.00298 (.00038)	AGE, AMS, Reg. Now, Curr. Exp.	.2526

				Dependent variable is log occ. SES		
20	−.3979 (.0815)	.1320 (.0114)	.02554 (.00129)		AGE, AMS	.2636
21	−.3517 (.0809)	.1277 (.0113)	.02626 (.00134)		AGE, AMS, Reg. Now, Curr. Exp.	.2880
22	.0157 (.0831)	.0843 (.0121)		.00809 (.00069)	AGE, AMS, Reg. Now, Curr. Exp.	.1779
23	.1014 (.0787)	.1151 (.0117)		.00253 (.00073)	AGE, AMS, Reg. Now, Curr. Exp., Fa. Stat., Reg. Bef., SB	.3034

[a] The first-stage regression equation used to compute this variable is
AFQT Hat $= -19 + 17.85$ COLOR $+ .0735$ FO $+ .5505$ FS $+ 4.434$ SB $- 5.472$ ROS,
$\quad\quad\quad\quad\quad\quad$ (2.83) $\quad\quad\quad\quad$ (.0309) $\quad$ (.1481) $\quad$ (.262) $\quad$ (1.282)
with $R^2 = .271$.

to income, while the contribution of an additional year of schooling ($\hat{\gamma}$ in regression 18) is equivalent to a 5.4 percentile improvement in the true ability score. "Purging" AFQT of random errors thus increases its contribution to income, even though it does not modify the estimated contribution of education. Observe also that a bound can be set on the effect of ignoring the H variable in Eqs. (9) and (10) derived from the error model. In particular, the gain in predicting income with the estimate of error-free AFQT more than offsets the loss due to lack of a measure of the direct influence of H. That is, the *ignored* systematic part of ability, the part of heredity that is uncorrelated with the variables defining

AFQT Hat, has a smaller variance than the variance of error in observed AFQT, since the R^2 is higher for regression 18 than for 19.[†]

The only novel result in Table 8 (regressions 17–19) pertains to the coefficient of the color variable in the presence of the AFQT Hat variable. It is insignificant now, indicating that all of the color effects were captured by AFQT Hat. Thus, we could have included the color variable in the definition of the B (background) set in Table 7 and excluded it from the version of Eq. (10) that we actually estimated. Taken at face value, this result implies that discrimination against blacks does not affect white–black differences in income once person-to-person differences in ability are adjusted for random measurement error. This outcome could not have been forecast on the basis of any previous literature. Since the number of blacks in the sample is very small, the result cannot be taken for anything more than an invitation to further work.

The model of Table 7 may be extended by adding equations connecting other indicators of social position, such as Occupational SES (O) and other current experience variables (Reg. Now, Curr. Exp.), to the unobserved ability variable. In Fig. 3 we sketch one possible extension.

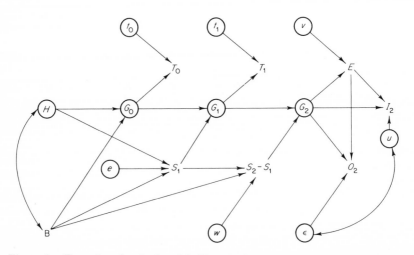

Figure 3. Extension of revised model of income determination to include occupational SES (O) and other current experience (E) variables (circles denote unobservables).

[†] Let $G = S + H$, and H be defined so as to be uncorrelated with S, where S now stands for schooling and all other "environmental" effects. Then using the observed T as a variable implies leaving out from the regression $-\beta t$, the error of measurement in T. Using $\hat{T} = S$ implies the leaving out of βH. The latter causes a smaller reduction in the explained variance than the former.

As shown, we now assume that the current experience variables (E) are causally dependent on ability, and that Occupational SES and Income are causally dependent on the current experience variables, as well as on ability. We leave unspecified the causal relationship between Occupational SES and Income.

In revising the structural equations of Table 7, we add equations linking ability to Occupational SES and Income. Both E and the color variable (C) are included in the equations for Income and Occupational SES. We alter the initial equation for ability (G_0) to include C, and recognize the unobservability of heredity (H) by replacing it with a disturbance (h), defined to be that component of heredity which is uncorrelated with our measures of personal background, color, and incremental schooling. Thus, in the extended model, Eqs. (2), (4), (5), and (7) remain unchanged, and we replace Eqs. (1), (3), (6), and (8) with

$$G_0 = a_1 B + a_2 C + h \tag{11}$$

$$S_1 = b_1 B + b_2 C + e \tag{12}$$

$$S_2 - S_1 = c_1 S_1 + c_2 B + c_3 C + w \tag{13}$$

$$E = d_1 G_2 + v \tag{14}$$

$$I_2 = \beta_1 G_2 + \delta_1 C + \eta_1 E + u \tag{15}$$

$$O_2 = \beta_2 G_2 + \delta_2 C + \eta_2 E + \epsilon. \tag{16}$$

As in our first error model, this extended version also includes Age and AMS, which are assumed to have an independent effect on Income and Occupational SES in Eqs. (15) and (16). For clarity, we have omitted Age, AMS, and C from Fig. 3, and Age and AMS from the revised, augmented set of equations (2), (4), (5), (7), (11)–(16).

Lacking measures of G, T_0, and h, we cannot estimate the extended model in its entirety. Just as in our initial error model, however, we can use equations derived from the extended model to identify the effect of errors in AFQT and to estimate the contribution of $S_2 - S_1$, this time with respect to Occupational SES.

Substituting (11) into (4), and (7) into (15) and (16), we have

$$G_1 = \gamma S_1 + a_1 B_1 + a_2 C + h \tag{17}$$

$$I_2 = \beta_1 G_1 + \beta_1 \gamma (S_2 - S_1) + \delta_1 C + \eta_1 E + u \tag{18}$$

$$O_2 = \beta_2 G_1 + \beta_2 \gamma (S_2 - S_1) + \delta_2 C + \eta_2 E + \epsilon. \tag{19}$$

These together with

$$T_1 = G_1 + t_1 \tag{5}$$

form a four-equation system with one unobservable latent variable (G_1), an indicator of it (T_1), and two current dependent variables (I_2 and O_2), both affected by this same latent variable. We estimate such a system in two stages, first estimating $\hat{T}_1$ (AFQT Hat) from the reduced-form equation given by the substitution of (17) into (5), and then substituting the resulting estimates for G_1 in (18) and (19).

The lower panel of Table 8 reports our estimates for the model extended to include (logarithmic) Occupational SES. The lists of regressors for regressions 20, 21, and 22 parallel those for regressions 17, 18, and 19 respectively. Regression 23 adds the background and SB variables to the list of regressors used in 22.

Before summarizing these results we check them for the extent the coefficient estimates satisfy the proportionality constraint of Eqs. (18) and (19), which is that $\beta_1\gamma/\beta_1 = \beta_2\gamma/\beta_2$ (or $\beta_1/\beta_2 = \beta_1\gamma/\beta_2\gamma$).[†] If our model is correct, then the coefficients of SI and AFQT Hat should be in the same ratio in regressions 17 and 20, or 18 and 21. These ratios, all of which are implied estimates of γ, turn out to be 4.8 and 5.1, and 5.4 and 4.9 respectively, values which seem close and which support the earlier interpretation of these results.

In general, the coefficients for SI and AFQT Hat in the Occupational SES regressions perform in a fashion similar to their behavior in the Income regressions. The coefficient of incremental schooling remains about the same when we switch to the AFQT Hat variable and eliminate the direct influence of personal background variables (except for Color, Age, and AMS) and preservice schooling (compare regressions 21 and 23). The coefficient for "error-free" AFQT is markedly greater than the coefficient for AFQT (compare regressions 21 and 23). An increase of a percentile in the "true ability" score adds about 2.6% to Occupational SES while the contribution of an additional year of schooling ($\hat{\gamma}$ in

---

[†] Our procedure for estimating Eqs. (18) and (19) is not fully efficient since it does not take into account the proportionality constraint. Efficient methods for the estimation of systems such as this one have been developed by Zellner (1970), Hauser & Goldberger (1971), and Goldberger (1972). Since the system aspects of this model are peripheral to our main interest (the role of schooling in income determination), we did not use such procedures to improve the efficiency of our estimates further. In another round of estimation using more efficient methods we would not impose the proportionality constraint on the coefficients of the color variable, nor on the coefficients of the current experience variables. Equations (18) and (19) do not contain such constraints since we expect variables such as color, region (representing, for example, regional cost of living differences), and marital status (representing differential supplies of effort in the market) to have rather different effects on earnings and on occupational status. This seems to be actually the case. For example, the estimated color coefficients in Table 8 are quite different in the Income and Occupational SES regressions.

regression 21) is equivalent to a 4.9 percentile improvement in the true ability score. And, allowing for direct effects of measured AFQT, schooling before service, and social background improves the fit only marginally (regression 21 versus 23). Thus, the results for Occupational SES suggest that ignoring (as in regression 23) the presence of random measurement errors in AFQT does not bias the estimate of the schooling effect (using SI) on Occupational SES.

5. Discussion and Summary

We have tried to compare our results to those of other similar studies, but without too much success. Most of them use total schooling instead of the incremental schooling variable on which we rely so heavily. Also, such studies tend to treat years of school as an error-free measure of educational attainment, a position that is hardly tenable in light of the extreme diversity of the educational system in the U.S.

Duncan's (1968) major study uses the same basic data set as we do, but defines the subsample of interest as white males age 25–34, includes both veterans and nonveterans, and introduces early intelligence and number of siblings. Instead of actual income he uses expected income. For his sample, when parental status, number of siblings, and early intelligence variables are introduced into a regression with expected income as the dependent variable, the coefficient of total schooling declines about 30%.[†] We cannot, however, be sure that this difference between Duncan's study and ours is due to the difference in populations sampled, because expected and actual income are imperfectly correlated (in our sample the correlation between the logarithms of these two variables is about .7), and because his results do not control for differences in labor force participation or the effects of different regions of origin, and do not allow for the correlation of the parental status variables with the left-out school quality variable.

Hansen, Weisbrod, & Scanlon (1970) analyze a sample of 17–25-year-old men rejected by the selective service system because of low AFQT scores, and conclude that schooling is a relatively unimportant income

---

[†] In addition to collating information from several samples, Duncan's study also uses correlations between the AFQT and other variables based on an extrapolation from the veterans subsample to the total sample. The use of these adjusted correlations would seem to be part of the reason for the discrepancy between our own results and those implied by Duncan's data. Although the assumptions which underlie the adjusted correlations appear reasonable, they do remain open to question.

determinant. The education coefficient drops about 50% when the AFQT variable is introduced in the regression of income on age, color, size of family of origin, intactness of family of origin, and education. It drops even further when such current success variables as job training and marital status are added. Their sample is special in that it concentrates on the very young and on blacks (about half of their sample is nonwhite versus 9% in our subsample). It is well-known that schooling–income differentials are rather low at the beginning of the labor force experience, and there is little evidence for a strong schooling–income relationship among blacks (see Hanoch, 1967). Both of these facts could help to explain the differences in results. Moreover, the correlation between AFQT and the omitted school quality variable is likely to be higher for their population than for higher ability groups, so that including AFQT in the regression overstates the bias in the education coefficient due to neglecting ability. For these reasons, then, we are not ready to conclude that using a larger number of low-ability men than was available to us within our own sample would alter our estimate of the bias in the education coefficient due to omitting ability. All of these considerations do remind us again, though, that we cannot take our sample as representative of the entire labor force.

Several other studies, based primarily on samples of males with relatively high social status, have also found a relatively small bias in the schooling coefficient due to left-out ability variables: Ashenfelter & Mooney (1968), Rogers (1969), Taubman & Wales (1970), and Weisbrod & Karpoff (1968). This last study can also be interpreted to show a rather significant effect on income of the quality of college schooling.

Our findings support the economic and statistical significance of schooling in the explanation of observed differences in income. They also point out the relatively low independent contribution of measured ability. Holding age, father's status, region of origin, length of military service, and the AFQT score constant, an additional year of schooling would add about 4.6% to income in our sample. At the same time a 10 percentile improvement in the AFQT score would only add about 1% to income.

Using a "clean" schooling variable, incremental schooling, we concluded that the bias in its estimated coefficient due to the omitted ability dimension is not very large, on the order of 10%. The earlier (before military service) schooling coefficient falls more, but we interpret this to be the consequence of the interrelationship between test scores and father's status variables with the other important omitted variable— the quality of schooling. Unfortunately, given the restricted nature of our sample, both as to the selectivity inherent in being a veteran, and in being relatively young (under 35), these results cannot be taken as representative for all males. Nevertheless, this is one of the largest samples ever brought to bear on this problem and we would expect these results to survive extension to a more complete population.

Our results also throw doubt on the asserted role of genetic forces in the determination of income. If AFQT is a good measure of IQ and IQ is largely inherited, then the direct contribution of heredity to current income is minute. Nor is its indirect effect very large. Of course, the AFQT scores may be full of error and heredity may be very important, but then previous conclusions about the importance of heredity are also in doubt since many of them were drawn on the basis of similar data.

Appendix

The formulas used in the text are all repeated variations on the excluded-variable formula.[†] Let the true equation be

$$y = \beta_1 x_1 + \beta_2 x_2 + e,$$

where all the variables are measured around their means (and hence we ignore constant terms) and e is a random variable uncorrelated with x_1 and x_2.

Now, consider the least-squares coefficient of y on x_1 *alone*:

$$b_{y1} = \sum x_1 y / \sum x_1^2 = \sum x_1(\beta_1 x_1 + \beta_2 x_2 + e) / \sum x_1^2$$
$$= \beta_1 + \beta_2 \sum x_1 x_2 / \sum x_1^2 + \sum x_1 e / \sum x_1^2.$$

Since the expectation of the last term is zero, we can write

$$E(b_{y1}) = \beta_1 + \beta_2 b_{21}$$

where $b_{21} = \sum x_1 x_2 / \sum x_1^2$ is the (auxiliary) least-squares regression coefficient of the variable x_2 on the included variable x_1.

Moreover, if e were to refer to the computed least-squares residuals, $\sum x_1 e$ would equal zero by construction. Hence, the same formula holds also as an *identity* between computed least-squares coefficients of different order. That is,

$$b_{y1} = b_{y1.2} + b_{y2.1} b_{21}.$$

[†] These formulas are given, in a different context, by Griliches & Ringstad (1971, Appendix C). See Yule & Kendall (1950, pp. 284–285) for the notation used here.

This same formula, with a suitable change in notation, applies also to higher-order coefficients:

$$b_{y1.2} = b_{y1.23} + b_{y3.12} \cdot b_{31.2} .$$

In what follows we shall assume that we are talking either about least-squares coefficients or about population parameters and we shall not carry expectation signs along. The discussion could be made somewhat more rigorous by inserting the plim (probability limit) notation at appropriate places.

The model we deal with can be written as

$$y = \beta_1 E + \beta_2 G + e = \beta_1 S + \beta_2 G + \beta_1 Q + e,$$

where $E = S + Q$ is education, S is quantity of schooling, Q is quality of schooling, G is a measure of ability (here assumed to be error-free), and Q is uncorrelated with S but is correlated with G. Then, estimating the equation with both G and Q excluded leads to

$$b_{yS} = \beta_1 + \beta_2 b_{GS} + \beta_1 b_{QS} = \beta_1 + \beta_2 b_{GS} ,$$

since $b_{QS} = 0$ by assumption. If G is included in the equation, then

$$b_{yS.T} = \beta_1 + \beta_1 b_{QS.G} .$$

Now, while b_{QS} is zero, $b_{QS.G}$ need not be zero. Given our assumptions we can write

$$b_{QS} = b_{QS.G} + b_{QG.S} b_{GS} = 0,$$

which implies that

$$b_{QS.G} = -b_{QG.S} b_{GS} < 0,$$

since both $b_{QG.S}$, the partial relationship of school quality to test scores, and b_{GS}, the relationship between test scores and levels of schooling, are expected to be positive. We also have

$$b_{QG} = b_{QG.S} + b_{QS.G} \cdot b_{SG} .$$

Substituting the formula for $b_{QG.S}$ into the formula for b_{QG} we get

$$b_{QG} = b_{QG.S} - b_{QG.S} b_{GS} \cdot b_{SG} .$$

Solving for $b_{QG.S}$, and recognizing that $b_{GS} b_{SG} = r_{SG}^2$, gives

$$b_{QG.S} = b_{QG}/(1 - r_{GS}^2),$$

which then gives

$$b_{QS.G} = -b_{QG}b_{GS}/(1 - r_{GS}^2).$$

The algebra gets a bit more complicated when S is divided into two components, which for notational convenience will be called B (before) and A (after) here. The model now is

$$y = \beta_1 B + \beta_1 A + \beta_2 G + \beta_1 Q + e.$$

Then

$$b_{yB.AG} = \beta_1 + \beta_1 b_{QB.AG} \quad \text{and} \quad b_{yA.BG} = \beta_1 + \beta_1 b_{QA.BG}.$$

Assume, as is approximately true in our sample, that A is uncorrelated with G. Since we have already assumed that Q is uncorrelated with both A and B, we have

$$b_{QB.A} = b_{QB.AG} + b_{QG.AB} \cdot b_{GB.A} = 0$$

$$b_{QA.B} = b_{QA.BG} + b_{QG.AB} \cdot b_{GA.B} = 0,$$

and hence

$$b_{QB.AG} = -b_{QG.AB}b_{GB.A}, \qquad b_{QA.BG} = -b_{QG.AB}b_{GA.B}.$$

Thus, we can see immediately that the relative magnitude of the biases in the two schooling coefficients depends on the size of $b_{GB.A}$ relative to $b_{GA.B}$. Now because

$$b_{GA} = b_{GA.B} + b_{GB.A}b_{BA} = 0$$

by assumption, we have

$$b_{GA.B} = -b_{GB.A}b_{BA},$$

which we can substitute in

$$b_{GB} = b_{GB.A} + b_{GA.B} \cdot b_{AB}$$

to yield

$$b_{GB.A} = b_{GB}/(1 - b_{AB}b_{BA}) = b_{GB}/(1 - r_{AB}^2)$$

and

$$b_{GA.B} \doteq -b_{GB}b_{BA}/(1 - r_{AB}^2).$$

Now, if A (schooling after service) were entirely uncorrelated with B

(schooling before service), then $b_{BA} = 0$ and its coefficient in the income-generating equation ($b_{yA.BG}$) would be unbiased:

$$b_{QA.BG} = -b_{QG.AB} \cdot b_{GA.B} = b_{QG.AB} \cdot b_{GB} b_{BA}/(1 - r_{AB}^2) = 0,$$

while the coefficient of schooling before service in the income-generating equation would be biased downward. In our sample, however, b_{BA} is actually negative and on the order of -0.3, implying that the coefficient of A is also biased downward, but only by about a third of the bias in the coefficient of B.

Acknowledgments

This work has been supported by NSF Grant No. GS 2762X. We are indebted to Mr. Paul Ryan for research assistance, and to E. Denison, O. D. Duncan, A. S. Goldberger, A. C. Kerckhoff, and K. O. Mason for comments on previous drafts. An earlier version of this paper appeared in *The Journal of Political Economy*, Vol. 80, May/June 1972.

14

Love and Life between the Censuses[†]

MARC NERLOVE AND T. PAUL SCHULTZ

Demographic phenomena such as marriages, births, migration, labor force participation, and even, to some extent, deaths, are conditioned and partly determined by economic factors. Such demographic phenomena in turn determine the characteristics of a population over time: its age distribution, location, educational attainment, and other important attributes, both economic and noneconomic. Economists have long been interested in demographic phenomena and their interrelation with economic phenomena. More often than not, however, they have studied such things as female labor force participation, migration, fertility, marriage, and so forth, in isolation. Yet, over an individual's lifetime, or the "lifetimes" of the households of which he may be a member, decisions on family size, consumption and savings, labor force participation, location, investment in various forms of human and nonhuman capital, and so forth, affect one another in a variety of ways.

While it would be highly unrealistic to view each individual or household as planning, at the beginning of life, a lifetime of consumption and investment decisions, numbers of offspring, and location, all of these decisions are taken jointly to some extent and their outcomes interact with one another over time. Moreover, when one considers a group of households, it is apparent that the aggregate characteristics of the group

---

[†] This chapter summarizes our longer study, Nerlove & Schultz (1970), to which readers are referred for detailed empirical results.

reflect the simultaneous nature of the determination of these decisions. For each individual household, decisions may be sequential; however, it is clear that individual households will take into account the constraints placed by present decisions on future opportunities for choice. Moreover, when we examine groups of households at a point in time, the total number of families making one sort of decision and that making another will reflect choices at different stages of a lifetime sequence; hence, factors that differ from one group to another may be expected to influence several types of decisions simultaneously and decisions that appear to be sequential for the individual family will be jointly determined for a group. This property of social aggregates has led some who have studied socioeconomic phenomena to prefer data on individual households to geographical aggregates.

Comparing individual households, however, does not circumvent all problems of simultaneity. In the analysis of time-series data, it is common to regard a variable whose value is determined at a previous point in time as independent of the contemporaneous disturbance in the relation to be estimated. In general, such independence cannot be assumed when dealing with cross-sectional data, either on aggregates or on individuals. All econometric relationships contain unobserved disturbance terms which are intended to represent the net effects of numerous factors, other than those included directly in the relationship, but which are too numerous or too difficult to measure to have been introduced as separate variables. Such disturbances are treated as stochastic variables and often assumed normal by virtue of the central limit theorem. In a cross-sectional context, however, such disturbances cannot be assumed independent of one another for the same individual at different points in time, as they often are for aggregate relationships in a time-series context. In general, such disturbances must be assumed to represent, at least in part, certain omitted variables, specific to the individual, which vary relatively little over time. Thus, although certain decisions may be taken sequentially by an individual or household, the measurable results of those decisions taken in the past may not, in fact, be independent of the current disturbance term in the relationship explaining another decision.

A simple example of the lack of independence between past decisions and current disturbances in a cross section occurs in the study of individuals' savings behavior. It might be expected that wealth has a negative effect on the propensity to save out of current income; yet wealth and the savings rate are positively associated cross-sectionally. The reason is simple: those individuals who have a high rate of savings for one reason or another, apart from the level of their wealth, are likely to have had such an above-average rate for some time. Since wealth is largely an accumulation of past savings, high levels of wealth tend to be associated with high rates of savings.

The same problem is encountered in a demographic context in the cross-sectional analysis of fertility as a stock of children ever born or now alive. In considering a relationship between the current birth rate and the average stock of living children that women of a specific age had in a prior period, it might be anticipated that the larger the stock the smaller the current increment to that stock, i.e., the lower the birth rate. But this expectation presumes either that across regions women have the same family-size goals or that regional differences in goals are uncorrelated with current stocks, i.e., that stocks are predetermined. It is only when the numerous and difficult-to-observe factors which have influenced family-size goals in previous periods are included in the relationship that one is likely to observe the anticipated inverse cross-sectional association between stocks and additions to the stocks of children. Unless a complete model can be specified and estimated, variation in prior-period stocks will be positively correlated with the disturbances in the relationship explaining current-period birth rates. A similar example discussed below occurs in connection with our attempt to take account of age-distribution effects on the variation of fertility among regions in Puerto Rico.

Joint simultaneous determination of several endogenous variables by several relationships describing behavior generally implies that the "explanatory" variables in one relationship determining one of the endogenous variables will not all be independent of the disturbance in that relationship. This is because some of these "explanatory" variables will be other endogenous variables determined jointly by the several relationships describing behavior. Moreover, as we have suggested above, lagged values of the endogenous variables or other variables which depend only on past decisions cannot be treated as independent of the disturbances in the behavioral relationships we may try to determine using either individual household or areal data. Because we often have a data base much richer in economic information at the aggregate level than at the household level, use of geographical aggregates appears justified, provided that due attention is paid to the effects of differences in the age distribution of the population among regions and other aggregation problems. Certainly in the study of social behavior we cannot afford to neglect data sources even if problems of interpretation and analysis may arise. It is in this spirit that we have undertaken our investigation of family decision making in Puerto Rico.

Our model of behavior consists of several relationships designed to explain or describe several interdependent household decisions. Our data base consists of figures on seventy-five small geographical regions (*municipios*) in Puerto Rico, for the census years 1950–1960 and to some extent for the intervening years. The key endogenous variables in our study of Puerto Rican demographic and economic structure in the 1950s are (1) family-size decisions, as reflected in crude birth rates, (2) female labor force participation rates, (3) marriage patterns, (4) income differences, and (5) migration decisions. The chief variables that "drive" our system, i.e., those which we have treated as exogenous, are death rates (both crude and for infants), educational attainments and current opportunities, characteristics of the industrial structure of each region (including the prevalence of unpaid family workers in the labor force and the degree to which a region may be considered agricultural), and the tightness or looseness of the labor market as reflected in the unemployment rate during the census week.

Our model contains five equations describing births, female labor force participation, income, and the form and prevalence of marriage. We have also included a rather highly disaggregated set of twenty equations describing migration in various age–sex classes.

Desired (or even realized) family size is unfortunately not an observed variable in the data analyzed; consequently, that part of our model focusing on fertility deals with the crude birth rate. Children-ever-born, parity progression ratios, and other such variables, are potentially valuable in studies of this sort. However, these particular figures cannot be constructed for the geographical regions in the period studied here. The equation "explaining" the crude birth rate does so in terms of the age distribution of the female population, income, female labor force participation, prevalence and form of marriage, opportunities for schooling, educational attainments, and mortality. The latter is measured alternatively by the crude death rate and by the death rate of children under one year.

Female labor force participation is "explained" by the age distribution of the female population, income, prevalence and form of marriage, the number of young children per woman, educational opportunities, and an index of industrial structure designed to reflect differences in the demand for female labor services in different regions.

We attempt to describe the variation in income in cash or in kind by female labor force participation, form and prevalence of marriage, numbers of young children per woman, the sex ratio, educational attainments, unemployment rates, and the degree to which the region is agricultural.

Marriages are considered to be of two types, legal and consensual.

Although the latter type has been decreasing in importance, consensual unions accounted for a quarter of all marriages at the beginning of our period. Each form of marriage is "explained" by the same set of variables: income, the sex ratio, the female age distribution, opportunities for adolescent schooling, the index of demand for female labor services, and the unemployment rate.

The ages of household members are among the most important determinants of fertility, labor force participation, and marriage behavior. If we were to observe the behavior of a household over its complete history, we might analyze the entire time-profile of decisions. Areal aggregates, however, reflect the behavior of many households at many stages of their "lifetimes." Consequently, areal aggregates will be determined importantly by the age composition of the population residing in the geographic unit to which the data refer. The sex composition of the population will also be extremely important because it will affect the nature of the households in an area. (The behavior of one-person households may be expected to differ quite markedly from that of households consisting of two or more persons.) During the period under consideration in Puerto Rico, extensive migration occurred from rural to urban areas, including the mainland U.S. Such migration greatly and differentially affected the age and sex composition of the populations residing in many of our geographic units of observation. Moreover, the migration decision is clearly constrained by, and jointly determined with, past fertility and present decisions regarding labor force participation. Thus, even if we had data on individual households, we would want to treat migration as endogenous to our model; it is necessary when the data used are areal aggregates because of the feedback effects of migration on the other variables of the model resulting from the effects of migration on the age and sex composition of the population in each region.

The migration equations of our model are more complex than the five other behavioral equations described above. Basically we assume that the probabilities of movement from one region to another depend upon differences in economic opportunity between the regions. Then the net absolute numbers moving from one region to another depend upon relative populations and these probabilities, so that our equations involve relative-population-weighted averages of economic differences. We also make some attempt to allow for the differential cost of moving within Puerto Rico as compared with the cost of moving from Puerto Rico to the mainland U.S.

Equations have been estimated using cross-section data for 1950 and 1960 and vital statistics for intervening years. Thus the birth rate equation uses eleven years of data, much of it interpolated, in an effort to make use of birth and death rates which are available for intervening years. The migration equations are estimated using only a single cross section because net migration, in this case, can only be estimated for each region over the entire intercensus period using forward survival methods based on life tables for Puerto Rico as a whole and the observed population in each region in each of the two census years. The remaining equations are estimated by pooling the data for the two census years and introducing a dummy variable to allow for a parallel shift of the relationship over the ten-year period. For reasons explained in detail in Nerlove and Schultz (1970), the birth rate equation is estimated using a transformation designed to allow for unspecified and unobserved random regional effects. Observations have all been weighted by the square roots of the relevant regional populations. Both ordinary least-squares and instrumental-variable estimation procedures have been employed and the results are compared.

Our model suffers from a number of important problems and short-comings which must be mentioned here. These are in addition to the usual problems involved in measuring the variables included.

First, and perhaps foremost in the minds of many who have studied fertility, is the absence of any reference in the model to knowledge of modern techniques of birth control, family planning programs, and the like. This, it must frankly be admitted, is a serious shortcoming of the present investigation. Knowledge of modern contraceptive and steriliza-tion techniques does appear to be widespread in Puerto Rico. We know of no data, however, that bear on the differential knowledge and availability of modern birth control methods among regions in Puerto Rico. Con-sequently, we must rely on the hope that these factors do not differ greatly among regions or over time, or are relatively uncorrelated with variables that do appear in our model, or that they have little effect on actual fertility. Some evidence that the link between knowledge about, and availability of, birth control methods may be tenuous is presented in two Rand research memoranda dealing with the Philippines: Koehler (1969), Harman (1970). It is, of course, always difficult to disentangle knowledge about, and use of, birth control methods from educational, economic, and religious factors. Another Rand research report on Taiwan (Schultz, 1971) does report significant effects on birth rates of a nation-wide family planning program. Thus the evidence is mixed; we face a difficulty about which we can do little at the present time in our study of Puerto Rico.

A second major source of difficulty with our model is that it is incom-plete. Its incompleteness takes two forms. The first is that the model has not actually been closed by the necessary demographic identities. The age and sex distribution of the population in each region is endogenous to the model since it is determined by past fertility, mortality, and migration. Moreover, the age and sex distribution greatly affects fertility, marriage rates, labor force participation rates, migration, and mortality. Except for mortality, which is difficult to treat adequately as an endogenous variable within the limitations of our data, there is, in principle, no difficulty involved in constructing the demographic identities necessary to close our model. Because the life tables available to us refer to Puerto Rico as a whole, we are not able to use identities in the strict sense of the word but only estimated approximations. Work on closure in this sense is under way.

A more troublesome lack of completeness arises because our so-called exogenous variables are not really exogenous at all, but rather are determined both interregionally and over time by many of the demographic and economic phenomena we seek to model. Unemployment rates (particularly persistent interregional differences among such rates) are determined partly by labor force participation rates and partly by employment opportunities which, in turn, are affected by the location of industry. The latter in turn affect the measure of the demand for female labor services, also treated as exogenous in the model. The industrial composition of a region is also surely affected by the nature of the labor force to be found there; textile and electronic firms are more likely to locate in regions where women have a greater propensity to seek gainful employment than in areas where they are less likely to do so. Educational opportunities available in a region, too, cannot be entirely independent of the desires of parents to see their children educated and of their willingness to bear the costs, including opportunity costs, involved.

Any model, however, must stop somewhere and must be closed somehow. Our model is no exception to the general rule that all models are incomplete in this sense. Some are simply more incomplete than others; we have broken off what we hope is a not too indigestible piece of the reality we are attempting to study.

On the whole our statistical results are quite variable and sensitive to the estimation procedures employed as well as to the inclusion or exclusion of certain variables. For the most part, however, regressions using the same sets of variables and the same estimation procedure for the two census years are quite similar.

Birth rates are strongly influenced by past death rates, form and prevalence of marriage, and the opportunity costs of children (as measured somewhat indirectly by female labor force participation rates). Age composition, income, and educational attainments had disappointingly unstable, and frequently unimportant, effects.

An interesting general lesson can nonetheless be drawn from the way in which our measure of age composition is related to the crude birth rate. In order to take account of the effect of the age and sex composition of persons living in a given *municipio* on the number of births observed there, we constructed a measure of the birth rate we would have expected in that *municipio* in each year from 1950–1960 on the basis of the age and sex composition and the (female) age-specific birth rates had they been what they were Commonwealth-wide in Puerto Rico in 1954. We were not able to observe age-specific rates directly for each *municipio* during this period, but we expected that our age-composition variable, which is essentially an "expected" birth rate, would be positively correlated with the observed birth rate and, indeed, would have a regression slope approximately equal to one. Ordinary least-squares regression, however, using data on all the *municipios* for the eleven-year period, yielded a highly significant negative slope. A little reflection suggests why: Consider two regions and suppose that region A has a high birth rate and region B a low one. The birth rate in A has very likely been high for some time because of various factors, only some of which are included in the birth rate equation. If this is so, under very general circumstances, A will have a younger population than B. Since little girls are given low weight in our index of age composition, the value of this index will be lower for A than for B. Thus, low values of the index tend to be associated with high birth rates and vice versa. For this reason, we need a transformation technique designed to allow for time-persistent regional differences. The technique, developed in Nerlove (1971) is summarized in the Appendix. The results based on the transformed data suggest a positive but weak relationship between the index of age composition and the crude birth rate.

The female labor force participation rate is negatively related to income (albeit weakly) in analyses using instrumental-variable methods but not in ordinary least-squares regressions. These findings do, we believe, illustrate the importance of accounting for simultaneity in models of this sort. The effect of young children is as expected, namely negative, but the most powerful explanatory variables are our index of the demand for female labor services and the unemployment rate. Educational and age composition variables have erratic, although sometimes significant, effects.

Our attempt to explain regional variation in income shows the importance of differences in educational attainments, rural–urban differences, and the effects of marriage and sex-ratio differences. The attempt to isolate the anticipated positive contribution of female labor force participation from the negative influence of income on the supply of female labor services to the market was unsuccessful.

Legal marriages are positively related to income and consensual unions negatively related. The opposite effects are observed for the variable measuring schooling opportunities for adolescents. Age effects, demand for female labor services, and the effects of differing sex ratios appear to be relatively unimportant.

The migration equations reveal quite mixed results for different age groups, but income and cost differences tend to show up strongly.

It would, we think, be premature to draw any firm policy conclusions from our analysis. Practically speaking, it represents more of a pilot study and an agenda for futher research than it does a finished piece of econometric analysis. Yet the differences among estimation procedures do demonstrate the *statistical* value of treating these family decisions jointly, and the apparent interactions between fertility, labor force participation, and marriage suggest the *economic* and *sociological* importance of doing so. Because the age distribution effects uncovered thus far appear weak, however, the dynamic interaction between economic and demographic variables that we had hoped to find is less well established. Much remains to be done in terms of improving the individual equations, the data upon which they are based, and in terms of applying the same basic structure to new and possibly richer data bases. Our study does, however, we believe, demonstrate both the need for, and feasibility of, simultaneous-equation models to describe the complex of family decisions of which desired and realized family size are but one aspect.

Appendix

ESTIMATION OF DYNAMIC RELATIONS IN A CROSS-SECTION OF TIME SERIES

Problems and methods of estimation using data on a number of individual units (firms, households, geographical areas, etc.) are discussed at length in Nerlove (1971). We only summarize the essential nature of the problem and its proposed solution here.

Suppose we observe a large number of individuals ($i = 1,..., N$) over a relatively short period of time ($t = 1,..., T$). Let x_{it} be a vector of K independent, exogenous, variables; let y_{it} be an endogenous variable, the current value. For simplicity, suppose that the relationship to be estimated contains only one lagged value of the endogenous variable y_{it}:

$$y_{it} = \alpha y_{it-1} + x_{it}\beta + \gamma + u_{it}, \qquad (1)$$

where α is a scalar coefficient, β is a $K \times l$ vector of slopes, and γ is a constant term. The disturbance u_{it} is intended to represent the net effect of numerous, individually unimportant, factors that have been omitted from the analysis, as well as any errors of approximation in the form of the relation. Since some of the omitted factors are likely to be rather specific to the individuals or geographical regions involved and time-invariant or only very slowly changing over time, the following model has been proposed for their stochastic structure:

$$\begin{cases} E(u_{it}u_{i't'}) = \begin{cases} \sigma^2 = \sigma_\mu{}^2 + \sigma_\nu{}^2 & i = i', t = t' \\ \sigma_\mu{}^2 & i = i', t \neq t' \\ 0 & \text{otherwise;} \end{cases} \\ E(u_{it}) = 0 \qquad \text{all } i \text{ and } t. \end{cases} \qquad (2)$$

If the observations are arranged in groups corresponding to the individuals, i.e., ordered by the first subscript, then by the second, e.g.,

$$u' = (u_{11}, ..., u_{1T}, ..., u_{N1}, ..., u_{NT}),$$

we can write the variance–covariance matrix of the disturbances as

$$E(uu') = \sigma^2 \begin{bmatrix} A & 0 & \cdots & 0 \\ 0 & A & \cdots & 0 \\ \vdots & \vdots & & \vdots \\ 0 & 0 & \cdots & A \end{bmatrix} \qquad (3)$$

where

$$A = \begin{bmatrix} 1 & \rho & \cdots & \rho \\ \rho & 1 & \cdots & \rho \\ \vdots & \vdots & & \vdots \\ \rho & \rho & \cdots & 1 \end{bmatrix}.$$

The parameter $\rho = \sigma_\mu{}^2/\sigma^2$ is often called the intraclass correlation coefficient in random-effects models in the analysis of variance. Our model of the disturbance in the analysis of cross sections over time is an example of a random-effects model.

The matrix $(1/\sigma^2) E(uu')$ has two distinct characteristic roots:

$$\xi = [(1 - \rho) + T\rho], \qquad \eta = (1 - \rho). \qquad (4)$$

Generalized least-squares for a model with variance–covariance matrix given by (3) amounts to using transformed values of the variables appearing in the equation to be estimated (1) rather than the original observations. If we write $\bar{y}_{i.}$ as the mean for the ith individual of y_{it}, $\bar{y}_{i.}(-1)$ as the mean of y_{it-1}, and $\bar{x}_{i.}$ as the vector of means of the exogenous variables, the appropriately transformed equation is

$$\left[\frac{y_{it} - \bar{y}_{i.}}{\eta^{1/2}} + \frac{\bar{y}_{i.}}{\xi^{1/2}}\right] = \alpha \left[\frac{y_{it-1} - \bar{y}_{i.}(-1)}{\eta^{1/2}} + \frac{\bar{y}_{i.}(-1)}{\xi^{1/2}}\right]$$
$$+ \left[\frac{x_{it} - \bar{x}_{i.}}{\eta^{1/2}} + \frac{\bar{x}_{i.}}{\xi^{1/2}}\right] \beta + \frac{\gamma}{\xi^{1/2}} + v_{it},$$

(5)

where

$$v_{it} = \left[\frac{u_{it} - \bar{u}_{i.}}{\eta^{1/2}} + \frac{\bar{u}_{i.}}{\xi^{1/2}}\right]$$

are disturbances having common variances σ^2 and zero covariances for all i and t. It is well known that estimates based on (5) for *known* values of ξ and η have optimal large-sample properties. As shown in Nerlove (1971), these estimates also have excellent small-sample properties; in effect, knowing ξ and η converts a sample on N individuals over T time periods into a large sample if N is large even if T is small.

The problem is, of course, that ξ and η are not known a priori, but must either be estimated or assigned some arbitrary value. Setting $\rho = 0$ implies $\xi = \eta = 1$, so that (5) reduces to (1); hence, the assumption $\rho = 0$ amounts to ordinary least squares on the "pooled" cross section of time series. It has been shown in the Monte Carlo experiments reported in Nerlove (1971), that ordinary least squares yields estimates of α which are seriously biased upward and estimates of σ^2 biased downward. The standard errors obtained are consequently far too small. The bias in the coefficients β will depend upon how the variables x_{it} are correlated with y_{it-1}; in the case considered, there was only one such exogenous variable and it was positively correlated with y_{it-1} so that the bias in its coefficient was toward zero.

Since $\xi = (1 - \rho) + T\rho$, one can see that the second term in each of the square brackets in (5) vanishes asymptotically as $T \to \infty$. The resulting equations express the observations in terms of deviations from individual means. Estimating α and β from such deviations is equivalent to estimating regressions having separate constant terms for each individual. As can be seen from (5), such regressions neglect the "between-individual" variation among the individual means as compared with generalized least squares. In the Monte Carlo experiments such neglect resulted in a downward bias in the estimated α and an upward bias in a derived estimate of ρ based upon the estimated residual variance plus the "variance" of the constant terms. In the case considered, a single x_{it} was positively correlated with y_{it-1} so that an upward bias in the estimated β was observed.

Several other methods of estimation, including an instrumental-variable method and a gradient maximum-likelihood procedure were examined. The method that appeared to show the least bias, mean-square error, and generally overall robustness against specification problems, was adopted for our empirical work. This is a two-round procedure based upon a first-stage estimate of ρ, and thus the weights ξ and η, from a regression using deviations from individual means; the second round then yields estimates based on transformed observations, as in (5), using the estimated values of ξ and η to weight deviations from individual means and the individual means themselves.

Let $\bar{y}_{i.}$ be the individual means of the dependent variables, and let $\bar{x}_{i.}(k)$ be the individual means of the kth independent variable. We suppress our earlier separate notation for the lagged value of the dependent variable. Let $\bar{y}_{..}$ and $\bar{x}_{..}(k)$ be the grand means of y_{it} and $x_{it}(k)$, respectively, and let b_k be the estimates of the slopes in a least-squares regression of $(y_{it} - \bar{y}_{i.})$ on the variables $(x_{it}(k) - \bar{x}_{i.}(k))$. If s^2 is the sum of squared residuals from this regression, our estimate of ρ is

$$\hat{\rho} = \frac{\hat{\sigma}_\mu{}^2}{\hat{\sigma}_\mu{}^2 + s^2/NT},$$

where

$$\hat{\sigma}_\mu{}^2 = (1/N) \sum_{i=1}^{N} \left\{ (\bar{y}_{i.} - \bar{y}_{..}) - \sum_k b_k(\bar{x}_{i.}(k) - \bar{x}_{..}(k)) \right\}^2.$$

The method may be used with instrumental variables as well as with ordinary regression.

15

Senate Voting: Problems of Scaling and Functional Form

JOHN E. JACKSON

1. Introduction

In a previous paper on Senate voting behavior, Jackson (1971a) used Guttman scaling to get an ordering of the roll-call votes taken on specific bills and the proposed amendments to them considered by the Senate in 1961 and 1962. The pattern of a senator's votes on these roll calls, summarized in his scale score, was used to measure his support for each legislative item. Linear regression analysis was then employed to estimate the weight each senator gave to his constituency and various leader and colleague variables in deciding how much support to give each bill, i.e. how to cast his votes. However, that analysis contains the implicit assumption that the scale scores measuring a senator's support for each bill constitute a cardinal variable. This assumption is clearly inappropriate for variables developed from Guttman scales, which only provide a highly aggregated ordinal measure of a senator's support for each bill. The question then is, "How much were the results reported in the earlier paper affected by making this assumption?" In this chapter, we examine this question by postulating an alternative stochastic model to explain a senator's support for each bill and using a different statistical procedure to estimate the influence of the hypothesized variables. We also employ this example to make several general comments about the choice of a particular model and estimating method.

The alternative model examined is the limited dependent variable (LDV) or "probit regression" model developed by Tobin (1958). Although this model still requires some assumptions that are not met by the Guttman scale variables, it does account for one of the most serious violations of linear regression. Thus it should provide some evidence about how much the previous results were affected by the use of linear regression (LR).

Section 2 of the paper indicates how the Guttman variables violate the assumptions of the linear regression model, sketches a nonlinear model designed to overcome some of these problems, and explains why LDV was selected as a compromise. Section 3 presents the Senate voting models, the variables used to estimate them, and the linear regression results. Finally Section 4 compares the LR results with those obtained from the estimated LDV models. Three types of comparisons will be discussed: Do the two techniques yield different conclusions about Senate voting behavior? How well do the two techniques fit the data used to estimate the models? How accurately do the alternative models predict voting behavior?

2. The Statistical Problem with Guttman Scales

Guttman scaling was originally developed as a means of analyzing sets of questions in surveys of attitudes; Guttman (1941) and Stouffer et al. (1950). It attempts to define and measure an attitudinal dimension on the basis of the questions' ordered, cumulative properties. If each of the questions in a series corresponds to a point on a single attitudinal dimension, then respondents agreeing with any one of the questions should agree with all less extreme questions. Empirically, the Guttman procedure orders the questions to minimize the number of "nonscale" responses. It then assigns each respondent to a group depending on which questions he agrees with and which ones he disagrees with.

In legislative roll-call analysis, the votes on amendments to a bill and the vote for passage of the bill are used as the "questions" and these are ordered from least to most support in accordance with the observed pattern of votes; Anderson, Watts, & Wilcox (1966) and MacRae (1970). An example of a bill that scaled perfectly is the extension of the Civil Rights Commission in 1961. The most extreme amendment was to make it a permanent agency. This was followed by an attempt to extend it for four years, an extension of two years, and an attempt to prevent consideration of any of the above. All senators who favored a four-year extension also favored a two-year extension, and those who opposed a two-year extension opposed a four-year extension and making it a permanent agency. Individual senators were then scored from four to zero depending upon which amendments they supported and which ones they opposed; for example, those voting to consider an extension but only for two years were scored a two. These scale scores are then used as the dependent variable in regression analysis.

There is an inherent difficulty in this approach. To illustrate, consider Fig. 1, in which the line $Y^* = a + bX$ purports to represent the expected relationship between Y (senator's preferences) and X (his

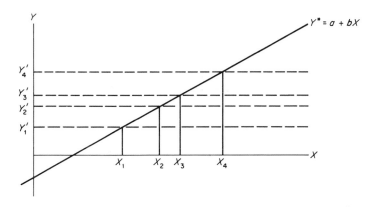

Figure 1.

constituency's preferences). More precisely, allowing for stochastic disturbances, the line represents the expected preferences of a senator given a value for X, i.e. $Y^* = E(Y \mid X) = a + bX$. His actual preferences, if they could be ascertained, would deviate randomly about the line and are represented by the expression $Y = a + bX + u$, where u represents these random deviations. In this case, the ordinary least-squares regression of Y on X would give unbiased estimates of the coefficients a and b since the values of the regressor X and the disturbance u are uncorrelated.

However, in the case of Senate voting there is no way to measure the content of the bill, and hence Y, directly. For some bills, there are no continuous measures of their content (e.g. units of Area Redevelopment) so that a senator's true preferences are not known. For other bills, the measures may exist (e.g. level of the minimum wage), but there is no procedure currently available for getting senators to disclose their preferences. The senator's votes on the various amendments provide a basis for assessing his preferences, and the Guttman scale combines these votes into a scalar measure. But it is clear that this measure may offer only a distorted picture of Y.

The dashed lines in Fig. 1 show where four different amendments might have been located on this underlying continuous dimension. For the Civil Rights Commission, say, the attempt to prevent the Senate from considering any extension corresponds to Y_1', the two-year extension to Y_2', the four-year extension to Y_3', and establishing a permanent agency to Y_4'. The Guttman procedure then assigns a score of zero to those senators who voted against all four amendments. Senators who voted for the weakest amendment, Y_1', but for no others, are assigned to the second group with a value of one, and so on, with the senators who voted for all the amendments assigned a value of four. The distortion arises because all senators with the same scale score are taken to have identical preferences, when in fact they may differ by as much as the distance between two amendments. For example, senators preferring either a 2, 2.5, 3, or 3.9 year extension of the Civil Rights Commission are all scored a two, and all senators who want at least a four-year but less than a permanent extension are scored a three. Because of this aggregation, each Guttman score contains an error component additional to the previously discussed stochastic disturbance. The problems created by this aggregation process are most severe for extreme values of X and will be discussed separately.

The Civil Rights Commission scale can be used to illustrate a second problem inherent in the use of Guttman scale scores as measures of senators' preferences. The Guttman scale only provides a rank ordering of the votes on a given bill, and thus of the senators' positions. There is no way to determine the "distance" between the amendments, and thus between the groups of senators on the underlying dimension. Using the scale scores directly as the dependent variable in a linear regression model makes the implicit assumption that the ranks reflect the actual spacing of the amendments along the Y dimension. In the case of the Civil Rights Commission this means that voting for a two-year extension rather than no extension constitutes the same amount of additional support for the Commission as voting to make it a permanent agency rather than merely permitting a four-year extension. This is clearly a strong assumption, particularly on bills where the underlying dimension is not as clear.

The most serious problem created by the use of Guttman scale scores in linear regression, however, is the systematic correlation they introduce between the explanatory variables and the deviations about both the senator's expected preference, Y^*, and his expected scale score. In

Fig. 2 let the line $Y^* = a + bX$ again be the senator's expected preference given X, let Y^{**} be the step function representing the expected Guttman scale score for each value of X, and Y_j the actual preferences of the senator given by $Y_j = a + bX + e_j$ where the e_j are

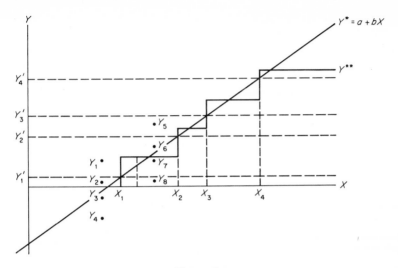

Figure 2.

error terms. There are two different systematic errors. The first systematic error is introduced by trying to approximate the line Y^* by the step function Y^{**}. For extreme values of X and hence of Y, the step function ceases to discriminate among senators. This error, defined as $Y^* - Y^{**}$, is negative for small values of X and positive for large values. In absolute value, it is largest for values of X less than X_1 or greater than X_4. This introduces a systematic correlation between these errors and X. If the amendments offered to most bills adequately covered the range of senators' preferences, the problem would not be serious because there would be few senators left in each of these tails. Unfortunately, the Senate does not spend much time considering extreme amendments, so that on many bills the tails are likely to contain a substantial number of senators with different preferences and different values of X. Worse yet, one senator may be located in one of these tails on a large number of bills. He may be following his constituency's preferences but that will not be reflected in his Guttman scale scores because he will be scored a zero or a four on most bills. Hence, the linear regression model will seriously underestimate the coefficients in this senator's model.

A second problem is the nature of the deviations about the expected

Guttman scale scores, Y^{**}. For X less than X_1, only positive deviations from the expected Guttman scale score (which is itself an erroneous measure of Y^*) will be observed. For example, Y_1 and Y_2 represent the presence of two different positive error terms while Y_3 and Y_4 are the result of two negative error terms of the same magnitudes. In the linear regression model, using a continuous dependent variable to estimate $Y^* = a + bX$, this pattern would satisfy the basic assumption of an error term with an expected value of zero. However, with the Guttman scale variable, this assumption will not be met; Y_1 will be scored as $Y = 1$, but Y_2, Y_3, and Y_4 will all be scored as $Y = 0$. Thus only positive deviations from the expected Guttman scale will be observed for values of X less than X_1. For values of X greater than X_4, only negative deviations will be observed. This problem is not as serious for values of X between X_1 and X_4. For example, Y_5,..., Y_8 represent the addition of the same error terms as entered Y_1,..., Y_4 but for a different value of X. The respective Guttman scale scores will be 2, 1, 1, 0, representing both positive and negative deviations from Y^{**}. Consequently for values of X between X_1 and X_4 the deviations from the expected Guttman scale will more nearly conform to the assumptions necessary for the linear regression model.

We now have two sources of measurement error which will be systematically correlated with the observed values for X. Both sources are associated with the limited range of the admendments offered to each bill and have the same implications for the use of the Guttman scale scores as dependent variables in a linear regression. Both the inability of the step function Y^{**} to approximate the line Y^* for extreme values of X, and the systematic exclusion of negative error terms for X less than X_1 and of positive error terms for X greater than X_4, tend to make low values of X associated with positive error terms in the Guttman scale data, and high values of X associated with negative error terms. This leads to a negative correlation between the error term and the explanatory variable, provided that $b > 0$. (If the effect of X on Y had been negative, i.e. $b < 0$, then there would have been a positive correlation between X and the error term.) Thus Guttman scale scores do not satisfy the necessary assumptions of linear regression, and ordinary least squares will yield systematically different results than it would if the actual values for Y could be observed. These violations of the assumptions may result in an underestimate of the true value of b as the fitted line attempts to fit Y^{**} rather than Y^*.

Zavoina & McKelvey (1969) propose an alternative model, called n-chotomous probit analysis. This is an extension of probit analysis to the case where there are n rather than just two groupings of the dependent variable. Their program uses a maximum-likelihood procedure to estimate the coefficients in the underlying multivariate model and the location of the $n - 1$ dividing points used to construct the Guttman scale. The assumptions required for their procedure are that the senator's expected preferences are a linear function of the explanatory variables, $Y^* = \sum B_k X_k$, and that the disturbance between this and his actual preferences on any bill, given by $Y = \sum B_k X_k + e$, is normally distributed with mean zero and constant variance. Further, the $n - 1$ dividing points used in the scaling procedure have aggregated this behavior into n ordinal categories.

The limited dependent variable technique to be used in our study represents a compromise between linear regression and n-chotomous probit analysis. The LDV model permits the measured dependent variable to be grouped at one end of the underlying dimension. This grouping then forms a limit value for the dependent variable. At all points above this limit, the dependent variable is assumed to be cardinal, continuous, and linear in the explanatory variables.

This limited dependent variable model is represented by the line W in Fig. 3. The model says that if the limit is a lower bound, the measured value of Y cannot be less than the limit, no matter how much less than X_1, X might be, or how large a negative stochastic disturbance might be included in the senator's actual preference for that observation. Suppose that, for reasons of constituency preference or purely random circumstances, a senator is willing to vote for more restrictive admendments than Y_1'. The LDV model in effect gives him a latent score of -1 or even a -2, even though this is not manifest in his value of Y.

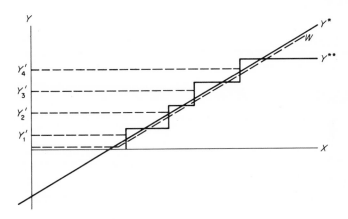

Figure 3.

(The same description holds, but in reverse, if the limit is an upper bound. Even though a senator might be willing to vote for stronger legislation, the $Y_4{}'$, he cannot be scored higher than four.) At all other points, W is assumed to follow the linear model of Y^*:

$$Y^* = B_0 + B_1 X_1 + \cdots B_K X_K \tag{1}$$

$$W = \begin{cases} L & \text{if} \quad Y^* < L \\ Y^* & \text{if} \quad Y^* \geqslant L \end{cases} \tag{2}$$

where W is the limited dependent variable, Y^* is the expected preference which is a linear function of the explanatory variables. In the LDV model the observed scale score Y^g is determined by

$$Y^g = \begin{cases} L & \text{if} \quad Y^* + u < L \\ Y^* + u & \text{if} \quad Y^* + u \geqslant L, \end{cases} \tag{3}$$

where u is a random disturbance. The parameters of the LDV model are estimated by maximum likelihood, given observations on Y^g, $X_1,\ldots, X_K$.

For our purposes, LDV represents a compromise between the linear regression model and the Zavoina–McKelvey approach. In the LDV model the dependent variable, once it passes the limit, is assumed to be cardinal and unbounded. This assumption is not valid for Guttman scales, so that the problems pointed out by Zavoina and McKelvey will still exist at these nonlimit points. In terms of Fig. 3, we will not do justice to Y^{**}, but will at least do justice to the threshold. The advantages of n-chotomous probit over LDV should decrease as the number of groupings increases and as the number of extreme observations becomes more concentrated at one end, rather than both ends, of the scale. Thus both LDV and LR become more appropriate as the number of amendments included (the number of dividing points) increases, and LDV would become more appropriate as the number of limit observations becomes concentrated at one of the limits.

Our problem now is one of selecting an estimating procedure for this behavioral model with the variables constructed from Guttman scales. The advantages of linear regression are that it is readily available and inexpensive, it has shown considerable robustness in the face of real-world problems, and it is the best-understood technique. The assumptions of the n-chotomous probit procedure on the other hand better satisfy the model and type of data at hand. However, it is not readily available in programmed form, most readers will not be acquainted with the technique, its robustness is unknown, and it is more expensive computationally. "Probit regression" appears to occupy a middle position in these considerations. The data at hand satisfy the LDV assumptions better than the linear regression assumptions, but possibly not as well as those of n-chotomous probit. LDV is not as widely used or understood as LR among social scientists, but is better known than n-chotomous probit.

When our study of Senate voting behavior was initiated, linear regression was selected because of its availability, computational efficiency, robustness and familiarity, and in spite of its inappropriate assumptions. Now that alternative models are feasible, the question arises whether the results and conclusions about Senate voring behavior would have been different had a more appropriate technique been used.[†] An answer to this question for the Senate voting study should provide information for social scientists more generally concerned about the problems of choosing a statistical technique.

3. The Voting Models, Variable Construction, and LR Results

A complete discussion of the models hypothesized for each senator and the votes used to construct the Guttman scales is given in Jackson (1971a) and will only be summarized here. The basic model specified for each senator was

$$Y^* = b_0 + b_1 C + b_2 L + b_3 W + b_4 P + b_5 R \qquad (4)$$

where Y^* is the senator's preference, C is his constituency's preference, L and W the preferences of his party's floor leader and whip respectively, P the preferences of the President, and R the position of his party's leader on the committee reporting the bill. Because the Democrats were the majority party, R refers to the Committee Chairman for the Democrats and to the Ranking Minority Committee member for the Republicans. The variables L and W respectively refer to Mansfield and Humphrey for the Democrats and to Dirksen and Kuchel for the Republicans.

This basic equation was altered in some cases to incorporate more specific hypotheses. If both senators from a state were in the same party, then we specified that the senior senator influenced the voting behavior of his junior partner, but not vice versa. For most Eastern Democrats, we specified that a notable liberal on the reporting committee also influenced

[†] Zavoina and McKelvey graciously made their program available. Unfortunately it arrived too late to be adapted to the local facilities and used in the following comparisons.

their voting behavior. An analogous variable was constructed for notably conservative Republicans. These Committee Liberal and Committee Conservative variables were based on senators with a generally liberal or conservative reputation, often a signer of a Committee's minority report. Occasionally, the opinions of regional or ideological leaders were included, such as Russell in the models for Southern Democrats.

Guttman scales were constructed for each of 36 issues in the 87th Congress (1961–1962), 18 from each session. In 32 cases, the votes comprising each scale were limited to the amendments on a single bill; in the remaining four cases the scales include roll-call votes taken on several separate bills. For convenience, however, we will refer to all 36 issues as "bills". With few amendments available on each bill, the range and thus the number of categories of each scale is limited. This should be offset by the advantages of having a clearer idea of what the scales are measuring. The votes used to construct these scales comprise 46% of all the roll-call votes in 1961 and 36% of all the roll-call votes in 1962.

The scales were standardized to a range of zero to four, with zero being the most conservative position, i.e., voting to limit the legislation as much as possible, in all cases. This range was selected because it corresponded to the modal number of rankings in the original scales. It also offered the best trade-off between the desirability of having a large number of groupings, and the disadvantage of having to deal with bills with fewer than this number of groups.

Those scales that had fewer than five categories were inflated to the zero-to-four range by multiplying each score by four divided by the scale value of the highest category. Thus if a scale had only four categories, they were scored as 0, 1.33, 2.67, and 4.00. On scales with more than five categories, the categories with the fewest frequencies were added to the adjacent larger groupings, and the categories rescored. This aggregation was continued until there were five groups, scored zero to four. For example, the initial distribution on the Area Redevelopment Act, namely

Raw scores	0	1	2	3	4	5	6
Number of senators	18	7	8	4	8	5	50,

was rescaled as

Scaled scores	0	1	2	3	4
Number of senators	18	7	12	13	50.

These scale scores provide measures for the dependent variable—the senator's voting behavior—and for some of the independent variables—the party leaders, the committee chairmen and ranking minority members, the committee liberal and conservative, the senior senator, and the regional and ideological leaders.

This still leaves the President and constituency variables to be measured. The President's preferences were measured by two variables, a Presidential Preference variable and a Presidential Dummy variable. The Presidential Preference variable was constructed from the *Congressional Quarterly Almanac*'s assessment of the President's position on each roll-call vote. President Kennedy's positions according to these assessments fit the previously constructed Guttman scales almost perfectly. These scale positions were then used for the Presidential Preference variable. The Presidential Dummy variable is simply a binary variable which equals one for the three bills where the President was reported not to have taken a public position on any of the votes, and zero for all other bills.

The Constituency Preference variable was derived from relationships between senators' voting behavior and the demographic and regional characteristics of their constituencies. This procedure, which has been used in several previous studies on the effects of constituency on voting behavior, is based on the assumption that demographic and regional characteristics are correlates of political opinions.[†] For example, the distribution of preferences will vary more between farmers and blue-collar workers than it does within each group. The mix of these groups in each state's population then, at least within fairly broad regions, should account for a high proportion of the variance in political opinion at the state level. Thus, we can use the distribution of these groups among the states to estimate the constituency opinion on each bill for each state.

Constituency preferences were derived for each bill by a regression of the scale scores of the senators voting on each bill against the characteristics of the states. To see how this fits into our general model,

---

[†] The justification for the use of demographic and regional characteristics to proxy relative constituency opinions has been stated by MacRae (1958, p. 256) as

> What we must investigate, if we are concerned with the connection between representatives and their constituencies, is the degree of association between roll call votes and constituency characteristics. If this association is high, we infer that in some way the constituencies have influenced the legislators. . . . For if the association is high, the representative may be said to represent relatively local interests, and this in itself has significance for the functioning of representative government.

Similar variables have also been used by Turner (1951) and Shapiro & Cherryholmes (1969).

consider Fig. 4. Here $Y_i(j)$ is the *unobservable* preference of senator i on bill j; $Y_i^g(j)$ is the scale score of senator i on bill j; $X_i(j)$ is a vector of the leadership and colleague scores relevant to senator i on bill j; $C_i(j)$ is the *unobservable* preference of senator i's constituency on bill j; Z_i is the vector of demographic variables for senator i's state (e.g. region, urbanization, income levels, unemployment); and $i = 1,..., 100$ denotes the senators, $j = 1,..., 36$ denotes the bills.

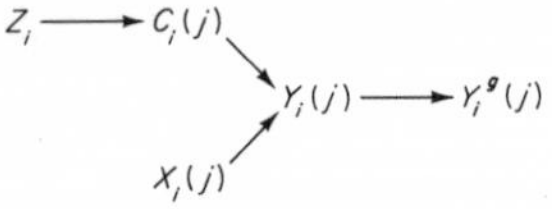

Figure 4.

Our main interest is to relate Y^g, or rather Y, to C and X. But C is not directly observable. Therefore, at this point, we estimate C by regressing the $Y_i^g(j)$ against the Z_i across all senators for each bill. The calculated scores from this regression, the $\hat{Y}_i^g(j)$, are denoted as $C_i^*(j)$ and interpreted as estimates for the $C_i(j)$. These estimated constituency preference variables, the $C_i^*(j)$, should represent the systematic effects of the preferences of various groups in a state and the distribution of these groups among the states in the country. The voting model for each senator formulated in Eq. (4) will then be estimated by relating $Y_i^g(j)$ to $X_i(j)$ and $C_i^*(j)$ across all bills.

This two-step procedure may introduce some bias into the estimates of the coefficients in each senator's model. This bias, when present, will mean the constituency coefficients are overestimated and the leadership and colleague coefficients are underestimated. This bias will be present if both of two conditions hold: (a) an important leadership variable is excluded from the individual senator's model or the influence of one of the included leadership variables varies from bill to bill, *and* (b) the preferences of this excluded leader or the variations in the included leader's influence are systematically correlated with one or more of the constituency characteristic variables. Suppose, for example, that Mansfield's influence on a few bills was strongest among non-Southern Democrats from states hit hard by the 1961 recession. In any attempt to predict votes on the basis of the constituency characteristics, region and unemployment will be good predictors because they are proxying Mansfield's influence as well as any constituency preferences. When the individual models are estimated using the predicted vote to measure constituency preferences, the constituency coefficient will be overestimated because the variable is measuring both constituency preferences and Mansfield's influence on these few bills. However, if Mansfield's influence on these senators is equally strong on all bills, this bias will not exist because Mansfield's preferences are included in each individual model.[†]

The most interesting result of the constituency models is the amount of variance in senators' voting behavior which can be explained by constituency characteristics. The coefficient of determination ranged from 0.220 for the National Wilderness Preservation Bill to 0.895 for extending the Civil Rights Commission. The civil rights issues, as a group, had by far the highest explained variation. Presumably, civil rights, in addition to being a very salient political issue, had the most homogeneous distributions of opinion within each state. This provided senators with a clear understanding of their constituency's preferences over this issue. Only three bills, the Cultural Exchange Program, the National Wilderness Preservation system, and Comsat, had explained variances below 30%. The latter two bills in particular were largely centered on questions of very little concern to a majority of people in most states. Consequently, it must have been difficult for a senator to get a clear idea of his constituency's preferences or the bills' impact on them.

4. Estimation of the Voting Model

The LR voting model for each senator was estimated by regressing the senator's Guttman scale score on each of the 36 bills, $Y_i^g(j)$, against his state's estimated constituency variable $C_i^*(j)$ and the vector of leadership and colleague variables, the $X_i(j)$. As measured by R^2, the voting models for the individual senators accounted for a high percentage of the variance. Table 1 shows the distribution of the R^2 values (corrected for degrees of freedom) for the senators, classified by region and party. The table substantiates the statement that the simple models explain a high proportion of the variance in senators' roll-call voting behavior. Only two models were not significant at the 5% level, as measured by the conventional F-test; these were Senators Tower (Rep., Texas) and Neuberger (Dem., Oregon).

We now turn to an examination of the limited dependent variable models and their results. The question of whether a senator's voting

---

[†] We are of course assuming that a senator's vote on bill j does not influence his constituency's preference on that bill, i.e. that $C_i(j)$ and $Y_i(j)$ are not simultaneously determined.

TABLE 1

DISTRIBUTION OF R^2 FOR INDIVIDUAL SENATOR'S VOTING MODELS

Groups[a]	Value of R^2							Total
	0.00–0.29	0.30–0.39	0.40–0.49	0.50–0.59	0.60–0.69	0.70–0.79	0.80–1.00	
E. Dem.	2	1	2	9	8	0	1	23
S. Dem.	0	1	3	2	5	4	3	18
W. Dem.	4	3	7	2	6	1	0	23
E. Rep.	0	2	2	7	3	3	1	18
W. Rep.	1	0	1	7	6	0	4	19
Total	7	7	15	27	28	8	9	101[b]

[a] The groups are Eastern, Southern, and Western Democrats, and Eastern and Western Republicans respectively.

[b] There were 101 senators' models estimated because of the death of Brigs (Rep., New Hampshire) and his replacement by Murphy. Each man's voting was estimated as a separate model.

behavior was better approximated by a LDV model with an upper or lower limit was quite easy to answer. The senators with many limit values generally had them concentrated at one limit. Table 2 shows the distribution of senators by the number of observations at their less frequently observed limit. For example, if a senator had been scored as four on 20 bills and zero on only three bills, he would appear under the three column in Table 2. This table supports the statement that few senators had many observations at both limits. The senator was given a lower- or an upper-limit LDV model depending on the limit at which he was more frequently observed.

TABLE 2

FREQUENCY OF THE LESS-FREQUENT LIMIT OBSERVATIONS

Number of less-frequent limit observations	0	1	2	3	4	5	6	7	8	9	10
Number of senators	17	28	19	11	8	9	1	4	2	1	1

Each of the 101 senators' models were reestimated using the LDV procedure. These results are compared with the linear regression results on three criteria. The first criterion is the goodness of fit to the 1961–1962 data used to estimate the models. The second concerns the number of times the null hypothesis of no systematic influence by an explanatory variable is rejected. The third criterion is the ability to predict the senators' voting scale scores on 25 bills in the 1963 session.

The estimated scores for the linear regression are just the calculated values of Y from the least-squares regression, denoted subsequently as $\hat{Y}^1$. The estimated scores for the LDV model, denoted as $\hat{Y}^2$, are the calculated expected values from the maximum-likelihood estimated LDV model, namely

$$\hat{Y}^2 = L[\hat{P}(Y^g = L)] + \int_L^\infty vf(v)\, dv, \tag{5}$$

where $\hat{P}(Y^g = L)$ is the estimated probability that the senator's preference is at the limit L, and $f(v)$ is the estimated probability density conditional on the senator's preferences being above the limit. These estimated probabilities are calculated from the estimated expected preference Y^* shown in Eq. (1) and the assumption that his actual preferences are normally distributed around this with some variance σ^2 which is estimated by the LDV procedure. For details, see Tobin (1958).

These estimated scores were then compared with the observed scores. For senator i on bill j, the LR prediction error is $Y_i(j) - \hat{Y}_i^1(j)$, and the LDV prediction error is $Y_i(j) - \hat{Y}_i^2(j)$. These errors for each model are then squared and averaged for each bill and for each senator. These mean squared errors will form the basis for our comparisons of the two models.

A. PREDICTION OF 1961–1962 VOTES

Table 3 shows the distribution of the differences obtained by subtracting the LDV mean squared error from the LR mean squared error for each of the 101 senators over the sample observations. The LDV procedure had a lower mean squared error for slightly more than half the senators, 54 out of 101. In 24 of the 35 cases where the magnitude of the absolute difference exceeded 0.050, it was LDV that had the smaller mean squared error.

TABLE 3

LR MEAN SQUARED ERROR MINUS LDV MEAN SQUARED ERROR FOR SENATORS IN 1961–1962

	$\leqslant -0.100$	-0.050 -0.099	-0.000 -0.049	0.000 0.049	0.050 0.099	$\geqslant 0.100$
Difference						
Number of senators	4	7	36	30	16	8

When related to the size of the mean squared error, these absolute differences are very small. The ratio of the absolute difference in mean squared errors was computed for each senator. This ratio was less than 0.10 for nearly 60% of the senators. It exceeded 0.30 for only eight senators, and most of these had very small mean squared errors.

A similar comparison may be made across bills rather than across senators. Table 4 gives the results. The LDV procedure out-performed

TABLE 4

LR MEAN SQUARED ERROR MINUS LDV MEAN SQUARED ERROR FOR BILLS IN 1961–1962

Difference	$\leqslant -0.100$	-0.050 -0.099	-0.000 -0.049	0.000 0.049	0.050 0.099	$\geqslant 0.100$
Number of bills	1	5	10	12	5	3

LR on this criterion for slightly more than half the bills, 20 out of 36. Again, the differences between the two methods are not substantial. Thus, in terms of goodness of fit over the sample, there is little basis to choose LDV over LR.

B. SIGNIFICANCE OF EXPLANATORY VARIABLES

The second comparison concerns the explanatory variables found nonsignificant (at the 5% level) by the two procedures. This comparison is made to see if the two techniques lead to contradictory conclusions about the influence of the different variables hypothesized to affect Senate voting. For example, if the LDV procedure accepted the null hypothesis of no influence by the party floor leaders more often than LR did, it would raise doubts about Jackson's (1971a) conclusion that Mansfield was an important factor in how non-Southern Democratic Senators vote.

In the regression model, the significance test is made by assuming that the ratio of an estimated coefficient to its estimated standard error is distributed as a t-statistic. The two-tailed test was used. For the LDV model, the null hypothesis was tested by comparing the log of the likelihood function when the variable was excluded to that value when the variable was included. Minus two times this difference is assumed to be distributed as a χ^2 with one degree of freedom.

The results of these calculations do not show any conflict between the two techniques. The two techniques led to different conclusions with respect to only 26 of the over 600 coefficients estimated. These differences involved the models of 23 senators. LR rejected a null hypothesis accepted by LDV in thirteen cases and accepted a null hypothesis rejected by LDV in thirteen cases. LR rejected the null hypothesis of no influence for the party leader (Mansfield or Dirksen) and other senator (Morse in Gruening's model, for example) variables more often than LDV, while LDV rejected the null hypothesis of no influence more often for the constituency and committee liberal/conservative variables. These discrepancies were quite small, however, never more than two or three for any variable.

These slight differences indicate that the two techniques yield the same conclusions about the significance of constituencies, party leaders, and the President. Thus, the conclusions reached in Jackson (1971a) are not essentially altered by using the LDV procedure rather than linear regression.

C. Prediction of 1963 Votes

Noticeable differences in the two procedures did appear when the two models were used to predict voting behavior during the 1963 session of the Senate. There were 86 senators whose voting behavior in 1963 could be predicted with their previously estimated models. Senators who were elected or appointed between the 87th and 88th Congresses and senators whose models depended upon the preferences of a senator who retired, died, or was defeated between these two Congresses were excluded. The results of the LR predictions are presented in more detail in Jackson (1971b).

Guttman scales were constructed for 25 bills considered in 1963 prior to President Kennedy's assassination. For each bill, the constituency variable was constructed in the same manner and using the same regional and demographic variables as for the 1961 and 1962 bills. Once the constituency variables were constructed, they were inserted into the LR and LDV models previously estimated with the 1961 and 1962 data, to compute predicted scale scores for each senator. In fourteen of the 86 models, the LR and LDV specifications are not precisely the same since nonsignificant variables were eliminated in each case. Differences between the observed scale score and the predicted scale score for each model were analyzed in the same way as were the differences for the 1961–1962 votes.

Figure 5 shows a plot of the actual scale scores against constituency for Senator Bartlett (Dem., Alaska) for the 25 bills in 1963. (Bartlett was selected because constituency was the only statistically significant

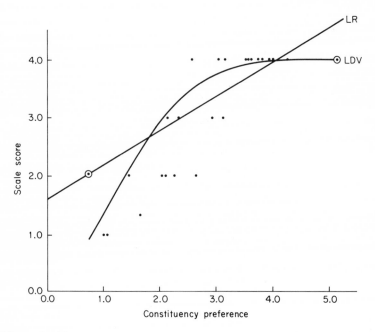

Figure 5. Plot of scale score versus constituency for Senator Bartlett, 1963 bills.

variable in his model.) The curves represent the expected scale scores for these bills using the limited dependent variable and linear regression models. This example is fairly typical in terms of the goodness of fit to the 1963 data.

TABLE 5

LR MEAN SQUARED ERROR MINUS LDV MEAN SQUARED ERROR FOR SENATORS IN 1963

Difference	⩽ −0.200	−0.100 −0.199	0.000 −0.099	0.000 0.099	0.100 0.199	⩾0.200
Number of senators	12	8	36	23	4	3

Table 5 shows the distribution of the differences obtained by sub-tracting the LDV mean squared error from the LR mean squared error for each of the 86 senators. Two-thirds (56 of 86) of the senators had lower mean squared errors with the LR models than they did with the LDV models. LR also had the smaller mean squared error in twelve of the fifteen cases where the magnitude of the difference was greater than 0.200. In most of these cases, however, the sizes of these differences are not substantial. When these differences were expressed as a percent of the LR mean squared error, half (46) were less than 10% and three-fourths (67) were less than 20%. The average mean squared error, for all 2073 individual voting scale scores from 1963, was 0.883 for LR, and 0.884 for LDV, again indicating a slightly better performance by LR.

The other comparison made with these predicted 1963 votes was on the basis of the individual bills. The difference between the LR and LDV mean squared error for each of the 25 bills is shown in Table 6. For

TABLE 6

LR Mean Squared Error Minus LDV Mean Squared Error for Bills in 1963

Difference	$\leqslant -0.100$	-0.050 -0.099	-0.000 -0.049	0.000 0.049	0.050 0.099	$\geqslant 0.100$
Number of bills	5	9	5	4	1	1

nineteen of the 25 bills, the LR mean squared error was smaller than the LDV mean squared error. The size of these differences as well as the distribution favored the linear regression estimates. In fourteen of the sixteen cases where the magnitude of the absolute difference exceeded 0.050, LR gave better estimates. Not only was LR more likely to have a lower mean squared error, but when there were large differences, LR was almost always the superior technique.

The overall conclusion is that, based on 1963 predictive ability, the linear regression procedure is slightly preferable to the limited dependent variable method. When these results are combined with the earlier results which showed very little difference between the fits of the LR and LDV procedures to the data used to estimate the models, and between the results of individual hypothesis tests, linear regression appears to be the more successful approach. These results, when combined with ordinary least squares' advantages in terms of computational efficiency, availability, and familiarity, argue that linear regression can be profitably used to test hypotheses which can only be represented by ordinal Guttman type data.

5. Conclusion

The principal finding of this paper is that the LDV model, which on a priori grounds seemed to be more appropriate for analysis of Senate voting behavior, did not yield results which were clearly superior to those obtained using linear regression. The two approaches gave essentially the same fit to the sample data and the same picture of which variables were significant. But in postsample prediction, linear regression produced slightly better forecasts than LDV.

There are at least two possible interpretations of our findings that linear regression and limited dependent variable give similar results. One interpretation is that linear regression is sufficiently robust to handle the ordinal variables produced by Guttman scaling. This should be of considerable encouragement to those social scientists forced to deal with ordinal or noninterval data. A contrary interpretation is that neither LDV nor LR is appropriate for data of this type: their assumptions are too strong for Guttman data. The facts that the models estimated with both techniques could reasonably predict voting behavior outside the sample and that the conclusions about the influence of constituency and the various Senate leaders were consistent with most prior opinions strongly suggest that the models and techniques have more substance than this second interpretation allows.

The decision about whether to believe the empirical findings about Senate voting behavior turns on which of the previous interpretations about the choice of technique one adopts. If the a priori arguments that LDV is more appropriate to these data and that it corrects many of the theoretical problems associated with LR are accepted, the conclusions and interpretations of the LR model should also be accepted. The LDV models then provide further evidence and justification for these conclusions. However, those who believe neither technique to be appropriate and maintain that the techniques are too similar to provide independent confirmation, may continue to reject the empirical conclusions.

Acknowledgments

This work was supported in part by a grant to Harvard University from Resources for the Future, Washington, D.C. The author wishes to thank Eric A. Hanushek, John F. Kain, and H. Douglas Price for their help and criticisms. Most of this work was done while the author was an Instructor of Economics at the U.S. Air Force Academy. While the views expressed here are those of the author and not those of the Academy, he wishes to express his appreciation for the environment which encouraged this work. RFF and the above individuals are of course exempt from any association with these views.

References

Allport, F. H. The *J*-curve hypothesis of conforming behavior. *Journal of Social Psychology*, 1934, **5**, 141–183.

Althauser, R. P., and Heberlein, T. A. Validity and the multitrait-multimethod matrix. In E. F. Borgatta and G. W. Bohrnstedt (Eds.), *Sociological methodology 1970.* Chapter 9. San Francisco, California: Jossey-Bass, 1970. Pp. 151–169.

Althauser, R. P., Heberlein, T. A., and Scott, R. A. A causal assessment of validity: the augmented multitrait-multimethod matrix. In H. M. Blalock, Jr. (Ed.), *Causal models in the social sciences.* Chapter 22. Chicago, Illinois: Aldine-Atherton, 1971. Pp. 374–399.

Anderson, L. F., Watts, M. W., and Wilcox, A. R. *Legislative roll call analysis.* Evanston, Illinois: Northwestern University, 1966.

Anderson, S. B., and Maier, M. H. 34,000 pupils and how they grew. *Journal of Teacher Education*, 1963, **14**, 212–216.

Anderson, T. W. *An introduction to multivariate statistical analysis.* New York: Wiley, 1958.

Ashenfelter, O. A., and Mooney, J. D. Graduate education, ability and earnings. *Review of Economics and Statistics*, 1968, **50**, 78–86.

Banks, A. S., and Textor, R. B. *A cross-polity survey.* Cambridge, Massachusetts: Massachusetts Institute of Technology, 1963.

Basmann, R. L. An expository note on estimation of simultaneous structural equations. *Biometrics*, 1963, **16**, 464–480.

Blalock, H. M., Jr. Correlation and causality: the multivariate case. *Social Forces*, 1961, **39**, 246–251.

Blalock, H. M., Jr. Making causal inferences for unmeasured variables from correlations among indicators. *American Journal of Sociology*, 1963, **69**, 53–62.

Blalock, H. M. Jr. *Causal inferences in nonexperimental research.* Chapel Hill, North Carolina: University of North Carolina, 1964.

Blalock, H. M. Jr. Path coefficients versus regression coefficients. *American Journal of Sociology*, 1967, **72**, 675–676.

350 REFERENCES

Blalock, H. M. Jr. Multiple indicators and the causal approach to measurement error. *American Journal of Sociology*, 1969, **75**, 264–272. (a)

Blalock, H. M. Jr. *Theory construction: from verbal to mathematical formulations.* Englewood Cliffs, New Jersey: Prentice-Hall, 1969. (b)

Blalock, H. M. Jr. Estimating measurement error using multiple indicators and several points in time. *American Sociological Review*, 1970, **35**, 101–111.

Blalock, H. M. Jr. Causal models involving unmeasured variables in stimulus-response situations. In H. M. Blalock, Jr. (Ed.), *Causal models in the social sciences.* Chapter 19. Chicago, Illinois: Aldine-Atherton, 1971. Pp. 335–347. (a)

Blalock, H. M. Jr. (Ed.) *Causal models in the social sciences.* Chicago, Illinois: Aldine-Atherton, 1971. (b)

Blalock, H. M., Wells, C. S., and Carter, L. F. Statistical estimation with random measurement error. In E. F. Borgatta and G. W. Bohrnstedt (Eds.), *Sociological methodology 1970.* Chapter 5. San Francisco, California: Jossey-Bass, 1970. Pp. 75–103.

Blau, P. M., and Duncan, O. D. *The American occupational structure.* New York: Wiley, 1967.

Bohrnstedt, G. W., and Goldberger, A. S. On the exact covariance of products of random variables. *Journal of the American Statistical Association*, 1969, **64**, 1439–1442.

Boudon, R. A new look at correlation analysis. In H. M. Blalock, Jr. and A. B. Blalock (Eds.), *Methodology in social research.* Chapter 6. New York: McGraw-Hill, 1968. Pp. 199–235.

Bowles, S. Schooling and inequality from generation to generation. *Journal of Political Economy*, 1972, **80**, S219–S251.

Briggs, F. E. A. The influence of errors on the correlation of ratios. *Econometrica*, 1962, **30**, 162–177.

Brown, J. W., Greenwood, M., Jr., and Wood, F. A study of index correlations. *Journal of the Royal Statistical Society*, 1914, **77**, 317–346.

Brown, T. M. Simplified full maximum likelihood and comparative structural estimates. *Econometrica*, 1959, **27**, 638–653.

Brown, T. M. Simultaneous least squares: a distribution free method of equation system structure estimation. *International Economic Review*, 1960, **1**, 173–191.

Burnham, W. D. and Sprague, J. Additive and multiplicative models of the voting universe: the case of Pennsylvania, 1960–1968. *American Political Science Review*, 1970, **74**, 471–487.

Campbell, D. T. From description to experimentation: interpreting trends as quasi-experiments. In C. W. Harris (Ed.), *Problems in measuring change.* Chapter 12. Madison, Wisconsin: University of Wisconsin Press, 1963. Pp. 212–242.

Campbell, D. T., and Stanley, J. C. Experimental and quasi-experimental designs for research on teaching. In N. L. Gage (Ed.), *Handbook of research on teaching.* Chicago, Illinois: Rand-McNally, 1963. Pp. 172–246.

Centers, R. *The psychology of social classes.* Princeton, New Jersey: Princeton University Press, 1949.

Chernoff, H., and Divinsky, N. The computation of maximum-likelihood estimates of linear structural equations. In W. C. Hood and T. C. Koopmans (Eds.), *Studies in econometric method.* Chapter 10. New York: Wiley, 1953. Pp. 236–302.

Chow, G. C. Two methods of computing full-information maximum likelihood estimates in simultaneous stochastic equations. *International Economic Review*, 1968, **9**, 100–112.

Christ, C. F. *Econometric models and methods.* New York: Wiley, 1966.

Cochran, W. *Sampling techniques.* 2nd ed. New York: Wiley, 1963.

Coleman, J. S. *Models of change and response uncertainty.* Englewood Cliffs, New Jersey: Prentice-Hall, 1964.

Cooley, W. W., and Lohnes, P. R. *Multivariate procedures for the behavioral sciences.* New York: Wiley, 1962.

Costner, H. L. Theory, deduction, and rules of correspondence. *American Journal of Sociology*, 1969, **75**, 245–263.

Costner, H. L. Utilizing causal models to discover flaws in experiments. *Sociometry*, 1971, **34**, 398–410.

Crano, W. D., Kenny, D. A., and Campbell, D. T. Does intelligence cause achievement? a cross-lagged panel analysis. *Journal of Educational Psychology*, 1972, **63**, 258–275.

Crockett, H. J., Jr. Psychological origins of mobility. In N. J. Smelser and S. M. Lipset (Eds.), *Social structure and mobility in economic development.* Chicago, Illinois: Aldine, 1966.

Cutright, P. National political development: measurement and analysis. *American Sociological Review*, 1963, **28**, 253–264.

Davis, J. W., Jr., and Dolbeare, K. M. *Little groups of neighbors: The selective service system.* Chicago, Illinois: Markham, 1968.

Denison, E. F. *The sources of economic growth in the U.S. and the alternatives before us.* New York: Committee for Economic Development, 1962.

Denison, E. F. Measuring the contribution of education. In *The residual factor and economic growth.* Paris: Organization for Economic Cooperation and Development, 1964. Pp. 13–15, 77–102.

Douglass, H. R., and Huffaker, C. L. Correlation between intelligence quotient and accomplishment quotient. *Journal of Applied Psychology*, 1929, **13**, 76–80.

Duncan, B., and Duncan, O. D. Minorities and the process of stratification. *American Sociological Review*, 1968, **33**, 356–364.

Duncan, O. D. Review of *Social area analysis. American Journal of Sociology*, 1955, **61**, 84–85.

Duncan, O. D. A socioeconomic index for all occupations, and Properties and characteristics of the socioeconomic index. In A. J. Reiss, Jr., with O. D. Duncan, P. K. Hatt, and C. C. North, *Occupations and social status.* Chapters 6 and 7. New York: Free Press of Glencoe, 1961. Pp. 109–161.

Duncan, O. D. Path analysis: sociological examples. *American Journal of Sociology*, 1966, **72**, 1–16.

Duncan, O. D. Ability and achievement, *Eugenics Quarterly*, 1968, **15**, 1–11.

Duncan, O. D. Some linear models for two-wave, two-variable panel analysis. *Psychological Bulletin*, 1969, **72**, 177–182. (a)

Duncan, O. D. Contingencies in constructing causal models. In E. F. Borgatta (Ed.), *Sociological methodology 1969.* Chapter 3. San Francisco, California: Jossey-Bass, 1969. (b)

Duncan, O. D. Inheritance of poverty or inheritance of race? In D. P. Moynihan (Ed.), *On understanding poverty.* New York: Basic Books, 1969. Pp. 85–110. (c)

Duncan, O. D. Unmeasured variables in linear models for panel analysis. In H. L. Costner (Ed.), *Sociological methodology 1972.* San Francisco, California: Jossey-Bass, 1972.

Duncan, O. D. Some linear models for two-wave, two-variable panel analysis with one-way causation and measurement error. In H. M. Blalock, Jr. *et al.* (Eds.), *Mathematics and sociology.* 1973.

Duncan, O. D., Featherman, D. L., and Duncan, B. Socioeconomic Background and Occupational Achievement: Extensions of a Basic Model. Final Report, Project

No. 5-0074 (EO-191), Contract No. OE-5-85-072. U. S. Office of Education. Ann Arbor, Michigan: University of Michigan, 1968.

Duncan, O. D., Haller, A. O., and Portes, A. Peer influences on aspirations: a reinterpretation. *American Journal of Sociology*, 1968, **74**, 119–137.

Eisenpress, H. Note on the computation of full-information maximum-likelihood estimates of coefficients of a simultaneous system. *Econometrica*, 1962, **30**, 343–348.

Eisenpress, H., and Greenstadt, J. The estimation of nonlinear econometric systems. *Econometrica* 1966, **34**, 851–861.

Ellis, R. A., and Lane, W. C. Structural supports for upward mobility. *American Sociological Review*, 1963, **28**, 743–756.

Featherman, D. L. The socioeconomic achievement of white religio-ethnic subgroups: social and psychological explanations. *American Sociological Review*, 1971, **36**, 207–222.

Fisher, F. M. Dynamic structure and estimation in economy-wide econometric models. In J. S. Duesenberry, G. Fromm, L. R. Klein, and E. Kuh (Eds.), *The Brookings quarterly econometric model of the United States*. Chapter 15. Chicago, Illinois: Rand-McNally, 1965. Pp. 588–635.

Fisher, F. M. *The identification problem in econometrics*. New York: McGraw-Hill, 1966.

Fleiss, J. L., and Tanur, J. M. A note on the partial correlation coefficient. *The American Statistician*, 1971, **25**, 43–45.

Fletcher, R., and Powell, M. J. D. A rapidly convergent descent method for minimization. *Computer Journal*, 1963, **6**, 163–168.

Geraci, V. J., and Goldberger, A. S. Simultaneity and Measurement Error. University of Wisconsin: Social Systems Research Institute Workshop Paper EME 7125, 1971.

Gibbs, J. P. Measures of urbanization, *Social Forces*, 1966, **45**, 170–177.

Gockel, G. Income and religious affiliation: a regression analysis. *American Journal of Sociology*, 1969, **74**, 632–649.

Goldberger, A. S. *Econometric theory*. New York: Wiley, 1964.

Goldberger, A. S. On Boudon's method of linear causal analysis. *American Sociological Review*, 1970, **35**, 97–101. (a)

Goldberger, A. S. Criteria and Constraints in Multivariate Regression. University of Wisconsin: Social Systems Research Institute Workshop Paper EME 7026, 1970. (b)

Goldberger, A. S. Econometrics and psychometrics: a survey of communalities. *Psychometrika*, 1971, **36**, 83–107.

Goldberger, A. S. Maximum-likelihood estimation of regressions containing unobservable independent variables. *International Economic Review*, 1972, **13**, 1–15.

Goldberger, A. S., and Olkin, I. A minimum-distance interpretation of limited-information estimation. *Econometrica*, 1971, **39**, 635–639.

Goldstein, S. Socioeconomic differentials among religious groups in the United States. *American Journal of Sociology*, 1969, **74**, 612–631.

Goodman, L. A. On the exact variance of products, *Journal of the American Statistical Association*, 1960, **55**, 708–713.

Griliches, Z. Notes on the role of education in production functions and growth accounting. In W. L. Hansen (Ed.), *Education, income, and human capital*. New York: National Bureau of Economic Research, 1970. Pp. 71–115.

Griliches, Z., and Ringstad, V. *Economies of scale and the form of the production function*. Amsterdam: North-Holland Publ., 1971.

Gruvaeus, G. T., and Jöreskog, K. G. A Computer Program for Minimizing a Function of Several Variables. Princeton, New Jersey: Educational Testing Service Research Bulletin 70-14, 1970.

Guttman, L. The quantification of a class of attributes: a theory and method of scale construction. In Paul Horst *et al.* (Eds.), *The prediction of personal adjustment.* New York: Social Science Research Council, 1941.

Hanoch, G. An economic analysis of earnings and schooling. *Journal of Human Resources,* 1967, **2,** 310–329.

Hansen, W. L., Weisbrod, B. A., and Scanlon, W. J. Schooling and earnings of low achievers. *American Economic Review,* 1970, **50,** 409–418.

Harman, A. J. Fertility and Economic Behavior of Families in the Philippines. Santa Monica, California: Rand Corporation Report RM-6385-AID, 1970.

Harman, H. H. *Modern factor analysis.* 2nd ed. Chicago, Illinois: University of Chicago, 1967.

Hauser, R. M. Educational stratification in the United States. *Sociological Inquiry,* 1970, **40,** 102–129.

Hauser, R. M. *Socioeconomic background and educational performance.* Washington, D.C.: American Sociological Association, Rose Monograph Series, 1971.

Hauser, R. M., and Goldberger, A. S. The treatment of unobservable variables in path analysis. In H. L. Costner (Ed.), *Sociological methodology 1971.* Chapter 4. San Francisco, California: Jossey-Bass, 1971. Pp. 81–117.

Hauser, R. M., Lutterman, K. G., and Sewell, W. H. Socioeconomic Background and the Earnings of High School Graduates. Presented at American Sociological Association meetings, Denver, September, 1971.

Heise, D. R. Separating reliability and stability in test-retest correlation. *American Sociological Review,* 1969, **34,** 93–101. (a)

Heise, D. R. Problems in path analysis and causal inference. In E. F. Borgatta (Ed.), *Sociological methodology 1969.* Chapter 2. San Francisco, California: Jossey-Bass, 1969. Pp. 38–73. (b)

Heise, D. R. Causal inference from panel data. In E. F. Borgatta and G. W. Bohrnstedt (Eds.), *Sociological methodology 1970.* Chapter 1. San Francisco, California: Jossey-Bass, 1970. Pp. 3–27.

Hilton, T. L. Growth Study Annotated Bibliography. Princeton, New Jersey: Educational Testing Service Progress Report 69-11, 1969.

Hodge, R. W. Social integration, psychological well-being, and their socioeconomic correlates. *Sociological Inquiry,* 1970, **40,** 182–206.

Hodge, R. W., and Treiman, D. J. Class identification in the United States. *American Journal of Sociology,* 1968, **73,** 535–547.

Hood, W. C., and Koopmans, T. C. (Eds.) *Studies in econometric method.* New York: Wiley, 1953.

Humphreys, L. G. Investigations of a simplex. *Psychometrika,* 1960, **25,** 313–323.

Hurwicz, L. Prediction and least squares. In T. C. Koopmans (Ed.), *Statistical inference in dynamic economic models.* Chapter 6. New York: Wiley, 1950. Pp. 365–383.

Jackson, J. E. Statistical models of senate roll call voting. *American Political Science Review,* 1971, **65,** 451–470. (a)

Jackson, J. E. Predicting Senate Voting Behavior: An Attempt to Evaluate a Model. Harvard University: Program on Quantitative Analysis in Political Science, 1971. (b)

Jensen, A. R. How much can we boost IQ and scholastic achievement? *Harvard Educational Review,* 1969, **39,** 1–123.

Johnston, J. J. *Econometric methods.* 2nd ed. New York: McGraw-Hill, 1972.

Jones, F. A note on 'Measures of urbanization,' with a further proposal. *Social Forces,* 1967, **46,** 275–279.

Jöreskog, K. G. Some contributions to maximum likelihood factor analysis. *Psychometrika,* 1967, **32,** 443–482. (a)

354

Jöreskog, K. G. UMLFA: A Computer Program for Unrestricted Maximum Likelihood Factor Analysis. Princeton, New Jersey: Educational Testing Service Research Memorandum 66-20, revised edition, 1967. (b)

Jöreskog, K. G. A general approach to confirmatory maximum likelihood factor analysis. *Psychometrika*, 1969, **34**, 183–202.

Jöreskog, K. G. A general method for the analysis of covariance structures. *Biometrika*, 1970, **57**, 239–251. (a)

Jöreskog, K. G. Estimation and testing of simplex models. *British Journal of Mathematical and Statistical Psychology*, 1970, **23**, 121–145. (b)

Jöreskog, K. G., Gruvaeus, G. T., and van Thillo, M. ACOVS: A General Computer Program for Analysis of Covariance Structures. Princeton, New Jersey: Educational Testing Service Research Bulletin 70-15, 1970.

Kahl, J. A. Some measurements of achievement orientation. *American Journal of Sociology*, 1965, **70**, 669–681.

Karpinos, B. D. The mental qualification of American youths for military service and its relationship to educational attainment. *Proceedings of the Social Statistics Section of the American Statistical Association*, 1966. Pp. 92–111.

Karpinos, B. D. Mental test failures. In S. Tax (Ed.), *The draft*. Chicago, Illinois: University of Chicago, 1967. Pp. 35–53.

Keesling, J. W. Maximum Likelihood Approaches to Causal Flow Analysis, University of Chicago: School of Education Ph.D. dissertation, 1972.

Kendall, M. G., and Stuart, A. *The advanced theory of statistics. Vol. 1, Distribution theory*. London: Griffin, 1958.

Kendall, M. G., and Stuart, A. *The advanced theory of statistics. Vol. 2, Inference and relationship*. London: Griffin, 1961.

Klassen, A. D. Military Service in American Life since World War II: An Overview. Chicago, Illinois: National Opinion Research Center Report 117, 1966.

Klein, L. R. *Economic fluctuations in the United States, 1921–1941*. New York: Wiley, 1950.

Klein, L. R. *A textbook of econometrics*. Evanston, Illinois: Row, Peterson, 1953.

Klein, L. R. Estimation of interdependent systems in macroeconometrics. *Econometrica*, 1969, **37**, 171–192.

Klein, L. R. *An essay on the theory of economic prediction*. Chicago, Illinois: Markham, 1970.

Kloek, T., and Mennes, L. B. M. Simultaneous equations estimation based on principal components of predetermined variables. *Econometrica*, 1960, **28**, 45–61.

Kmenta, J. *Elements of econometrics*. New York: Macmillan, 1971.

Koehler, J. E. The Philippine Family Planning Program: Some Suggestions for Dealing with Uncertainties. Santa Monica, California: Rand Corporation Report RM-6149-AID, 1969.

Koopmans, T. C., and Hood, W. C. The estimation of simultaneous linear economic relationships. In W. C. Hood and T. C. Koopmans (Eds.), *Studies in econometric method*. Chapter 6. New York: Wiley, 1953. Pp. 112–199.

Koopmans, T. C., and Reiersøl, O. The identification of structural characteristics. *Annals of Mathematical Statistics*, 1950, **21**, 165–181.

Koopmans, T. C., Rubin, H., and Leipnik, R. B. Measuring the equation systems of dynamic economics. In T. C. Koopmans (Ed.), *Statistical inference in dynamic economic models*. Chapter 2. New York: Wiley, 1950. Pp. 53–237.

Krauss, I. Sources of educational aspirations among working-class youth. *American Sociological Review*, 1964, **29**, 867–879.

Kuh, E., and Meyer, J. R. Correlation and regression estimates when the data are ratios. *Econometrica*, 1955, **23**, 400–416.

Land, K. C. Principles of path analysis. In E. F. Borgatta (Ed.), *Sociological methodology 1969*. Chapter 1. San Francisco, California: Jossey-Bass, 1969. Pp. 3–37.

Land, K. C. On the estimation of path coefficients for unmeasured variables from correlations among observed variables. *Social Forces*, 1970, **48**, 506–511.

Lawley, D. N., and Maxwell, A. E. *Factor analysis as a statistical method*. London and Washington, D.C.: Butterworths, 1963.

Lazarsfeld, P. F., and Henry, N. W. *Latent structure analysis*. Boston, Massachusetts: Houghton Mifflin, 1968.

Lenski, G. *The religious factor*. Garden City, New York: Doubleday, 1963.

Logan, C. Legal Sanctions and Deterrence from Crime. Indiana University: Department of Sociology Ph.D. dissertation, 1971.

MacRae, D., Jr. *Issues and parties in legislative voting*. New York: Harper, 1970.

MacRae, D., Jr. with Goldner, F. *Dimensions of congressional voting*. Berkeley, California: University of California, 1958.

Madansky, A. Determinantal methods in latent class analysis. *Psychometrika*, 1960, **25**, 183–198.

Madansky, A. Spurious correlation due to deflating variables. *Econometrica*, 1964, **32**, 652–655.

Malinvaud, E. *Statistical methods of econometrics*. 2nd Revised ed. Amsterdam: North-Holland Publ., 1970.

Marschak, J. Economic measurements for policy and prediction. In W. C. Hood and T. C. Koopmans (Eds.), *Studies in econometric method*. Chapter 1. New York: Wiley, 1953. Pp. 1–26.

Mason, W. M. Working Paper on the Socioeconomic Effects of Military Service. University of Chicago: Department of Sociology, 1968.

Mason, W. M. On the Socioeconomic Effects of Military Service. University of Chicago: Department of Sociology Ph.D. dissertation, 1970.

Miller, C. R., and Butler, E. W. Anomia and eunomia: a methodological critique of Srole's anomia scale. *American Sociological Review*, 1966, **31**, 400–406.

Mood, A. M., and Graybill, F. A. *Introduction to the theory of statistics*. New York: McGraw-Hill, 1963.

Morgan, J. N., David, M. H., Cohen, W. J., and Brazer, H. E. *Income and welfare in the United States*. New York: McGraw-Hill, 1962.

Mosbaek, E. J., and Wold, H. O. *Interdependent systems: structure and estimation*. Amsterdam: North-Holland Publ., 1970.

Neifeld, M. R. A study of spurious correlation. *Journal of the American Statistical Association*, 1927, **22**, 331–338.

Nerlove, M. *Estimation and identification of Cobb-Douglas production functions*. Chicago, Illinois: Rand-McNally, 1965.

Nerlove, M. Further evidence on the estimation of dynamic economic relations from a time series of cross sections. *Econometrica*, 1971, **39**, 359–382.

Nerlove, M., and Schultz, T. P. Love and Life Between the Censuses: A Model of Family Decision Making in Puerto Rico, 1950–1960. Santa Monica, California: Rand Corporation Report RM-6322-AID, 1970.

Olsen, M. E. Multivariate analysis of national political development. *American Sociological Review*, 1968, **33**, 699–712.

Pearson, K. On a form of spurious correlation which may arise when indices are used in the measurement of organs. *Proceedings of the Royal Society of London*, 1897, **60**, 489–497.

Pearson, K., Lee, A., and Elderton, E. M. On the correlation of death rates. *Journal of the Royal Statistical Society*, 1910, **73**, 534–539.

Pelz, D., and Andrews, F. Detecting causal priorities in panel study data. *American Sociological Review*, 1964, **29**, 836–848.

Peters, C. C., and VanVoorhis, W. R. *Statistical procedures and their mathematical bases*. New York: McGraw-Hill, 1940.

Rangarajan, C., and Chatterjee, S. A note on comparison between correlation coefficients of original and transformed variables. *The American Statistician*, 1969, **23**, 28–29.

Rao, C. R. *Linear statistical inference and its applications*. New York: Wiley, 1965.

Reiss, A. J., Jr., with Duncan, O. D., Hatt, P. K., and North, C. C. *Occupations and social status*. New York: Free Press of Glencoe, 1961.

Rickard, S. The assumptions of causal analyses for incomplete sets of two multilevel variables. *Multivariate Behavioral Research*, 1972, **7**, 317–359.

Rivera, R. J. Sampling Procedures on the Military Manpower Surveys. Chicago, Illinois: National Opinion Research Center, 1965.

Robinson, W. Ecological correlations and the behavior of individuals. *American Sociological Review*, 1950, **15**, 351–357.

Rogers, D. C. Private rates of return to education in the U.S.: A case study. *Yale Economic Essays*, 1969, **9**, 89–134.

Rosen, B. C. Race, ethnicity, and the achievement syndrome. *American Sociological Review*, 1959, **24**, 47–60.

Rothenberg, T. J. Structural Restrictions and Estimation Efficiency in Linear Econometric Models. New Haven, Connecticut: Yale University, Cowles Foundation Discussion Paper 213, 1966.

Rothenberg, T. J., and Leenders, C. T. Efficient estimation of simultaneous equation systems. *Econometrica*, 1964, **32**, 57–76.

Rozelle, R. M., and Campbell, D. T. More plausible rival hypotheses in the cross-lagged panel correlation technique. *Psychological Bulletin*, 1969, **71**, 74–80.

Schuessler, K. *Analyzing social data*. Boston, Massachusetts: Houghton Mifflin, 1971.

Schiller, B. Opportunity stratification. *American Journal of Sociology*, 1970, **76**, 426–442.

Schultz, T. P. Evaluation of Population Programs: A Framework for Analysis and its Application to Taiwan's Family Planning Program. Santa Monica, California: Rand Corporation Report R-643-AID, 1971.

Schuman, H. The religious factor in Detroit: review, replication, and reanalysis. *American Sociological Review*, 1971, **36**, 30–48.

Sewell, W. H., Haller, A. O., and Ohlendorf, G. W. The educational and early occupational status attainment process: revisions and replications. *American Sociological Review*, 1970, **35**, 1014–1027.

Sewell, W. H., Haller, A. O., and Portes, A. The educational and early occupational attainment process. *American Sociological Review*, 1969, **34**, 82–92.

Sewell, W. H., and Shah, V. P. Socioeconomic status, intelligence, and the attainment of higher education. *Sociology of Education*, 1967, **40**, 1–23.

Sewell, W. H. and Shah, V. P. Social class, parental encouragement, and educational aspirations. *American Journal of Sociology*, 1968, **73**, 559–572.

Shapiro, M. J., and Cherryholmes, C. *Representatives and roll calls*. Indianapolis, Indiana: Bobbs-Merrill, 1969.

Siegel, P. M., and Hodge, R. W. A causal approach to the study of measurement error. In H. M. Blalock, Jr. and A. B. Blalock (Eds.), *Methodology in social research*. Chapter 2. New York: McGraw-Hill, 1968. Pp. 28–59.

Simon, H. A. Causal ordering and identifiability. In W. C. Hood and T. C. Koopmans

(Eds.), *Studies in econometric method.* Chapter 3. New York: Wiley, 1953. Pp. 49–74.

Simon, H. A. Spurious correlation: a causal interpretation. *Journal of the American Statistical Association,* 1954, **49**, 467–479.

Spearman, C., and Holzinger, K. The sampling error in the theory of two factors. *British Journal of Psychology,* 1924, **15**, 17–19.

Stacey, B. G. Some psychological aspects of inter-generation occupational mobility. *British Journal of Social and Clinical Psychology,* 1965, **4**, 275–286.

Stouffer, S. A. *et al. Measurement and prediction.* Princeton, New Jersey: Princeton University Press, 1950.

Sullivan, J. L. Multiple indicators and complex causal models. In H. M. Blalock, Jr. (Ed.), *Causal models in the social sciences.* Chapter 18. Chicago, Illinois: Aldine-Atherton, 1971. Pp. 327–334.

Swamy, P. A. V. B., and Holmes, J. The use of undersized samples in the estimation of simultaneous equation systems. *Econometrica,* 1971, **39**, 455–459.

Taubman, P., and Wales, T. Net returns to education. In *Economics—A half century of research, 1920–1970: 50th annual report.* New York: National Bureau of Economic Research, 1970. Pp. 65–66.

Theil, H. *Economic forecasts and policy.* Second edition, Amsterdam: North-Holland Publ., 1961.

Theil, H. *Principles of econometrics.* New York: Wiley, 1971.

Tobin, J. Estimation of relationships for limited dependent variables. *Econometrica,* 1958, **26**, 24–36.

Tukey, J. W. Causation, regression, and path analysis. In O. Kempthorne *et al.* (Eds.), *Statistics and mathematics in biology.* Chapter 3. Ames, Iowa: Iowa State University Press, 1954. Pp. 35–66.

Turner, J. *Party and constituency: pressures on congress.* Baltimore, Maryland: Johns Hopkins Press, 1951.

Turner, M. E., and Stevens, C. D. The regression analysis of causal paths. *Biometrics,* 1959, **15**, 236–258.

U. S. President's Task Force on Manpower Conservation. *One-third of a nation: a report on young men found unqualified for military service.* Washington, D. C.: U.S. Government Printing Office, 1964.

Wald, A. Note on the identification of economic relations. In T. C. Koopmans (Ed.), *Statistical inference in dynamic economic models.* Chapter 3. New York: Wiley, 1950. Pp. 238–244.

Wang, M. W., and Stanley, J. C. Differential weighting: a review of methods and empirical studies. *Review of Educational Research,* 1970, **40**, 663–705.

Warren, B. L. Socioeconomic achievement and religion: the American case. *Sociological Inquiry,* 1970, **40**, 130–155.

Wechsler, D. Manual for the Wechsler Adult Intelligence Scale. New York: Psychological Corporation, 1955.

Wegge, L. L. A family of functional iterations and the solution of maximum likelihood estimation equations. *Econometrica,* 1969, **37**, 122–130.

Weisbrod, B. A., and Karpoff, P. Monetary returns to college education, student ability, and college quality. *Review of Economics and Statistics,* 1968, **50**, 491–497.

Werts, C. E., Jöreskog, K. G., and Linn, R. L. Comment on 'The estimation of measurement error in panel data.' *American Sociological Review,* 1971, **36**, 110–112.

Werts, C. E., and Linn, R. L. Path analysis: psychological examples. *Psychological Bulletin,* 1970, **74**, 193–212.

Werts, C. E., Linn, R. L., and Jöreskog, K. G. Estimating the parameters of path models involving unmeasured variables. In H. M. Blalock, Jr. (Ed.), *Causal models in the social sciences*. Chapter 23. Chicago: Illinois: Aldine-Atherton, 1971. Pp. 400–409.

Wilks, S. S. *Mathematical statistics*. New York: Wiley, 1962.

Wiley, D. E., and Wiley, J. A. The estimation of measurement error in panel data. *American Sociological Review*, 1970, **35**, 112–117.

Wold, H. O. A., and Jureen, L. *Demand analysis*. New York: Wiley, 1953.

Wonnacott, R. J., and Wonnacott, T. H. *Econometrics*. New York: Wiley, 1970.

Wright, S. The method of path coefficients. *Annals of Mathematical Statistics*, 1934, **5**, 161–215.

Wright, S. The interpretation of multivariate systems. In O. Kempthorne *et al.* (Eds.), *Statistics and mathematics in biology*. Chapter 2. Ames, Iowa: Iowa State University Press, 1954. Pp. 11–33.

Yee, D. H., and Gage, N. L. Techniques for estimating the source and direction of causal inference in panel data. *Psychological Bulletin*, 1968, **70**, 115–126.

Yule, G. U. On the interpretation of correlations between indices or ratios. *Journal of the Royal Statistical Society*, 1910, **73**, 644–647.

Yule, G. U., and Kendall, M. G. *An introduction to the theory of statistics*. 14th ed. London: Griffin, 1950.

Zavoina, W., and McKelvey, R. A Statistical Model for the Analysis of Legislative Voting Behavior. Presented at American Political Science Association meetings, New York, September, 1969.

Zellner, A. An efficient method of estimating seemingly unrelated regressions and tests for aggregation bias. *Journal of the American Statistical Association*, 1962, **57**, 348–368.

Zellner, A. Estimation of regression relationships containing unobservable variables. *International Economic Review*, 1970, **11**, 441–454.